DADDY
THROWS ME
IN THE AIR

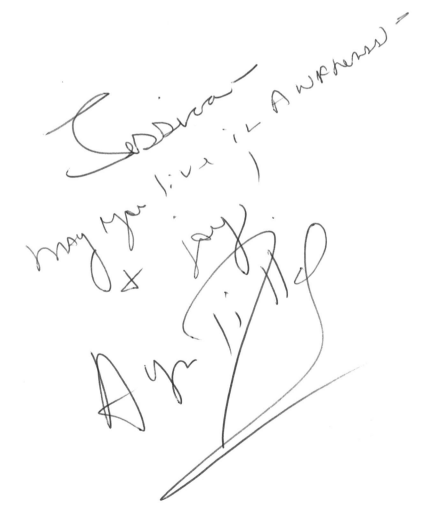

DADDY
THROWS ME
IN THE AIR

Remembering Childhood

*'How your imprints, memories and perceptions of them
create your beliefs, choices and ultimately your life.'*

AYN DILLARD

*A Return To Childhood And Growing Up For The Purpose
Of Awareness, Healing, Forgiveness And Joy!*

Columbus, Ohio

The stories and memories in this book are told from
my perception. Others may have different perceptions.
This book is written for the intention of awareness,
understanding and forgiveness leading to healing.

Names have been changed or left out for the privacy
of those living.

"Life can be understood by looking backward.
But it must be lived fully in the present looking forward."

Published by Gatekeeper Press
3971 Hoover Rd. Suite 77
Columbus, OH 43123-2839
www.GatekeeperPress.com

Cover design by JudithSDesigns&Creativity

ISBN: 9781619848030
eISBN: 9781619848047

Printed in the United States of America

DEDICATED TO

Every child and adult but especially to those who think or thought as a child or as an adult that something must be 'wrong' with me and everyone else is 'okay.'

With much thanks and love to my Aunt Sandra.

CONTENTS

THE PURPOSE

THESE STORIES ARE FOR REMEMBRANCE and awareness leading to the release of limiting imprints beliefs and emotions, along with the understanding from where they derive. An important awareness is that wherever we land on earth, whatever our circumstances, it is the perfect place for us. Our soul is placed to accept, rise above, integrate, release, understand, forgive and or to break against to become more than what we were when we first arrived.

Have you ever wondered why out of all the memories we have and are created in our lifetime, why specific ones we recall more often and stay with us, appearing to be the ones more significant? Perhaps these are the ones imprinted to bring us to our greatest awareness, healing of negativity or the ones that sustain us in positive feelings of love and joy. Our memories, imprints and perception of them are what create our beliefs about ourselves, others, our world and guide us as we travel through life.

Until we become aware of them, their impact, examine them for their true meaning, we will be guided by them as if on remote control. When we are able to view them objectively, examine them from all viewpoints, release the ones needed to exit, we will be at awareness and more able to live our lives at choice.

These stories are truth from my childhood and life based upon my perception of the imprints which created my belief system that created my life. Understanding the imprints along with hidden messages from childhood, I am then more able to see myself and others with clarity.

As you read my stories, you may experience your own remembrances—my stories will trigger yours. And once you begin this journey of awareness, more imprints and memories will surface for you to examine. One may lead to another, onward to more awareness and clarity. Our imprints and memories of them are what create who we are and who we become. The truth of your childhood is imprinted in your mind, body and spirit. Imprints can even flow generational through family lineage.

Most of us have similar feelings in childhood—circumstances and situations are just different. Individual perception of what occurred is different even within the same family. Our placement in the family, psychological makeup, our astrology, personality and our age when circumstances and experiences occur will allow that each one of us be imprinted differently. Some people are more impressionable and are easily imprinted. Other people are more able to resist imprints. We are all unique and individual. It's when the pain of our repetitive experiences becomes great that we will want and need to look within to find out why. Memories and imprints are there to reveal our core wounding. Self-refection and awareness are keys to growth and ultimately the healing of our souls.

If you are a parent, you may experience sadness or guilt as my stories bring up similar ways that you interact with your children. Be aware that what you are doing, or have done is because of your imprints and experiences carried forward from your parents and ancestors along with the beliefs of your world in the time you were growing up.

An awareness is that when an individual becomes a parent, the event in itself does not automatically transform them into knowing how to guide or care for another human being. More often than not, parents will treat a child as they have been treated, how they treat themselves or flip into the opposite and try to make up for what they perceived was lacking in their childhood. Whatever it is or becomes, it is an experience that molds the individual for life based on their perception of it.

Some people become parents and display their issues of control, anger, hurt, hate, insecurity, etc. onto the child. Perhaps, for the first time in their lives these 'parents' are able to have control and feel powerful over someone else. Since children are truly dependent, often there is no immediate consequence to these negative actions, but the effects will certainly be recognized eventually by the child either by harm to self or to others. Our wounded children can do hideous things to themselves, others and out into our world.

Children come to this planet to exist, but also to teach parents by reflecting back to them their individual imprints and beliefs regarding who they are. This awareness shown can, if the parents are open to it and become aware, give them the opportunity to look at themselves and life in a whole new way. Doing so enables them to progress further in their soul's growth. Becoming a parent can be a kind of reflection of the imprinted self. Ideally parents and children will grow together if open, aware and self reflective. If not, damage may be imprinted.

If a parent has a lack of self-awareness and self-reflection and is stuck in their self importance and negative imprints then uses a child for their ego gratification, the process may be negated. A war of wills may develop which is harmful to both parties because no constructive energy flows between the individuals. Some parents project and imprint their lack, unhappiness, depression, anxiety and fear onto their children. Other parents project and imprint their hope, ambition and love onto theirs. Whichever and whatever it is, it's for the child to incorporate, break against, learn from, deal with or to overcome.

Awareness is that in the child/parent relationship, one is not more important than the other. One has just been on the planet longer and the one, who has been on the planet longest, may not always be the wisest. Sometimes the parents are in kindergarten and the children in graduate school—just in different places and levels in earth school. Children will carry and reflect back aspects of that which the parent truly is, not what they pretend to be or who they may want to think or wish they are.

All relationships are for the purpose of growth and development between the people involved, be it child/parent, romantic, friendship or business. In each relationship there is healing, breaking against, harm done, fun, learning, etc. and in most there is a mixture of all.

Memories and imprints are experienced daily. Some we choose to keep and others we flush away. It's in our energy—the ones that attach to us and stay. This book is to assist in release of negative and harmful imprints, but you can't release something if you have no awareness of it. So awareness is paramount.

If you find that you are in the same situations over again and don't understand why, it's because you are being guided by imprints. Become aware of the memories that come into your mind and examine them. Understand where your imprints come from, see all sides, and accept what occurred in order to be able to break free and to be at choice. Becoming aware is the beginning of having the ability to disengage and create a different outcome. If you listen to the same song over and over again, pretty soon it will repeat in your mind without the CD even being played. That's exactly how our imprints guide us. When you get tired of the same imprint controlling your life, it's time to create a new reality. "Until you make the unconscious conscious, it will direct your life and you will call it fate." Jung

If you are a child or young person reading these stories, understand your parents and other adults did the best they were able with the knowledge they had at the time.

When an individual is aware of abuse in any form, physical, mental or emotional and allows it to continue, the abuse is done not only to the abused, but also to the abuser.

Any negative emotions with the feeling attached to them that my stories bring up are ready to be honored and released. Negative emotions brought up by this book can be helped into release by using 'The Process' in the 'Emotional Wisdom' section.

Everyone comes from a different place in this life—different circumstances, financial, educational, racial, cultural or environmental. Everyone's imprints and perceptions are different. Even though we are similar, we are all individual.

The stories in this book will create triggers for awareness and healing and the ripple effect will go out into our world.

This is my story—my imprints and perceptions. My life is my gift to you.

"Difficulties exist only so that in overcoming them,
we may grow strong. Only those who have
suffered and overcome are able to help others."
—Ayn Dillard

*"A changed thought system can reverse cause—and—effect
as we have known it. For most of us, this is a very difficult
concept to accept, because of our resistance to relinquishing
the predictability of our past belief system and to assuming
responsibility for our thoughts, feelings and reactions. Since
we always look within before looking out, we can perceive
attack outside us only when we have first accepted attack as
real within."*
—Gerald G. Jampolsky

INTRODUCTION

IT WAS TIME TO HEAL. I had to stop creating a life that I could not live. It was time for the pain and suffering to stop. There was too much pain. I will die if the pain continues. Why does my life keep ending up in the same place? Abusive marriages, divorces, lawyers, legal suits—people in my life that had alcoholism, mental illness and abusive behavior, all telling me that I am the problem. Why did I keep creating and recreating everything I did not want and vowed not to have in my life?

In the process of the healing—soul searching—reading of books—discussing—studying—therapy; seemingly insignificant scenes from my childhood kept entering my mind. The scenes were overpowering me, forcing me to look at and relive the feelings that I was having at the time. I began writing down the stories and discovered very meaningful messages that I was given as a child, messages that imprinted me and shaped my life's existence. These scenes and the feelings they created caused me to experience a repetitive pattern. It did not matter, if the imprints were intended to create this pattern, only that it was the pattern it created in me. Until I was genuinely ready and able to look at my imprints and beliefs, where they came from and release them—the pattern would remain.

The pattern created was that of fear and stress. Fear that I was not good enough. Fear that something was wrong with me because I was constantly being criticized for being me. My interests or desires were not acceptable to my parents because they did not have the same interests or desires. They mostly criticized me, instead of supporting me. I felt—not smart enough—pretty enough—talented enough or even worth taking up space on the planet. I began continual negative self- talk. My parents did not need to keep criticizing me because I was constantly criticizing myself. It was like listening to a song over and over again. Soon it played continually in my head, without the song being played.

I could barely breathe. As a child I was often sick with respiratory problems. My mother and father smoked. I detested smoking and discovered that I am highly allergic to it. So unknowingly, my parents were subjecting me to a toxin that was literally making me ill. This can be a metaphor in that it's a physical example of something my parents unknowingly did that made me ill. They also inflicted many words and behaviors upon me which emotionally fractured me. But I didn't realize this until I became aware.

Before the age of twelve, I was outgoing but then became very shy. I didn't want to draw attention to myself, so I kept to myself. I did whatever I could to survive, to try and fit in which was to deny who I am. I learned to pretend that I was happy when I wasn't just to get through the day. I was told by verbal messages and nonverbal messages that I was nothing. I pretended so much that I almost forgot who I was. I was an emotionally sensitive child, but tried to pretend that I wasn't, to feel 'safe'. When I showed my feelings, I was negated, even attacked and told my feelings were wrong. Therefore, I tried to do what was expected. I denied my feelings. I forced feelings deep down inside and tried to believe that I was wrong and everyone else must be right. All the while I knew that nothing felt right or correct about doing this. I learned to give my power away. I learned to become a victim. I learned to cut myself off from my feelings and to deny my instincts.

In my confusion and pretending, I learned to negate how to evaluate others. At times, I temporarily lost my God-given intuition. I was so needy for love and acceptance that I settled for what I could get. I did whatever I could to try and create a life. I tried to create a family that would love me, but for some reason, I could not create what I wanted. I kept recreating the same existence that I so desperately was trying to get away from.

I unknowingly gave my power away to others, in order to try and get what I so deeply desired—which was acceptance, validation, connection and love. But by so doing, I didn't receive anything but more of the same indifference or criticism. I brought people into my life who criticized me for being me. They wanted to control me, take from me or change me—instead of to love and support me. They wanted me to be what they wanted me to be—not what I wanted.

I became a fractured soul. I felt desperate. I almost collapsed and even thought about suicide at times. I thought if no one likes or wants me, 'Why am I here?' But my inner strength for survival and belief in God helped me to keep trying to find my direction, to heal my soul, to find my purpose and place in this world.

When I was forced to go back to my parents for help, they punished me by saying that I was a failure and could not create a marriage or a life. When I could not pretend any longer and wanted and tried to confront the truth as I saw and felt it, they did not want anything to do with me. They excluded me from family events. They wanted me to shut up and to go away. They wanted a child that could pretend nothing was wrong. They wanted me to tell them that they were wonderful parents. They could take no talking or questioning because they did not want to look at themselves. So clearly, they could not give me answers about the way I felt and why I felt so lost. They did not want to hear about my feelings. That was too difficult, too real and too painful for them because then they would need to look at themselves. It was easier for them to say that something was wrong with me. They blamed me as they pointed their finger stating; "We are fine. Nothing is wrong with us. It must be you. No one else feels the way you do. We have no problems until you come around. Your sisters don't have any problems. It's only you!"

My parents blamed me for the abuse I suffered. It seemed as if they thought I purposefully brought it on myself. They pulled away and would have little to do with me until I was a 'success' in their eyes. So then they could feel like 'good' parents with a 'successful' daughter. But even at those times of my life when I had success and was happy, my family would still criticize and exclude me, which confused me even more. It seemed as if nothing about me could please them.

Why was I born into this particular family? They obviously did not like anything about me. Why did I have to experience so much pain? Was I being punished for some really awful thing I did, of which I was unaware? Were other people as unhappy and full of fear as I was? I wondered if there was some reason, some positive reason, or outcome for all the pain and all that I endured.

After almost a lifetime of hurt and pain, I realized I had lived the majority of my life in insecurity, fear and stress, and this made me come from a place of weakness. Most of the choices I made came from a place where I was frozen in weakness and fear. Being in fear and stress disconnected me from my inner core and the source of my higher-self, my aware-self, my God-self. Only at the same time, I felt a deep connection to God. Therefore it was confusing. While I thought separating from my authentic self would keep me 'safe' and I did this automatically to survive. I also felt like the hand of God was guiding me.

Being in almost continual fear and stress, clearly I was out of balance. Therefore I was not able to make the best choices for myself. I was for the most part just trying to escape the life that I had been reared in. Other people subconsciously sensed my fear, neediness and weakness. So if they had the need or desire to control me for their benefit and purpose, they could. They were able to sense my weaknesses and utilize them in whichever way best suited their agenda and goals. This left me open like a sitting duck waiting to be attacked, used or destroyed in whichever form it came.

Therefore, unconsciously I was bringing the same experiences to myself over and over again. Consciously, I wanted love and acceptance, but subconsciously, I kept repeating the same negative pattern because I had no awareness that my imprints and beliefs of my 'wounded inner child' were running my life. It was as if I was sending out radar for these negative experiences to occur and reoccur in my life. So that, hopefully and eventually, I might become self-reflective and aware by what was occurring and release the need for these experiences.

When a child experiences constant fear and stress, they shut down parts of their brain. They stay in the 'fight or flight' mode or may shut down completely. This creates havoc in their whole system. They do not think or absorb clearly what is being said or what is going on around them. They are overly concerned with trying to stay 'safe'. They are affected mentally, emotionally and physically because these three are inseparable. Some people may even stay locked emotionally at whatever age it is that they become fractured and never emotionally develop past this age.

Fear is the lowest vibration with unconditional love being the highest. In our society, oftentimes fear is used to control. Parents use fear with children because most religions and society in general uses fear to keep people in the place desired. Control and fear are taught repeatedly in our world. An individual living in constant fear and stress will either attack outward or attack inward. When we feel that we have no choice but to believe what others say about us, we relinquish our individuality. These negative experiences close down our inner light—our true essence and keep us in a place of darkness negating our ability of the awareness to see clearly.

The stress experienced in childhood will be triggered over again when similar situations occur. The person will react in the same manner by either attacking outward to society or inward harming self in various ways. The stress will eventually build until it turns in on itself. A pattern will be created in a person's brain and emotional system—creating the energy vibration that they emit into the world. They will automatically subconsciously and repeatedly draw to them the same negative experiences. There will be no choice involved. They have been imprinted. That is why it's also important to limit what young children and teenagers are exposed to daily on television by games and social media, etc.

My parents and others did not intend to harm me. They would not intentionally do anything that would deny me anything and everything I am or want to be. They were acting out of their own psychology along with their imprints, perceptions and belief systems that had been stamped upon them. They were doing and treating me as they had been imprinted and how they perceived things should be. Even when the best of intentions are coming from parents, they can still be creating fear, stress and low value in their children. Therefore my parents were behaving in a manner they hoped would keep me and them 'safe'. But ultimately it was 'safe', so they did not have to look at themselves.

Parents may wonder why when children are struggling and

'not successful', that is in their estimation, and exclaim with much frustration; "What did we do wrong? We gave them the best that we had to give. We gave them everything." Truth being, the parents gave their children exactly who and what the parents really are, not who or what they think, wish or pretend that they are. Then the parents sit in judgment of the children, while really the judgment is of self. Many parents' conversely will be more than happy to take credit when a child excels or is successful in some endeavor.

The best a parent can do is to love a child unconditionally and discipline them with understanding and guidance along with their own intense self-reflection. The catch being, parents can't give unconditional love unless they have experienced it themselves. Therefore until the parents look at themselves with full awareness, self-reflection and responsibility, the history will continue to repeat itself in whichever form it takes.

The greatest gift a parent can give a child is to love, accept and honor themselves, faults and all in self-reflection. Then children will more naturally receive what they need to complete their soul growth and will automatically know that they are loved. Children need to know that it's okay to make mistakes and to be authentically who they are, while learning and striving to become more of who they were meant to be.

A child more often than not is a mirror of their parents in some form or another and, at times the mirror is cracked or even broken. And if a child takes on that crack and is assaulted or hit repeatedly, the child will eventually break, fall apart or even shatter. But then of course, when a child grows and matures and is at awareness, there is a choice to either stay in the mirror, break against it or to step through it and out of it. The key is becoming aware. It's like waking up from a dark and deep sleep. Perhaps ultimately, it is for the parent's as well as the child's awareness and growth that a particular soul chooses to become their child.

Every child wants and deserves to be loved, valued and supported as a unique individual. Doing so will give them the strength coming from their core to tackle whatever life throws at them. When parents honor a child for their individuality and instill a sense of peace and self- worth, this inner strength will be with the individual no matter what their circumstances in life. Unfortunately, you cannot give what you do not have.

What the individual perceives intellectually and emotionally to be true, they arrange into their belief system. This is done so the individual can make sense of their world which becomes their reality. What we feel emotionally is what creates what we think and believe as true. The reverse is also valid. What we think is what creates how we feel emotionally and we believe as truth. An individual's imprints and beliefs define who they think they are. It serves as their guideline as to how to live. What we think of ourselves and others determines our life and the quality of it. Quality of beliefs = quality of life. Emotions are to serve you, not control you.

We walk around trying to find people who will match our beliefs about ourselves and the world. When it does, it feels right. When it doesn't, it feels strange or wrong. Even if abuse, negativity and unhappiness feels right—if that's our imprints that is what we will feel comfortable attracting and staying in, even if we are in pain. It's what we will choose either consciously or unconsciously. Some become comfortable in their pain, so they choose to stay and wallow in it. To do so, feels 'safer' than becoming aware, confronting imprints and change. Confronting imprints and becoming aware takes courage and the mustering of internal strength.

It's the strong who better deal with change not the weak. When you have been negated and abused on any level, when you first experience acceptance, kindness and love, you may feel leery and uncomfortable in it. Until you become able and can allow yourself to accept and feel worthy of it. When you have been abused, negated and diminished, it becomes difficult to allow yourself to become vulnerable. It takes strength to do so.

"Intelligence is the ability to adapt to change." Stephen Hawking— and I will add, even if it is scary and uncomfortable in the beginning.

Children adapt to whatever circumstances, environments and situations they find themselves in, in order to get attention, love, feel nurtured, and to survive. In their adapting, they become imprinted. Children have a need to know that parents are not always 'right'.

Parents are complex and have many sides to them. They make mistakes and have character flaws.

Just like a mother who cautions her child to stay in the yard to avoid possible harm, so too does the belief system want to keep you safe. Just like a child wants and needs to grow up and leave the yard so too an individual wants and needs to grow past the imprints of limiting beliefs.

The dictionary's definitions of belief and systems are: BELIEF—intellectual acceptance of anything as true, SYSTEM—a combination of parts as a whole—in an arrangement. Thus are created imprints in your brain, your emotions and your body.

Awareness is the first step to change. Concept being, do not run from your pain instead embrace it. Self reflection, no matter how painful, will lead to awareness. An individual cannot conquer negativity by resisting it, only by recognizing, seeing and owning it in self-reflection. By recognizing and owning the negativity, the choice is that it may be transmuted into other forms. The energy that expresses itself by negativity is the same energy that expresses itself in the positive. Therefore, negativity may be transmuted into the positive. By recognizing this truth in your life, you can shift negative beliefs into positive ones.

In writing my stories and analyzing my imprints, awareness and healing occurred and the hurt began to drop off. I could understand my feelings and reactions, while also understanding the behaviors and actions of the people involved. I was then able to view the scenes from my childhood and life from an observer's viewpoint. This released the grip the past had on me, thus enabling me to forgive the people involved. I was then more able to be at choice—to either keep the imprint, to change it or to release it. This released the need to recreate the past to try to change the outcome. I was also more able to see into and through people and their motives more clearly. I learned that it was 'okay' to feel comfortable, but if I wasn't comfortable, I could choose to get away from the situation or the people. I learned to listen to myself, evaluate, and not deem myself 'wrong' for being me or what I felt. Instead, I honored it. I could also walk into the uncomfortable and hold it outside myself as I further examined it along with its intention.

I wanted to stop recreating the imprints from my childhood. I had enough pain. I wanted to be able to create in my life that which I wanted.

If you are ready to ask, who am I, why do I think as I do, behave as I do, make the choices that I do, and what am I comprised of? Then you are ready to hear the answers and create change in your life. You will also become brave enough to become the change.

We will keep creating the same things until the past is looked at with awareness, acceptance and understanding then integrated into our future lives. While sharing my stories, I realized that everyone has similar stories, just different circumstances.

Experience = Imprint and Perception of = Belief = Life Created.

This book reveals the process of how imprints occur and a process to assist in releasing beliefs about yourself and others. Through awareness and 'The Process', you will be able to assist in healing, releasing stress, imprints and limiting beliefs that you have held onto that are holding you back from achieving the life and results that you desire. Look within with awareness. Are you satisfied with the way you are feeling and the life you're living?

The process to healing the 'inner child', releasing negative imprints, limiting beliefs and emotions is: Awareness—Understanding—Acceptance—Forgiveness into Love, Peace and Joy! It is a mental process that will lead you to emotional wisdom. We all have an Intelligence IQ and also an Emotional IQ and they work in tandem to create your life. 'Emotional Wisdom' will naturally lead you into awareness in the physical which will guide you to your 'Body Wisdom'. When the mental, emotional and physical are in balance—you and your life will flow more smoothly towards the direction of your heart's desire including better mental, emotional and physical health. You will even find that you will feel, look and behave more youthfully. You will have more energy because you will not have the weight of negative imprints blocking your energy flow and holding you captive. You will feel more often than not, in balance, integrated and self-actualized.

When you become aware and are at choice to release the negative, the rest will fall into place. Have constantly changing flexible beliefs of yourself and others. Your life is the creation of your mind and the reality you create is to give you the opportunity for your soul's growth.

Fall in love with yourself and your journey into awareness, so you may experience an internal and everlasting peace and joy.

When each one of us can be led to our true self and be able to develop our individual talents with loving guidance, fulfillment will be the order of the day. Peace will be more present in each individual able to be manifested in our world.

Read my stories—remember your childhood—read them to your children—discuss them—talk about the feelings experienced. Write about your memories and imprints. Become aware. Break through the limiting imprints and belief systems from the past—the negative imprints and belief systems of your ancestors. Let examining your life become a grand adventure!

You more readily love and accept others when you love and accept yourself

> "A person is never himself but always a mask; a person
> is never his own person, but always represents another,
> by whom he is possessed. And the other that one is,
> is always ancestors. . . ."
> —Norman O. Brown

Now begin the journey back with me . . .

PROLOGUE

A BEAUTIFUL, YOUNG WOMAN LIES ON a gurney being rolled down a dimly lit corridor into an austere operating room. The thin silhouette of her body is revealed under the sheet as she is transferred onto a metal table. Her dark brown hair is the only alive color in the room. Overhead fluorescent lights glare onto sharp instruments. Doctors and nurses in surgical masks surround. With her wrists secured, fear begins to overwhelm just as electroshock is given and sedation takes a deeper effect.

A doctor selects what looks like an ice pick and aims it directly into the corner of one of her richly colored brown eyes. Poking it in then up into her brain, he wheedles it around. Finished with one, he precedes to the other—to forever sever her emotional connections—tearing apart and destroying pieces of her innate individual essence.

THE LITTLE SPIRIT

ONCE UPON A TIME, THERE was a little spirit who dreamed that when she came to earth that she would be loved. She dreamed of being happy and having the security of being in a home surrounded by people that would love her and see her as a special, unique spirit with her individual talents.

Looking down from Heaven, she searched for a man and woman who really wanted a baby. She looked for two people she thought would love her and help her to be the best little spirit she could be.

She made her choice, a couple who had been trying for three years and hadn't yet conceived. She thought these are people who really want a baby and will appreciate me for being me.

She landed on this planet, but soon realized that her Mommy and Daddy only loved her when she was like they wanted her to be. They wanted her to make them proud. It didn't seem to matter if she was happy or not, only that they were pleased. She had thought when observing them from Heaven that they would love her just because she was who she was and because she chose to be with them.

She recalled how much they appeared to want a baby when she looked down upon them from above. She wondered why now that she was with them that they didn't seem pleased with her. She realized and learned that on earth much of the time, love can be complex, confusing and often about control. She loved her parents with all her heart, so she tried really hard to be what they wanted her to be and to please them.

Her parents put her in frilly dresses and took lots of home movies of her. They loved it when she danced and flirted with her eyes. She was full of life and fun. She was their precious little doll. She learned that on this planet to be loved, you need to please. If you are pretty, smart and do what 'they' say, then you will be worthy of acceptance and love. She learned these lessons well—far too well. She did the best that she could and tried to be what they wanted—what they would be proud of. She wanted their love and acceptance more than anything on earth. Therefore, she learned to act and pretend to be happy when she wasn't.

She almost forgot what it felt like being in Heaven and being loved for the totality of her being. She began to lose herself in her efforts to try and fit in, to be loved and accepted on earth. She soon realized she was living a lie. Only she still dreamed of truth and not living lies.

When she remembered her experiences in Heaven, she knew that if you lived your truth, you would be true to others. By living in truth—there is no fear—no reason to hurt others. She knew that living a lie would only hurt her, but she was willing to do just that if she could receive love from her parents. She would do anything to feel loved. She would even lose herself.

Her parents didn't notice. They did not or could not fully see her, or her true spirit. If her parents could have seen her true spirit, they would have loved her unconditionally, but they were only able to see her through their imprints and beliefs and see her as an extension of themselves. If they thought of her as being good, they felt good about themselves. If they thought of her as being bad or a failure, they didn't like her and felt bad about themselves. They could only be proud when she was good, whatever 'good' really was. In fact much of the time, they didn't even want to be bothered by her. They just wanted her to be with them when it was convenient.

Pretending made her unhappy because she didn't know who she was anymore. Other people seemed not to notice or to see her much less her true essence. They tried to make her into what they wanted her to be because she couldn't see who she truly was any longer.

Her daddy kept saying that he wanted a boy child. This made her sad. Didn't he know boys and girls were the same only different?

The little spirit was young and had not been away from Heaven long enough to forget. She still had memory of wisdom. She knew that we have male and female energies inside our brains—so it doesn't matter which human body we are in on the earth plane because it's only an earthly experience. Male and female are both lovable, both are good, both are needed and both are equal. One isn't better or more desirable than the other.

She took ballet and loved to dance. Her parents said ballet will ruin your legs. "We don't like muscular legs." She liked classical music. They said, "We don't like classical music. We like 'big band' music."

Pretty soon, the little spirit realized nothing she could say, do or feel mattered or was right before their eyes. It seemed as if she could do nothing that would please them and to get the acceptance and love that she so desperately desired. Oh, they paid for ballet lessons and gave her what she asked for, but they criticized even as they did so.

She thought something must be wrong with me. I don't fit into my family that I chose on earth. So, why am I here? Why don't they love me? Why don't they see me? She wanted to go home—back to Heaven with the other spirits. She still remembered and understood the ways and laws of Heaven. She did not understand why she was on Earth. She did not understand the rules here.

She believed in her parents but they didn't believe in her. They wanted her to have their beliefs and likes instead of her own. She found that she lived with people, who belittled her pain, laughed at her dreams, tormented her for caring and ignored her fears. This hurt her so badly—she thought she might die from the pain.

The little spirit asked herself repeatedly and to anyone who would care or listen, "Do you know why my parents don't love me? Don't see me? Don't know who I am?"

After trying and trying and so much pain—so much pain, she didn't know if she could breathe or live. She decided she would have to be what she wanted to be. She would have to be true to herself or she might die.

She was good and dreamed of goodness. She dreamed of a place where all people are honest, living in their truth and in their authenticity. Although this was very challenging even difficult, perhaps even impossible to do on earth, she decided, she would listen to herself—her feelings—her emotions—her body and get to know herself. She couldn't worry anymore if they loved her or not, because she knew by now, they never could or would see her.

Only God and the other spirits in Heaven knew her true soul and spirit. So why was she here on earth? Remember, she came to earth to be loved?

After searching and asking the question over and over again. "Why am I here on earth if no one loves me and can truly see me?"

She found the answer. She found the answer in her pain, in her suffering and in her asking. The answer is—for her to be herself and to love herself. The answer is for her to heal her soul. It didn't matter who loves or likes her, as long as she was true to herself and her soul. She knew in her heart that all she needed to be was who she truly is all of the time. The answer was to be true to her soul.

The little spirit almost lost who she is trying to be, for the sake of what others wanted her to be. Therefore it took her a long time to figure out who she truly is. All the trying to be what others wanted her to be had made her forget her true worth and she had become terribly confused.

All the obstacles and hurt that were shown to her were for her to break against and to make her stronger. It might have been nicer and easier if all had seen her in the beginning for her true spirit and who she was in her soul. But they did not. Perhaps, it was not in God's plan for her that it be that easy. Therefore she chose to do it for herself. Perhaps, this was the plan all along. She learned self-love and to live and be in internal peace.

If everyone found the way to this place—this place of love, peace, and acceptance of self—peace would reign on this planet and beyond.

Sometimes, you need to go backward before you can go forward. It may feel painful to go back and experience all the emotions and feelings of this little spirit but through the pain will come a joy . . . a joy that passes all understanding. Go back with her now, see what you see, feel what you feel and remember her journey. It may be a bit like yours.

Now the journey on Earth begins . . .

PART ONE

CHILDHOOD—
CONCEPTION TO ELEVEN

IT'S OKAY FOR 'YOU' TO BE A GIRL

I am at conception

ALL DURING MY CHILDHOOD AND life, my Dad told the story of how he always wanted a boy. He wanted a boy so that he could teach him all kinds of things—sports—business—how to make his way in the world.

My parents tried to have a baby for three years without success. So when I'm conceived, it's a successful and happy occasion. They spent a lot of time thinking of names, primarily boy's names. The names they liked; Michael, Andrew, David or Gary.

Of course they had a baby girl and named me, Natalie. They said, "They're very happy to have me, even though, I am a girl." My father stated, "Since you are the first born, it's okay that you're a girl."

I felt relief and thought to myself, 'But, I'm happy to be a girl! So it's nice to hear that it's okay to be who I am. All my life I wondered, would my dad have liked me better were I a boy?'

My parents kept trying to have a boy. Three years after me, a second baby girl is born. Dad commented in frustration, "I guess, the second one is okay being a girl, too." Then when, the third and fourth girls are born, my father gave up on having a boy. He said he didn't want any more girls—so no more children. He had a vasectomy.

I think to myself in relief. 'Thank goodness! Since I am the first born that it's okay for me to be a girl,' as I wondered what my younger sisters felt like, since they were really supposed to be boys. I felt that I disappointed my father by just being me. So what must my younger sisters feel like? Did they feel wrong for being who they are before they ever began life?

I always wondered why my father wanted a boy so intensely. Why did he feel they were more desirable? Would I feel more love from him if I were a boy? Would he have been more proud of me? Would I have been more accepting of myself if I had been a boy because then I would have pleased my father? He might have been more accepting of me had I been a boy. Feeling more accepted I might have been able to pull that acceptance into myself.

I learned to play baseball and to climb everything while also being a girly-girl. I was a tomboy in overalls then could put on a frilly dress and be a total girl. I have both inside of me.

My father now has three grandsons. He's overjoyed. He has a granddaughter, too. She is eight and already verbalizes that her grandfather likes boys better than he does girls. She actually commented, "Grandpa likes boys more than girls. He does more for the boys. He likes to be with them better than he does me."

Why wasn't my father given a boy like he so wanted? Were all the girls put in his life, so he'd learn to love and respect the female side of himself? It appears, at times, my father is uncomfortable around women and does not know how to communicate and relate to women. Does that reveal that he does not own or communicate with his female side—his emotional side? He pushes down and stifles his emotions or he pushes them off onto others.

Perhaps all the women were put in his life, so he could have the opportunity to learn to own his emotions and to express them. But then at times, he appears to love his girls more than life itself. He seems to relish their femininity as he provides for and protects them. He is very kind and respectful of females usually. And at times, he does show his emotions and is sensitive and caring.

My awareness is, male and female are equal energies. We carry both inside ourselves. The right side of our brain is female which is emotional, intuitive, creative and feeling. The left side is male which is analytical, language, reasoning and intellectual. We are both, need both and both are equal; one is not more valuable. It's a balance and more complex than it is simple. Parts of the brain overlap and share duties then of course; we are all unique and individual and created accordingly.

What does it mean if you don't like one side? That you don't like or accept a part of yourself? You deny a part of yourself, therefore making it nearly impossible to have a positive relationship with the opposite sex.

Can you imagine life on earth, having male without female or female without male? Life would be pretty one-sided wouldn't it, if not downright boring? If we only had the ability to be analytical and not emotional or emotional without being analytical, we would not be whole and at balance. And, there would be no creation because it takes the connection and implosion of male and female to create life.

When an individual gets stuck, more in one side of their brain and ignores the other, is when they have trouble even chaos in their body, mind and spirit. And this distortion will be manifested into their life and interaction with all they relate to because they will not be able to see or understand both sides of self or others. Male and female create the whole. That is why men and women are drawn to one another and compelled to be together in union.

Simplistically, males are most usually bigger and stronger than females. They protect and provide. He is the thinking, analytical brain. Females are usually smaller and softer. They are emotional and nurture. She is the feeling heart. A wise male will always protect his lady's heart. The female energy will assist a man in processing his emotions, while the male energetic aspects protect her to do what God intended her to do. Together with their strengths and weaknesses, they thrive in joint effort and creation. Therein is the balance. When we are functioning out of the integration of both sides of self, we are at our most effective. Being able to use the Right side, the feminine and the Left side, the masculine in union even simultaneously, an individual will be more in balance with the capacity to be analytical and emotional at the same time or quickly alternating. By balancing the male and female energies inside ourselves, we are more accepting of both sexes. We will have no judgment that one is better than the other. We are more at one with ourselves, able to value others and more able to function at our true potential with the ability to think through our heart. Thinking through the heart is the key to awareness and understanding. I enjoy that I am female and also enjoy the male side of myself. There is power in acceptance. There is power in feeling whole. The highest reach of what love is on earth—the merging of male and female.

DADDY'S LITTLE GIRL

Birth until two

I'M MY DADDY'S SPECIAL LITTLE girl. My daddy loves me more than anything and above all others. When I cry lots and can't go to sleep, Daddy takes me for a ride in the car. If I still can't get to sleep, my daddy puts me on his chest until I am able to fall asleep. Sometimes, Daddy's chest is the only place where I am able to fall asleep. I feel the warmth of his body as I hear and feel his heart beating. I feel safe lying on my daddy's chest. I feel loved and warm.

My Grandmother, NaNa, tells everyone that I'm my daddy's special little girl. She says that we look so much alike that he must have just spit me out and my mother had nothing to do with it. I like being Daddy's special little girl. Everyone says that I am.

Everyone wonders why I cry so much. The doctor said that I have colic. I know that I cry so much because I'm not sure that I like being on earth. I miss the safety of Heaven. It's strange here. I don't feel that I belong or fit in. I'm afraid because everything is so different than in Heaven.

I hope that I chose the right parents. Parents who will love and take care of me parents who will help develop my talents and abilities, parents who will teach me how to live and to be happy, I know that the parents you choose on earth are very important because they set the stage for everything else that happens in your life on earth.

I'm worried because something just doesn't feel right. I'm worried and that is why I cry. I cry to say, notice me and hold me. I'm scared. Mommy and Daddy please don't leave me alone. I need you both to love me. I cry a lot. If I cry a lot, you won't be able to ignore me or leave me alone. If I cry a lot, you will have to give me attention.

My daddy's attention feels the best. I feel like my daddy will love me and protect me more than my mommy will. I'm so little. I need to feel that I am loved and protected. I will die if you don't hold me, touch me and feed me. My life is in your hands, Mommy and Daddy. I'm so little that daddy can hold my whole body in one of his hands.

When I'm born, I'm premature and am put into an incubator. They put me into a glass box. I'm afraid in there. I want my mommy. I need and want the touch and feel of human flesh.

My mommy is tired and sleeping after giving birth to me. It was difficult form mommy to give birth. It took a long time. It was rough on both mommy and me. My Daddy and Grandmother are worried because there are things that are wrong with me. The doctor tells my Grandmother not to give out any information about me yet and to wait until the next morning. She wants to tell the whole town that she has a granddaughter and to announce my birth in the society section of the newspaper.

My daddy is so worried that he goes home, gets drunk then falls asleep. The doctor doesn't tell Mommy his concerns about me. No one wants to worry Mommy.

The doctor and nurses work on me all night long. The next morning, Daddy comes to see my mommy. He is very worried to find out the outcome. But when he enters Mommy's hospital room, he sees, I'm in her arms and that I'm fine. My mommy says, "Look at our little girl, isn't she beautiful!" Daddy is so relieved.

Maybe, this is why my Daddy is so close to me. He was so afraid that something was going to be wrong with me and that he might lose me. Anyway I'm my Daddy's special little girl. He takes tons of home movies of me. He takes movies of me day and night. He even makes a movie of a whole day in my life with me as the only star.

My mommy likes me but not as much as Daddy does. Mommy gets real tired of taking care of me. She cannot handle my demands. She gets tired of my crying. Having a baby is more than she thought it would be. She pretends to like having a baby, but she really doesn't like it all that much. She had a baby because she thinks women are 'supposed' to want to have one. She wanted a baby because Daddy wanted one, but Daddy really wanted a son. He even tells people this.

My mommy wants attention. She doesn't like Daddy giving me so much attention. Sometimes, she even wishes that I would go away. She never tells anyone this, but I can feel what she's feeling. She wants all of Daddy's love and attention. She doesn't want to share him. She doesn't like the fact that he loves me so much.

I'm the first grandchild on both of my parents' sides of the family. All of my grandparents shower a lot of attention on me. They dote on me. I'm the first special little grandchild.

My mother's mother, NaNa, loves me the most. I'm very special to her. My mommy doesn't like that her mother likes me so much. Mommy wants all the attention from everyone. She wants my Grandmother's attention. She feels like I'm coming between her and her mother and my daddy and her.

I want Mommy to love me more than anything, but I cannot feel her love. I try so hard, but I cannot feel it. She's tired and unhappy much of the time. She has no energy and her eyes look dead.

I cry and cry. I want to go back to Heaven. I think, perhaps that I knew even then that my stay on earth was going to be difficult. It would have helped, if I could feel that Mommy loved me, but maybe the reason that I couldn't was part of the plan for my life.

When I'm about one-year-old, Mommy goes into a catatonic state. I'm playing in her room. She is on the bed and she doesn't move. I go to her and try to make her play with me but she will not move. I cry and cry, 'Mommy! Mommy! Where are you Mommy? Where did you go? Are you going away because you don't love me? Please, don't leave me Mommy! I need you Mommy! I need you to be here for me. I need you to teach me things. Please Mommy, answer me! Where are you?'

Daddy comes home from work and finds Mommy and me this way. My daddy takes me to live with my Grandmother. I love my Grandmother, NaNa, but she isn't my mommy. I live with my Grandmother for about a year until Mommy is better.

When my Mommy comes back, she's not the same. My daddy tries to pretend that everything is the same. Only it isn't. He takes more home movies, Easter movies and Christmas movies. It appears as if everything is 'okay' in the movies, but it isn't.

Daddy wants a baby boy. Mommy gets pregnant again. Nothing is the same. Everyone is pretending that Mommy is okay. Mommy isn't okay. My mommy dislikes me even more than she did before she went away. Now she is going to have a new baby. Why doesn't my mommy like me? Why doesn't she love me? Why is she having a new baby? Aren't I enough? I wish I was a boy. Maybe then, I would be good enough. Then they would love me and not want another baby. After the new baby arrives, Mommy gets angry when my Daddy shows me attention. She wants all the attention for her and the new baby.

My awareness as an adult looking back, I am amazed at what I went through as a baby. I had colic. When I was one year of age, my mother had a nervous breakdown, probably postpartum depression but not much was known about that then. As far as I was ever told no clear diagnosis was given of her. I go live with my Grandmother in another state, until she is able to leave the institution. After about a year, my mother comes home and a year later has another child.

As a one-year-old, I had a lot to deal with. I have never felt that my mother loved me. She shows little affection to or for me.

Thank God, I had a few years of feeling loved as my daddy's special little girl, a few years and then not as much for the rest of my life.

Mother resented the attention my Father gave me and she did all her life. I never understood this until I looked back and saw this weak and indulged woman who lost being the center of attention when I was born. By having a mental breakdown, she certainly received attention and got me out of the house. She escaped from having to deal with me or the reality of being a mother by escaping into mental illness. By becoming mentally ill, she didn't have to deal with anything. By going catatonic, she closed out the world. In her catatonic depressed state, she shut down and closed out her emotions. She escaped from having to deal with any and everything.

My father was working all the time and they were in the process of building a new house. Since my father was working all the time my mother was left to make most of the decisions for the house and to care for a new baby. This was more than she could handle. She had been a pampered child and woman. So she escaped from the responsibility of it all by falling into a catatonic state of mental illness.

My father did everything he knew to do, to get 'his family' back to 'normal'. My father had his plans and goals. He wanted to make a lot of money and have a son to carry on his name. It would not do to have a mentally ill wife.

My mother's feelings for me must have been severed during her nervous breakdown and the methods used to treat her. After electroshock and other treatments, my mother was given a treatment that is no longer practiced. She was given what is referred to as a transorbital or prefrontal lobotomy. This procedure cuts some of the nerves to the brain. The emotional feeling area of the brain is severed in the frontal lobes. The premise being that then an individual is able to go through life without their feelings overwhelming them. I believe that this operation cut the few feelings that my mother had for me. She lived the rest of her life with little to no emotional affect. She had few interests and didn't show excitement or affection.

I understand this must have been horrible for my mother. So horrible that it cannot be put into words. It was horrible for me, too. We all lost; all three of us, my mother, my father and me. What a nightmare, we all endured, each in our own way.

I can look back now as an observer and in awareness to see all sides of this terribly difficult time and experience. I love and forgive us all for our needs and desires. Did any of us have our needs met? I think not. All of us went through much gain and loss and so quickly.

This situation and the decisions made concerning it affected us all for the rest of our lives. The dynamics were put into play to be carried forward. Perhaps these dynamics were there from the beginning, when we three chose to spend this lifetime together interacting and reacting with each other, trying to get our individual needs met and to achieve our purpose and goals living our life on earth.

For a long time, I hated my mother for having a mental breakdown and leaving me. I hated my father for pretending Mother was okay when she wasn't. I hated my mother for not wanting me to have my father's attention. I hated my Father for pulling away from me, not showing me attention and treating me like I was the cause and problem. If my father showed me attention and Mother noticed or was aware of it, she would give him Hell. Then he would pull away from me. Therefore, I lost everyone and in every way.

I hated my father for telling me that if I hadn't been born my mother would not have gotten sick. I hated my father and mother for not owning their responsibility and instead pretending we were a 'normal' family. Nothing about our situation was 'normal' and no amount of pretending could make it so or different than it was.

I hated my father for denying my feelings and emotions. His pretending everything was fine caused me to deny my feelings and emotions. I pretended everything was fine, also. I hated them for blaming me for the things that they still to this day cannot own as their own.

I honor my suffering and feel my pain. By not resisting it and walking right into it with awareness, I overcame most of it. It was my trying to escape from it that hurt me the most. When I tried to pretend that everything was okay, as my parents did/do, is what almost did me in. By staring the loss, fear, hate and hurt straight in the face in awareness, it allowed it to diminish. I feel my hate and my pain. I acknowledge my feelings, all of them, my pain and my disappointment. Therefore I am aware of the situation and able to see all sides of it allowing me to release it. I no longer feel the need to keep recreating the dynamics in order to try to change the outcome.

The gift Mother gave me is the awareness and ability to express and own my feelings. I feel things deeply and am emotionally expressive. Observing mother having little or no emotions, I felt the subconscious need to carry them for her. Sometimes I hid them, but I always had them. Today I have learned to honor and to genuinely feel my feelings and the emotions connected to them. I experience them all and express them with the full joy of feeling and being alive.

At times, I have become overly emotional. I would feel so deeply that I would get stuck in the right side of my brain. I would become so emotional that I temporarily cut off the left side, the thinking/analytical side. At those difficult periods in my life, I painfully wished that I might have a frontal lobotomy. I thought that not feeling must be wonderful because, at times I felt so much pain and frustration that I thought I might go crazy or die. It seemed as if the people in my life and the universe were treating me in such a way to try to break me—trying to make me suffer so much that I either went crazy, completely lost who I am or took my life. At those times, I thought wouldn't it be wonderful not to be able to feel anything, to be able to go through life without feeling, like my Mother does. But the reality is, if I can't feel the pain then I can't feel the joy. I have the ability to experience deep love and intense joy and for that I am grateful.

With awareness, I now release the negative as soon as possible and hold onto the positive. If I don't allow myself to feel all emotions including the negative, I can't truly feel the positive. I feel the pain and I feel the joy. When I shift into the left side of my brain, the analytical, I can pull out of my emotions and into my thinking brain and be able to observe, become aware, understand, accept and forgive to better process my emotions.

Thank you Mother for showing me that I never want to stop feeling. I want to experience and feel everything. Thank you, Mother for showing me the way to joy and bliss on earth.

We are sentient beings. We are on earth to feel and experience all our emotions. Doing so heals us and expands our soul. Many of us are afraid to experience our deepest emotions and when we observe others experiencing theirs, it makes some uncomfortable. Many cannot handle it and even turn away. Some may even judge them as acting crazy or weird. The reality is, when we do this it shows us that we are not able to handle our own feelings with all the emotions connected to them. Therefore, we become fearful even intimidated when someone shows theirs. But even as we are doing this, we go to movies, plays, operas and listen to music that serve to stimulate our emotions.

Our world operates by trying to control human emotions and the feelings connected to them. Many times, we reward people who can hide their feelings. While at the same time we seek out 'entertainment' to have our emotions triggered by artificial means or we drink, do drugs, etc., to either feel more or to feel less. By experiencing naturally what we feel is how we grow and develop our true soul's destiny.

Did my mother give her emotions up, so that I was more able to fully experience mine? Was this the plan, the gift of our life together? Did I experience and feel so much, so that she did not have to? Did she experience emotion by observing mine? But since she could not handle her own emotions, she judged and ridiculed me for mine.

My father, was he able to stay in this distorted relationship out of commitment and duty? Or did it become comfortable living with someone who had few feelings and emotions, so he did not have to have as many of his own?

I became the strange one, the unusual one, the one with the feelings and emotions. I took all of them in from my parents and they watched as my pain ate away at me. Then they criticized and ridiculed me for having my feelings and constantly told me I was wrong for having them. My feelings and emotions are the only way in which I survived. My intense sensitivity, that sometimes I expressed and many times did not express, is the only way that I stayed sane in the 'crazy making and toxic' family that I grew up in.

I can still feel like I am my daddy's special little girl in my heart even when he treats me as if I do not exist. I hold that special feeling in my heart as I nurture and heal myself.

Peace comes from accepting others without demands or expectations. I am always precious to myself and to God even when no one else is able to recognize it.

I own my feelings and emotions. I allow them to flow through me in awareness. I am so blessed to be able to fully feel and express my emotions, a blessing that was taken from my Mother. What and how we feel is many times, how we know what our intuition is telling us.

I honor myself for my survival. I forgive, which is letting go of the past and therefore, the means for me correcting my misperceptions.

I am able to experience peace and internal joy.

WHEN I WAS TWO—I NEVER MET A STRANGER

I am two

I'M TWO YEARS OLD AND no matter where my mommy and daddy take me, I never meet a stranger. I say 'Hi!' and 'Bye-Bye!' to everyone. I ask them all sorts of questions. People respond to me with attention and affection. I'm out going, friendly and not afraid of anyone. I'm confident. I like people and people like me.

Mommy and daddy think this trait is cute, even though it's a lot of trouble for them to chase me down. They wonder where I get my outgoing personality. They laugh and tell relatives about how friendly I am. My grandmother laughs and inquires, "Why is she so outgoing and friendly? None of us are like this. She wants to talk to everyone."

My family except for my daddy tended to keep to themselves.

In a restaurant I walk around exploring and visiting—table to table. All the people talk to me. Mommy and daddy are worried that I'm bothering people. They chase me down and apologize for me. The people always say, "No! No! She's not a bother. She's so cute. Let her stay. We enjoy talking with her."

So off I go, chatting away—table to table. Anyway I like it when Mommy and Daddy chase after me. It's fun! Onetime, a sailor gives me a dollar. I don't know what it is. I run back to Mommy and Daddy and show them what the sailor gave to me. My parents try to return the money, but the sailor won't take it back. He says that he doesn't have a family and he wants me to have the dollar because I am such a beautiful little girl.

Later in my childhood and as a preteen, I became very shy and intimidated of people. I became afraid that people don't and won't like me. I started to think that something was wrong with me. I believed that no one could possibly like me or want to talk to me. I began to act like the rest of my family. I became outgoing no longer.

I guess my life experiences up to this point taught me that people didn't like me, or perhaps I learned to dislike myself. Whatever the reason, I became shy instead of talkative. I felt inferior to everyone for some reason and in some way. Perhaps I was taking on belief systems that were not my own. Maybe, I began to think and feel as my mother and family feel. From the age twelve to age fourteen, I was a shy and withdrawn young lady. I barely talked even in school.

My awareness is, now that I am in my forties, I feel as if I am that two year old again. I love to talk to people and to be social. I find people interesting if not fascinating. I now live in another state from my parents and it's the best thing that I ever did. I am now able to be me. The real me; without their continual criticism, judgment and influence, and I love exploring and expressing who I am. I love being me. I have come to know me and I like me.

I am aware that the more I am in touch with myself, the more I enjoy people. The closer I feel to God, the more I enjoy everyone. Everyone has something to share, like and enjoy about them. I speak to people everywhere, I like hearing their stories and about what they do and think. I am not as critical of myself any longer. I accept myself for who I am. Therefore, I feel, enjoy and am free.

The two year old didn't have time to develop limiting beliefs about people and the world. Therefore, she could reach out to everyone and expect that they reach back to her in a positive manner.

Granted, people and children need to be aware of safety in this day and time, but we can all smile and be friendly to one another.

If we all truly liked and valued ourselves, there would be no need for concern that we might be harmed by being open and friendly to one another because then, no one would have the desire to harm another.

I truly believe that people are basically good at heart. I am glad I have recovered the two-year-old in me. People enrich and enhance my life on earth. I believe this is a major reason that we are on earth, to react and interact with one another. While learning more about ourselves in the interaction; I am grateful for this awareness.

MY GRANDMOTHER'S CLOSET

I am one and a half to two

THERE ARE SO MANY SHOES in here! I can't wait to try them all on. The clothes are hanging down and when I walk through them they brush me in the face. There is a pink silky nightgown. I like to walk through it because it feels good on my face.

"Natalie, what are you doing?"

"Nothing, NaNa!"

"Darlin', get out of NaNa's closet!"

"I want to try on your shoes!"

"No, darlin', get out of my closet. I don't want you to play in there!"

I run down the hallway from the closet into my grandmother's bathroom. She's relaxing soaking in her bathtub. I put my hand into the bath water and splash her.

"Don't get NaNa's hair wet!"

I laugh as I continue to splash her. Then I run back to her closet, run through the clothes and sit down to try on another pair of her high heels. I walk back to the bathroom to show my grandmother how well, I can walk in her high heels.

"Natalie, I told you to stay out of my closet. Emmett, will you get Natalies out of here! So, I can enjoy my bath!"

I run back into NaNa's closet to hide. My grandfather, Mimi, walks in and says, "Stay out of NaNa's closet."

I love my Mimi. Even when he's angry, he's got a twinkle in his eye.

I run back into the bathroom, where my NaNa is. She says for me to sit down and talk to her. So I do, for a minute and then I run out and back into her closet.

"Lordy Natalie, you're like worm in hot ashes. Now stay out of my closet!"

"I want to try on your shoes, NaNa!"

"Emmett, get Natalie out of my closet!"

My grandfather, Mimi enters, "Natalie, get out of the closet or I'm going to take my belt off and spank you." His eyes are twinkling. I know he won't take his belt off and spank me. He's just saying this because he's doing what NaNa says to do and he's trying to get me to obey him. Like good luck with that, grandpa.

I run out into my grandparent's bedroom and jump into Mimi's chair. He follows me. Then picks me up and sits down with me in his lap rocking back and forth. I relax against his chest for a minute. Feels good, feels nice but now, I must go exploring once again. I pull up as he tightens his hold.

"Stay with me", he says. "Let me hold you." I pull away and run. He laughs, "Can't stay still for a minute, can you?"

I run back into the bathroom to see what my grandmother is doing. Then I run back into her closet. I hide way back under all the clothes, hanging down.

Oh! No! She's coming in. She reaches in for her nightgown. I stick my head out and say, "Boo!" She jumps then laughs. "I told you to stay out of my closet!"

"Did I scare you, NaNa?"

"Yes, you scared me. Now hop up on the bed with me and I'll read you a story before bedtime."

I love my NaNa and Mimi so much!

At the age of one and a half, I was staying with my grandparents because my mother was in a mental institution. My beautiful Mother was being given a prefrontal lobotomy.

When I was in college, I called my grandmother to ask if I might stay with her one summer. I couldn't stand the thought of going home to be with my parents. I always felt safe and loved when I was at my grandmother's house. I needed to feel loved and protected at this time in my life. I felt alone and horrible around my parents.

My then boyfriend was planning to get a job in the town that my grandmother lived in. So, I had the great idea that I could stay with my grandmother. I thought that she would want me to stay with her because I knew how much she loved me.

When I asked her if I could stay with her for a few months in the summer, she said that she would think about it. Then her answer was, no. She said that she did not want to have to cook and take care of someone. I told her I could take care of myself. After all, I was nineteen. I would probably be out with my boyfriend most of the time anyway and I was planning to get a part time job. I did my best to convince her that it would be a good idea and that I would be no trouble to her. She had a huge house and I could live at the opposite end of it. My grandmother still said, no. That it would not be a good idea. My grandfather had died the year before. I found out later that the reason, NaNa did not want me to stay with her was because of her new boyfriend. She wanted privacy to be with him,

It hurt deeply when I discovered the reason that she denied my visit. I felt somehow betrayed. My grandmother changed after my grandfather died. While he was living, she was the proper Southern society wife but after his death she reverted back to being the wild flapper of her youth. I knew that she still loved me dearly. Only something was different.

My NaNa, my grandmother on my mother's side, was never the "traditional" type of a grandmother. She was a master bridge playing, cruise going, scotch drinking, cigarette smoking, one arm bandit pulling, man crazy woman. She was a hoot and certainly not the cookie- baking type. She was more the embarrassing me to death asking, if I enjoyed 'oral sex', just after I was first married kind or Grandmother.

She had been the first born daughter of an incredibly indulgent kind and Godly man, my great grandfather, who owned a bank and a mercantile store in a small Southern town. He would loan young servicemen the down payment for a house right out of his pocket, if they could not come up with it. He would walk home from the bank and ask people along the way to eat dinner at his house. He asked that his wife, always prepare more than needed for just this reason. He believed strongly in education and NaNa graduated first woman in the class in her college at the age of sixteen. NaNa was a Cadillac driving, flapper of beauty, indulged, intelligent and wild as a buck. She was engaged to one man then went to a party and met my handsome grandfather. She saw him wearing a white turtleneck against his dark hair and olive complexion and that was it! They were together ever since. The man that she was engaged to didn't speak to her for many decades. That was my wild and crazy, exciting, self-indulgent, irritating as Hell grandmother whom I adored.

She taught me how to play cards. We spent many afternoons and evenings sitting on her bed playing card games while she sipped iced coffee. My grandmother and I are both hot-natured and she would crank the air conditioner to the lowest it would go.

Today when I look back on my feelings at the time, I understand that she had needs and desires that took precedence over mine. I understand, but it still hurt. I had thought that I was so special that she would not put anyone before me.

My awareness is that she put herself before me and that is okay, even if it hurt and pissed me off at the time. I know that I am and always will be special to her.

Knowing and feeling how much my grandmother and grandfather loved me, gave me a deep sense of comfort for all of my life. Even when they were angry and correcting me, I still knew they loved me. They never called me stupid or made me feel like I was awful even when they were angry. I knew if they were angry that they still loved me, even adored me. Sitting in my grandfather's lap while he smoked his pipe and watched his movies was the best. He was so handsome and a very kind and loving man.

It was as if they knew that making mistakes was okay. It was like they had this awareness because they had made mistakes and choices that, perhaps they wish, they had made some differently. They both lived full, exciting and fruitful lives. They accepted me. Therefore, I accept my grandmother for who she is.

I always felt safe and secure at their house. I knew that no matter whatever happened in my life that they would always love and treasure me. They valued me. They accepted me. They saw my true spirit as I saw theirs. It's called understanding, acceptance and forgiveness -sometimes, easier to come by with grandparents than it is with parents. I thank them for their wonderful gift.

ICE CREAM SODA

I am three

ICE CREAM! ICE CREAM! ME! Me! Me! I want! I want! I want
ice cream! Daddy and I are sitting on the stools at the counter
of an ice cream store. I feel really small. I am looking up at my
Daddy. I can just barely see over the counter. I can hear the noises—
the blenders—the glasses clinking. I can see the tall glasses on the
shelves above me and the shiny silver glasses that the people put the
ice cream in, to make ice cream sodas.

The man behind the counter is shaking ice cream up in one of the
silver glasses. I'm excited! I like ice cream. I want to be able to see
over the counter. I want to be big! I want to see over the counter and
be able to see everything that's going on back there.

My Daddy hands me an ice cream cone. Yummy! I begin to lick
it. It's so good! I ask, "Daddy do you want a taste?" My Daddy takes
a taste. "Daddy, where's your ice cream?" He answers, "It's coming.
Mine is being made now."

Then the ice cream man puts a tall, really, really, big glass full of ice
cream in front of my Daddy. The really big glass is filled with all the
colors of ice cream—lots of chocolate—nuts—whipped cream—and
a cherry on the top! It's so pretty! I ask, "Daddy, can I have a bite of
your ice cream?" My Daddy gives me a bite. Then he begins to eat his
ice cream.

I like my Daddy's ice cream better than mine. It's prettier and it
tastes better, too. I state. "I want an ice cream like yours Daddy!" He
responds, "You are too little. You won't be able to eat all this ice cream.
Now eat your ice cream cone." My ice cream cone isn't interesting
after seeing and tasting my Daddy's ice cream.

"I want another taste of yours. Can I have another bite? I want a
big ice cream, too." Daddy says, "Eat your ice cream cone. I will give
you another bite in a minute." I respond, "I don't like my ice cream
cone anymore. It isn't as good as yours." He says, "Eat your ice cream
cone or you'll have to go sit in the car."

"I want a big ice cream too. I'm big and I can eat a really big ice cream! Please Daddy I want a big ice cream! I want a bite of yours! Please Daddy! I want some more of yours!"

Daddy shouts, "Eat your ice cream cone before it melts!"

"I don't care if it melts. I want a bite of yours. Please Daddy, give me a bite! Please Daddy, give me a bite! I want another taste!"

Then SPLAT! Daddy turns his ice cream over on my head. Startled, I cry. The ice cream is so cold. It's running down my face and onto my clothes.

I'm in shock by the cold of the ice cream running down my face. I'm crying. Daddy shouts at me, "Stop your crying. You are such a pain in the neck! I'm so tired of you! I can't even enjoy eating ice cream around you!" Then he picks me up in his arms and carries me outside. I'm crying really hard now. I want some more ice cream! Why is my Daddy taking me outside?

My awareness is that it is obvious that my father could not handle the frustration in him that I created by my wanting his ice cream. His reaction and behavior accomplished nothing positive and created more stress for the both of us.

Having what I wanted withheld from me while watching another person having it, was more than me, as a three-year-old, could handle. My father tried shock treatment to get me to shut up and not ask anymore. He took his frustration out on me. His decision denied him the pleasure of his own ice cream. Then of course, he blamed me because he could not blame himself.

Wasn't it natural for a three-year-old to want something so enticing and to feel left out when told they were too little to have something so big, pretty and special?

My awareness is I was told to be satisfied with what I had and not to want or ask for more. What his actions taught me was, if I ask for more I will get it turned on my head. In that instance, my Father taught me to settle. I did settle for less in many instances. In my life when I expressed that I wanted more, better or something else, I did oftentimes have it turned on me. I learned not to ask, until I realized that I could and would get what I wanted for myself. As in, when and if someone tells me I can't have it then I go get it. There is a flip side to this awareness, in that a person needs be satisfied with what they have and not always want more. In wanting and being satisfied, there is a balance as to when to strive, when to be satisfied and when to settle. It's an individual thing and it depends on circumstances, ability and desire.

Letting a child fully experience something may neutralize the intense desire for it. While if it is held back the desire will intensify. Being told I was too little only made me feel unworthy and wanting of it even more to prove that I was big enough. All I wanted was to be like my Daddy.

Perhaps, it would have been possible for him to put me in his lap and share the experience of having such a big ice cream treat. I only wanted to be like my daddy! I wanted a big pretty ice cream, too!

Once as an adult, I went into an ice cream store and ordered and ate the biggest ice cream sundae they had. It was a blast

DADDY THROWS ME IN THE AIR

I am three

MY GRANDMOTHER AND AUNTS ARE visiting. They're watching as my daddy throws me up in the air over his head. I'm laughing, enjoying the attention. Daddy is proudly showing off his little girl and his ability to entertain her. My grandmother warns, "Be careful. Don't throw her too high or she'll hit her head!" Daddy states, "No! No! She likes it. She's fine!" He continues to throw me up and to catch me as I squeal in joy.

Then BAM my head slams into the ceiling. Startled, I cry in shock and pain. My daddy, grandmother and everyone tries to comfort me.

When I don't stop crying, in the time frame that Daddy thinks is enough, he gets angry. He says, "It doesn't hurt that much.

Your head didn't hit that hard! Go to your room if you can't stop crying!" After he says this, I cry harder and go to my room and sit on my bed.

My head is hurting as I reflect, 'Why am I being sent to my room? Did I do something wrong?' I'm feeling a deep hurt in my heart because I don't understand why I'm being sent to my room. I didn't do anything wrong. My Daddy hit my head on the ceiling and now, he's angry at me. I'm so confused and all I want is Daddy's love and attention.

My grandmother comes in—sits beside me, holds me and tells me not to worry. She informs, "Your daddy is acting silly. Men are like that. You have to pretend they are right when they are wrong to make them feel better. Now stop crying. So you can come out of your room and join us." Even in my three-year-old mind, I thought as I stared into my grandmother's face, 'Huh? I have to pretend to make a man feel better when I am hurt? This is too silly and wrong.'

Awareness is that this is an example of how I learned to deny my genuine feelings and emotions.

As an adult, I can consciously understand that my father couldn't stand the fact he hurt his precious little girl. After all, he didn't mean to hurt me. He was trying to give me pleasure and to make me laugh. When he hurt me he got embarrassed in front of my grandmother. He had to punish me when he couldn't cope with his own feelings of what he had done. This is how my Father often related to me. This is how I've lived my life in relationships, especially with men. I deny my feelings and emotions and put theirs first, which of course in the big scheme of things, not only hurts me but creates distortion in the relationship.

At three-years-old, I only had the feelings of a child—confusion, wanting comfort, attention and love—which became unacceptable emotions. My Father couldn't tolerant or accept my emotions of hurt and pain because it made him feel badly about himself for being the one who inflicted it. So I tried to deny my feelings to please him and confusion and anger was stored inside of me instead. I saw that in order to get what I desired, which was love and attention, that I needed to suppress my true feelings and emotions. I was actually punished, sent out of view—for expressing my emotions and for being unable to suppress them on demand. Therefore I became stuck in those feelings because I was forced to suppress them. From what my grandmother shared with me—it created the beginning of the belief system and imprint that I could not be genuine around men and that I needed to suppress my emotions to make them feel better about their selves.

When a child stuffs their emotions to please parents or authority figures, they will either implode the negativity into themselves by negative self-talk or other self-destructive acts. Or, they will explode their feelings and emotions outward in acts and deeds done to others and into society. This imprint of suppression incorporates into the energy field of the person and can serve to bring to them more of the same because they are living a lie concerning their feelings and emotions. By denying their true feeling and not being able to express them fully, they will not connect in true intimacy with another in a romantic relationship. If you are always denying what you feel to make another feel better, there can be no real connection because emotions and feelings and sharing them honestly are the way we connect with one another on a deeper level of intimacy.

Emotions and feelings must be acknowledged and released in some way. If they are stifled and buried, they will resurface. The way to release the feelings is to have them, experience them, own them and then release them. The more you allow yourself to feel and let the emotions move through you, the more you will release and heal. Feel the feelings without judging them—just honor what you are feeling. Parents need be aware to let children honestly express genuine emotion. Of course, too much emoting and acceptance of it can lead to a coddled and weak child. I was not coddled or indulged in this way. I was taught to suck it up. As in many things in life, there is a balance and a fine line.

Our feelings and emotions are who we are and nothing is wrong with them. Human beings were put on this planet to experience our emotions—all of them. Feelings and emotions carry power. Emotions are energy. We humans consist of energy—the energy of our emotions and our feelings manifest and create our expressions or not—even in our physical make-up. Stifling emotions can create illness in the mind and the body.

The way my pent-up feelings and denial of emotions were manifested in me was by negative self-talk that lead me into abusive marriages, where my feelings and emotions were further denied because I allowed them to be. I drew this to me because that is how I learned to behave and survive as a child. I felt that I was not good enough or worthy enough to have my feelings and emotions acknowledged. I thought that I needed to deny myself in order to be loved and accepted which was a lie because I was not loved and accepted by my doing this. Doing this even blocked my love and acceptance of self. It was imprinted on me. I learned to deny my feelings or be sent to my room, punished and ignored. Therefore, I was taught to deny who I really am and my inner knowing of what is right or wrong, how it feels and how to express it.

I'm sure my father learned something similar from his parents. He can only accept positive feedback. When negative feedback brings emotions and feelings that he cannot handle, he denies his part in them and pushes them off onto others. He blames others. So he will not have to deal with himself, his feelings or his part in it. Of course, many men reared in the time frame that my father was, have been taught to deny their feelings causing much stored up pain.

How different would the outcome, 'imprint' of this story have been if my father had owned his feelings of his discomfort of hurting me? If he had apologized to me, held and nurtured me, until I released all my emotion—I would then have felt loved and appreciated for my feelings and honored for myself and my emotions. I would have seen my emotions and moods were acceptable and were worth something and that I along with my feelings had value. Therefore I would be able to recognize my self-worth. I would have been able to release my hurt feelings and emotions instead of denying them and burying them as if they were unacceptable.

Parents—own your feelings and accept your emotions. Otherwise, your children will carry them for you. Let your children express all of their feelings; hurt—anger—love—discomfort—whatever their feelings are—honor them. Doing so will enable their feelings to flow through them allowing them to be in touch with their emotions—their true and individual identity. By releasing the pain and destructive feelings, positive feelings can be fully owned and experienced.

When emotions and feelings are denied we separate from self and deny who we truly are. By letting all emotions flow, an individual can live life to the fullest. They will be able to acknowledge and experience all their emotions and live life fully in present time, instead of trying to relive the past to create a different outcome. By releasing denied and suppressed emotions from the past, peace may be experienced and joy will abide in the individual. To be able to fly and feel free, you need to be aware of the emotions and the feelings attached to them that weigh you down and release them.

If you find you are in a relationship that you want to be close and intimate and feel that you can't fully express yourself when you are hurting or when you are happy. If you can't express and share the fullness of you for fear of being shamed, blamed or negated and feel you have to shut down or stifle parts of yourself—it probably would be better to get out.

All emotions are acceptable, so feel them all, to be at total acceptance of self so you can be receptive and accepting of others.

THE SNOWSUIT

I am three

IT'S REALLY COLD OUTSIDE. MY Daddy is lying on the sofa. My Mommy is talking to him and the TV is on. I'm dancing around playing, being silly and trying to get some attention. Daddy warns, "Careful! Stay away from the furnace."

I continue dancing, fall and land on the furnace. I land on my left leg and my hands. I am stuck. It burns. I cry.

Daddy rushes over and pulls me off the furnace. My leg is burning and my hands hurt. Mommy and daddy rush me to the doctor's. The doctor wraps my legs and hands in white bandages.

Mommy takes me to get my bandages changed and for the doctor to look at my leg and hands again to see how they are healing. The doctor says that I will have a crisscross mark on my left leg for a while, but as I grow it will go away. My hands will be sore, but will heal just fine. The doctor puts sticky stuff on them and wraps them up in white gauze.

We come home from the doctor's office. I'm wearing my puffy, gray snowsuit. It's difficult to move in this snowsuit but Mommy says I have to wear it because it's cold outside.

With me still in my snowsuit, Mommy puts me in the middle of her big bed and tells me that she will be right back. I lay on the bed waiting for her. I can barely move wearing the snowsuit. I fall asleep. I wake up. It's getting dark outside. I'm so hot in this snowsuit

I'm frightened. I feel an awful alone scared feeling down into my tummy. 'Where's my Mommy?' I pull my shoes and socks off because I'm hot. It's difficult to move or to do anything in this snowsuit. I try to take it off, but I can't. My leg hurts and I can't use my hands very well.

"Mommy where are you?" I call out. I roll over and off the big bed onto the floor. I go out the front door while feeling terribly frightened. My heart is pounding. I have this horrible feeling in my tummy. Where's my Mommy? Did she leave me? I'm about to start crying.

As I walk barefoot down the sidewalk wearing the bulky snowsuit, Mother comes around the corner and sternly asks, "Where are you going? Why can't you ever mind me?"

I'm so happy to see her, but she's angry. "Mommy I got scared!" She snaps, "I just went to the neighbors for a few minutes. Why don't you ever mind me? Get back into the house. Why are you barefoot? You're going to get sick! You're such a pain in the neck!"

I want to tell her about how frightened I got being left alone, but since she's angry at me, I don't. I so badly want her to hold me, but she doesn't. She's angry at me. So I stuff my fear and pain inside and feel like I am wrong and 'bad' for wanting to be with her.

Remembering that feeling of waking up hot and alone wearing that puffy gray snowsuit; I can even now easily recall my feelings of total panic. I felt deep fear even terror that my Mother had left me and was not coming back. The feelings of intense abandonment had been triggered in me at the age of three-years-old.

Whenever I have broken up with a boyfriend, proceeding or during a divorce, I have that same deep feeling of abandonment, fear and panic. During and right after some sort of break up from a loved one, I will awaken for a certain period of time with the exact feeling in my gut that I had when I missed and desired my Mother so badly on that day. It is a feeling of being left alone to die. The feeling aches into my soul. It is a feeling of utter abandonment and it is exactly the same way I felt at three-years-old when my mother left me on her bed. As the feeling dissipates, I know that I am healing from the hurt of the break up or the ending.

I wonder why, as adults we can't put ourselves in the child's place. It would seem to me that my mother would have been able to see and understand what I was feeling. I was injured and left alone wearing a stuffy snowsuit. Why wasn't she able to see my face and feel my terror? Why did she leave me there? Why didn't she realize that I was scared and looking for her? Why didn't she realize all this and hold and comfort me instead of getting angry? She didn't do these things because she did not have the ability to see, be aware, recognize and to understand my feelings. She was more concerned with herself and her inconvenience. She was consumed and stuck in her own needs and emotions so she was not able to have awareness of mine. My mother doesn't show much feeling, but when she does it is usually negative, angry, unhappy or hysterical.

An individual who is totally consumed with their own feelings is unable to empathize with others. Their inability to observe and have empathy causes them to miss the import signals from loved ones. Their loved ones will learn to stuff their feelings and deal with them in the best way that they know how. This may be by addictions, over-eating, self-hate, promiscuity, etc. anything that will help them stuff their feelings, and or escape from their pain. I dealt with mine by trying to stuff them and to try and be the best little girl that I could be, so as not to bother anyone.

The best thing a person can do for themselves and others is to sense their feelings, recognize and acknowledge them. Then they will be more able to recognize feelings and emotions in their children and friends.

I kept recreating that terrible sensation of abandonment in my life to see if I could fix them. I couldn't until I stayed in the feelings and felt them into my core to be able to really see and to feel where they were coming from. Then I could release them to see that I lived through them just fine.

Ultimately, I need no one but myself. I will never abandon me. Therefore no one has the power to abandon me.

I wonder if my mother could have recognized what I was feeling and nurture me instead of shouting at me. Might I have healed the abandoned part of me sooner, or was it what I needed to be shown in order that I experience it and do it for myself? Did I need to feel the extreme sense of abandonment and aloneness for me to recognize that I am never alone?

For years, if I looked closely at my left leg, I could see the slight scars of the crisscross that the floor furnace left, but today the slight scars are gone. And I do not carry the feelings of abandonment any longer.

I am never really alone. I will never abandon myself. I am safe. I am always in the arms of God.

The pain and hurt that I am shown and feel is what I am able to look at, understand and release.

SITTING UNDER MOMMY'S DRESSING TABLE

I am three

DADDY IS READING THE NEWSPAPER while lying on his bed. His legs serve to hold the newspaper as he reads it. One leg is bent with the bottom of his foot placed on the bed then the other leg rests across it to create a frame, so the newspaper rests perfectly there for him to read it. My mother has a glass and wood dressing table that sits across from the bed. There is a space under and in the middle of the dressing table where the chair can fit. So that Mommy can sit at her dressing table, look into the mirror to do her hair and make-up. And it's where I can fit perfectly. I decide to sit in this space and mimic the way that my Daddy is holding his legs to read the newspaper. Sitting in the space with the glass top above me, I try to sit just like my Daddy sits. I observe him and place my legs just like his. I do it! I am sitting just like my Daddy. "Daddy! Daddy! Look at me! I am sitting just like you are. Look I am big like you!"

Daddy looks up from his newspaper long enough to say, "Good for you!"

I am so happy that my Daddy notices me and that I accomplished sitting like he does. I sit there for a while then get bored. So I rise my body up and as I do so, I also lift up my legs. Doing so, my legs kick the glass table top above me. It falls down to break in pieces on top of me and all around me. Pieces of glass land on my head and face. I scream and cry out! A piece of glass hits my face right on my nose. Blood drips down my face.

Daddy jumps up and immediately picks me up. He looks into my face. I have a cut on my nose with blood running down my face. "Oh my God, your nose could have been cut off!" He rushes me to a doctor's office. I have a cut across the bridge of my nose that the doctor sutures together. He says that I will probably have a slight scar on the bridge of my nose for the rest of my life. He was correct I do even to this day. I have a slight scar and it serves to remind me of that day when I was mimicking my Dad sitting in the space under Mother's dressing table.

What is the awareness in this memory? Clearly that children try to mimic every little thing that parent's might do. They are observing when a parent has no clue that they are. Dad had no real awareness of what I was doing as I observed him reading the newspaper. He was focused and busy reading the newspaper. That is where his attention was. While my little three-year-old self, was observing him— mimicking his exact position wanting to be just like him. So I found a place right across from him to mimic the way that he was sitting. And by so doing, I have a scar that will forever be on my nose. Barely noticeable, but there all the same, a clear example of what children carry from parental mimicking and observation. I wanted to connect with and to be just like my daddy.

Children observe everything and will try to be like, even mimic what they observe. This is a clear example of an imprint that is actually a scar on the bridge of my nose that will be there for the rest of my life. An example of how intensely imprints are on our children— small and large.

What familial imprints are you unknowingly carrying that aren't as obvious as a scar on your nose, but are there all the same guiding your life choices? Parents, what are you modeling to your children?

GOING TO THE BEACH

I am three and a half

WE'RE GOING TO THE BEACH—JUST my mommy and me. We're in the car. I have a new pail and shovel. I am going to dig in the sand.

Mommy is driving the car. I'm talking to her. I'm acting silly and

I start singing. So, she will notice me. The song I'm singing is a song about the devil making it rain. Then God making the sun come out. Mommy likes my song. She asks me to sing it again. When I sing, act silly and cute my mommy will talk to me. She'll laugh, notice me and talk to me. I am pleasing her. So I keep singing. I want her to laugh and I want her to smile. She's pretty when she smiles. She's nice when she smiles.

It's really hot outside. The sun is shining in through the car windows. The sun is real bright!

We stop at a gas station to fill the car up with gas. We get some soda pop and my Mommy buys me some gum. I'm so happy to be with my Mommy. It's just Mommy and me. I'm a big girl. My mommy and I are big girls on our way to the beach together.

Mommy buys me some sunglasses and a cap to wear at the beach. She's wearing sunglasses and a cap, too. My mommy and I are just alike. I want to be just like Mommy.

We get back into the car and resume our way to the beach. When I stop talking or singing, Mommy gets quiet and she stays quiet for a long time. I don't like it when she's quiet for a long time. It scares me. I want my mommy to talk to me.

I feel if I am entertaining. Then she will notice me. I start talking and singing again. She likes it when I make up stories to tell her. I like to pretend, make believe and tell stories. She likes it when I sing. She likes the song about the rain and the sun. So I sing it for her over and over again. She asks me to sing another song. My mommy says, "I'm tired of that one. Do you know another one?" I make up some other songs to sing. She laughs and says she likes my songs. I'm so happy that Mommy likes my songs. I feel so happy being with my mommy.

I'm tired of singing and telling stories now. It's hard work to sing and tell stories all the time. I get tired. So I just look out the window at all the cars going by. I look out across the land.

When I look over at Mommy, she's frowning—not smiling. She looks unhappy. I think to myself, 'Mommy, don't leave me—don't go inside yourself and leave me.' Sometimes, my mommy goes inside herself for a long time and doesn't talk to me.

I sing, talk to her and tell her stories, so that she will stay with me.

I think if I entertain her, she will stay with me and not go away in her mind. It makes me sad and scared when my mommy goes away.

I ask, "Mommy, do you want me to sing again?" She responds, "No, that is okay. Look out the window at the big bridge." I look out the front of the car. I see a big tall bridge up in the air. It's up in the air, so a boat can go by. When the big bridge comes down, I will be able to see the ocean.

Yay! The ocean! I'm so excited! I stand up to see over the dash board of the car. The bridge comes down and there it is the ocean. I think the place we are going is called Galveston beach.

Now that we are closer to the beach, all I want to do is look out the window. The water is big—really big water. Birds are all over. Mommy says they are seagulls. I like the seagulls. There are big white birds flying up in the sky. They have big wings and make noises. They fly over the water then dive down really fast to get a fish. I like the birds flying. They're beautiful. The ocean smells so good. The salty air is refreshing and it feels cooler outside—the breeze off the ocean feels good.

We're almost to the beach. I'm so excited! I'm going to run on the beach and dig in the sand with my shovel.

I like being alone with my mommy. It's just my mommy and me. It makes me feel good in my heart to be with Mommy.

The ocean—the beach—a pail—a shovel—and my mommy—all I need to be happy!

When I recall the memory of this day spent with my mother, I can still feel every sensation. I can also remember the stress I felt wanting to have her attention. The feelings I had thinking I was responsible for her moods and reactions, the stress of believing that I could control whether she was happy or not. I wanted my mother to be happy and to show me love and attention. But my mother had a severe mental issue and had been given a prefrontal lobotomy. She never showed much attention or happiness to anyone.

My mother's intentions were not to create this stress in me—in fact, she had no idea that I was feeling this way. Through my eyes, the eyes of a three and a half year old—this was my perception. My imprint and perception were that if my mother was not giving me attention, and or looked unhappy or if any other negative emotion was apparent on her face or in her manner—that I was responsible. I believed it was my fault. I had either done something wrong or she did not love me.

Where did this belief come from? I had very little to do with my mother's reactions or the expression on her face be it happy or sad. But, at the age of three and a half, I sure felt I could control her by entertaining her by the mere singing of a song.

My main concern was pleasing her. My desire was to please her, to be noticed by her and for her to respond to me in a positive manner. I wanted and needed her attention.

My awareness is that children want to please. It is in their heart and soul. Therefore, they may feel that they are responsible for actions, behaviors and feelings that have nothing to do with them. When a parent is aware and notices a child trying to entertain them for the purpose of changing the parent's mood, they should acknowledge what the child is doing. Then if the parent is sad, thinking or whatever their mood may be, they can let the child know what their feelings are and why. The child will then be more able to release the idea that they are responsible for their parent's moods. Children take everything personally and they think the world revolves around them.

Children can more understand if you state, I am sad or I am worried about this or that. Then children have a chance to understand and may not bring unnecessary feelings into themselves. You will not protect a child by not sharing your feelings, both good and bad. Children see and feel what you are feeling anyway.

From a parent's mind to a child's mind there is no barrier. No wonder children suffer trauma even when the parents hold it all in and pretend all is well. Children both subconsciously and consciously sense and know and it encourages them to pretend, create over activity, even to be naughty to get attention or to keep silent in order to protect their parents—anything to keep their world safe so they have the chance of feeling loved and protected. Each child will respond differently depending on their individual personality and psychology.

Share honest emotions and feelings with your little ones. Release the need for them to carry your burden. Let them know that it is okay to feel all different kinds of feelings and that they are not responsible for what another person is feeling. Your child will then be more able to express their inner feelings to you, when the need arises.

We are all responsible for our own feelings. But we all have an effect on one another especially with those whom we share love. Feelings are visitors, let them come and go . . .

IF 'I LOVE LUCY' WAS MY MOM

I am four

I WANT HER TO BE MY mom. She's so funny! She's always laughing and doing silly and funny things. She's the silly and funny lady on TV.

If she were my mom, we would laugh, have fun and she would love me!

She'd hold me and tell me how wonderful I am. She'd tell me that she's happy to have me for a daughter. She'd say that she always wanted a little girl just like me. In the hope of my imagination, 'I Love Lucy' plays dolls and games with me. She rocks me to sleep and kisses my face. I make-up all sorts of stories in my mind, like mini TV shows, pretending that she's my mom. We have so much fun and I feel so loved.

On Sundays my parents and I go for a drive in the car. One Sunday, I beg them to take me to 'I Love Lucy's' house. I beg and beg and start crying. My parents tell me that she lives far away in California in Beverly Hills. They say that it's too far to drive to her house on a Sunday drive. I keep insisting, crying and begging for them to take me to her house anyway. They can't convince or console me.

My parents tell this story and think it is a cute story about how inconsolable I am. They tell about how I keep crying and how they cannot convince me that, 'I love Lucy', lives too far away for us to go visit her. They think this is just a cute childhood story about a child who likes the 'I Love Lucy' show.

My reality at the age of four was I really did, with all my heart and soul want her to be my mother. I sincerely believed that she would give me the attention that I did not receive at home from my own mother.

What I thought of as a four-year-old from watching her character and show on TV is that, 'I Love Lucy' will love me. I will be safe with her. She will talk to me and laugh with me. She is fun and we will have fun together. She will notice me. She will appreciate me for just being me. 'I Love Lucy' will value me.

Clearly I was a child aching for love and attention. I was trying to have my needs met anyway that I could think of even if it was through the TV and the hope in my imagination. My fantasy of having a TV character as my mother helped me believe that I could have a chance at receiving love and attention from someone. Even if it was someone I had never met and really knew nothing about but her role on a comedy show. All through my childhood this was my favorite show. Many people loved her show. I just had this different little twist to it. I thought that she would be the perfect mom.

Awareness is how sad and desperate I was at the age of four for love and attention that I would put my hope for it on an actor on TV. As I grew up, I didn't idolize rock stars or other actors like many young people do. I got it out of my system at the age of four to understand that it's futile. Clearly children and young people that over idolize actors, singers, rock stars, etc. are missing and lacking something in their home environment and life to do so.

Lucille Ball was a funny and entertaining woman but what we see on TV or in the movies when someone is acting in a part does not reveal the truth of that person or their life. I recall reading that Lucy's children missed her because she worked so much and that her husband was a womanizer. Her life wasn't perfect and she wasn't a perfect mother like I thought she would be from watching her play a role on TV. No one is perfect and no one has a perfect life—no matter how it may appear, what you might think or create in your imagination by watching an image that is orchestrated.

Wherever you are in your life, it is your life. It's your circumstances for you to enjoy, learn from and integrate, to break against or to let go of, to become more of who are and were meant to be. Your circumstances are yours. Let your focus be there, don't envy another's. What you think you see—might not be what really is.

CLIMBING THE FENCE

I am four

THERE ARE MEN ALL OVER my backyard. They're bringing all these metal and wire things and putting them around my yard. What are they doing?

"Mommy, what are those men doing in the backyard?"

"They're building a fence around the yard, a fence to keep you in."

I go back to my room and play with my dolls. I'm pondering this fence thing. 'Nothing can keep me in the backyard. What's Mommy talking about? I'm never going to stay in the backyard.' As the day goes on, I go back and forth from my room to the family room. I look out to the backyard and watch as the men build the fence.

My mommy and Grandmother, NaNa, are taking care of my baby sisters. My grandmother comments to Mommy. "I hope this fence can keep Natalie in the yard. So you won't have to run all over the neighborhood chasing her."

I enjoy going all over the neighborhood trying to find new friends. I like to roam all over and explore. I like to meet new friends, go into their houses and play with them. I like to see other people's houses and how they live. I run all over the neighborhood and Mommy has to come looking for me. I don't do this to bother my mommy or to make trouble. I run all over the neighborhood to find someone to play with, to explore and to feel free. I think there must be someone, somewhere in the neighborhood that will talk and listen to me, someone somewhere that will see me for me and like me.

One day, I'm playing in a friend's house several streets away from my street and Mommy can't find me. She's worried and goes up and down the streets looking for me. She knocks on door after door asking, "Is there a little dark-haired girl in here? She is my daughter. I can't find her." It's a very hot day and my Mommy is going to have another baby.

When my Grandmother hears about this, she tells Daddy that he must put a fence up to keep me in the backyard. My grandmother is worried about me getting lost or someone hurting me and she's worried about Mommy having to chase me down. So that's why they are building a fence around my backyard.

I continue playing in my room occasionally coming out to check on the progress of the fence.

When the fence is finished and the men are gone, I run out into my backyard. I size up this big tall wire thing. Then I begin to climb it. I put first one foot and then the other and before I know it I am at the top. I notice the sharp wire at the top and lift myself cautiously over it. I'm careful not to get my dress caught on the wire.

I'm over! I'm out! I am free! No one can keep me in. I like to go all over the place and nothing can stop me!

Daddy arrives home just in time to see my dress fly over the top of the nine foot fence he ordered built just to keep me in.

Later in life, my parents tell this story with humor and laughter. Dad expresses a little anger at the fact that he spent a lot of money on an extra tall fence to keep his little girl in and to keep her safe. And just as it was completed, she climbs it. I can tell by the way he tells the story that he is amused, proud and frustrated all at the same time. He called me his little rebel and while he wanted to keep me safe, he was also proud and admired my fearless and exploring soul. "Go get 'em Tiger", he would often say to me.

I remember living in that neighborhood and roaming all over it. I was always looking for somewhere to go, someone to play with and to talk to. I was a lonely lost little girl looking for a place to feel welcomed and at home, while also looking for adventure and fun. I would escape whenever and as often as I could. I would go up and down the streets, ringing doorbells to see if there were any children for me to play with.

There were teenage girls who lived next door and I loved to go to their house and look at all of their pretty clothes and ball gowns for parties. I knew that someday, I would be grown-up like them and have beautiful dresses. I liked being at their house because their mother talked to them and me. It was fun talking about 'big girl stuff'. I couldn't wait until I was grown-up. I hoped my mother would pay more attention to me when I was older.

There was a lady down the block who would give me candy and talk to me. I would pretend that it was Halloween when it wasn't, to give me justification to ring her doorbell and talk to her. She, of course knew it wasn't Halloween every other day, but she pretended with me. She always had a piece of candy to give me. She was really nice. She invited me in and we talked about all sorts of things. Maybe she was lonely, too. She said all of her children were grown. She told me stories about her children and what they used to do when they were young. I wished that I could live with her because she gave me attention. She made me feel special.

My awareness is that I was a lonely little girl and I did not feel like I fit into my family. My mother gave me little to no attention. I didn't feel special in my family and certainly not to my mother.

I can also see the symbolic reason for the fence. My parents of course, wanted me safe and secure, but they also wanted me to stay where they could watch me and for me to be just like them.

I am not like my family in most aspects and I was always looking for adventure and a way to find my identity apart and away from them. I hated coming home. I hated wearing shoes. I wanted to run around the neighborhood barefoot and free.

At the same time, I needed my family more than anything. I needed their love, attention and nurturing. I was looking for these things outside my home and in other people. I was an emotionally starved child and I would climb over any fence I had to for my freedom and salvation.

I applaud myself for my creative resources. I just ventured out and looked for fun and attention. I was a fearless little girl. At the age of four, I was fearlessly roaming around the neighborhood looking for adventure along with love and acceptance. Even at the age of four, I instinctively knew that I had to get away from my family and look elsewhere for most of what I needed to survive and thrive.

I lost that little girl for a while. I built an imaginary fence in my mind which closed off my love and acceptance of self. The imaginary fence in my mind held fear and negativity. Since life dealt me some difficult blows; I had become even more fearful and negative. I kept drawing this type of interaction to me. My belief system created the fence in my mind, a fence that I had to tear down piece by piece in order to find myself.

All the fences you put up in your mind along with fighting the fear only holds it in place to be experienced over and over again. Whatever you are not able to face has the ability to become bigger and to even, do you in. Once you face your fears squarely on, they will diminish. They will be released.

I love that fearless little girl and I allow her to live fully in me. I have faced many of my fears.

Much of the time, I am fearless and full of trust in myself and my creator. I am my own best friend. I do not need to keep roaming and looking, unless I choose to. I have myself in my own backyard.

Just like a fence can keep you in your yard, so can limiting imprints, perceptions and beliefs keep you in a life guided more by them than by choice. Become aware of imprints, examine them and from where they came. Are they really yours or do they actually belong to those around you, an ancestor, a friend or parents? Imprints you are carrying which would be better served being released from your energy.

Just like a mother who cautions her child to stay in the yard to avoid possible harm, so too, does the belief system want to keep you safe. Just like a child wants and needs to grow up and leave the yard, so too, an individual wants and needs to grow past the imprints of limiting beliefs

NAIL IN MY FOOT

I am five

RUNNING AROUND MY NEIGHBORHOOD WAS the best. I explore far away from the street where I live. I lived in a new subdivision where there were many houses under construction. The kids I ran with considered houses under construction wonderful entertainment almost like an amusement park. I was the youngest in the group but it didn't faze me because I was a daredevil and the most adventuresome. I led the pack. I never saw a ladder I couldn't climb or a roof that I couldn't stand atop off.

It was a hot summer and I would run carefree and barefoot. I hated to wear shoes. Mother could get me to wear them hardly ever. It was a glorious adventure to explore street to street, through backyards, into houses under construction, climbing the ladders to roof tops and standing high upon them with the best view of my world that I could have.

Running, climbing, skipping, jumping all over until one day, I stepped on a nail and it stuck straight out of the ball of my foot. I hopped on one foot back to my backyard. I sat down in my 'made especially for me' little outdoor lounge chair. I yelled loudly, "Daddy! Daddy!" He rushed over to me. When he saw the nail sticking out of my little foot, his face flooded in horror. "Dang, Natalie!. How in the world did you do that?"

I shrugged and am sure showed a bit of fear. "Get it out, Daddy!"

"Hold on, Tiger. Let me get something to pull it out." He rushes into the house.

I sit in my little lounger looking at my foot with the nail sticking out of it, wondering, 'Why is Daddy taking so long? I want this thing out.' I shout, "Daddy! Daddy!" No answer.

So with all the strength I could muster, I hold the end of the nail and pull! The nail comes right out. It didn't even bleed or hurt that much. It felt like a kind of yucky pulling sensation then it was over.

Daddy rushes out of the house holding a tool, some cotton and a bottle of stuff. When he sees the nail is out of my foot, he looks in my face in amazed shock. "You pulled that nail out on your own!?"

"I got tired of waiting. So I pulled it out."

Daddy picks up the nail and inspects it. "Thank God, no rust." Then he stares me in the face with concern and amazement.

"Daddy, it didn't hurt much or even bleed that much."

He responds, "You're something else, Tiger!"

He puts liquid on the cotton then on my foot to clean it. He puts a bandage on my foot as he lectures. "I don't want you ever playing at those houses under construction again. Do you understand me?"

"Okay Daddy", I respond.

With my foot all taken care of, Dad takes the supplies back into the house. When he's gone, off I go as quickly as I can. I rush off to continue my exploration of the world. When I look back on this memory, I am amazed at myself, my bravery and my resilience. I just pulled that nail right out. I wanted it out, got tired of waiting so took care of it myself. I wasn't afraid. I knew what had to be done. I did it then off I went.

I admire my spirit of adventure and my 'suck it up—I'll take care of it myself' nature. What a brave little girl I was at five. I explored my world, while I pushed every boundary my parents set. My explorations were some of the happiest most fun, educational and inspirational of my childhood. Sure, I stepped on a nail or had other mishaps occasionally, but the gains were well worth the small discomforts. So what if I stepped on a nail, it was a minor inconvenience and I was able to pull it out all by myself.

Life begins and takes off at the edge and end of your comfort zone.

HANGING FROM MY KNEES

I am five

I HAVE A SWING-SET IN MY backyard. There is a cross bar at the side of it. On that bar, I like to hang by my knees for so long that I get dizzy. Then I flip over to land on the ground flat on my back and watch the world spin around me. I like it when the skirt of my dress hangs down over my face, so no one can see me. Of course, I wear shorts under my dress that way no one can see my under panties.

On this beautiful day, I am hanging from my knees, looking up at the sky. The sky is blue with puffy white clouds floating by. Some of the clouds are in the shape of angels. I feel like I belong somewhere up in those clouds, up in the sky, up in the Heavens instead of here on earth. I hang by my knees looking up with an ache in my heart and soul with a sincere knowing that I belong and want to be back up in sky—higher than the birds and back home with God.

THE 'SUSIE WALKER' DOLL

I am five

SHE'S TWO FEET TALL WITH long auburn braids, so pretty with a checkered dress, lace petticoat, shoes, socks and bows in her hair. She walks and talks and I want her for Christmas more than anything. When she's on the TV, I show my mommy. "Look! See! This is what I want, what I have to have. She walks and talks, Mommy!"

I think to myself, she'll be my friend. I'll play with her and love her. She'll never go away or get mad at me.

On Christmas morning, she's under the tree. She looks so pretty that I'm afraid to touch her. My Mommy says, "Here she is, the doll you asked for! Santa brought her to you." I keep looking at her and by the end of the day I'm finally able to pick her up. She's the most beautiful doll I've ever seen. I love her more than anything. I'm going to take the best care of her in the whole wide world.

I play with her. Take her hair out of the braids. Brush her hair. Take her clothes off then put them back on again. I try other doll clothes on her. I'm having the best time.

I go out to show Daddy how pretty her hair looks out of the braids. My Daddy shouts, "You're ruining that doll!"

I run back into my room and sit on my bed. Daddy comes in and shouts, "You're ruining that doll! Don't you know how to take care of your things? Where are her clothes? Her hair isn't supposed to be taken out of the braids. That doll was very expensive. You should take care of her. Maybe, if I take her away! You'll learn to take care of her!"

He put my doll up very, very high in the closet on a shelf then says, "You can have her back when you learn to take care of her!"

I am horrified. I sit on my bed and look up at my doll. She's scared to be so high up on the shelf. But I can't get her down and save her or I'll get into trouble.

Couldn't Daddy see that I love her more than anything and I would never hurt her? I only brushed her hair and changed her dress. She gets tired of the same clothes and hairstyle. If she has to go away, I won't love her so much. It won't hurt as much that way. I lay on my bed and cry.

A few days later, my daddy gave my doll back to me. But the feeling was never the same. I didn't understand how he could take away something that I loved so much. Besides, Santa had brought her to me. Santa knew I'd take good care of her. I must have done something really wrong for my daddy to take her away. It hurt so badly inside. I was afraid to play with her again, afraid to love so much. Afraid to brush her hair, so she just sat in my room.

As an adult, I can understand that my father's actions were from his belief system developed in him, as a child based on his experiences from his parents, and the world he grew up in. His intentions were not to harm or to hurt me, but to teach me what he thought was important, which was to keep my doll nice and perfect so she would last longer.

My child's view was to smother my doll with love by all the attention I could give her. My father grew up very aware of the depression. When he was a child, did not have the money to purchase things he wanted. He started working when he was fifteen. His value on material items is that you take good care of them so they will last.

In this time frame, he was a young husband with four children under the age of five. That doll was probably expensive and my parent's made sure that I got her for Christmas because I asked for and wanted her. But in his punishment, my father was not focusing on his little girl's feelings. Had he been aware of her feelings, he would not have acted in the manner in which he did. Instead, he was treating me the way that he had been treated as a child from the imprints that he carried. He was operating out of his imprints and his belief system. This was the only way he knew to respond. His belief system was not appropriate for me in this situation.

At the age of five, all I knew was the hurt. The stress that this incident caused in me developed a fear of loss. It was extremely traumatic for the doll that I loved and wanted so intensely to be taken from me. From my perspective, at the age of five-years-old, she was taken away because I loved her too much. I was showing my love in the only way that I knew how—by constantly playing with and doing for her.

My father did not have a clue that the whole purpose for the doll was for me to have something to play with and love. From his perspective, I was supposed to put her on a shelf and admire her.

When a child asks for something and a parent answers the request. The parent must truly give it to the child, not take the gift away for punishment. Then on the flip side, children need to be taught how to care for their belongings, to appreciate them and to keep them nice. But ultimately, the choice is the child's as to how to treat belongings. My father might have suggested that I keep my doll nice, so she will last longer. He could have explained how to do that and give me some insight into caring for her. But for a little girl to do the expected of combing a doll's hair and changing her clothes and then be punished for it, is insanity and crazy making. Also in my equation, I didn't have a mother cognizant enough to step in, soften the punishment or to guide Dad.

At the time, it hurt me so much that I did not know what to do. So I decided to cut off my feelings and not love or care for the doll because I could not stand the pain of her being taken away again. I could not stand the pain of the loss. As far as I understood at the time, she was taken away for the reason, I believed which was I loved her too much.

Playing and actions that a parent may perceive as destructive may really be expressing love or fun. Playing is the intention of toys and dolls and certainly at the age of five-years-old. If the doll was too precious and only for the purpose to look at her then it was not the toy for a five-year-old.

Children can be taught to care for their belongings without harsh and severe punishments that result in cruel treatment and negative imprints. Parents might look through the eyes and heart of the child before deciding if punishment is in order.

The type of interaction I received concerning my 'Susie Walker' doll created a fear in me of caring too much. I did learn to take good care of my belongings but that is a trait of my nature that I was born with. This experience taught me that if I loved a person or an object that it or they would be taken away or would go away. Also, I may do something wrong and be punished if I am not being or acting 'perfect', whatever 'perfect' is? That my actions might cause the person that I love to go away and I would not know what I did to lose their love. Just like with the doll, I did not know what I did wrong, except to show my love for her and she was taken away from me at the very moment that I was giving her love.

I created exactly what I took into my beliefs. I had been imprinted. I have lost every person I've loved, or have chosen inappropriate partners which produces the same results, not having love. So I will not have to experience the pain of losing it or receiving love only to have it shattered. Thus, proving to myself over again that I must do something 'wrong' and do not deserve to have things I want and to love and be loved.

I am aware of this imprint and limiting belief. I own it and understand my father was doing the best he knew how to do. He was acting out of his imprint. This awareness helps me to understand him. Therefore, acceptance and forgiveness are able.

Forgiveness is the answer and positive relationships are the result. I am able to experience love and know that it will not go away. I am worthy of giving and receiving love. I am worthy of receiving what I desire. I am always in the eternal love of God.

THE PINK ROOM

I am six

MY FRIEND MELISSA LIVES IN the most beautiful pink room. It's just perfect. It has beautiful pink curtains and a beautiful pink bedspread. She pushed two twin beds together, so her bed looks huge. Sitting atop the bedspread are a whole lot of stuffed animals and dolls resting on the pillows.

She has a big picture window that overlooks her backyard. In front of the window trimmed with the pink curtains, her desk and chair are placed. She can look out to her backyard when she's coloring or writing at her desk. Her carpet is pink, too. She has pretty pictures hanging on her walls. The room is bright and cheery. My friend, Melissa has everything that I wish I had.

Her closet is filled with darling clothes. She has lots of dresses, shorts, slacks and tops to wear while she plays. She even has two older sisters to teach her all about stuff—like how to act around boys and what clothes are cool.

Her house has a big front porch. We play on the front porch a lot of the time. 'Roly Poly' bugs and 'June bugs' flock to her front porch, we like to play with these bugs. We also like 'Lady bugs' a whole lot. She says that the 'June bugs' come to her porch because her mother's name is June. I wish my mother's name was June. Then maybe bugs I can play with would hang around my house.

Melissa and I sit on her front porch for hours playing games with the variety of bugs that choose to live there. We also play the game of 'jacks'—you know, 'ball and jacks', on her front porch. We play the game of 'hop scotch' on her drive way. Her sisters really know how to draw a neat 'hop scotch' board using colored chalk.

Melissa and I wear our hair alike. We both have long dark hair. We both wear our hair in ponytails. We are best friends.

I love to spend the night at Melissa's and I do so a lot. We stay up late with her older sisters watching the scary shows that are on TV real late on Saturday night. I love hanging around her older sisters. I wish I had an older sister that could teach me things, look after me and show me what is cool. Sometimes, we all sit outside in her backyard and tell scary ghost stories. We like to scare ourselves. It's so much fun!

Melissa lives right next door to me, but it seems like a different world. We're living in a rental house. Daddy says that we will not be here long. So it isn't worth fixing up the house. Mother says that some of the neighbors treat us badly because they know we live in a rental house. As if we're not as good as they are because we rent instead of own. I guess it's better to own.

I go over to their houses to play with these kids whose families say this about us. Their house is real pretty. The girls have a beautiful room. They have lots of toys and dolls but their room isn't as pretty as Melissa's room. I don't think that they are any better than my family. They just have a prettier house. Anyway, they treat me very nice.

I know all this upsets my mother, but it doesn't bother me so much, except I want a beautiful pink room, too. I know my daddy is going to get me one someday. He says that we won't be in this rental house for very much longer.

My daddy is starting a new business and is working very hard. He's hardly ever home. He says that once he gets his business going really good that we'll buy a house. I look forward to when we can buy a new house.

We only have one car. Everyone else in the neighborhood has two cars. My mom and dad share a car. It's difficult sometimes. My mom sometimes has to take a taxi. Maybe that's why those people don't think we're good enough for them. I think riding in a taxi is fun but it's inconvenient for my mother.

My sisters and I don't have a lot of pretty clothes. We have clothes just not a lot of them. Our rental house is big but the colors in it are awful! Mother doesn't like the colors either. My room is the darkest, darkest green. I hate that color! It's not a little girl's color. It seems like night, even in the daytime because it's so dark in my room. Daddy says it's not worth painting because we're going to move soon.

I get sick with the chicken pox, measles and the mumps while we are living in this house. I have to spend a lot in time in bed in that awful dark green room, resting and healing.

When I have the chicken pox my mother says that I need to stay in the dark so that my eyes will not have damage. I can't look at my picture book, color, read or watch TV. It's an awful time for me because I have to stay in that dark, dark room. I can't scratch either because if I do the chicken pox might scar my body. I try to be real good and do what my mother says to do. Lying here in this dark room is lonely and awfully sad. I can't go outside to see the beautiful sun. I can't see my friend Melissa, until I'm well again.

I lay in this dark green room still and quiet. I try to find some reason, some purpose for being in this awful room. I think maybe, God put me in this dark green room, while I have the chicken pox. So that it was certain that my eyes don't get hurt because in this room, it's like nighttime even in the daytime. Thinking this, helps a little, as I suffer in this room waiting to get well. I don't want to hurt my eyes because I love to read. I wish that someone would come in, visit me or read to me, but no one does.

Then one day mom poked her head in and says that she's going to run a quick errand. She says for me to stay in bed and that she'll be right back. "Do I want anything?"

I'm feeling much better today. I've been in this awful dark green room for what seems like forever. I'm ready to get out. My mother had said earlier today that my fever had broken.

I hear the door close as she leaves. I open my door—free at last. I venture into my mom and dad's room. It's bright and sunny. I love it in here!

I turn on the TV. Cartoons are on! I haven't seen cartoons in a long time. It's so good to watch TV again. I hope I don't go blind! I'm feeling better and the chicken pox is almost gone. I start jumping on the bed. It feels so good to move. Jumping on the bed and watching cartoons, I feel well again! I'm back to myself again!

Then I hear the door. Mother is coming in with my little sisters. I smooth out the bed spread; turn off the TV then race back to my room. I get into bed quickly, but I'm scared! What if God punishes me and makes me blind because I disobeyed my mother and got up too soon? I'm so scared and worried because I watched TV in the light and I jumped on the bed when I was supposed to be quiet and still. I'm scared. I pray. "Please, God, don't make me blind, I won't do it, again! I promise!"

Mother comes to my door and gives me some candy. She takes my temperature. I don't have any more fever and haven't had any since yesterday. She says, "I think it's okay if you get up now. You're well!"

What a relief! I decide to tell her what I did while she was gone because my conscience is bothering me. She says, "That's okay. You're well!" Hooray! I can come out of this dark dungeon into the wonderful bright world again!

I hated that dark green room and the time that I spent recovering in it. I think that it would almost have been fun to be sick in a room like Melissa's. I hope that someday I have a beautiful, bright, pink room.

Then one day daddy says that we are moving to a new house. We all go to see it. It's beautiful and all new. Daddy says, "Yes, you can have a pink room. You will share it with your younger sister." I'll be able to pick the colors and decorate it because I'm the oldest besides my sister likes pink, too.

We move into the new house and my mother gets a decorator. I get to help her decorate my room. The curtains are pink and our bedspreads are pink. I have a desk with a bulletin board made of cork framed in pink fabric. I can stick pictures, party invitations and notes on it with tacks. We have tall pink shelves to put our toys and dolls on. There's a big picture window that looks out into the backyard. We have a closet full of pretty dresses. We have shorts, slacks, and tops to play in. My mother gets a new red station wagon. Daddy gets a new car, too.

I invite my friend Melissa over to spend the night. She likes my pink room. We're sad that we don't live next door to each other anymore but I don't live that far away. We still can visit each other and spend the night at each other's houses. I always want her to spend the night at my house because I don't want to leave my pink room.

At Christmas time, my daddy even lets us get a tiny pink tree to put on a table in our room. I'm so happy! My daddy got me, my pink room! My dream came true.

Looking back at this particular memory brings so much awareness to me. I felt like I was not as good as the other people in the neighborhood because we were renting our house. I was very conscious of how this feeling affected my mother. It did not feel good to have the worst house on the block. It did not feel good, to not have clothing and a room equal to my friend's. I felt left out even though I was treated well.

Apparently, mother felt snobbery and she conveyed those feelings to me. I realized that we did not have what the rest of the neighbors had and I saw how it affected my parents. I saw my father working, gone from us all the time to make money and to have success. So we could have what he wanted us to have and what we wanted to have.

I experienced living in an awful room and could not wait to get out of it. I experienced isolation, how to cope with it and how to try to make the best of it. To this day, I cannot stand being in a dark environment and dark green may be nice on a car but I avoid it almost totally. I experienced my father achieving success enough to give us our dreams. He made all of our material dreams come true. I saw that dreams can come true, when you work hard. I wonder what my feelings and awareness would have been had my father not been so successful?

I have the awareness that when I disobeyed my mother. I thought God was going to punish me and make me blind. This shows that a belief in a vengeful God had been created in me by the age of five.

I experienced what it is like to have a best friend. She accepted me and loved me even when I did not have a lot of material things. She shared her sisters, her room and toys with me.

I saw how important material things are to my parents and to others and that some people judge others by what they have or don't have at any given time. I saw how your life can change overnight just by having money. The people are not any different. They just have more money and material items.

I saw, experienced and learned a whole lot that year. What I experienced created many of my beliefs that I've carried with me all my life. As an adult, I have driven by that house and around that neighborhood. I have many warm memories of everything but that dark green room.

Later in life, I learned that during that time frame of my dad building his company and while we were living in that rental house that there was a situation when dad and his partner didn't know if they could make their payroll or not. So they went to Vegas and rolled the dice. Dad later told me, "That he knew when he rolled those dice that it will either make us or break us." Well, the dice were on his side. They were able to make their payroll then able to go onto build a large and successful company. What a brave risk taker my Dad was. He had four children under the age of five, a new business and a completely dependent wife and he took the risk of rolling the dice. He always told me that he had an Angel on his shoulder that guided him.

Even though, I had an abundance of material things, I was not a pampered child. My father taught me to value what I was given and what I had. Also even though I loved my pink room, many nights after I crawled into bed and was laying there snuggled under the covers. Just before I would fall asleep, I would say in my mind's eye with a knowing in my heart that I want to go home. That even though I was in my earth home and in a beautiful pink room that I knew I had another home and I missed it.

Children see everything. They take it all in to form who they are and who they will become. They perceive through their own individual perceptions. They are continually being imprinted by beliefs that will guide their life.

THE DEVIL'S SONG

I am six through nineteen

ALL OF MY SISTERS AND I are running around the break-fast table. We're going wild! We're chasing each other, running around the table, pushing the chairs in and out as we go if and when they get in our way. It's summertime. We've been home all day. We're bored! We are four children home all day and we're going wild!

Our housekeeper, Lilly, is ironing across the room from us. She keeps telling us to settle down. She says "Shush! up! You all be quiet!" She walks over and claps her hands and starts singing. "Sha Na Na Na! Sha Na Na Na!" She raises her hands above her head and wiggles her fingers as she sings. "Sha Na Na Na! Sha Na Na Na!"

She's singing funny words. We stop and look at her. "What are you singing? What are you saying?"

She just keeps on singing. "Sha Na Na Na! Sha Na Na Na!"

Our curiosity stops us in our tracks. "What are you doing?"

She stops singing for a minute to answer. "You're bad children. The devil has got hold of you. I'm singing the devil's song to free you from his spell!"

We burst out laughing. "We don't have the devil in us! We're just being wild and silly! There's no devil around here!"

We calm down to listen to her story about how the devil gets into little children then they act wild and crazy.

"We don't believe you! That song doesn't work!"

"Oh, yes it does! You children have calmed down, haven't you?"

She's correct. The spell was broken. We're settling down and listening to her stories. Lilly goes back to her ironing and we gather around her sitting on the floor to listen to more of her stories.

My mother walks in and comments, "You all sure are being good today and so quiet. We tell her that Lilly sang the devil out of us. She responds, "What?"

After that day, we always wanted her to sing the devil out of us when we were acting wild. We acted wild sometimes just so she would sing it. Sha Na Na Na! Sha Na! Na! Na!

She took care of our house and all of us for most of our childhood. She was a wonderful good hearted woman. She had known much hardship in her life.

One day, I was having difficult times with a boyfriend at school. When I was in high school, I would sit on the counter in the kitchen and talk to her about my life's troubles and ask for advice. She would be ironing and we would talk and talk. She would give me her insights and opinions. She had some real sound, common sense advice as I recall. We would discuss and talk about lots of things. She would share stories about her life. I would listen intently. Then I would ask what to do about this and that and she would listen then offer suggestions.

I spent many afternoons sitting on the kitchen counter sharing my day and talking with Lilly. It was comforting to come home from school to have Lilly always be there in the kitchen ironing. She was a special and needed addition to my family and like a mother to me.

Then all of a sudden after being with our family about fourteen or fifteen years, Lilly is gone. I do not know why, but my parents let her go. It was a strange and heart-breaking experience. My parents just said that she had been with us too long and wasn't doing her job well any longer. They appeared to have no feelings at all about it. It was just a matter of fact thing to them.

One of my sisters became extremely upset about losing Lilly. My parents responded as if something was wrong with my sister to be so upset about it. One day, Lilly was in our house cleaning, ironing and being there for us. Then the next day, she was gone! It was scary to have her be gone so quickly and with no warning. It was also upsetting that my parents showed no concern. The fact that someone could be in our house almost every day for fourteen years then because she did not do things correctly or displeased them in some way—was gone.

It made me wonder that if I did not do things 'correctly' or displeased them would I be likewise dismissed. The answer to this is, yes and I eventually was.

Later, I was to learn that Lilly was let go because my mother was jealous of the attention and affection in which we regarded her. I thought of Lilly as more my mother than my actual mother was because Lilly listened and talked with me. After that, we talked to Lilly occasionally on the phone. One day years later, I was driving in my car and saw her standing at a bus stop. I turned around to go see her but by the time I got back to where she was, the bus had come and gone. That was the last time I ever saw her.

I will always remember with fondness sitting on the kitchen counter talking with her and listening to her stories about her life.

She offered me nurturing when no one else would or could.

I thank her for her gift to me.

THE WILLOW TREE

Birth until ten

SHE SITS ON A BENCH under the big beautiful willow tree in the front of her house. I run over to sit under the tree with her. The branches fall over the bench to partially hide us. The sun is flickering through the leaves. It's like magic! We sit on the bench and talk. My grandmother is so beautiful. She is tall and thin. She has long dark hair with some gray in it. She wears her hair on top of her head. Her skin is translucent. It's white and soft. Her eyes are a soft grayish color. Her voice is soft, too. She speaks calmly and slowly. I know that she loves me very much. We're talking about flowers and trees.

It's almost time for dinner. So we go inside the house. As we enter the house, aromas of a roast cooking and freshly baked chocolate cake are in the air. My grandmother is a wonderful cook.

I follow my grandmother into the kitchen. She asks me if I want to help her ice the cake. Yummy! It is incredible chocolate icing and I get to lick the spoon! She comments, "I know that you like being at your other grandmother's better because she has such a big beautiful house and all your aunts are there to have fun with. Over here, there's just 'Daddy D' and myself in this small house but I'm glad that you're spending this time with me." I respond, "I like being at your house, just you and me. You make good food, are beautiful and you're nice!"

I'm icing the cake and watching her as she makes everything ready for dinner. She's working hard to make a nice dinner for us. Later on, everyone will be here for dinner but for right now, it's just her and me getting things ready.

She looks like a queen to me—like a royal person. She carries herself in this manner. It's the way that she walks and talks. She's a royal person that should live in a castle. A queen in a castle is how I envision her and she's just temporarily trapped in this little house.

She has a kindness about her. Although, she has a sad and faraway look in her eyes and she's quiet and calm. She has a 'knowing' look in her eyes as if she sees and knows things but chooses not to speak about them. She appears peaceful. I can't imagine her yelling or getting angry. I wonder if she ever got angry and yelled at my daddy when he was a little boy.

She wears clothes that are old and out of style. Yet her clothes and the way she looks have a certain quality about them. She wears long skirts with pretty soft blouses and old style shoes. She has elegance. She carries herself like a queen. Her carriage is like that of royalty. She has an apron around her waist now as she busily prepares our dinner. Her long hair is up in a roll all around her head. I bet if she wore pretty, more stylish clothes that she would really look so beautiful that it would be unreal, because she even looks beautiful wearing the old-timey, unstylish clothing that she wears.

She's class, quality and all that is good. She looks like an angel to me. Her name is Gabriella. Her name even sounds like the name of a princess or a queen or perhaps even an angel, but I call her "De De".

I overheard my mother talking about 'De De'. She said that her husband 'Daddy D' talks cruelly to her. He says hateful things to her and makes her cry. My mother says that she cannot imagine anyone being cruel to her because she's so sweet to everyone. She does not have a mean bone in her body. My mother says that 'Daddy D' told my grandmother 'De De', if she was drowning and his mother was drowning at the very same time that he would save his mother and let her drown.

When I heard my mother saying this it made me feel sick inside even like I might throw up. It made me hate my grandfather. How did he, even ever think to say such a thing and why would he say it at all?

I don't get to spend enough time with her but when I am with her she gives me her undivided attention. I love to watch her take her hair down out of the roll atop of her head. Her hair is very long and very beautiful. She only wears her hair down when she's sleeping.

She's getting ready for bed and she's brushing her hair. I'm sitting nearby and talking with her. She's sitting at her dressing table. Everything is neat and organized on her dressing table. Her silver brush and comb and everything are carefully placed on white lace doilies. Her house is not big but it's neatly organized. Her bedroom is beautiful with a dressing table and a big four poster bed.

I only remember going to the store with her one time and she purchased all these little dolls, games and toys for me. When my daddy saw what she had bought for me, he said, "Mother, you shouldn't waste your money on things like this. Natalie has a room full of dolls and toys." I still remember that day and the little things she got for me just because she wanted to give me things that I wanted. So I don't feel that it was money wasted. I also knew that she didn't have much money which made what she bought for me even more special. It was a special memory to last forever that showed how much she loved me.

The house with the willow tree out front, my Daddy bought for his parents with the money he got when he was recruited out of high school to be a pitcher with a professional baseball team.

My grandmother 'De De' became very ill when I was about eight-years-old. She became so ill that she went to stay with her sisters, in their family home in a small town in the South. She had three sisters and some of them never got married. They still lived in their very large family home.

We all went to visit her. I overheard my parents saying that it'll probably be the last time that we get to see her. Hearing this made me feel heartbroken. I didn't want to think about my grandmother dying and I felt a little afraid to see her. My father had said that she was very ill. Cancer had eaten up her body. And that it made him sick that his beautiful mother had bile coming up through her mouth. Her tummy wasn't working correctly.

The house she was now in was totally great. It was one of those big old white houses that had lots of trees around it. There was a great staircase and an upstairs that had an open level all the way around it, so you could see to the room below. I think there might even have been three stories to the house. The house seemed as if it went on forever. I thought this is where beautiful Gabriella must have lived when she was a princess.

I wondered why she had married my grandfather and moved to that little house. Except of course she had a great front yard with the willow tree that my Daddy bought for them. She could sit on the bench under the willow tree and watch traffic go by and no one would see her sitting there because the branches hung over so far. I wonder if she misses her willow tree. She told me that she would sit on the bench under the willow tree often and that it was her favorite place to be. When I visited her, I would spend hours sitting on the bench under the willow tree—playing, dreaming and feeling the magic of the earth combined with the universe.

My grandmother was in a downstairs bedroom. A whole lot of people were coming over to see her. Her sisters were cooking a lot of food. My sisters and I were running all over the house, up and down the stairs and all around the floor with the open level around it.

My mother called to me and said, "You all be quiet! You're disturbing your grandmother. Natalie, she wants to see you now."

I felt a little frightened but I badly wanted to see her. I walked into the room and around to the side of the bed that she was lying on. I stood back from the bed, hesitant and a bit fearful. I had never been around illness or someone soon to die. I looked into her face. She said in her peaceful calm voice, "Look Natalie, I'm wearing my hair down the way that you like it." I smiled at her. She looked so tiny, thin and frail as she asked, "Would you give "De De" a hug? I stepped forward and hugged her very gently. I didn't want to hurt her. She looked into my eyes for a very long time, studying my face as if she wanted to make sure she remembered. She asked, "Are you frightened?" I nodded my head, yes. She responded, "That's okay, I understand. I want you to know that I love you a whole bunch and will forever."

"I love you, too." I replied as I leaned over and kissed her gently on the cheek. She closed her eyes and smiled peacefully. I felt so sad inside.

Her sisters said that I needed to leave now to let her get some rest. As I was leaving the room, I turned to see her lying there with her eyes closed. Her sisters were all around her caring for her. She looked calm and peaceful.

I never saw her again.

One night, I was running through the hallway and the phone rang. I picked it up, just as one of my parents picked up the other phone. I heard someone say that 'De De' had taken a turn for the worse and was dying. I burst out crying. My heart broke. My mother quickly got me off the phone.

My mother and father went to the funeral. They didn't take us girls because they didn't think a funeral was something that we needed to go through at our young ages.

I remember this woman as I described her in these memories. The last time that I looked into her face is imprinted on my soul.

She represents everything good to me. She represents a calm knowing. I visualize her sitting under the willow tree. I hold this woman in my heart and know that her spirit watches over me. Each time, I see a willow tree, I think of my beautiful grandmother, Gabriella.

The place where I live now has many willow trees. When my niece was visiting one summer, we were driving down the street where willow trees line the road. She asked, "What kind of trees are those? I love them! They are beautiful! I wish I had one at my house." I answered, "They are willow trees. I love them, too! Your great grandmother used to have a large one in her front yard. When I was a little girl just a bit older than you are now, I used to sit on a bench under a willow tree with her. She responded, "Cool!"

My niece would have loved 'De De'. They are a lot alike, caring loving, giving and seeing more than they express verbally to the world.

My father grew up in a home where he observed his father saying and doing hateful, degrading things to his mother. He observed his father controlling his mother by hurting her, using fear and manipulation. Even if he did not like what he was seeing, he took it all in. His beliefs about how to treat a woman and the value of a woman were developed in this environment.

My father observed his beautiful mother dutifully cook, clean while staying calm and quiet. I know that he loved her very much. He would talk about her often but rarely mentioned his father. Yet, he must have had some disrespect for her that she would allow her husband to degrade her. She was doing what her beliefs and society told her to do. Be a good housewife and dutiful to your husband. This is the relationship that my father observed which developed an imprint on him. My father was a kind man and treated my mother most of the time like a queen.

Dad told me the story that when he was a school boy and his mother would come to school for PTA meetings and such that the other women would laugh and exclude her because she didn't wear and couldn't afford fashionable clothing. This hurt was imprinted deep into him. He worked hard and long hours to provide for his family. He was driven and when my father became a financial success, he told my mother that he wanted his girls to have the best of everything. He didn't care the cost. He afforded us to have the finest designer clothing, jewelry, houses and accoutrements that there could be. My mother had an abundance of gorgeous clothes and jewelry as did his girls and he took great pride and pleasure in our having them. He was a generous, giving man, unselfish, even though he made enough money for him to have all his dreams realized, too. He put his girls first and foremost.

He told me once when I was just a little child. "Stick with me kiddo and you will be wearing diamonds the size of acorns." And he made good his promise. My father kept all his promises. He was a man of his word. Sometimes, the imprint of deprivation can be the stimulus to create much drive and success.

My grandmother appeared to be calm on the exterior but inside she was being eaten up. She did this to herself by holding her emotions, anger and pain of submission inside. She developed the disease of cancer of her ovaries and it physically and literally ate her up. I find it interesting that the cancer that killed my 'De De' started in her female organs. She was in a relationship with a man who abused her as a woman. For whatever reason, she could not, did not own her feminine power.

A bit of this imprint and belief system was passed down to me. Except that I rejected it as soon as I had the awareness of it. I most usually feel and express my emotions. When I am diminished or abused, I exit. I also have had problems in my reproductive system. I had an ovary removed when I was in my thirties. Happy to say, all is well now. There are many similarities between my grandmother and myself. I identify with her much more than I realize. I love to cook for and to give to those whom I love.

As a child I observed the feelings and emotions that were being transmitted between my grandmother and grandfather. A belief was being developed in me when I visited with them. The imprint that women were not worth much and that no matter how 'good', beautiful or giving a woman was, it did not matter to 'some' men.

My grandmother's value and worth were that of an angel. But why didn't she, couldn't she fully claim her worth? She died young. She died with the people who loved and valued her all around her. It gives me strength when I recall her memory.

An imprint and memory of comfort is of my Angel Gabriella sitting under her willow tree.

After my dad's mother's sisters sold their family home. My father took care of all of them for the rest of their lives. He sent them money every month.

"When our hearts turn to our Ancestors, something changes inside us." Russel N. Nelson.

COMIC STRIP

I am six or seven and years after

HE'S SITTING AT THE DESK in his living room drawing pictures for me. He draws funny pictures of a man. It's a picture of a man's face from the front, from the side, sometimes wearing a hat and sometimes not. He draws these cartoons for the newspaper. He tells me that he draws a comic strip for the 'funny papers'.

He says things that he thinks are funny then laughs at them. I don't think what he says is funny at all. When he talks to me, I don't understand what he is saying. I don't like his voice. It is gruff. What he says doesn't make any sense to me. I don't like his stories and I don't like talking with him. I don't like to be around him.

My grandfather, my father's father, 'Daddy D', is a small, thin man with straight gray hair. This seems strange to me because my daddy is a big tall man.

My mother told me that he says very cruel things to my grandmother, 'De De'. That he says cruel things to her and makes her cry. After I heard this, I really and so much more didn't like being around him. I didn't want to look him in his face.

When I'm in a room with him, I avoid him by standing back and behind the other people that are in the room. I don't like to get close to him or to hug him.

I think, he works for the railroad, but I'm not sure. He and my grandmother don't look as if they belong together. She's kind, tall and beautiful. He's small, angry and cruel. I wonder why she likes him. I wonder how she could love him. They are married. So they must be in love, right? I don't think they share a bedroom because when I was watching my grandmother brush her hair, while she was getting ready for bed, my grandfather wasn't around. She was in a bedroom that was hers. Maybe, he's just gone a lot or something—doing the railroad work.

Why would my grandfather say cruel things to my beautiful grandmother?

After my grandmother 'De De' died, my grandfather married another woman. This woman was icky inside and out and had several icky daughters. They all moved into my grandmother's house. The house that my father bought for his parent's when he was only in high school. The house didn't feel the same with these new people in it. The elegance and refinement were no longer there. My grandmother, Gabriella was elegant and beautiful. These women were nowhere near her quality.

While visiting my grandmother's house for the last time, the icky girls showed me a trunk that held my grandmother's belongings. I looked inside and there were clothes, books and lace things. Items that she had on top of her dressing table like her silver hairbrush and comb, seeing the items in the trunk made me ache for my beautiful and kind grandmother, Gabriella. It felt as if my heart was breaking to view her belongings.

I reached inside the trunk to touch her things to feel close to my grandmother. The girls said that I would have to buy some of my grandmother's things if I wanted them. I was just a kid. I didn't have any money to buy anything from them. I would have liked to have some of her belongings. These girls didn't even know my grandmother and they had custody of her things. This made me feel deeply unhappy inside. It was strange for them to be in her house. I had her in my heart and my memories of her. No one else could have them and they weren't for sale.

My mom and dad didn't like this new wife and her kids. They were arguing with them. I never told my parents about the trunk and what the girls said to me. I didn't want to talk about what had occurred. It hurt me deep inside and I didn't want to upset my parents any more than they already were. I didn't want to bring back the sad feelings that I had inside of me, while looking in my grandmother's trunk knowing that I couldn't have her things, unless I gave money to these icky strangers.

I wish so badly that I could have had a piece of the lace—the white lace that was on her dressing table. I wish I could have had her silver hairbrush. I wish that I could have had something of hers to hold, to touch and to keep forever.

My grandfather died and left the icky lady a widow. I think the icky woman and her children ended up with my grandmother's house. She called my dad and asked for money. With a voice full of anger and disgust, my dad told her, "No, I have my family to provide for." How I know this is that dad was on the phone in the kitchen and I was eating a snack and listening. When dad got off the phone with the icky woman, he chuckled in disgust and said, "Now, ain't that a kick in the head." He let out a sarcastic chuckle then hugged me and said, "I love you, Tiger. Get to bed."

That is pretty much all I remember about my father's father.

While writing all of these stories I thought that since I didn't have much memory of my grandfather that perhaps, he wasn't that important to my life. That is incorrect. He is part of where my father got his imprints that guided his life. This man that I remember was cruel and this man had been my father's role model.

My own father never talked about this man much. So I don't know what he thought of him. My grandfather didn't have much money so based on what I know about my father, he probably thought he was a failure. I do know that my father took care of his father financially, at times.

I wonder did my grandfather feel like a failure. Is that why he was cruel to my grandmother? Had he observed his father being cruel to his mother? Did he take all his frustration out on my grandmother because she just took it? She was kind, loving, giving and he took advantage of these traits in her.

Was he intimidated by her beauty, her calm knowing and peaceful appearance? So perhaps, he tried to disrupt her serenity to create the same insecurity and stress in her that he had in himself. If he hurt her and made her cry, therefore temporarily making himself feel powerful and in control. This is what insecure and weak men do— men with little to no self-awareness.

For some reason my grandmother didn't, couldn't, own her power. Therefore she allowed this man to abuse her and shake her up inside. She let it eat up her insides, despite her calm exterior.

My grandmother Gabriella was from a wealthy family and she was beautiful and refined. She married beneath her in every way. I feel as if my grandmother outclassed my grandfather by a country mile. So perhaps, he put her down to make himself feel better about who he is.

I don't know all that much about my grandparents' parents, what they did, or how their families lived. What matters is that my father observed his father treating his mother in a degrading manner. My father was not like his father. He had success and money and he was usually generous and kind to his wife and daughters. Even if at times, he held things over our heads and beat us up with them. He mostly was kind and did things to try and teach us lessons about money, resources and life. But I wonder if his father's attitude about women and what my Dad observed was the reason why my dad wanted sons so much, as if girls weren't somehow as valuable. Since he saw his dad, degrade his beautiful and kind mother.

The imprint of the shame and lack of being poor as a child prompted my dad to develop his talents to work hard and to provide well for his family, he was driven towards success. He always bought us the best and when we went out to eat or traveled, it was in the best fashion and quality that the world offered. We lived in beautiful homes with the best of furnishings and wore the finest of stylish clothing.

My father adored his mother. She was tall with long dark hair and my father got his good looks from her.

This man 'Daddy D' had a great impact on my life, as did his parents and his parents before him. It doesn't matter that I didn't know these people in the flesh. They had a great impact on my life anyway.

All of an individual's ancestors line up to create much of whom they are, what they believe about themselves, and others. Both the positive and the negative aspects of the people are passed down, generation through generation. What is interesting, is that most often the negative imprints dig their template in deeper than the positive ones. Their negative energy lies hidden, while they guide lives with many times little to no awareness of the harm being done to self and those around them while limiting lives to the full expression of who they really are or might become.

My dad had a self-reflective side to him. He was usually able to see things from another's point of view and life circumstance—eventually. I think he tried to overcome and negate most of his negative familial lineage imprints. His feelings of being inferior and his shame of being poor and in lack as a child stimulated him to become more than his family ever could have imagined. He loved women and for the most part treated them well. He enjoyed pampering women. It gave him great pleasure to give to others. He was more like his mother than his father.

After my grandfather 'Daddy D' died, I did get my grandmother's silver hairbrush and an emerald and diamond ring that her father had given to her. For Christmas, one year, my dad had the emeralds and diamonds made into a ring for me. At the age of thirteen, I put that ring on my finger and wore it every day. Having it on my finger and able to look down at it made me feel that my grandmother was always with me.

One day, I looked down at my ring and the center stones were missing. I freaked out. I had been in two college classes that morning. I immediately called the university and told them what I had lost and which classes I had been in. And like some miracle from Heaven, someone found the stones and turned them into the lost and found. I got my grandmother's stones back and this made me unbelievably grateful.

Many years later, I was divorcing my first husband. It was a heated divorce. He wanted everything from the marriage even after he had gambled away most all our money. He had affairs, an illegitimate child with his secretary and was an alcoholic. But he was still pushing to go to court to try and take everything left materialistically from of the marriage and from me. During this time, my house was burglarized. What was taken is the wedding ring that he had given me which he was trying to get back in the divorce, my grandmother's diamond and emerald ring along with my chest of Tiffany silver flatware. Tiffany replaced the silver, but the rings were not itemized in our insurance. Therefore, I received a small amount of compensation for them.

I lost my grandmother's ring forever. And I know in my heart that my ex-husband was the one that had the house burglarized. He lost in court. I was awarded what remained of our marital assets with the divorce being granted to me on the grounds of extreme mental cruelty in a no-fault divorce state. My attorney set a legal precedent.

This weak and nasty immoral, addicted man from the wrong side of the tracks had married me mostly for benefit of my family's money and their influence. I had married him right out of college. I was attracted to his fun, good looks and sense of adventure or was there something else underlying driving my attraction to him that I did not realize at the time? My dad came from little and made a great success; therefore, I thought this man and his ambition could do the same. I married beneath me as my grandmother did before me. And this man in the end stole my grandmother's ring.

I had become like my grandmother whom I loved so much and had so much compassion for. Her DNA ran through me even as I vowed to never let that happen to me. When I look back at this man that I married, I can realize his image that he created to attract me and who he really was. They were not the same. He was fun, outgoing, handsome and friendly in college. But when he got out into the world as a man, his character revealed he was the lowest of the low. He was always out for himself. He didn't love or care about me because he had no comprehension of what love is. And when I met him, I had no ability to see past the fake imagery of his creation.

It's not until one becomes aware, self-reflective and in full honesty of self that they are able to say. "Okay, that is where this comes from. I don't like it and I choose to eliminate it from my belief system." But the imprint can be so deep that it becomes enmeshed in your energy and may attract the same negativity, even as you vow not to let that happen. You can become exactly what you think you are resisting.

Until it's seen, owned and examined on all levels, negative imprints lie hidden, like guided missiles towards destruction.

It's up to each individual to look at what is being passed on, both to and from the past, then weed out and release that which serves no more. Release what is detrimental to self, to our children and to our future. The awareness and release of these negative imprints allows us to be free and at choice, to be all that we truly are in our lives. Instead of being guided by hidden imprints from others.

Love is not fear. Love is not control. Love is not abuse. Love is kind acceptance of self and others. Love is honesty and respect.

Until we can truly love and accept ourselves, we will continue to hurt and harm not only ourselves, but the people closest to us, our wives, our husbands, our children, our families and our friends.

It's out of our own frustration, self-lack, lack of understanding, lack of awareness and lack of self-reflection that we do harm to others and ultimately ourselves.

Jesus treated all women with the deepest respect. We honor all women by showing them the same love and respect that Jesus showed to women. Women have been abused and put down by men–sometimes very crudely and cruelly. But Jesus is the perfect man, the man God wants every man to emulate. This is the kind of man God wants every woman to know in her life.

PRESS HARDER!

I am eight

IN CLASS WE ARE PRACTICING writing capitol letters in cursive. I write so softly that my teacher can't see my letters. She tells me continually to press harder with my pencil. I try to make myself do this, but I can't. I write so lightly even I can barely see it.

I was shy - very, very shy. I was quiet as a mouse in school. I didn't talk much, but did make good grades. I tried hard to be very good all the time. I didn't want to get in trouble or draw attention to myself. So I tried to be quiet and good in order not to be noticed.

The teacher is walking around the room and looking at our papers. When she passes me, she bends down and instructs me to press harder with my pencil. "Write, so I can see how nicely you make your letters."

I tentatively turn to her and quietly says, "Okay, I will try."

She responds, "Don't try. Do it!" I jump startled. I knew she was beginning to get frustrated and angry and it frightened me. She bends close to my face and softy states, "I am trying to help you. If you don't write darker, no one can see what you write. And from what little I can see, you write beautifully."

She continued walking the room looking at the papers of the other students and watching as they write. Occasionally she picks up a paper and makes a comment.

I try to press harder with the pencil but can't. For some reason, I just can't! And I don't know or understand why. I try so hard to do as the teacher asks, but can't. She's getting close to my desk again and my heart begins to pound. Then she picks up my paper and in a very loud voice states, "Write darker or I will give you a failing grade no matter how well you write.- how can I grade something that I can barely see?!"

I look down at my desk in shame and humiliation. She embarrassed me in front of the whole class. I am shaking inside but try not to show it—to avoid further humiliation. Putting my paper down in front of me, she continues, "Do you hear me? Write darker or you will fail this class!"

I look up at her with tears in my eyes and nod, "Okay, I will."

I sit in my seat staring at my paper trying to hold back tears. I am so hurt in my heart. I don't understand why I can't write harder. I am trembling inside and my head is spinning. I feel frantic as I wonder— 'Is something wrong with me?—Something must be wrong with me.—I am told this often enough at home - they must be correct.'

Then I take a breath and try again. I force myself with everything I have to press harder with my pencil. And I do make a darker capitol 'S'. When I see it, I sigh in relief.

I continue pressing harder and I can see my letters now. It makes me happy that I can see my letters, because before this, even I couldn't see my own writing - and now I can. I take a breath and proudly think, 'I 'can' do it.' I even realize that I write pretty, now that I can see it. I feel so relieved, proud and happy both at and for myself.

The teacher walks by and looks at my paper then smiles down at me. "Good job young lady. Now, I can see your beautifully formed letters."

Our smiles meet. She is proud of me and I am proud of myself.

This is a memory of how shy I was as a young school-aged child. That at times, I tried not to be noticed or even seen. It was as if I wanted what I wrote along with myself to be invisible. I thought that something was wrong with me. I felt criticized a lot at home and it diminished my self-confidence. During these years of childhood, I was internally diminishing myself to match how I perceived I was being treated.

Might sound silly now, as an adult, but at that time it really was scary to press down harder with my pencil—so that my letters could be seen. But I did it because of my teacher's prodding even humiliating way. Her pressure and challenging me - worked. As an adult at times, I can still feel myself as that scared little eight-year-old sitting at her desk—not feeling good enough—shaking inside - not feeling worthy to be seen or even to be alive. Even to this day I can still feel emotionally and physically the way my teacher's loud words startled my heart and served to break me open, challenging me to try harder into developing my self-confidence and awareness.

During different time frames in my life, it took everything I had to muster up the courage to break through fears of not being good enough and to allow myself to be seen, heard - to write - to speak in a public forum before many—to dance on a stage and to stand up for myself. Each time I overcame my fear, it built my confidence a bit more. There is nothing wrong about feeling unsure and insecure. We all do at times. The key is to overcome those feelings by trying—even the act of trying makes one feel better—to try and fail - so what—to never try—you will never know that you might have succeeded.

Also I was embarrassed to be called out in front of the class. I was worried about what the others might think of me. But no one noticed, they were concerned with themselves—not me. Most people don't notice when you might think they are. What matters is your image and what you think of yourself—not what others think at any given moment. More often then not, they don't care, even remember or would change their opinion at a moment's notice.

Your opinion of self is what matters. After I wrote my letters darker, I forgot my worry and insecurity about what I thought the class might think because I had accomplished a task and was pleased with myself. What I thought of myself is what mattered. Showing clearly that when a person thinks well of themselves—what others may think matters not.

Sometimes we need to be startled, pushed and challenged in order to grow and to reach past where we are at any given time. Usually those in our life who challenge and push us, do so out of caring and are put in our lives for just that purpose. It's up to us to listen, rise to the challenge and to become more aware.

SELLING GIRL SCOUT COOKIES

I am eight and for years after

IF I WORK REAL HARD to sell tons of these cookies, I'll win an award. The award is a little stuffed bear, but that's not the most important part. The most important thing is that I'm going to sell more Girl Scout cookies than anyone else. I'm going to be the best! I'm going to win the top award!

I told my mom and dad my goal. They said I could order a lot of cookies, but that I needed to make sure that I could sell them before I ordered them. My parents said they would buy a few boxes, but didn't want to be stuck with a whole bunch of them. They said, "We don't want to be eating Girl Scout cookies forever!"

I'm wearing my Brownie uniform and beanie. My troop leader said we must dress in our full uniform to be official. I've put the boxes of cookies in my little red wagon. I've got an envelope with some money to make change for the people buying. I'm ready to go all over the neighborhood. It's a beautiful fall day and I'm ready to be the winner!

Mother said for me to be careful and not to go, too far away, but I don't care. I'm going to go as far as I need to go to sell all of my boxes of cookies. The troop leader said that if and when we sold all of the cookies we ordered that then we could order more. That is what I am planning to do. I'm going to sell all of my cookies today. Then quickly order some more. The troop leader said, "First come, first serve!" Well, I'm going to be the first!

Off I go, street to street, block to block. After about five streets, I've sold almost all of the cookies. There was only a lady at one house that said someone had gotten there before me. Hooray I'm beating everyone!

It's getting cold outside, but I keep on going. I'm really far away from my house by now. I'm starting to get into another area where the houses are much larger.

I enjoy looking at all of the houses. I like to look in the door of the houses while the people are buying the cookies. I love to see all the pretty interiors. It's interesting to see how all the different people decorate their homes. What colors they choose? Whether or not, the house is neat or messy? It is surprising to find that the houses that are pretty and neat on the outside are sometimes the ones that are messy and unattractive on the inside.

People can be like that, too!

As I'm walking along pulling my almost empty wagon, I see a beautiful 'Thunderbird' sitting in a driveway in front of me. I know this car. It belongs to a really beautiful lady. I've seen her at the Country Club. She has beautiful blond hair that she wears on top of her head. She is tall and slim. She looks like the movie star, Grace Kelly. She wears beautiful clothes, jewelry and looks like a beauty queen all the time.

I'm going to go to her house to see if she would like to buy some cookies. Her house is beautiful like she is. It's big and sits on a corner. It's one of those long, low ranch houses. I really like it. I would love to have a house like this one when I'm grown-up and married. It's going to be fun to see inside this house. I walk up the front walk and ring the doorbell. No one comes at first, so I ring it again. Then I hear footsteps. A housekeeper answers the door.

I ask if they would like to buy some Girl Scout cookies. As I am saying this, two darling little red-headed children come to the door—a boy and a girl. Of course they start jumping up and down exclaiming, "Yes, yes, please, please, we want some cookies!" The housekeeper asks me to step inside the door. She says, "Wait here, Miss." She walks down a hallway to the back of the house. I hear her say, "Ma'am, there's a little girl selling Girl Scout cookies."

I'm standing in the middle of the entry hall with the darling red-headed children. They are running all around me excited about the prospect of having some cookies. The house is very lovely just like the lady and her car.

The housekeeper comes back and says, "Step back here Miss, the lady of the house is resting." I grab my last four boxes and follow her back to the lady's bedroom with the little children jumping up and down beside me. I feel a bit uncomfortable. I'd wanted to see her house and now I'm going into her bedroom.

I enter the room. She is lying in her bed wearing a beautiful pink satin robe. She looks pretty. The TV is on. I say, "I don't want to disturb you, but I am selling Girl Scout cookies." She smiles and asks, "How much are they?"

She has a kind way about her. She asks me if I've sold a lot of boxes. I respond that I just have four more to go and then I can get more cookies to sell. If I can sell all of those, I might win a prize. She looks at all the different kinds of cookies and says that she will buy four boxes.

The little red-headed kids are going wild with excitement. She looks over at her excited children and smiles. I can tell she loves them very much. She tells her children to settle down and to go into the other room, so she can think and pay for the cookies. The housekeeper comes in and takes the children away.

The lady gets up and reaches for her purse. It takes her awhile to find her money. I look around the room. It's so pretty! I wonder what it must feel like to be so beautiful, have two beautiful children and live in such a beautiful house.

I say, "I'm sorry that you are sick." But she doesn't really look sick to me. She looks just sad and tired. Maybe she just needs some rest.

She leans over and hands me the money. She smells like liquor. She smells like my parents do when they have a party. What a shock this is to me. If she is sick, why is she drinking gross, terrible, old, nasty liquor? I look beside her bed on her night table to see a bottle of liquor and a glass with some liquor in it. I recognize the bottle because my parents have one like it.

I get the money for the cookies, say thank you then leave.

I feel strange about what I have just seen. This beautiful lady with everything in the whole world is lying in bed drinking liquor in the afternoon. It gives me a sick feeling inside.

While walking back to my house, I decide that I want to be just like her but without the liquor part.

I sold all my Girl Scout cookies that day. I ordered more and sold them, too. I sold the most cookies in my troop. I won an award and a Girl Scout stuffed teddy bear.

All of this was great, but what made the biggest imprint and impression on me was the experience of seeing this lady that I admired, in a whole different light. Whenever I would think of her, it would make me sad.

A few years later, I overheard my parents talking. They were talking about their trip to Las Vegas. They were talking about a couple who had gone on the trip with them. They were talking about the beautiful blond woman and her husband. Her husband owned a big car dealership and they were in Vegas with a group of people including my parents. Mother was saying that this woman was much younger than her husband and the rest of the people on the trip. Mother said that this woman didn't like hanging around everyone else. She acted as if she was bored all of the time. Mother said that she didn't really blame her because she was so much younger. She probably really was bored to death. Mother said that this woman came from a family with a lot of money and that she was spoiled rotten. Mother said her husband couldn't control her. Apparently, the couple had a fight because this woman wouldn't cooperate and socialize with the people her husband wanted to entertain in an attempt to get their business. Mother said the woman left Las Vegas, early one morning because her husband had beaten her to a pulp. Mother said that no one saw her after that. Her husband never said a word about why she had gone home.

I was about twelve-years-old when I overheard this conversation. I had never heard of a man hitting his wife. I was shocked. This lady was so nice and beautiful. I couldn't imagine a man wanting to hit her. Why did her husband want to control her? Why, when my mother was talking about it, did she sound to me as if she thought the lady should have let her husband control her? And that she should have done what he said, even though mother did understand why the woman would be bored.

I thought after hearing this story that this was why the lady drinks and looks so sad, even though she appears to have everything. She is so beautiful. I just couldn't imagine anyone wanting to hit her.

Approximately twenty years later, I crossed paths with this woman again. I was running a ballet school and I taught two of her children ballet. She had a new husband and two new children— little dark-haired girls. When I saw her in the waiting room, I recognized her immediately. She looked pretty much the same just a bit older. She was still very beautiful. Her children were two of my favorite students. The other two red-headed children were now young adults.

She didn't recognize me because I was only an eight-year-old child when she last saw me. She did remember my parents.

Then a few years later, our paths crossed again. She had gotten a divorce and she was looking for employment. I was running an art and interior design business. She worked for me part time for a while. Several times during this period when I spoke with her on the phone, trying to train her and assist her in building her business, she had been drinking and she slurred her words.

My awareness is, how interesting it is that it can seem like a person has everything and they are still unhappy. Of course, what does having everything mean? What is everything? Quite obviously, this beautiful lady was very unhappy inside and nothing could make her happy. It appeared to me that she lacked love of self. Her unhappiness wasn't that she had too much money which made her uncontrollable as my mother had suggested, but that she lacked love of self. Just by the fact that she would be with a man that would hit her because she didn't do what he said reveals this.

Of course this is just speculation on my part. No one can really know what goes on in another person's mind, in their home or in their life. What appears one way may really be quite another.

I recall this woman because there was something about her that reminded me of myself. Perhaps I was able to see and feel how lonely and lost she was and with a knowing that she did not love herself because at the time, I was having trouble loving myself. Even at the age of eight, I could relate to this woman. I could have an understanding of her. There was fragility about her to which I could relate. I did grow up to be like her in ways, but not in the way I had imagined on that day while selling Girl Scout cookies. The way I became like her was that I did not know my full worth either for a while and in a time frame of my life. I had a husband who drank. I loved him very much and he could be wonderful but when he drank he sometimes got bizarre and anything but fun. We had many long talks and arguments about his drinking. He would try to quit but then wouldn't. One night when he was drunk, we were arguing and he pushed me. When he did that something clicked in me and the very next day, I filed a restraining order. I had the locks on the house changed. A lady in the domestic violence office said that she was shocked that a man could have done that to me because I am so beautiful which was exactly what I had thought about that lady some thirty years ago.

Of course most everyone knows that the way one appears on the outside has nothing to do with it. It has to do with what is going on inside.

I got out of that marriage quickly and no man has ever touched me in a hurtful manner physically ever again. I claimed my worth in that regard quickly. It was one of the most difficult things I have ever done to end this marriage because I loved him. But I loved myself more and after my first marriage and its horror, I was not going to subject myself to another man with addictions and behaviors that did nothing but harm me and him and destroy our marriage. The weekend after I kicked him out of the house, I cried the whole week.

It was continual sobs. I sat in the closet with his perfectly spaced GQ suits and bawled. I wrote little notes to him and put them in the pockets of his suits.

That ex-husband has since sobered up and got counseling. He told me along with much apologizing that my doing what I did, is what made him realized how horrible he had become. That he lost the woman he loved because of his addiction and behavior.

And if this wasn't enough to this tale, after my divorce, I was running my interior design business. I loved being single without the trauma and drama of a man's issues. I was enjoying taking care of myself being on my own and independent. During this time frame, one of my girlfriends from high school who had just remarried threw a wine and cheese art party in her home to help me promote my business. She lived in a gorgeous home. I was excited and appreciated her doing this for me. She, of course was my age and the man that she married was none other than the owner of the car dealership. The man who was once married to the beautiful blond woman who bought Girl Scout cookies from me so many years ago. He was my parents' age. So clearly this man likes younger women. The night of the party was great. It went well and I acquired new clients. During the evening, I kept my eye on the car dealership man, the new husband of my friend. All I could think about was what my mother had told me that he did in Vegas to his beautiful blond wife. His actions at the party that night showed him to be encased in a shell to promote and protect his image. He was arrogant, selfish and self-serving along with being braggadocios and pompous.

When my girlfriend showed me though their house and we were alone, I inquired if he treated her well. She smiled and responded, "Oh yes, just look at our house." I didn't believe her answer. What does a house have to do with how he treats her?

She inquired of me, "Are you going to remarry? I saw you with that handsome man at Picasso's. His family is mega-wealthy. Isn't he a pilot and don't they own an aviation company? They have their own jet. What a catch." In that time frame, women who were unmarried or divorced were to be in ways pitied. Therefore, she wanted me to be married, so I would be 'okay' again in her eyes.

I responded, "He's a man I see occasionally. No. I am not ready to remarry, if ever. I like being on my own."

I could tell by the expression on her face that she thought I was crazy not to want to marry this man. I learned early on that marriage is only as good as the people in it. A beautiful house, money or whatever else does not matter unless there is respect, honor, fidelity and genuine love and no addictions.

Some women think that they are safe if they are married or stay in a marriage. While being in a marriage can be the most unsafe place a woman can find herself both psychologically and physically.

About that car dealership man, I heard years later from my father that he lived out his life in agony, had issues with his heart and diabetes along with clots in his legs—so bad that he had to be completely sedentary.

It's fascinating how people and memories intertwine throughout our lifetime showing us—teaching us—mirroring to us.

"We bring to ourselves that which, we think we are. By being yourself, you help others be themselves. When you recognize your own uniqueness, you will not need to dominate others or cringe before them.

"Our life is the creation of our mind." Buddha

IT'S BUMPY AND I AM SCARED!

I am eight

WE ARE ON OUR WAY to Florida for a family vacation. I am sitting beside Daddy on the airplane. The little girls are sitting somewhere behind us with Mommy.

The airplane is bouncing up and down lots and way too much for my comfort. I feel as if I could throw-up any minute and if I did that,

I would be so embarrassed because I am eight-years-old and not a baby. But it's really, really bumpy and I'm really, really scared.

I am trying to act grown up, but I get so frightened that I can't anymore and I turn to Daddy, "I'm scared, Daddy. Why is the airplane bouncing so much? I feel like I could throw up!"

He responds, "It's okay Tiger, airplanes are meant to withstand turbulence."

"But—but, Daddy, I feel sick to my stomach."

"Here's an airbag, hold onto it just in case you need to throw-up."

I take the bag and hold it tightly in my lap while trying very hard to not be afraid.

Then the airplane bounces up high then down low as my stomach does the same. "Daddy, Daddy! Is the plane going to crash?"

"No, everything is fine. The airplane is doing what it's supposed to do. It is built to withstand turbulence."

"Okay Daddy, but I am still scared."

The plane bounces roughly again. I grab hold of Daddy's arm, "Daddy!"

"Okay, Tiger, remember when we were fishing that time and your Mother caught a fish and when she reeled it in and it flip flopped inside the boat, how she jumped up, screamed and almost turned the boat over?"

I laughed, "Yes, I do, Daddy and it was so funny!"

Daddy kept telling me stories, real and made up, one after another, until the plane touched down in Miami. He kept my mind off the turbulence, off my fear and off my needing to throw-up. He kept me focused and even laughing and enjoying myself. Even at the age of eight, while this was the perfect distraction, I knew what he was doing. And as I knew this, I loved him so very much for his doing of it.

I love the memory of sitting beside my dad when I was scared riding in turbulence in an airplane and he told me story after story to keep my mind off my fear. So clearly, your mind, even while in intense fear can be distracted and occupied in order that you stay out of fear and in control, relaxed and in present time. Daddy taught me this by example, when I was eight-years-old that to occupy my mind with funny and interesting things and the fear will dissipate. I love you Daddy for this lesson, thank you! I recall this imprint of awareness as often as need be.

If when emotional, you flip into your thinking brain, it will alleviate or may even clear the emotion. Being more in the analytical side of your brain will bring you into present time—to be in the moment and out of the emotion of fear or the anticipation of fear and the 'what if's'.

When I am in stress, emotional pain, fear, anticipation or dread, I will oftentimes, do a task, such as clean my house, workout, focus on something physical and or mental that will pull me out of my feelings and emotions. Doing this gives me release to either work through the issue, come back to it refreshed, put it more into perspective or to release it completely. Staying and being in present time puts most things into perspective. It's the anticipation of fear of the future and or anticipation of the 'what if's' or the negatives that messes us up and freezes us in emotional fear.

Of course we need to prepare for the future and the 'what if's' in life as best that we can, but some things we have no control over or won't know until they happen. As human beings, we are vulnerable at times. Some things are out of our control. So it's better to live happy and positive and turn it over to God.

DON'T LOOK IN THIS CABINET

I am nine

CHRISTMAS IS FAST APPROACHING. EXCITEMENT is in the air. We've given our Christmas lists to mom and dad. They told us that they'll make sure that Santa Claus gets them. My sisters and I tell mom and dad over and over, reminding them daily of all the things that we want for Christmas.

I want a Brownie doll, a Girl Scout watch, a bike and a record player. I want the Girl Scout watch absolutely the most! I feel as if I'll be a real grown-up with a watch especially a Girl Scout watch.

Mother comes home with lots of packages takes them into her room and closes the door. Later when I check, there is nothing there. No packages are in her room. I knew that mom and dad bought some of the gifts and I knew Santa brought some of them. My younger sisters didn't know this yet. I'm three years older than they are. I know a lot more things than they do.

I wonder what mom bought. I'm terribly curious! One day, I'm snooping around and mother catches me. She warns, "Don't go through any closets or cabinets in our room. If you do, you'll spoil some surprises." I ask her if any of my things are in the cabinets. I ask specifically about the watch. She answers, "It's Christmas. I'm not talking. Wait and see! Christmas is about surprises!"

I didn't care about surprises. I just had to know! So one day when I'm sure that mom isn't around, I climb up to the cabinet where I suspect she has put some of the packages. I climb up the drawers using them as if they are steps, and crawl into the large cabinet at the top. I'm very quiet and very careful. I open all the different sacks and packages. I find some things I recall my younger sisters asking for. Surely, there's something for me, too.

Then hooray! I find a Brownie doll and a Girl Scout watch. I feel excited to know that I'm getting these things especially the Girl Scout watch. After seeing, the watch I'm totally satisfied and carefully exit the cabinet. I take great care to put everything back exactly the way I found it.

I spend the next few days before the arrival of Christmas dreaming of wearing that Girl Scout watch. How cool I'll be and feel with it on my wrist.

Then Christmas morning arrives. We all hurry in to see what Santa Claus has left for us. With four little girls, there's a lot of loot—all sorts of toys, games, bicycles in varying sizes and lots of dolls with their accessories.

We decided on Christmas Eve where we wanted Santa to put our gifts. I go to the area where I know my gifts will be. I see a lot of the things that I had asked for—a bike—a Brownie doll—a record player but no Girl Scout watch.

My heart sank. I look around at my sisters' things. Nope. No, Girl Scout watch there. They're too little anyway. I don't think they can even tell time. But what if it had gotten mixed up in their stuff, I'd just die if one of my younger sister's got my watch by mistake.

I'm sure I saw a Girl Scout watch in mom's cabinet. That's the main thing I want. "Oh! Where is it?"

I run into my mom's room. She's still in bed. We got up so early, like five or something. My mom said she was going to rest a little longer but for us to go on in to see what Santa left. Daddy was up playing with us and helping with our toys. But mom was still in bed. I run into my parents' bedroom and jump on her side of the bed. I sit beside her. I guess my jumping woke her up. She opens her eyes and sleepily asks, "Did you get what you wanted from Santa?" I respond, "Yes, I did—but—um—well . . ."

I couldn't ask her directly about the Girl Scout watch because then she would know. I had sneaked a look in her cabinet. I'm scared that maybe God is punishing me for looking in the cabinet and not obeying my mom. Maybe my mom found out that I'd gone into the cabinet and is punishing me by not giving me the watch. What if she returned it to the store?

I was sure I had put everything back just like I'd found it. I feel guilty for sneaking and doing what my mom said not to do. That was why the Girl Scout watch wasn't there because I am really bad. I'm being punished. My heart is pounding. I guess my mom suspected something was wrong because she says, "Go look again, maybe you missed something."

I race back into the family room. Toys are everywhere. My youngest sister is even riding her tricycle in the house. Daddy is telling her to wait until we go outside but she won't. There's so much activity and mess. But where's my Girl Scout watch? Will I ever find it? I go over to where Santa placed my things. I look again and yes! There's a little box with the Girl Scout name on it. I open the box and there it is my watch! I put it on and feel—oh so happy, grown-up, cool and everything else that is good! I feel as wonderful as any nine-year-old girl can feel with a new bicycle and Girl Scout watch!

You know I really wish that I had listened to my mom and not looked into the cabinet. I did spoil my surprises. Sometimes, it's nicer not to know. To let surprises happen especially at Christmas.

What awareness! As an adult releasing the need to always know the outcome and be in control can be a difficult process. Allow life to be a surprise. We do not always need to know the outcome. Many times, we have no way in the world to control the outcome of situations in our life. Sometimes what you expect or want is not what you get and many times it works out for the best this way. Also sometimes what you really want and are looking for is right in front of your eyes but you can't see it because you are looking so hard for it or trying to find something else that you think might be better but isn't.

Let go and let God! Trust that what is truly yours will be yours.

Release the need to control all situations. Allow Surprises! Many times what will be will be, no matter how hard you try to know and control the outcome. Relax and go with the flow . . .

Also it's interesting that when I did not find my much desired gift, the Girl Scout watch from Santa, I immediately thought the reason was because I was being punished. That God or my mother was punishing me by not giving me the gift that I wanted the most.

The same belief that most of us have, if something happens 'bad' or that we deem is bad, we think we are being punished by a judging and vengeful God.

Where does this automatic response come from? Is it the religious dogma and Puritan ethics that instill a fear of God? And perhaps, is having that fear, at times might be a good thing? So we are kept on our path with surprises, twists and turns along the way of our journey on earth.

PLEASE LET ME GO WITH YOU!

I am nine

MY BEST FRIEND MELISSA IS at my house visiting. We're having the best time playing together. It's really hot outside. So we're spending most of our time playing indoors. My younger sisters are beginning to bother us. At times, it's difficult to play with my younger sisters getting right in the middle of what we're doing. They're real cute and we do play with them occasionally, but sometimes we older girls just need time to be alone. So we decide even though it's terribly hot outside that we'll go for a bicycle ride.

Melissa and I go into the garage and get the bikes. We ride out to the end of the driveway. We look at each other. Boy! It's hot! One hundred degrees or something! The heat is blasting up to us from the concrete on the driveway as the heat coming from the street is overwhelming us. We can barely look up because the sun is very bright as it beats down on us.

We decide to ride down to the creek. It's cooler under the shade of the trees at the creek. It will feel good to sit on the cool rocks under the trees and dangle our feet in the water.

Just as we start to go, my younger sister Dana pulls her little bicycle with training wheels out of the garage to go with us. We shout, "Dana, you're too little to ride with us. It's too hot for you. Go back into the house!"

Dana replies, "I want to go with you. I'm big! I want to go, too!"

We warn, "We're going to ride real far away and you're too little to go that far. We're going to ride real, real fast. You're just too little. Now go back into the house."

Dana insists that she's going to go with us. We begin to ride off and she follows. We stop and turn back and shout for her to go back home. This is so frustrating. Can't we do anything without my younger sisters hanging around us?

We state, "Dana, we want to be alone. Please, let us ride our bikes alone. We'll have to go slow if you go with us. We want to ride fast and we want to go far. You can't go as fast or as far. You're too little. We will ride with you another day. Please, let us be alone!"

Dana says, "No! I want to go with you." She's almost crying now. "I can ride fast. Please! I want to be with you. I can go far. I'm a big girl. I want to go to the creek with you! Please, let me go with you!"

I don't remember Dana ever being so insistent before. She's really bugging us!

We state, "No! Dana, go back! You can't go with us."

We start out. We shout back to her. "We're going to go real fast now. You go back into the house and out of this heat. It's much too hot for you. You're too little to be out here."

Melissa and I look at each other. It's even too hot for us. The heat is awful! But we start out again to ride to the deep shade and cool water of the creek. Only, here comes Dana.

We're getting sick and tired of her persistence. The heat is really beginning to get to us. We are ready to get out of here and go to the creek.

"Dana, please go back to the house. We're going now." We begin to ride real fast. We are almost down to the end of the block. As we turn the corner, we see Dana out of the corner of our eyes. She's halfway up the block. She's peddling very fast to keep up with us and she's crying. Her face is bright red.

Melissa and I look at each other. I'm worried. I hope she's okay. My heart is pounding. My heart is breaking. I feel as if I have a knife in my heart to see her this way. Melissa says, "Come on let's go! She'll get tired and go back home." I respond, "No, we need to take her home. She is too little to be out in this heat." We turn and bicycle back to her.

There she is, my little red-headed sister crying her eyes out because we're riding too fast for her. When we get up close to her, we see how red her face is and I get frightened. She's so little and cute with her curly red hair and big blue eyes. The way she looks with her bright red face makes me worried. I feel as if I'm going to faint from the heat. So what must my little sister feel like? My heart feels as if it's going to break. She tried so hard to keep up with us and to be with us. She did a good job too. She's crying more and more while saying, "I just wanted to be with you." I hug her. She's so red and sweaty with salty tears all over her face. Her pretty blond curls are dripping with her perspiration. We turn our bikes around and walk with her back to our house.

I ask, "Dana, why didn't you obey us and stay home?" She replies, "I want to be big like you. I want to be with you and play with you." My heart is breaking and I'm so worried because she's still so bright red. I'm scared that she's too over heated. I would die if anything happened to my little sister.

I feel guilty for wanting to ride my bicycle alone with my friend. After all, being alone with my friend isn't as important as if something happened to my little sister. We take her into the house and get her some water. We all have lots of cool water to drink. Melissa and I feel better after drinking the water, but Dana is still real red in her face.

We call out, "Mother! Dana is really hot. What should we do to take care of her?" Mother walks in looks at Dana then states that Dana is okay. We say that we want to put her in a cool bath to make her feel better. Mother says that a cool bath isn't necessary and for us to be sure not to make a mess. All mother cares about is whether we make a mess or not.

"But mother, she's so hot. We need to do something." Mother asks again that we not make a mess.

We decide to put her into a cool bath anyway. We know we have to do something to make sure that she will be alright. Melissa says that she heard it was best to put over-heated people in a warm bath. But a warm bath sounds terrible after being out in that heat. So we run a cool bubble bath for Dana. We play with her in the bath tub. Her face finally stops being red. She is laughing and enjoying the attention. We got her out of the tub and wrapped her in a big towel. We dressed her in a fresh shorts outfit then we stayed in the house for the rest of the day and played with Dana in the air conditioning.

I can still feel the ache in my heart when I recall seeing my younger sister Dana peddling as fast as she could to keep up with my friend and myself. The tiny girl with the red curls working so hard to try to keep up with her older sister. When she looked up at me with her beautiful blue eyes, I felt such guilt. I felt selfish for wanting time alone with my friend. There was nothing wrong with me wanting and needing to be alone with children of my own age and away from my younger sisters. There was nothing for me to feel guilty about. Why did I feel such guilt? I am a caring person. Why do I remember this so vividly? I see this fragile little girl trying so hard and it breaks my heart. She reminded me of a piece of myself. I want to hold that little girl again and love her.

Older sisters—younger sisters, little sisters want to be with older sisters. Much of the time older sisters don't want little sisters around.

I release the guilt for wanting to be alone with my friend and acknowledge the caring I gave to my younger sister.

Reality is that later in life—this sister turned on me when I needed her. None of my younger sisters, ever in my life showed me caring, concern, nurturing or empathy. I was always the one giving to them.

SUNFLOWER SEED SUMMER

I am nine, ten and eleven

SHE LIVES ACROSS THE STREET from me. We walk to school together almost every day. I walk down and across the street to meet her and then we walk to school. We love walking to school. It's a magical journey.

Our neighborhood is a new one and not all of the lots are filled. Lucky for me since I love playing around house's under construction and climbing to rooftops that my parents usually bought in new developments.

Along with the construction, there are fields full of wildflowers. My best friend Jane has a field beside her house. We walk through the wildflower fields on our way to school. Sometimes, we pick some flowers to give to our teachers.

Today is the last day of school. So we pick out a very special bouquet of flowers to take to our teachers. Jane and I don't have the same homeroom teacher. So, we hardly ever get to see each other at school. But after school and in the summer, it's another story. We're together all of the time—inseparable. We're looking forward to summer vacation and our adventures together.

There's a creek between us and the school. We can take either the street route or the more exciting one through the creek to get to our school. If we're running late, we'll take the street. If we have more time, we elect to take the creek. We adore the adventure of the creek. It's like a world of its own—private and full of mystery.

We go behind the houses and walk down the slope. Then step on these huge flat rocks to get over the creek without getting wet. It's so fun! We cross at the shallow end. Further down the creek, there's a deep part that is shaded by many trees. The foliage is very dense at that part of the creek. It's a mysterious and magical place.

The creek is a fantastic place to play on weekends. Exploring the creek is one of our favorite things. On one side, if you follow the creek far enough, you'll run into horses and all sorts of wonderful sights. We spend hours and hours exploring the creek. We pretend all sorts of things. We're 'Huck Finn' and his friends one minute then pirates, the next. When we're up by the area with the horses, we're girls of the Old West. We've been left behind by our wagon train and the Indians are about to attack. When we're down by the deep part of the creek, we're lost on the ocean. Our ship has sunk and we're abandoned. We're in magic land. This creek can take us all over the world.

We like to explore everywhere. We walk all over the neighborhood. They're building lots of new houses. We climb all through the houses under construction. If there's a ladder left behind by the construction workers, we'll climb up to the roof of the houses. We'll stand up to view what seems like forever, as far as our eyes can see!

My friend Jane and I have the best time, all of the time. Our favorite time is summer. We take turns staying at each other's houses. We run around outside barefoot. We like to eat sunflower seeds— tons and tons of sunflower seeds. We buy them in little packages and shell them ourselves. Our fingers get all shriveled from the salt but we don't care. We just keep on eating them. No telling how many bags of sunflower seeds we go through in the summertime. There is never a day without sunflower seeds in the summer.

We spend the long hot afternoons in one of our houses eating sunflower seeds and reading. We spend more of our time at Jane's house because I have so many younger sisters. My younger sisters like to hang around us. This annoys us because we like to have our privacy.

Jane has one older sister. She's lots older and she doesn't bother us at all. In fact, she makes faces at us. She thinks we're weird and she's always telling on us to Jane's mother. Jane's mother doesn't get mad at us and she doesn't bother us. So we're left alone to scheme, play and explore on our own at Jane's house. The only thing is her sister's room is no man's land. We're never allowed in there, unless we're invited.

We like to read mystery books, such as 'Trixie Belden' and 'Nancy Drew'. A lot of packages of sunflower seeds and a 'Trixie Beldon' book and we're in hot summer heaven. Sometimes we pretend that Jane is 'Trixie', because she has blond hair like 'Trixie' does. And I'm her friend 'Honey', because in the books her friend has long dark hair like me. Then off we go to create our own mysteries and adventures.

The best treat in the world is when we go to the 'Five and Dime' store with one of our mothers. Then we are able to purchase yummy sunflower seeds, 'Pez' candy with container along with fireball red, grape and sour apple gum. A package of sunflower seeds is only a nickel. They are put into larger packages where you can get six for a quarter. That's our best day at the 'Five and Dime', when we can buy a couple of large packages. We each get fifty cents a week for allowance. So we can buy pretty much everything we need to have a great summer.

When we buy a book, we need to save up for it or ask our mother's for help. They usually help us purchase a book because they like for us to read. At the 'Five and Dime', we spend our time looking through the books. We like to check out the whole selection. I've got almost the whole collection of 'Trixie Beldon'. I love to read!

Sometimes we hop on our bikes and ride all over the place. We ride down to the creek. We ride around to another part of the creek that we usually don't go to on foot because it is too far. We explore as if we're discovering the new world. We check out the rocks, the fish, and the foliage as we explore up and down the banks of the creek. We pretend we're on a treasure hunt.

It's cooler down under the trees by the creek. We sit on the side and dangle our feet into the cool water. The large flat rocks that we sit on feel cool to the backs of our legs. The water is so clear that we can look down from where we are sitting and see the fish swimming. We can see clear to the bottom of the creek. It's so peaceful and cool in our special place by the creek. It must be almost like what Heaven is like.

It seems as if we are real far away from our houses. We pretend that we are—perhaps, even lost somewhere in another land.

One day while we're far away down by the creek, it starts to thunder storm. It begins to rain hard and to thunder loud. We get further under the branches of the trees then go to a part of the creek that is partly sheltered by a big rock. It's almost like a cave. We're in uncharted territory now. We sit under the big rock looking down and watch the water rush fast by us. The water is falling off the leaves of the trees. It's so beautiful! We'll remember this day for a long time. We feel as if we're sharing some magnificent adventure being in a secret place far back along the creek while it rains. It feels like no one knows where we are and that no one could find us if they were looking. It's exciting and scary at the same time. We pretend that we're lost in the woods and we're going to try to find our way home when it stops raining.

Finally the hard rain stops. Now it's raining lightly. The sun is trying to peek out. The reflection of the sun makes the rain glisten on the leaves. So it looks like it is raining drops of gold.

We wish we could stay here forever, but know we need to be heading back. This day's adventures are coming to an end as we walk along the creek back to our bicycles. As we ride our bikes home the water is rushing fast past us and down the drains on the sides of the streets. We are all wet and it's so excitingly fun. We ride real fast, lifting our legs off the pedals and straightening them out to the side as we coast home. Wheeee—what a fun ride!

Some days we take out across the neighborhood on foot. Since it's a new neighborhood, there aren't fences separating the yards. We can walk street to street and block to block. We like to snoop around in people's backyards. It can be a very interesting thing to do.

As we're walking between the houses one day, we see huge giant sunflowers. They are bright yellow. We can't believe they're so big and beautiful. We go up close to them to investigate. There are the sunflower seeds in the middle just like the ones we eat. The only difference is, they're not roasted in their shell and salted. We pull some out and take a taste. Um, pretty good. But not as good as our special bags harvested from the 'Five and Dime'.

We talk about the idea of growing our own giant sunflowers. But how do we roast the seeds, salt them and put them into a bag—so on and so forth? So we cancel that idea. But WOW! Sunflowers are beautiful! Now when we eat the seeds, we feel as if we're eating a little bit of the sun.

Summer evenings are the best. We get to stay out late until around nine or nine-thirty. We like to play 'statues' with the other neighborhood kids. It's a game, where one kid turns around and the rest of us wiggle and jump until the kid with their back to the group yells, freeze! Then the kids all freeze in the position that they're caught in—whatever that position may be. Then the kid who had their back to the group tries to guess what each kid is. Hence, the game 'statues', get it?

The best nights are when there are 'lightening bugs' darting around. They look like little stars floating close to the earth. We run all around trying to catch them. We try to catch them and put them into glass jars. We're not too successful in accomplishing this since they fly really fast.

One day when we're at Jane's house, we decide to paint our toe nails and finger nails. We decide to paint them alternating colors— one pink then one blue—pink then blue. Not just any shade of blue— Popsicle blue. Our favorite Popsicles are the ice blue ones and the banana ones. So it makes perfect sense that we paint our fingernails and toenails the color of one of our favorite Popsicles.

Jane's older sister thinks that we're gross but we don't care. When we're all through painting our fingernails and toenails, we think they look spectacular.

We're eating our sunflower seeds and reading our mystery books. It's difficult to keep fingernail polish on while eating sunflower seeds. So our nails look pretty chipped and gross. Now they're half blue and half pink and half blue and half pink . . .

Jane's sister tells us that we should read something worthwhile like the Bible. We respond, "I'm so sure. Have you seen how big the Bible is? We study it in Sunday school that's enough, thank you!" Her sister tells us that if we don't read the Bible, know it and live by it that we will go to Hell.

Jane's mother tells us that Jane's sister is going through a 'Bible phase' and not to let her bother us. She says for us to go ahead and read our mystery stories.

Jane's sister is fifteen and carries a lot of weight with us even if she is weird. She's older. I mean, she's in high school. We think maybe, it might be cool when you get older to read the Bible. Besides we sure don't want to go to Hell. Maybe, if we start reading the Bible in elementary school, we'll get a head start and make sure that we don't go to Hell.

So we go to her parent's book shelf and get a Bible. Then burst into Jeannie's room and say that we are reading the Bible like she is. She's so impressed that she lets us sit in her room. She actually invites us into her very private—private 'off limits' room. Alright, we made it into the princess's room, but there's one big drawback. We can't eat our sunflower seeds in her room.

We sit there on the floor of Jane's older sister's room huddled together trying to read and comprehend the Bible. We have to keep asking her sister what the words mean. It's the most difficult book that we've ever read. We're asking her questions over and over. She's really getting annoyed with us. She says, "You be quiet or leave!" She tells us that we're messing up her concentration.

We respond, "We're reading the Bible, like you told us to and we're not leaving!" After all, we gave up our sunflower seeds to sit in her room to read the Bible. So we stay and keep asking her questions. She gets madder and madder and then all of a sudden she yells, "Get out of my room, you God damned brats!"

We jump up and stare at her in disbelief. Those are the worst words that we've ever heard coming from a child. She used the name of God in vain. Even two little ten-year-olds knew she was breaking one of the Ten Commandments.

So we went back to reading our mystery books and eating our sunflower seeds. We'd always thought she was weird and we were right.

Those summers spent with Jane running all over our neighborhood were the best memories Exploring the creek—bicycles—sunflower seeds—climbing on roofs—reading mysteries—games outside after dark—'lightening bugs'—chipped blue and pink fingernails, the best of summer days! We had such fun and adventure, except for the Bible reading part.

Summers full of happiness, adventure and joy!

I later discovered and realized that people who tell others what they should or should not do concerning religion, the Bible and God are usually many times not very God-like themselves. Later, Jane and her family moved to another state. When I next saw Jane, she told me that her older sister went wild in college, had sex with lots of boys and got pregnant. All of her intense Bible reading and preaching to us, didn't guide her so well, huh?! Or perhaps, the reason she was so intense about the Bible in high school was because she felt her wild side wanting to act out and tried to suppress it. Who knows?

I believe religion is man-made and spirituality is of God—the source of all wisdom and truth. We do not need others to tell us what we should or should not do because we can talk to God anytime we want. God is here for us all the time and in every single moment—at the creek, reading mysteries, eating sunflower seeds or reading his word—he is in it all.

Jane and I later read the Bible together and enjoyed the stories. I had a housekeeper that told us very colorfully about the stories in the Bible.

I do not believe that an individual can judge as to whether

anyone is going to Heaven or not. I believe we all live forever. It is an individual decision to choose to live in either the dark or the light. It has been my observance that some of the 'religions' on earth that claim they are living by God's book and God's laws are only using their religion to control and to judge others. Their main concern seems to be putting fear into people so that they control them and rule over others on earth while benefiting themselves. As in asking for monetary donations so they can live big and large—therefore, they are really living in the dark.

We are on the planet of dualities: good and bad, negative and positive. It's our individual choice in any given moment. Organized religion is a creation of the mind of man.

A spiritual connection to God is pure, of the heart and soul—and is of God.

RINGING DOORBELLS AND RUNNING AWAY

I am ten

WHY IS THAT GIRL WALKING down the street in her short shorts and high heels, wiggling her hips? She looks really stupid. She looks the fool. Who does she think she is? My friend Chris and I are observing her from across the street. Chris lives one street over from the street where I live. We're playing in Chris' front yard. Chris lives across from the girl who walks up and down the street in her short shorts and high heels. This is the second time that we've seen her do this. She looks silly and bizarre. We stop playing when she walks by and stare at her. She doesn't even speak to us. She just walks on by, as if she's the queen of the neighborhood or something. She acts as if she owns the street and the whole neighborhood.

The high-heeled, short shorts girl is a couple of years older than we are. She's a real snob. We stare at her cold and hard trying to torment her, but she acts as if she could care less.

Chris and I are running around playing ball having a great old time, until this girl walks by wiggling her hips wearing her high heels. The high-heel girl goes into her house and comes out again. Now she's wearing real bright red lipstick. She parades by us again, so we look at her and I ask, "Why are you wearing high heels with your short shorts and why are you wearing lipstick?"

She responds snootily like we are stupid kids who know nothing about anything. "I am practicing walking in high heels. My mother got them for me last week and when I finally do wear them to church, I don't want to trip and fall. This is my first pair of high heels. They're difficult to walk in, but you two girls wouldn't know that because you are too young to wear high heels. How old are you—second grade?!"

What a mean girl! She knows we're older than second grade because she sees us at school.

"We're in the fourth grade. We're going to get high heels pretty soon too—maybe even next week."

We want her to think that we're grown up, too!

She laughs, "You're little girls! You're way too young to wear high heels!"

"We're lots older than we look!" We respond back trying to sound as old as we possibly can. "Why are you wearing all that lipstick and make-up? Aren't you too young for all that lady stuff?"

"My mother lets me wear make-up anytime I want! I can't wear it to school or to church, but anywhere else—mother says I can wear it. Besides it won't be long now, until I can wear it all the time. Nice talking to you two. Bye—now! I need to go in and paint my fingernails."

With that, the short shorts girl wiggles off across the street and into her house.

We are left feeling like two slobs. We're all messed up and sweaty from playing ball and running all over the place. We feel intimated and smashed into 'kiddie ashes' by this girl wearing high heels with her short shorts. We scheme. What can we do to get back at her? Paper her house? No, we can't stay out that late. Well, what? We need to do something that will annoy her, but that she'll never know we did it.

We had heard about kids who would ring doorbells and then run away to annoy people. The kids said that it works real well because the people have to keep answering the door and then no one is there.

Hey, that's a neat idea! Let's do it! Okay, when? How about Sunday night? I'll meet you over here about seven o'clock. We can meet before it gets dark. Then when it gets dark we can begin our torment of the high heels girl. We are ready. We are excited. We are going to show her who's cool and really grown up.

Sunday comes around. After I eat dinner, I run over to Chris' house. She's waiting outside for me. She states, "I've been watching the house and I don't think anyone is home."

We go into Chris' room and play board games. Her window faces the short shorts girl's house so we can peek out to see what's happening. It's getting darker and darker. Then we see their car drive into the driveway and into their garage. We wait awhile to let them get into the house and settled in.

We're starting to get nervous and ponder chickening out. It's getting late and I need to be getting home soon. We summon our courage. Okay—let's do it! We go outside and sneak up to the house. We have it all planned out. We run up to the door and ring the doorbell twice. Then we run back fast around to the bushes. We can't run back across the street to Chris' house like we want to do because then they would be able to see us.

We go up to the door. We ring the doorbell twice. We run like crazy around to the bushes. We did it! We're breathing hard and fast. What fun! What a rush! It's both scary and fun at the same time. We could see when the front porch light comes on.

It works! We did it! It's fun! Let's do it again! We wait a little while then do it again and it works again. I'm becoming tired and I have to walk a block over to my house to go home. So I say that's enough. It's getting cold out and we're both shivering. I want to go home but Chris says. "Come on, just one more time. It's so fun!" We agree to do it just one more time.

We start up to the front door and as we are going up the steps the father steps out from the side of the house and shouts, "Girls!" We take off running. He comes after us and grabs us. He states, "Girls! I'm taking you into the house and calling your parents."

We're so scared! We're shaking. We say that we're sorry. But it doesn't do any good. He takes us into the family room. There she is the snooty short shorts girl. She's smirking at us. She's in her pajamas all warm and cozy. I'm thinking that I wish I was home cozy in my pajamas. My mother and daddy are probably wondering where I am. It's getting so late.

The man asks us who we are then he recognizes Chris. He has her call her parents and tell them what she did and then he lets her go home. Next, he asks me who I am and my phone number so that he can call my parents to tell them what I did so they will punish me. I give him my phone number. He calls my father and tells him about what I did. He tells my father that he should spank me.

The snooty short shorts girl is laughing real low under her breath. It's so embarrassing. I want to get out of there so badly and go home. I want to go home to my warm house, put on my pajamas and snuggle into my bed. I want to be home with my momma and daddy.

The man says go on home now. Your father promised me that you would be punished. Do you live far? Do you want me to walk you home? I answer, "No! I live one street over. I can go by myself."

I want out of that house so fast and so bad. This man scares me. I want to go home to my parents. I exit the front door and run like the wind to my house. I know I'll be safe when I get to my house. I'm freezing cold as I run and so scared! I haven't stayed outside by myself this late ever before. I see something scary in every shadow. I hear dogs barking. I run as fast as I can. I want to be home safe at my house. I'm shivering inside and out. I want to be safe in my bed and at home.

When I enter the house, my father is waiting for me. He asks, "Why were you out so late? Your mother and I were worried."

I answer, "Chris and I were doing things." Dad asks, "Why were you ringing those people's doorbell and running away?" I reply, "Because we don't like the girl who lives there. She's real snooty."

He states, "That is no way for you to behave." And he starts to take his belt off.

I'm tired, shivering and scared after all that has happened, I just want to go to bed. I say, "I'll never do it again. It was a stupid thing to do." Then my dad starts hitting my legs with the belt as he says, "This will teach you not to ring doorbells and run away." I put my hands down to protect my legs and my hands get hit. I say, "Daddy, I won't do it again. Please stop hitting me!" He responds, "I told that man I will punish you and I am." I'm crying. He leaves the room.

I hate him for hitting me. Why didn't he believe me when I said that I would never do it again? He did not teach me to stop ringing doorbells and running away by hitting my legs. He taught me to hate him. I had already learned my lesson by the fear of being caught. Why did he hit me because that man told him to? He doesn't even know that man and his snooty daughter. Why doesn't my daddy believe me? I hate him! I hate him! I hate him for hitting me! I already knew that what I did was wrong. I told him so and told him that I would never do it again and he still hit me with a belt! I will hate him forever! I will hate him for the rest of my life!

The next time, I saw Chris I asked her if she got into trouble. She said, "No. My mom and dad were angry at that man for scaring me and making such a big deal over nothing. They think those people are weird and snooty." She asked me if I got in trouble with my parents. I responded, "No, my parents said the same thing yours said. What a big deal over nothing."

I was too shamed and embarrassed to tell her that my father had hit me with a belt. I felt humiliated that my father had hit me and he taught me nothing, but to hate him for what he did.

My father hit me with a belt one other time. I don't remember why he hit me, only that he did. The reason I remember that particular time is because of the trauma associated with being hit. Being hit with a belt did not teach me a lesson. It taught me to be humiliated and to hate him. I was filled with hate for him for humiliating me. Reflecting about my experiences, I do not believe that hitting children accomplishes anything positive. It is demeaning. I did feel as if I would have liked to yank the belt out of his hand and hit him back. Being hit did not reinforce the lesson learned because I do not except for this one 'ringing the doorbell' time, remember why I was hit, only that I was hit. The other time I was hit, I was crying hard. My father came back into my room and made me tell him that I forgave him for hitting me. He told me to stop crying or he would give me more to cry about. He said that he spanked me for my own good and that it hurt him more than it hurt me.

Dad did what he thought was right which was to hit me with a belt then when I cried, he could not own his own feelings of hurting me. So he had to push that off onto me, too. In order for him to feel okay about what he had done. What this did was damage beyond repair, my love and respect for him. He was basing his beliefs on the Puritan ethics of 'spare the rod, spoil the child'. These beliefs can be the basis for abuse of children.

Actually, I am not sure that my father knew what to do in this regard. He was just trying to make sure that I turned out 'good'. He also in many ways reared me as he would a boy by being overly harsh and punitive. He used tough love when understanding and communicating would have served to teach me and brought us closer. His being unnecessarily punitive towards me harmed my feelings for him. I was basically an extremely well-behaved child. Ringing a doorbell and running away was the worst of my childhood crimes.

That night of the 'ringing the doorbell' incident, I had suffered enough and had learned my lesson by the time I had gotten home. What my father needed to do was look into my face, talk to me and really hear me. Had he done that, he could have seen that I didn't need further punishment and that I had learned my lesson. Had he hugged me and sent me to bed after talking to me, it would have made me feel safe, loved and nurtured instead of feeling fear and shame. He humiliated me by hitting me and taught me nothing except fear.

I can only imagine what this does to children or people who have had more violent abuse. Hitting is abuse in my book. It is negative reinforcement and it beats a person down and destroys their spirit.

My awareness is that children should rarely if ever be spanked. Physical punishment does harm and creates the chance for more physical abuse. Humiliating a person tears down their individual boundaries and negates the opportunity for real worthwhile communication. I lost respect for my father for hitting me, so any chance for any real communication was lost at that time. I pulled away from wanting to open myself up to him and to be close to him for a long time.

Negative reinforcement creates fear and anger. Positive reinforcement, truly listening, hearing your child and seeing into their heart and spirit will create communication that will last and build a positive productive individual. But having written my opinion on this, I will also add that under certain circumstances, a father may need to corral a boy or young man by physically reprimanding them, when there is no other recourse or as a last resort. With some children and young people 'this way', may be the only way to get through to them. We must instill right and wrong in our youth to protect them and to guide them on the higher path. Sometimes perhaps, tough love is needed.

WHEN I GROW UP I WANT TO HAVE LOTS OF KIDS

I am ten through about fifteen and then into adulthood

I WANT TO HAVE A BIG white house like my grandmother NaNa, only I want it to be bigger and filled with lots and lots of children. I would like to have eight children. I want my husband to make a lot of money. He'll be really handsome and will love me a whole bunch. We'll be happy all of the time!

I select names for my future children, changing them often. Sometimes I'd add or subtract a child in my pretend world based on what names I like or dislike on that particular day. The only thing, I didn't change is that I wanted to have many children.

I imagine my children as mostly girls with long hair, but I throw in a few boys. My father always wanted a boy and I think that if I have some. It will make him happy.

I envision living in this huge white house with all my children in utter bliss. My parents will come to visit us and they'll see what a wonderful happy family I have. They'll see what a good, kind and loving parent is really like, by observing me. Then maybe, they'll love me.

I play different scenes of the same scenario over and over again. It gives me great comfort to pretend these stories in my mind. I look forward to the day when I can leave my mother and father to have my own happy family. Then I will feel loved and will love my children more than anything. I just know that I'll be able to make my children happy. I'll talk to them. I'll make them feel good about themselves. I'll never yell at them or hit them. I'll never drink too much and say things I don't mean. My husband will not drink too much. He'll spend a lot of time talking to our children and me. He'll always be home on time for dinner. We'll be more important to him than his work, money, golf, football on TV or anything else. We'll be the most important things in the world to him.

The most significant part of my dream is that when my parents come to visit me, they'll see what a wonderful successful person I am and they'll love me and be proud of me. They'll see that I'm loved and lovable. Then they might be able to love me, too.

In my fantasy, I think that I am able to show them what a real happy family is like.

In reality, when I get married I decide very quickly that I don't want to have children. By the time it's time to start thinking about having children. I realize that I'm married to a man who drinks too much. He stays out late, supposedly, on business and came home drunk, like my father sometimes did. He's always late for dinner if he comes home at all. He only cares about golf, drinking, gambling and sports on TV. All he wants to do is party. He's disgusting and obnoxious when he's been drinking. He wants me to drink with him. But I don't like to drink all that much. I like to have a glass of wine with dinner sometimes but that is about it. My focus is on dancing and physical fitness. My husband does not care about these things. So I make the decision that children will not be happy in our marriage because I am not happy.

I feel as if I'm living my childhood all over again. I'm being criticized for being me. It is Hell revisited. I don't want any children of mine to have to go through what I'd gone through as a child. I didn't think this marriage was going to last and I didn't think having children could/would help it.

I figured out early on that if a man and woman aren't happy together. Children only make it worse and not better. I'll go one step further and say if an individual isn't happy and at peace with themselves children aren't the answer. Their children experience sheer misery. I learned this from my parents. I grew up in misery much of the time. So I made the decision that children wouldn't/ couldn't make me happy nor could I make children happy if I weren't happy.

I wanted to make sure the pain that I had suffered in childhood would not be inflicted on anyone else. I thought if children have to feel so unhappy then I can't bear to have any.

One time I had a scare, I thought, I might be pregnant. I'm working as an assistant manager at a clothing store. The manager, an older lady told me that my symptoms sure sound as if I might be pregnant. I make an appointment with a doctor for tests. While driving home from the doctor's office, I'm filled with panic. I don't want any children and certainly not with the man I am married to.

I didn't realize how deeply I felt about this until that day. I start hitting my abdomen and crying. I'm filled with fear and panic. I cry out, "Please God! Please don't let me be pregnant! I don't even want to be married to this man. I just can't be pregnant!"

I took the pregnancy test. Now all I need do is to wait until the next day and call the doctor's office. I don't sleep at all that night. I go to work the next day feeling very upset. The manager is teasing me about the possibility of my being pregnant. I laugh and pretend that if I am pregnant that I'll be happy. I act in this way because I feel it's expected of me. Women are supposed to be happy if they think they might be pregnant, right?

I call the doctor's office to get the results from the test. I hold my breath until the nurse says, "No, not pregnant." I'm so relieved that

I can barely speak. The manager thinks I'm upset because I am not pregnant and asks if I would like to go home.

I did go home because I had been so stressed out about the possibility of being pregnant, being tied to this man and bringing a child into a home like I came from that I did need a break. I went home, fell asleep and the next morning my period arrived. Thank you, God!

I love children! I have always loved children. I love them too much to ever bring them into a home that is not happy. It is not about what children can do for you. It is about what you can do for your children. You cannot do for your children what you cannot do for yourself and your children certainly should not and cannot handle the weight of your issues and problems. You cannot give what you do not have to give.

Having a child is a sacred duty. Often times, it appears that it is done with very little thought in our society today.

I observe children and can usually spot their hurt and loneliness. Because of my experiences as a child, I can look into their eyes and know if they are happy or if their soul is being diminished or even destroyed by lost and unhappy adults in their lives. Children have always gravitated to me. Perhaps, they recognize that I can truly see and understand them. I am sensitive to them on a level that I believe is unusual. Children like being seen in the truth of their spirit, sometimes adults not so much.

If we fail our children out of indolence, indecision, by being violent, excessively strict or needy, we will have failed all of society and thwarted the universe's plans for a peaceful world.

Every person who heals and releases the hurt in their heart will be one step closer to healing the world. So our children can enter and grow up in a peaceful and joyful world. Our children will then be able to reach their true potential with as little pain and hurt as possible on this earth plane. I wonder if cruelty to a child whether it be mental, emotional or physical carries with it karma that you will be dealing with either later in this lifetime or in future incarnations. Our children are our future . . .

PART TWO

TEENAGE YEARS—
ADOLESCENCE

ELEVEN TO SIXTEEN

PART TWO

TEENAGE YEARS— ADOLESCENCE

ELEVEN TO SIXTEEN

TEETH KNOCKED OUT

I am eleven

ALL OF US LIKE TO go to the driving range with daddy. Daddy hits golf balls at the practice range over and over again to try and get his golf swing just right. My sisters and I run all over the place. Mother sits in the car and watches as daddy practices hitting the balls.

We get tall bottles of grape and orange pop out of the soda machine. Mom doesn't let us have pop like this at home. So it's a special treat. She doesn't like for us to drink this kind of stuff. Mom says it's bad for our teeth. Daddy lets us have it occasionally. I like the way you reach down into the pop machine to lift out the chilled soda pop. Some of the time, daddy will let us take turns hitting golf balls. He takes a rest, while we take our turns showing him how far we can hit the ball. Who cares if most of the time we miss the ball. It is fun trying!

One of my favorite things is to go up to the window and get more golf balls for my dad. I like carrying the wire baskets full of the balls. The balls might be white or they might be yellow. The yellow ones can be seen easier at night. I like the yellow ones better. I guess because they are different. Then there are the ones with holes in them. They don't go far. They are safer if you are playing with them up close. So if you get hit with one. You won't get hurt—like your teeth won't get knocked out.

There is a miniature golf course in the same area. I ask daddy if we can go play. I've played miniature golf before at a friend's birthday party. Daddy responds, "Your little sisters don't know how to play." I state, "I'll teach them. It'll be fun! Please! Please! Please!" Daddy finally says, "Okay, but be careful and watch after your sisters." He gives me the money. We're all so excited. We run to the car to let mother know where we're going and what we are up to.

I feel really grown-up. I go up to the window, ask for the golf clubs, get our balls and score card and pay for them. Then we're off to begin our game. We go to the first hole. It's really cute with a windmill at the end by the hole. I think miniature golf courses are neat. How do they think up all the little things to do? This is much better than regular golf.

Each of us selects the color of ball that we want. This takes a while. Little sisters can be tedious trouble at times. Dana wants to go first. Being a good older sister, I let her. She says she knows how to play. She's seven. She steps up to the place where you stand to hit the ball. I step back behind her. She swings the club, but not the way you are supposed to swing a club in miniature golf. She swings like she's playing real golf. Her club comes back and slams hard into my mouth. I'm stunned! I put my tongue up to the front of my mouth and parts of my two front teeth fall on my tongue. I'm shocked. I'm scared. I say that we have to go tell mom and dad. We have to go. I go back and give the equipment to the person at the desk. Then we all run back to the car where mom is waiting.

I yell, "Mom! Mom! My teeth are knocked out!" Mother says let me see. "Oh! My God! Go show your father." My sisters are crying. Dana keeps repeating, "I didn't mean to do it." Another sister says, "Why did this happen to my prettiest sister?" It's chaos.

I run up to daddy and show him my teeth. He says, "Oh! No! Go to the car. I'll be there in a minute."

We all run back and sit in the car. My daddy continues hitting golf balls. My mom is upset. She says angrily, "Why doesn't he come? We need to go get this taken care of." Then finally, my daddy gets into the car. Mom and dad start fighting about why daddy didn't quit hitting the golf balls immediately. Daddy says that he was worried and was trying to figure out what he should do.

We drive home. Mom puts my sisters to bed. They look at my mouth and my teeth. Daddy calls a dentist and tells him what happened. The dentist says to come to his office right now. My daddy and I get in the car to go to the dentist's office. By now, it's real late at night. It seems really weird to be going to the dentist's office late at night.

Riding in the car to the dentist's office feels strange. It's dark nighttime and I am in the car going to the dentist alone with my daddy. It's not often that I get to be alone with my daddy. He's usually working or all my sisters are around. It feels really good being alone with my daddy. I feel safe. He says, "Don't worry everything will be alright. We'll get your teeth fixed, Tiger." In that moment, I feel protected and loved by my daddy. I have his full attention and I know that he will fix everything. I respond, "Daddy, I am not afraid. I'm glad that my teeth got knocked out because now, I feel close to you." I scoot closer to my daddy. Daddy looks at me as if he is going to cry and he kisses my forehead. I feel so close to my daddy. "Don't worry, Tiger. I promise everything will be alright."

The dentist looks at my teeth and says that I'll need to have caps. He makes an appointment for me the next day.

The next morning, I walk to school as usual. It feels funny having my two front teeth almost gone. Mom tells me that she'll come get me at school when it's time to go to the dentist. I don't remember if any of my friends noticed my teeth. But I tried not to talk or smile. I am quiet and still unto myself waiting to hear what to do next. I'm not at school very long when they page me over the loudspeaker to go to the office. Mother picks me up and we go to the dentist's office to get my teeth fixed.

My mother said that when she looked through the front window and watched me walk to school that day that she thought I was the bravest eleven-year-old she had ever seen.

On that night riding to the dentist's office with my father was a wonderful feeling and memory because I felt so close to him. I felt his concern, attention and protection of me. I forgot about my teeth being knocked out because it was so great to feel loved and cared for. I could feel how determined he was that he make everything okay. That's the way I remember that night. I wasn't afraid because I knew my dad would make everything alright.

The dental work as it turned out was an ordeal that lasted for years. The decision the first dentist made about the size of the caps that he put in my mouth created all sorts of problems. I had to have root canals on both my front teeth and endured years of having crowns changed. The first ones the dentist first put on were silver according to him to protect my teeth.

My parents went with the dentist's recommendations even though dad said that he questioned it. Dad became furious over the dentist's recommendations as the years progressed. Because of this dentist's decisions, I spent almost a year without smiling and I loved to smile and used to smile a lot. My bite was messed up. It became a big mess in my mouth which thankfully has been corrected but what an ordeal to endure at an age that is difficult anyway. While going through puberty and being somewhere between being a child and a teenager.

I became aware because of this experience that doctors and dentists aren't always correct. It taught me to become aware and trust my instincts concerning health matters.

Interesting that sometimes trauma must be created before closeness and attention are shared.

THE HAIRCUT

I am eleven

I WANT TO HAVE A NEW grown up hairstyle. I've had a ponytail for such a long time. I've been looking through magazines, studying the pictures and see most of the girls have shorter hair. I want to have a cute, short, stylish hairstyle, too. All the girls in the magazines have short, straight hair. The length of their hair is just below their chin. My hair is below my shoulders, thick and wavy and it gets in my way. So I wear it in a ponytail most all the time. I feel like a baby.

Many of the girls at school are getting their hair cut short. So I ask my mom if I can get my hair cut short, too. She asks, "Are you certain you want to get your ponytail cut off?" "Yes, I am sure!" I answer. She makes an appointment with her stylist. The appointment is on Friday afternoon just before a birthday party at a friend's house. My hair is going to be new—a surprise for the party.

I get my hair cut just like in the picture that I show the stylist. It looks real cute. I love it! The hair-dresser blows my hair dry with a blow dryer. My hair is straight, full and beautiful. I look real old—like a teenager! I barely recognize myself. I'm excited to go to the party to show off my new hairstyle. The party is fun and everyone loves my hair. I feel so grown-up and sophisticated.

The next day, when I wake up my hair looks kind of wild. I'm use to sleeping with my hair in a ponytail. In fact, my hair was always in a ponytail. I go outside to play. I'm doing my usual Saturday stuff—running all over out-of-doors playing with my friend, Jane. We go inside her house and I go into the bathroom. I take a look at my hair in the mirror to admire my new, grown up, sophisticated self. Oh my goodness! My hair is standing out all over the place. It's frizzy and awful. I look terrible! I look like a wild woman! It's real humid outside and I have the kind of hair that gets frizzy in rainy weather. What am I going to do? Jane comes in and we try to do something with my hair but it's too short to put it in a ponytail. Jane still has her ponytail. I wished I still had mine. I don't like this new haircut. It's too much trouble to take care of. I don't know how to fix it right. Jane says that she liked my ponytail better, too. Then Jane's older sister and mother come home. When they see me, they ask, "What did you do to your hair?" I reply, "I got it cut." Trying to hold my chin up, I say, "It's the newest style." They state that they liked my ponytail better.

Immediately, I tell Jane that I have to go home. I run across the street barely holding back the tears. I run into the house and run into my bathroom to try to do something with this awful hair. I'm crying and call out for my mother. She comes in to try and help, but no one can do anything with my hair. I'm stuck with this awful frizzy hair until it grows out and I can put it into a ponytail again. Mother says you will get use to fixing your new hairstyle. It will just take practice. Nothing she says can help. Something comes over me. I'm overwhelmed by the realization of what I have done. I was trying to be so grown up and sophisticated. Instead, I look like a wild woman. I'm crying very hard. I go out to the family room where my mother is sitting on the sofa. I'm crying so hard. I don't remember ever crying this hard since I was a baby. I'm crying and saying, "Mother, I'm so ugly now. I will never be pretty again. I wrecked myself!" I'm crying uncontrollably. Mother takes me in her arms and onto her lap. I'm crying so hard, the hardest, I ever remember crying. I'm saying over and over again how ugly that I think I am because of my haircut. My mother is holding me and saying that it will grow, not to worry and to stop crying. That it will be alright. I'm sitting on my mother's lap as if I am a baby. Straddling her lap and leaning into her body. It feels so good to be sitting on my mother's lap and having her hold me close. She smells good, a fresh clean smell like flowers—only not. I relax and let my body go limp as she holds me. I sense that this will be the last time my mother holds me like this because I'm too old for my mother to hold me like a baby. Then I snap out of it and realize as I come back to my senses. I'm not a baby, so why am I sitting in my mother's lap crying? I push back but my mother pulls me close to her again, as she says, "Don't get up. I haven't held you like this in so long. It feels so good to hold you. I don't get to hold you anymore, since you have become such a big girl." I stay there for a minute more feeling the closeness and comfort of my mother as her smell permeates my being. Then I pull back and away and get up because I feel embarrassed. Embarrassed by the closeness, by the feelings and embarrassed by thinking, 'I'm too old to be sitting in my mother's lap'.

After crying so hard though, I feel a lot better. My hair will grow and until it does I can figure out something to do with it. I will think long and hard before I take another picture into a beauty shop again and say, 'Give me this hairstyle'. Actually, I don't think I have ever done so again. Also, as a grown up and since styles have changed from the stick straight to more wavy or individualized. I realize that when my hair goes wild, it's actually a cool look.

I recall how good it felt to hold my mother and to be in her arms while sitting in her lap. It was the last time that she ever did hold me like that in full childhood abandonment of joining as one with my mother. I remember that feeling always. The imprint is on my heart. I wonder if my mother remembers . . .

My awareness is I wonder why as we get older, it is sometimes so difficult to be close to our parents? I wonder why as a child, I believed I was a 'baby' if I sought comfort from my mother? Where did this belief in me come from? Where does this belief come from in our society? But as we grow up, it's emotionally healthy to separate from our mothers to become autonomous with the ability to self-comfort.

Those who don't separate from their mothers, lose who they are and may stay as weak, needy children for their whole lives.

Many, many years later, one evening my mother had a stroke and was rushed to the hospital. I was an adult living in another state. Daddy called and told me that her stroke was so bad that it was futile to operate. They were letting God take care of her. I made airline arrangements to go see my mother the next day. Early that morning, around three or so, I had a dream-like memory of my mother holding me as she did on that day when I was eleven, distraught about my haircut and thinking, 'I was ruined and ugly'. I felt her arms around me. The warmth and love coming from her was magnificent and much stronger than it had been even on that day. Tears ran down my face as I felt my mother's love and felt the essence of her so very close to me.

The next morning early, Daddy called to tell me that mother had died about three that morning.

In the months thereafter, when I would get up in the middle of the night to use the restroom or I might just awaken for no reason, I would smell the fresh fragrance of my mother. This occurrence stayed with me for several years in the most unexpected times but usually at night, late when I was quiet and to myself. And in places strangely, where there were no odors. I wear no perfumes and can't stand artificial odors. This fragrance came from nowhere in the places where I lived.

In times of stress, loneliness or unhappiness and just sometimes for comfort, before I go to sleep, I pull into me the memory and feelings of being in my mother's lap and her holding me close to her heart.

SHOW DADDY YOUR BRA

I am eleven

MY BREASTS ARE BEGINNING TO grow. They're beginning to show through my clothes. One of my teachers at school tells me that I need to start wearing a bra. I tell my mom.

My mom doesn't think that I need a bra yet. But the other girls my age are starting to wear them and besides, my teacher says that I need one. If a teacher says something parents usually listen.

So we go shopping for my first bra. I am embarrassed. My mother and the sales lady are laughing at how cute and little the bras are. Mother says that she didn't know they made a bra so small. I wish they both would shut up. They're embarrassing me!

I think the bras feel and look weird. I want one badly though because most of my friends have one, but at the same time I don't want one. The bra feels uncomfortable on my shoulders and on my back. Mother says that I'll get use to the feeling and pretty soon I'll forget that I'm wearing a bra.

The name of the bra is 'Grow Cups' for preteen girls. I wonder, how much more will I grow? I'm not sure I want to grow much more.

We purchase two bras. I wear one home. It feels weird and uncomfortable. It feels like I have on too many clothes under my blouse. Well I guess, I'll get used to it like mother says. I really did want it and I guess that it's part of growing up to be a woman. I can show my girlfriends at school tomorrow. That'll be fun!

I ask my mother not to tell my dad. She doesn't say anything when I ask her this. So I hope that she heard me.

When my dad comes home, I can hear them talking. I'm in the hallway getting ready to come into the kitchen. I overhear my mother telling my father about my new bra. She's laughing and saying how cute and little it is. I walk in and angrily state, "Mother, I asked you to not tell!" She says for me to show daddy my bra. He's never seen such a little bra before. They're both laughing!

I respond, "No way! Leave me alone!" Then I run out of the room. I hate them both! Mother can never keep a secret! I hate them both for embarrassing me. My father is a man. I would never show a man my bra.

I am not sure why they were so insensitive to my privacy and boundaries. My best try is to believe that they still thought of me as their little baby girl—so it seemed natural to them for me to reveal all and everything to them.

Their insensitivity made me extremely uncomfortable and I did not feel they valued me as a separate human being and that they only saw me as an extension of themselves.

I am sure that it is difficult for parents to watch their little ones grow up but parents think and remember how difficult it is for children to experience all the changes in their body.

Respect children as separate individuals. Respect their feelings and their bodies. Children are separate individuals. Separate from their parents. Children's bodies belong to them and not to their parents.

MOTHER, I NEED TO TELL YOU A SECRET

I am eleven

I AM GROWING UP AND IT feels weird. My body is changing. I'm getting hair in places, under my arms and other places. It feels funny. I feel funny and strange.

I think every woman gets this but I'm going to ask my mother about it. First, I need to get her alone. I don't want anyone else to hear.

One night, she's walking down the hall coming from her bedroom and she's alone. Now is my chance. I run up to her and say, "Mother, I need to tell you—ask you something. It's a secret." She asks, "What is it?" Keeping my voice very low I tell her, "I have hair down there."

She responds in a surprised stern tone, "Well, I hope that you won't tell anyone!"

I felt terror! Embarrassment! Shock! I run fast into my room! I wanted her to tell me that it was okay and that I was normal. What did she think? That I'd go around blabbing about this? I'm so sure! I need her to explain things to me! Did I ask something wrong? Aren't I supposed to ask my mother questions like this? At school they told us to ask our parents questions about growing up and stuff.

Is something wrong? Did I do something wrong? Is this something to hide?

My mother never said another word to me about that evening or my question. I felt embarrassed and unsure of what was happening to my body but I would never dare ask her or tell her anything again.

Later I learned from her that her mother had never told her anything about sex or 'growing up'. So she didn't really know what to say. But my learning this later didn't help me at the time.

I have always wondered why we are so hesitant, nervous and embarrassed to discuss the happenings within our bodies. We treat our bodies as if they are separate from us. Our generation has changed some, but still beliefs of not discussing sexual things forthright and honestly seems to prevail.

I believe all of this goes back to the religious dogma and Puritan ethics our culture has developed and unfortunately hangs on to.

Once all of us accept our bodies' growth and development as normal and that there is nothing wrong or unacceptable about our body. Children growing up will feel more comfortable in their skin. Then we all will feel more comfortable in our bodies.

God created us in his image. He created our bodily functions. So what's shameful about them? Nothing!

My mother rarely talked to me about much of anything. What I learned, I learned mostly from my girlfriends, their mothers and reading

THE CHRISTMAS STOCKINGS

I am eleven or twelve

I WANT TO MAKE MY MOM and dad something special. We all have stockings. They don't have any. I know I'll make them the most beautiful Christmas stockings in the whole world. I've saved my allowance and have about five dollars. I'm going to the 'Five and Dime' to purchase all the items that I will need to make the stockings.

I spend hours looking at all the decorations. I find some plain red and white stockings. I get glitter, bells, holly and bows—the perfect decorations for the perfect stockings. I have just enough money to get what I need—the stockings, glue, green and gold glitter and the other adornments. I purchase all the stocking ingredients and hurry home to my room to create.

With the glue—scissors—glitter—my work is in progress. First, I spell mom and dad on the white furry part at the top of the stockings with the glue. Then I sprinkle the glitter on the glue. WOW! These are going to turn out better than I imagined. Mom and dad will love them and love me for making them. When I'm not working on the stockings, I hide all the stuff under my bed.

My grandmother, NaNa and aunts come to visit. I show my grandmother the stockings. She thinks they are beautiful and encourages me. "You're so creative and sweet to make them for your parents." I tell her that I need more stuff to put on the stockings and I don't have any more money. I can't ask my Mom for more money because the stockings are a secret. My grandmother gives me some money. When we all go out to do errands, I have the opportunity to secretively buy more decorations for the stockings. They're turning out so well, better than the ones in the stores. My parents are going to LOVE them!

My mom enters my room unexpectedly and says, "What's all this mess? You're making a big mess! I have enough to do with Christmas coming and visitors without all of your mess." I respond, "Momma, I'm making a Christmas surprise!" She responds, "I don't care what you are making. Clean up this mess! You're getting stuff in the carpet and the maid has just left for the day. CLEAN IT UP!"

I'm upset but think to myself, 'When she sees what I've made, she'll forget all about the mess. The beautiful Christmas stockings will please her so much'.

A few days later after changing, arranging and letting the glue set, the stockings are ready. My grandmother and aunts think they are beautiful.

I run up the stairs to give them to my mother and father. My mother says, "They're pretty—but your dad and I don't need stockings. Santa doesn't visit us and besides there's nowhere to put them."

I don't remember what my dad said. My heart is broken. I had worked so hard. I wanted to please my parents to give them something from my heart. I wanted their love and attention.

I thought the stockings were pretty and that mattered, too. I thought they would look pretty hanging with all the other stockings, but my mother didn't think they would. She said that it would be too cluttered. My grandmother said that she loved my stockings. Her saying this made me feel better.

I kept the stockings in my room until it was time to pack up the Christmas decorations. Then I stuck them in the boxes with all the other decorations.

Many years later—in a different house, we were getting out Christmas decorations and my mother pulled the stockings out of a box. She said, "These are pretty. Wonder where they came from? Let's hang them on the fireplace hooks". I said, "I made them mother. I made them for you and daddy. Don't you remember?"

She had a blank look on her face. I'm not sure if she even heard me but she did put them on the fireplace hooks. She never said a word about whether she remembered me making the stockings or not. I didn't want to say anything more about the stockings because it hurt me so deeply that she didn't even remember that I'd made them.

The stockings are hung up every Christmas and no one remembers where they came from or who made them.

But I do! They were made with all the love I had. When I see them I remember. I remember the little girl and how she loved so much and wanted to please and make her parents a gift from her heart. I love that little girl and hold her in my heart forever.

My mother could not—would not acknowledge my love for her. She did not—could not see or feel the joy and love that I was feeling as I made my gift for her and my dad.

As an adult, I know my mother doesn't like holidays. She doesn't like having extra things to do. She can barely get through her day doing ordinary things. Holidays are just an extra bother for her and she can't wait until they're over. She dreads putting up a Christmas tree. She is always stressed and angry in the holiday season. She has no joy!

It's sad to me because I love the holiday season. I love to decorate the house and putting up the Christmas tree is one of the most joyous things I do at Christmas!

One year, many years later during the holiday season, my mother called to say that my father and she were going to their Yacht for Christmas. She stated that she was so glad because she did not have to deal with all the Christmas stuff. She went on and on about how she was so sick of Christmas. Then she asked me what I was going to do for Christmas.

At the time, I did not have the money to even purchase a tree. I wanted a tree badly, but it would have been an extravagance for me to get one that year. I answered my mother by saying, "Not much, perhaps, I'll spend the day with friends." She asked, "Are you going to put up a tree?" I replied that I did not have the money for a tree. She either didn't hear me or she just ignored what I said and asked, "Aren't you going to lots of parties?" I responded, "Sure there are always lots of parties."

When I hung up the phone, I cried. I thought isn't it bizarre that a person who wants a tree so badly, can't afford one? And some people, who can buy anything they want, think Christmas is a bother and it's too much trouble to put up a tree.

I do understand that all the decorations and celebrations can get over done and that going away on a Yacht is a nice way to spend Christmas, too.

Another year, after a divorce and I was alone in my house. My ex-husband had moved his grand piano out. I got the biggest Christmas tree that I could find and placed it in the corner where the grand piano once was. It took me days to decorate the tree, pulling a ladder around it the higher I went up to place the ornaments on the tree. After it was completed, it was fabulous! I would turn the lights on and lay under the tree as if I was a child. I cherish this Christmas memory!

I love the holidays, but some negative feelings come up. I don't like to give gifts to my parents because I never feel that they like what I give them. It feels good to give to them because I love them, but I feel they are critical of whatever it is that I give. They are critical of what I give them just like they are critical of everything about me. My mother is always so full of stress at the holiday season that she can't enjoy and truly see all the love that is trying to be expressed.

I believe the best thing about Christmas is the love that it gives us for the opportunity to express—the giving of love and remembrance of the birthday of Our Lord and Savior Jesus Christ

MOVING TO A NEW HOUSE

I am twelve

MY MOM AND DAD ARE looking for a new house. They're looking at really large houses. On the weekend, we all pile into the car and go searching for houses. It's so much fun looking at all the magnificent houses.

I guess that my daddy has made a lot of money because we're looking at really, really—I mean truly big houses. They have swimming pools and one of them even has a bowling alley. Mother doesn't like the one with the bowling alley. She thinks it's too big. I don't think it's too big. I think that it's perfect. It would be too cool to have a house with a bowling alley in it.

We keep looking. Then finally, my mom and dad find a house they both like. They take all of us to see it. It's white and it sits on a corner.

It's on the side of a hill. The backyard has a lot of trees. There's even a balcony off the kitchen with a tree coming up through the middle of it. It's really cool! I love it!

The front of the house is higher than the back. In the front, it's one story and in the back it is two. The house even has a carport. I will have my room downstairs next to the playroom. It will be private away from all my younger sisters. I'm hoping my parents decide to buy this house.

Mom and dad tell us that if we all like this house that this is the one that they'll buy. They say to me if we get this house that I'll have to change school districts. They tell me that I'll have to leave all my friends and start junior high with a new group of kids.

I reply, "I want this house. I can make new friends." They inquire, "Are you sure?"

"Yes! I'm sure! I want this house!"

How little I knew at the age of twelve. The house was great! I loved it, but moving to a new school at the age of twelve was really rough. I had moved before at the age of six and it had worked out beautifully. I had been popular at the school where I was attending.

Moving at the age of twelve to a new school was a totally different story. I felt like odd man out. I was so alone. All of the other kids had known each other since kindergarten. They had their friends and their little cliques. They were not looking for any new kids to join them. I was one of the few new kids that knew no one and fit nowhere. Plus, I was going through puberty and feeling unsure and awkward about myself. I felt that no one at the new school liked me.

Moving at this time in my life was an awful decision. I did not know at the age of twelve, how important friends are or that sometimes it can be difficult to make new friends and to fit in. Up until that move, I had always been one of the most popular kids—one of the leaders. Now I was seeing what it felt like to be on the outside. At twelve, it was a difficult lesson because of all the changes in my body and in my life.

I did not have the necessary tools to make that kind of decision for myself. That move changed my life for the worst. I grew a lot emotionally but also suffered a lot of trauma.

The choices we make decide our course in life—at any age.

When I expressed my dislike for the new school and the kids, my parents said, "It was your decision, now live with it!"

I hated myself for the decision I made at the age of twelve. I thought it was my fault that I had no friends. I thought it was because I moved to a new big house and I was being punished. I thought I could not have a big pretty house and friends, too. I thought that I had ruined my life by that decision. I had ruined my life by changing schools. I believed that my life and happiness were over. My life was over at the age of twelve. I wanted my friends back!

A twelve-year-old child does not have the ability to make this kind of decision. I did not know how to foresee the outcome.

My parents thought they were doing the wise thing leaving the decision up to me. If I had said that I did not want to change schools, we would not have moved to this new and wonderful house. How could a twelve-year-old make a decision like that—a decision that would affect the whole family?

Of course, the outcome might have been different. I could have loved the new school and made a lot of new friends. I had no way of knowing that the results would be disastrous. Based on my past experiences, I thought the outcome would be great. My last move to a new school had been no big deal. I had made many new friends and really fast!

Perhaps, what occurred and the decision made was what was intended for my life's experiences. We never really know the outcome of the choices we make, until we make them.

What we learn can change our destiny and give us growth that will benefit us for a lifetime. We learn to be resourceful. We look into ourselves, learn about ourselves, stretch and grow. Although often times, this awareness cannot be appreciated until much later and after many years have passed.

A KISSING PARTY

I am twelve or thirteen

A PARTY, A 'REAL' TEENAGE PARTY! I'm so excited that I can't stand it! A boy and a girl party! It's going to be at a really cool girl's house. She's way popular and too neat. Plus, she has two older brothers. Her brothers are going to chaperone the party. They're in high school. So they're lots older than we are. I have never been to a party where the parents won't be there.

It's going to be so cool! We're going to have chips, dips and soda pop. We might even turn the lights off and play 'kissing' games— kissing games like 'spin the bottle' and some other teenage party games.

My special boyfriend is going to be there. He's from my old school. The one I went to before I moved. He and some of his friends are planning to come to this party. He is the leader of the coolest group. I can't wait!

I wear his first name initial around my neck. He tried to kiss me another time at a party when we were playing 'spin the bottle'. He missed and instead kissed the corner of my lips. It felt funny but it made my stomach have butterflies. I got all sweaty but I still want to try it again.

At the last teenage party, the first time I ever played kissing games, the girl who had the party, her parents played, 'spin the bottle' with us. It was funny! All of us kids were really embarrassed, but we tried to act real cool as if we had done it a million times before. I think her parents knew it was our first time. Her mother is a teacher at our school.

I can't wait to see my boyfriend. Since I moved into the new house, we don't get to see each other often. We talk on the phone a lot. Sometimes we talk on the phone until really late at night. We fall asleep holding the phone to pretend that we're together. He told me that he holds his pillow at night and pretends that it's me. He said that he'll love me forever. I'll love him forever, too. He told me that his dad is going to get him a convertible when he's sixteen. We're going to drive all over town in it. I just know that someday we'll get married.

I'm so nervous about this party. What shall I wear? She said casual. I know I'll wear slacks and an oversized oxford cloth button down shirt with the shirt tail out and loafers. That'll look cool!

My dad drives a girlfriend and me to the party.

At the party all of us are talking. Everyone seems nervous. The boys are on one side of the room and the girls are on the other side. We're playing records and dancing a little.

It seems as if we're all just waiting for it to get a little later, so we can play the kissing games. The girl who's having the party—her brothers kept coming in and out. They're real nice. They come in and say, "Okay, the party is almost over. We're going to turn out the lights." Her brothers tell everyone to grab a partner and to find a place to kiss. We all look around at each other in a kind of shock. This is what we've all been waiting for all night, but what do we do? Then her brothers turn the lights out and it's dark.

My boyfriend takes my hand and leads me into a hall closet. It's so dark. We're laughing, nervously. He puts his arm around me. It feels good to be close to him. I put my arms around his neck. A hanger hits us in the face. We laugh! This is awkward but fun. We just stand there giggling and talking. Then he kisses me. He doesn't miss this time. It happens so quickly. He puts his arm around me again and we hug. It feels amazingly good to be close to him. I never want to leave this closet. I feel safe and warm. This is really a wonderful feeling— being in love is wonderful. I guess being married must be the most wonderful thing in the world. Married people can hold each other like this every night.

We can hear the other kids now. Someone turns the lights on and everyone starts coming out of their hiding places. We step out of the closet and immediately separate as if we don't even know each other.

Parents are beginning to arrive. My father is here to pick me up. When I get into the car, my father asks, "Why were all the lights off in the house when I drove up?" "I don't know." I respond. He asks what we did at the party. I respond, "We played records, danced and ate snacks. He asks, "Did you play kissing games? I answer, "Yes, we played one kissing game." He states, "Be careful kissing boys because you can get into trouble if you go too far!" I respond embarrassed, "I know! Okay!"

What a relief! That was all he said. How embarrassing. All I did was kiss one time. What did he think we did? He makes me feel bad just for one kiss. I can't wait to get away from him. I want to get into my room, so I can think about how special this night was.

The next day, he and my mother corner me in the breakfast room and start talking to me. They're saying things like; 'Be careful kissing boys—you can get in trouble kissing and going too far. They say, 'you would not want to do anything that you wouldn't be able to tell your husband, would you?' Dad, even says, 'If you get pregnant, I will disown you.'

I think that I know what they're talking about but I wasn't doing anything wrong. We just kissed. My parents were embarrassing me. They always make me feel as if I'm doing something wrong. I state, "We only kissed one time!" They respond, "We understand, but we want you to be careful!" I say, "I will!"

The first time I had sex was with the man I married. I believe sex is to be between two people in love and in a commitment. The man I married had no morals. He screwed everyone within his radar even while we were married and even had an illegitimate child while we were married. He was the worst lover I ever had, but I didn't know that at the time. Therefore, it was a big waste saving myself for him.

Of course as an adult, I understand what my parents were trying to convey. I wish they had emphasized also that I be careful to select a man that had equally high morals.

For me, love must be there before sex is involved. I have always felt this way. Sex is like a kind of physical worship between a man and woman in love. It is a belief that I was born knowing. Sure sex can be kinky, fun, raunchy and more, but first comes love and commitment as its basis. I unfortunately, have selected men who do not have this same type of morality or belief.

It saddens me that many young people today have lost the true meaning of sex and they engage in it as if it was nothing special. I have pity for them as they may be destroying their ability to genuinely connect and share physically in a committed and genuine love. To delay sex when you are getting to know one another and growing in love, can be very exciting. Kissing and petting can become off the charts excitement. No reason to have sex too soon.

Awareness also is when a female who is connected to her body, mind and soul has sex. She will become hormonally attached to the man. God created it this way, to keep parents connected in order to protect and rear their off spring. So be careful and guard yourself from having sex with someone that you really don't want to feel this strong of a connection with and certainly not with someone that you don't know well because you may become connected to someone that you don't really want to be. The sexual connection will cloud your ability to make a clear decision. Sex is a precious gift from God.

HIDING MY UNDER PANTIES

I am twelve

IT'S ONE OF THOSE PERFECT days at school, a beautiful crisp fall day. I have on a short gray wool skirt and a white oxford cloth shirt with a button down collar. I'm wearing a light blue sweater vest and white socks with black suede penny loafers.

At my school, we put dimes in the slots where the pennies are supposed to go in the loafers. This is one of the ways to tell if a person is cool or not. My hair is in a ponytail. My hair looks really good today. I feel really good!

I'm talking to my boyfriend. We are standing beside my mother's red station wagon. She's waiting for my sisters to get into the car. So I still have time to chat with my boyfriend. We're talking and flirting. It's really fun. He slips me a note. I just know that I'm going to love him forever.

My tummy starts to feel a little funny—not bad—just funny—a

little crampy or something. It is weird how I feel. At the same time, I feel strange—I also feel good. What's going on? I've never felt this way before.

It's time to go. All the kids are in the car. Mom says, "Hop into the car. Let's go home! Tell your friend, good-bye!"

Riding home in the car, I start feeling tired. It's funny the way I'm feeling. I don't have time to feel bad. I have ballet class to go to after I get home. I need to hurry and get something to eat then change into my ballet clothes and go.

We arrive home. I run into the kitchen and grab some cookies. Then I go down to my room. I have a cool room. It's downstairs by the playroom. It's private. There's even a separate entrance to my room from the outside. I begin to take off my clothes to put on my tights and leotard for ballet class.

My panties feel wet. I look and there's blood all over my under panties. I panic, but I know what this is. It's my menstrual period. I saw the 'Molly grows up' movies at school that told us about what's going to happen, but I still feel weird! I'm not sure that I'm ready for this to happen and for me to become a woman.

My mother put a huge blue box of Kotex in my bathroom cabinet along with a strange looking elastic belt.

I feel so strange and embarrassed. Should I tell someone? No! I really don't want anyone to know. This is my secret. I'm going to keep this a secret! It's my body and I'll figure this out on my own.

I get the big blue box and the package with the elastic belt out of the cabinet. This belt thing feels terrible. Maybe I have it on wrong. Okay, I'll read the instructions. Put the end of the Kotex thing in here—okay—got it! Are you kidding me? I can't wear this! Everyone will see that I'm wearing this thing through my leotard. This Kotex thing is huge!

These things aren't made for skinny girls like me who take ballet. I wonder what the other girls do. All girls have this—all girls go through this, but this belt thing is the worst! I know, I'll use safety pins. I'll pin this Kotex thing to my panties. Yeah, that works better.

I wonder if anyone else ever thought about doing this. Well, shoot! It still shows through my leotard. I feel a little sick to my stomach, too. Maybe, I shouldn't go to ballet. But I love ballet. I look forward all day to ballet class.

Okay think, what do other girls do? Some of the older girls wear long tee shirts over their ballet clothes, at times. That's it! I'll wear a tee shirt over my leotard and tights. Yes, it works!

Now that's figured out. What can I do with my bloody under panties? I don't want anyone to know what has happened to me.

I know. I'll hide them. Where? Out in the woods somewhere? I run up the stairs and go out the side entrance. I run across the street. There are woods behind the houses. I go back into the woods. I go really far back. I can put my panties inside this log then cover it with leaves. No one will ever know, but if someone finds them. Will they know they are mine? Oh, how would they know? No one could ever guess they were mine. Great! Good idea! Got rid of the panties!

It feels so good out in these woods. The wind is blowing through the trees. It has gotten colder outside and cloudy. I feel good out here, close to nature. It feels good having this secret about my body. I feel all close to nature and the earth and strangely calm inside.

My body feels different. I'm not sure what I think about how I feel, but I do feel kind of good in a strange way like I want to be quiet and private to myself. As if, I want to hold myself close.

I run home and mother takes me to ballet class. I get through class okay. Although, I feel as if everybody knows that I have this huge thing between my legs. I wonder if my ballet teacher ever has this problem. I begin to look at women in a whole new way. Wondering? Are they wearing one of these huge things between their legs, too?

A few days pass. I feel relieved no one has said anything. I guess, I don't look any different even though I feel different. Of course, I have told some of my girlfriends at school. Most of my friends have already started their periods a few months earlier. So cool, now I fit in!

Then one night, my father yells for me to come upstairs. I run up the stairs and into the living room. He says, "I want to ask you something. Do you have anything to tell your mother and me?" "No." I respond, "Why?"

"Are you sure?" I answer, "Yes." Then he says, "The maid found blood in your under clothes. Why didn't you tell your mother? She's so hurt? You should tell your mother these things!"

I'm totally embarrassed. I scream at him. "It's none of your business! Leave me alone!" Then I run downstairs to the safe haven of my room. Didn't he ever think of me? Doesn't anyone ever think of me and my feelings?

My mother—who cares? Why would I tell her? She doesn't care anything about me! I can't tell my mother anything! She never even talks to me! I wish they would both just go away! I will never tell them anything ever! They don't understand my feelings! Some things are just too private and too secret to tell! I never wanted to see my father again! He knew MY secret!

He never said another word about this to me, neither did my mother.

Looking back I wonder why I went to such lengths to hide my panties. Was it because I was growing up and wanted to keep some things to myself?

My privacy boundaries were crossed. My parents did not respect my privacy. I felt violated and I did not even really know what that meant at the time. I was not their little doll anymore. I was a separate growing up young girl.

My father was trying to create, actually force a mother—daughter moment, when he should have stayed out of it. I was not close enough to either one of my parents to share this private growing up moment with them. I handled it on my own just fine. My parents intrusion into my privacy made me feel angry. Thank goodness, they created mini-pads and tampons.

SUGAR IS SALT!

I am twelve or thirteen

IT IS APRIL FOOL'S DAY! What a blast! This is the day you can play all sorts of tricks on people.

My friend Linda is spending the night. We're going to plan some really neat tricks to play on my parents. My parents don't laugh much and I think some tricks might make them laugh and have some fun.

We're going to wait until they go to sleep. Then sneak up to the kitchen to figure out the best tricks that we possibly can, to make my parents have a fun April Fool's Day.

Linda says she has played tricks on her parents and they always thought the tricks were funny. So we decide we might play some of the same tricks on my parents. Since she tried them out on her parents, we know that they'll work.

Everyone in the house is asleep but us. We slowly climb up the stairs to the kitchen. So we'll have just enough light to see what we're doing, we turn on the light in the pantry. We snoop through the pantry looking for ideas. Okay, what shall we do?

Linda says the first thing we can do is exchange the sugar for the salt. She says that her parents thought it was funny when she played this trick on them.

Cool idea! We pour the sugar out of its container then fill it with salt. We're giggling. Can't you just see their faces when they put salt into their coffee. Okay, what else can we do?

The first thing, my parents do when they get up is to have their coffee. So, what can we do to the coffee? What looks enough like coffee that we could make an exchange without there being any notice? Nestle chocolate drink mix? No dirt, dirt would work! We're amazed by our clever ideas. We sneak outside through the back entrance to scoop some finely ground dirt out of the flower bed. We sprinkle the dirt into the coffee container laughing as we do. This is going to be so cool!

Linda comments, "Your parents are going to just die when they drink their mud coffee with salt in it. It's going to be so funny! They're going to laugh their heads off! Now what else can we do?"

I'm beginning to feel uneasy about all this. "I think we have done enough." She responds, "No we haven't! I bet we can think of a lot more funny April Fool's things to do!" I say, "No, this is enough to do." She says, "What a party pooper, you are!"

We run back downstairs full of excitement for what tomorrow will bring when my parents wake up to their April Fools surprises.

Linda and I stay up real late watching the late shows on TV.

The next morning, we're sleeping very soundly, until we hear blood chilling screams coming from the kitchen.

My mother sounds hysterical. She's screaming and yelling for my father to come into the kitchen.

I wake up startled and quickly. My heart jumps into my throat. I freeze up inside. Oh, no, apparently my mother doesn't think our tricks are funny. Please, God, don't let mother yell and scream in front of my friend.

Linda and I sneak up the back stairs to the kitchen. We wait and listen. My father comes into the kitchen as my mother is screaming and telling him about her coffee. She's actually almost crying.

My father yells for me. I'm scared to death. What can I do? What's going to happen to me? I was only playing a joke!

Linda looks frightened, too, but she says. "What's the big deal? It's only an April Fool's joke."

We muster up our courage and walk the rest of the way up the stairs to the kitchen. We nervously say, "April Fools! Did we surprise you? Pretty good tricks, huh?"

My mother is hysterical and crying. She's going on about how her coffee is ruined and what a brat I am.

I say, "Mother, it's only a joke. We were just having some fun. I thought that you would laugh and think it was funny. It's April Fool's Day, you know, the day when people play jokes on people."

My very angry crying mother says. "Not only did you ruin my morning cup of coffee! Now, I'm going to have to pour all of the coffee out because you put dirt in it. You are a brat! My whole day is ruined because of you!"

My father is trying to go along with my mother's angry tirade, but he's chuckling under his breath. He comments, "The kids were just trying to do some tricks. Relax, it's no big deal. We can get more coffee."

When my father says this, my mother just glares at me and I feel a chill go down my spine. I feel my mother's hate for me. I feel how she cannot stand it when my father sides with me. She wants to always make sure that I get into trouble and that my father is aware of how 'bad' I am. She likes to make a scene and make sure I get punished.

So she continues to rant and rave, until my father finally gets angry and yells at me. He yells his usual things about what a naughty brat I am.

Linda and I both apologize then go back downstairs. We only meant to have fun and make jokes but what we did was make my mother upset. Nothing we did turned out to be fun. It was upsetting for all of us.

When I look back at this scene, I can remember the excitement I felt wanting to create some innocent fun for my parents and me. I was trying to reach out and touch them in a 'fun' way. It made me excited to hear that my friend's parents responded to her jokes in a positive manner. It gave me hope that my parents might respond in the same way. I hoped that my parents would laugh and say what a funny idea. Then we could all have a good laugh together and feel close to one another, but as usual with my parents, nothing seemed to get the reaction that I was looking for.

As an adult, I can understand that it must have been frustrating for my mother to endure muddy, salty coffee. I am sorry that I upset her and that she did not appreciate my April Fool's joke, but looking back, I still think it was funny.

My awareness is that my mother and father never do appreciate my sense of humor. It is like we are on a different wave link. Most of the time when I am teasing or trying to be funny, they take it as though I am being serious then I get into trouble.

I do not show my sense of humor to them anymore. I am tired of being criticized for my humor and my light heartedness. I show my humor and fun side to people who will enjoy and appreciate it for what it is. The sad thing to me is that I feel like I cannot be myself when I am with my parents. I feel like I have to watch everything I say to them for fear of being criticized.

My awareness is that I can always be true to who I am but can show different sides of myself to different people as is appropriate to do so.

All of us have different ideas of what we think is humorous.

Some people do not seem to have any sense of humor. Then I've met others who thought they were funny and I did not get their humor at all.

Everyone is an individual and what is funny to one may make the other one cry. The awareness is to see humor from both sides. The perspective a person is coming from decides whether they will think something is funny or not. We all have varying degrees of sensitivity. Humor is based on an individual's perspective.

"Men are disturbed not by things that happen, but by their opinion of the things that happen."

—Epictetus

YOU'RE TOO FAT—NO, YOU'RE TOO SKINNY!

I am twelve and thirteen

A BALLET CLASSMATE AND I GO to the little burger joint in front of the ballet school. We order cokes and large orders of French fries. Yummy, greasy, salty, French fries with lots of ketchup, I'm not used to eating this kind of food. But it tastes so good today that we decide to go back for the same treat for several days in a row.

Then the ballet teacher says to me in front of the whole class. "Natalie, you're putting on some weight! A dancer can't be fat. Please, take care of this!"

I think to myself while I am feeling embarrassed beyond belief, 'No, no, this isn't my real stomach. It's full of coke and French fries. It'll go away.' But I respond, "Yes, Ma'am."

After that humiliation, I vowed to myself, no more French fries. In fact, no more food! I'll become the thinnest dancer there ever was.

So, the starvation diet begins. But before I totally start the diet of the century, I have a bowl of ice cream with bananas. My mother walks by and comments, "Keep eating like that and you'll get fat!" I think, 'Wanna bet?' but say, "No, I won't! I'm starting my diet tomorrow."

Next day, I begin my diet. I slowly stop eating so much. I get books on diets and nutrition. I get magazines like Glamour and Mademoiselle to read what the models say about dieting and how to get and stay thin. According to the magazines, the only things models eat are celery and carrots.

It's difficult to stay at the dinner table and eat what my family is eating. They eat fattening stuff like steak and mashed potatoes. According to the books and magazines that I read, a person should never eat this kind of food. So, I eventually stop eating with my family. My mother doesn't say anything at first. Then, she gets angry at me. Her anger makes me eat less because I think she must want me to be fat because she cooks all that fattening food.

Most of the time, I eat cereal because I read somewhere that one of the top models lives on cereal. So, I think, good idea!

I begin to drop off pounds fast and to get really thin. I wasn't really overweight in the first place. My dad comments, "You look pale. You're getting too thin. Do you feel okay? Eat something!"

At times I get so hungry, I eat a whole box of vanilla wafers with lots of milk or I'll eat Fritos and dip them in peanut butter. Of course, I know these things are over the top fattening, but I get so hungry, I don't care. I lose control and eat them anyway. Then the next day, I go right back to starving myself.

It feels really good being so skinny. I feel very in control of my body. I like my flat stomach and I can dance pulling all movement from my core. This is a powerful and centered way to feel. A dancer is all about being in control of their body. I feel great and look great in the ballet studio mirror. I have a real flat tummy now. When I started my period, my body changed. It got puffy and I didn't like it at all.

My mom is worried. When she picks me up from ballet class, she talks to my ballet teacher about my eating habits. Then we have a conference with my ballet teacher. My ballet teacher looks at me and says, "Dancers need to be thin but they also need to eat to keep their strength up." As she's saying this, I'm thinking, you're the one that said I was getting fat and now you're telling me to eat. I feel confused, but know that I'm going to stay thin no matter what. Anyway, I think my ballet teacher is saying this just to make my mother happy. So, I don't listen to a word that either of them said on that day.

Then, I guess my body changed or something because all of a sudden I could eat almost anything I wanted and not gain weight. I must be growing or something. I went to ballet class almost every day after school and also danced often in my room for hours. So I was getting lots of exercise and movement.

My body became thin and I would eat a healthy diet of normal lunches and dinners with some snacks and still stay the weight that I desire.

I love to eat. So, this was beyond great! I read the books on nutrition and learn the healthy things to eat to keep me strong. I try to eat mostly healthy food like veggies, lean meat and stuff. But I can even eat a whole pizza and still be okay, just as long as I don't do it every day. My sisters don't like the fact that I can eat a lot and not gain weight. They call me names like "stick woman".

I guess I was lucky because for about a year, I was almost anorexic but I got over it on my own. When I was growing up, they didn't know much about that affliction.

All of my life, I have been very aware of weight and how my body looks, feels and moves. I learned young and on my own the healthy way to eat.

We all have a skeleton that is our base frame like a piece of furniture has a metal or wood frame. A sofa for instance, can be fluffy with a lot of padding and stuffing and it looks good. It is one style built on the frame. Or a sofa might have lots less padding and fabric that is pulled tightly to the frame and that looks good too. It is just another style built on the same frame. Of course, frames can be different sizes, just like people can be large boned or small boned. They are all attractive in their own way. Padding and stuffing can be changed to change the look of a piece of furniture just like people can lose and gain weight. They just have a different look—a different style. Variety makes life interesting. It is all a matter of taste and style which can change and shift all the time and usually does. You can change your appearance and style on the outside but it is still you on the inside.

The secret is to have love for self at all times, no matter what your weight or size and to release judging yourself by someone else's standards. You can change yourself, if and when you desire, but always know that you are perfect just the way you are.

Who you are; what and how you think and believe on the inside creates what you look like on the outside. Your individual and particular beauty, the essence of you, will always shine through your eyes.

Create your exterior how you desire. Be whatever size, shape or weight that you choose to be. You will manifest what you think of yourself through to your outside appearance.

Children's bodies are changing all the time from fuller to thinner until they arrive at their destination. I was not aware of this when I was growing up.

Eat healthily, exercise, drink plenty of wonderful cleansing water and you will be healthy from the inside out. Move your body in whichever exercise you enjoy. Movement is a key element to moving energy through your body. When I was going through so much emotion as a child and even for all of my life, when I dance and move, I always feel better. It's a great release.

Think beautiful thoughts about yourself and your body. If you want to change it, do so, but feel love and acceptance of self until you do. We are all beautiful and God made us all!

BALLET IS RUINING YOUR LEGS

I am twelve

BALLET IS MY LIFE. I dream of being a famous ballet dancer. It's all I want in the whole world. I'm the youngest member in the corps de ballet.

I read and study about ballet. I read about famous ballerinas. I love the stories about Anna Pavlova. I listen to classical music and ballet music. I see myself dancing all the great ballets. I pretend I'm a world famous ballet dancer.

I go to all the ballet performances that come to town. I usually invite a girlfriend to go with me and we have a wonderful time. The theater is downtown. It's fun to go downtown to the beautiful theater to see the ballets. When I see a performance by one of the famous dancers that come to town my imagination soars. I see the whole ballet in my head over again with me starring in the lead role. I dream and pretend these scenarios over and over in my head. I buy the records and play the music of the ballets continually. I see myself doing the steps, the turns, the leaps that the dancers do in the ballet.

My ballet teacher is a famous ballet dancer. She sometimes dances in performances with her husband. After I see them dance, I stare at her in awe the next time I take class from her. I think she's regal and beautiful, especially when she's on the stage dancing. It's the way that she carries her body and the energy of her movements. There's something magical about being on stage performing in a ballet.

My parents don't share my interest in ballet. I think they thought it cute when I was little. They enjoyed going to the recitals. My mother always wanted me to take tap dancing, but I didn't like tap. She tapped danced when she was a young girl.

As I get older and begin to like ballet even more, I talk seriously about becoming a ballet dancer when I grow up. My parents' interest change, they don't want me to like ballet that much. They don't enjoy going to the ballet. I don't think they ever went to one, unless I was in it. They don't like classical music. They think both ballet and classical music are boring.

Sometimes there are dancers on TV—like on the 'Ed Sullivan Show' and I make a special attempt to watch these shows. If my parents are watching the shows with me they'll say, "Look at those ugly, muscular legs of hers. If you keep taking ballet, your legs will become just as ugly as hers!" I think the dancers are beautiful. I realize that many people do like the dancers and the ballet but not my parents.

My parents take me to ballet class and they purchase classical records for me. They buy me books on ballet and drive me and friends to see the ballet. But, as they're doing all of this, they're saying negative things. They're saying negative things about what I do and what I love most.

They comment often that they think ballet dancers' legs are ugly and their bodies are too muscular, and that the way a ballet dancer looks is unattractive and way too skinny. My father states, "Women shouldn't have such muscular bodies. It's not pretty and not feminine."

My parents worry that I'm going to ruin my legs. They say that when I grow up to be a lady, I'll have big muscular legs like a man. My parents also inform me that ballet dancers don't make much money. They take me to ballet class but offer the opposite of encouragement.

I like and develop my body to be lean and muscular. I watch what I eat. So, I'll be thin and able to dance lighter and have more strength in my body. Everything in my life is ballet. I dance for hours in my room. I imagine dancing in at ballet and accepting flowers on stage after the performance of a lifetime.

I ask my parents repeatedly to go to ballets with me. I exclaim, "You'll love it!" I want them to share my love of the ballet and the beautiful music. Their reply, "No, thank you, we will take you, but we do not have to go with you. We like to dance to 'Big Band' music."

I don't understand because I like all kinds of music—classical, rock and roll, jazz and 'Big band'—it all sounds good to me. It just depends on what I'm in the mood for. I like to swing dance and do the 'twist'. I like all kinds of dancing. So, I don't understand why my parents don't like ballet.

Each time Mother takes me to ballet class, she says, "I don't know why you like ballet so much. It's ruining your legs. Ballet is making you have muscles in your legs and they're ugly!"

All the talk about my legs being so muscular starts to make me self-conscious when I'm anywhere but ballet school. At ballet class, I notice my legs aren't very muscular compared to the other dancers' legs. I wish they were stronger and more muscular, but when I'm with my family, they're continually commenting about my legs.

My mother never worked out a day in her life, except she took tap and ballet when she was a girl. She did not study ballet seriously, as I did. Physical fitness is a foreign concept to her. She is not athletic at all. Therefore she does not know the feeling of being in a fit muscular body. The feeling of being in your core, in your center and the knowing that you can control and make your body do just about anything that you ask it to do.

I guess that my father definitely had the opinion that women should not have muscles. When he was younger, he was a professional baseball player. He is an athletic person. Apparently, he believed physical fitness was for men only. Their personal beliefs in this area did a number on my mind. For most of my life, I thought I had ugly legs because they have muscles and definition.

Until the world began working out and I looked around to realize that I have great legs. I get compliments about them often. People have commented, "Wow! Your legs are great! You have beautiful legs." Hearing comments like this surprised me at first and also served to heal the insecurity that my parents laid on me about my legs and my body.

My parents expressed their opinion in this area repeatedly trying to get me to conform to their beliefs. But all they did was to make me feel self-conscious and interfered with my enjoyment and desire to become a ballet dancer. When I was with my family, I felt that what I liked and enjoyed was not acceptable. Therefore, I did not feel acceptable to them. So I became unacceptable to myself in ways and on some levels. I eventually quit ballet and did not study it at the college level.

My self-esteem was damaged instead of being built up by my accomplishments in ballet. Looking back, I realize that I accomplished quite a bit at a very young age.

It is a normal occurrence that children have interests other than ones their parents have or want them to have. My awareness is to support and praise accomplishments in whatever form they take. Encourage children to develop their own unique and individual talents. Support their efforts.

Why would a parent expect their children to have tastes only like themselves? Perhaps, this may arise from insecurity on the parents' part. If a child enters into a field and excels in an area that a parent has no knowledge of, maybe their insecurity is triggered. The parent's defense system criticizes, instead of supports, in order to feel superior. Of course, what they are really trying to do is to feel equal. Anytime a person is feeling either superior or inferior, it is a defense mechanism being triggered, which shows they do not feel equal.

This type of human interaction unfortunately occurs many times in all kinds of relationships. So why wouldn't it occur in the child—parent relationship? When one person puts another one down for their likes or dislikes, it is because of fear, insecurity and lack of knowledge. Insecurity and fear—because what they think and like is being shown as not to be the 'correct' choice. Therefore an insecure person feels that they need to do whatever they can, to try to make themselves feel secure. Even if it means harassing and criticizing their children for having their individual dreams and desires.

Parents cannot live through and completely control their children's likes and desires. When they try to, it hampers the growth and individuality of the child.

Why would anyone criticize a body part of another human being especially their own child? Is it, perhaps, because they cannot accept their own body? Maybe they feel inadequate or unattractive and to avoid looking at their self and their feelings, they project that negativity outward onto others.

Criticizing a physical aspect of a child will never do anything but harm the child's self-esteem. Society expects an acceptable physical norm, but in reality, there is not just one but many. My parents negated a part of my body while putting more value on their own.

How one judges self is how they will judge others. If you accept self, you will more easily accept others. You don't have to like everyone, but you will accept who they are and move on. It is all just a matter of beliefs and perceptions—tastes and opinions.

When a person feels beautiful on the inside, they will feel good on the outside. They will then, more often than not, be able to see and appreciate the good and the beautiful aspects of others. The focus will be on the positive more than the negative.

Interesting thing is, as I got older and kept my fitness routine, my Father would comment how fit and good looking I am.

Ballet is the most difficult physical art form in the world. Ballet taught me physical and mental discipline and for that I am eternally grateful. Ballet stresses that your competition is within yourself as reflected in the studio mirror. Each day you work to improve your body, your grace, your strength as reflected by your movements.

Physical fitness and working out have saved my life many times. There were times, I was so emotionally down and depressed that I didn't want to move. The discipline that I learned from ballet forced me to move, when at times, it took everything that I had in me to do so. I could have chosen to sit on the sofa and eat, but instead I forced myself to move which shifted the energy in my body and mind. Working out and physical fitness are gifts that you give yourself just as healing your emotional body—only you can do it.

Bodies of all sizes and shapes are acceptable and beautiful in their individual unique way. What is that famous quotation? "Beauty is in the eye of the beholder."

MY LAST HALLOWEEN

I am thirteen

I HAVE TO TAKE ALL OF my younger sisters, 'trick or treating'. What a drag! Well, I guess I can get all dressed up like a 'beatnik' or something. Then maybe, it won't be all that boring.

Halloween is on a school night and mother will not let me go to my friend's house. I have to stay at home.

I love Halloween! I like to run around in the dark with my friends. I especially like it when it's cold and windy. When the weather is like that, Halloween is really haunting. It's fun to scare yourself by pretending a monster is after you.

This might be my last Halloween because I'm getting older. I'm getting too old to 'trick or treat' with my younger sisters. I wish I didn't have to take them around the neighborhood house to house, but I'll make the most of it. I'll dress up and get candy too.

I feel tall and awkward. I grew fast or something because all of a sudden I'm taller than everyone. I'll just stand in the back of the group. That way no one will notice me.

Everyone is ready and it's beginning to get dark. So off we go!

The wind is blowing and it's cold outside. It's a perfect Halloween! The wind is howling in the trees. The leaves on the trees are making rustling sounds. It's all so spooky and fun, I love it!

We go from house to house, up and down the streets. Our neighborhood has lots of hills which makes it even more fun and scary.

After being out for about an hour and a half walking up and down the hills, we're heading back to our house. It's getting late and everyone is getting tired.

We have three more houses to go before we're back at our house. The house that we're going to next is real pretty. It sits on the other corner opposite from ours and has a bridge to walk across to get to it. It's fun to walk over the bridge.

The lady who lives there appears nice. I've seen her driving her car in the neighborhood. She's pretty and friendly. It'll be fun going to her house. I think she has some sons around my age or maybe, older.

We run across the bridge and go up to the front door. We ring the door bell and yell, "Trick or Treat!" The lady comes to the door and looks us all over. She comments about all the little children's costumes and says how cute or scary they look. Then she looks up at me and turns up her nose. She makes a sarcastic comment about the fact that I'm too old to be 'trick or treating'.

She comments, "You're a bit tall aren't you? Don't you think you're too old to be 'trick or treating'? You're taking candy away from the cute little ones. It's horrible how you older children ruin the holiday for the children."

Hearing this coming out of her mouth is my worst fear. I feel so uncomfortable, I could die. I am tall for my age, five foot three and very thin. What this woman said to me and the way she said it, cut right through me. I felt embarrassed, awkward and wanted to crawl into a hole.

I told her that I was taking my little sisters out, but she shot me a dirty look. I felt like I had committed a crime by the way this woman looked at and spoke to me. Then she said, "If you are only taking your sisters out, why did you take the candy and why do you have a candy sack?"

I wanted out and away from her fast. I didn't respond to her and told everyone to hurry up that we are going home. I wouldn't let my sisters go to more houses after that experience.

When we got into our house, all my younger sisters got their pajamas on and then poured all their candy out on the floor in their bedrooms.

I went downstairs to my room and took a shower. I felt ugly and dirty after the way that lady had spoken to me. What she said and the way that she said it, hurt my feelings into my heart. I already felt awkward and weird about my appearance and all the changes of the new school and the new neighborhood. To hear those critical words come out of her mouth, when I was doing as my parents asked me to do, hurt me into the core of my being. I had seen her around the neighborhood and thought she was pretty and that she would be a nice person.

I got into my bed that Halloween night and cried. I thought something must be really bad wrong with me for a lady in our neighborhood to say those things to me.

This woman became a friend of my mother's and they played bridge together in a club. After that Halloween night, I have seen her and been around her all of my life. I do not really have an opinion whether she is 'nice' or not anymore, but I'll always remember her stinging words. The words she said to a thirteen-year-old child taking her sisters 'trick or treating'. I wondered what would make her say such comments to a child.

Years later, at a society luncheon event, I decided to share with her what I remembered about that Halloween and how it had affected me. She was shocked. She said she did not remember saying those things and she always thought all of us girls were darling. She even had hopes that her son and I would date because she thought me such a doll. So I had spent years agonizing over something this women had said when she didn't even recall saying it.

This incident makes me aware of how easy it is to affect a child or anyone by our 'innocent' comments. This woman meant no harm. She was just voicing her opinion, but she was voicing her opinion to a sensitive, insecure young girl. I took her words to heart because I was at a sensitive time in my life and was insecure in myself. If she had said that when I was feeling secure, I might have just thought her rude and blown it off.

What was the purpose of her cruel and berating remarks? Had she had a difficult day and was just taking her frustration out on a kid or was she a bitter woman who really didn't like children, unless they were little and adorable? Had she had some liquor that night while answering the door for 'trick or treaters', so her judgment was flawed? Who knows? It really does not matter.

All I know is that at the time, her remarks cut deeply into me. Are we ever truly aware of what we say and how we say it affects others? But on the flip side, sometimes harsh remarks can stimulate us to look at self and to change. Only in this instance, there was nothing

I could change. I was tall for my age and I was doing as my parents asked me to do and I got nailed for it by a neighbor.

Awareness is why did I let this affect me so deeply? Granted I was a child and did not realize at the time that this woman was being a grouch. I automatically took it into myself and to heart that something must be wrong with me. I had such low self-esteem at the time that I automatically took her critical remarks as if I was doing something 'wrong'. Actually, I was doing something I did not really want to be doing, to help my mother and my younger sisters.

The reality is when someone says ugly and hateful things they are usually talking about how they feel at the time. It is more a reflection of them and not you. If a person truly loves themselves, they usually don't say hurtful cruel things to others, especially to a young child. But also awareness is that sometimes, you can be overly sensitive and take something to heart that the person saying it doesn't even recall.

This lady was placing her opinion on me without knowing anything about what was really going on. How grumpy does a person need to be to verbally attack a child, 'trick or treating'?

When I look back on this event, it seems so insignificant, but I have remembered the way I felt at the time all of my life. This lady had no awareness of how much she affected the young girl she spoke to on that Halloween so long ago. She never realized it or even thought about it.

We are constantly, day by day, bringing up emotions and feelings in one another as we react and interact with each other.

So the awareness is that you never know how much you affect people by what you may say or do. Also why do we let what people say to us affect us so much, at certain times in our life? Why do we let their critical remarks injure our self-esteem? That is our issue to look at, not theirs.

When we are secure in ourselves, we will not feel the need to talk negatively to others. And when we are secure in ourselves, we will not take negative, critical things other people say into ourselves and allow them to affect us.

The goal is to respect ourselves and others.

I can forgive this woman. She had no awareness of how much she hurt me. It was my own insecurity which allowed this incident to affect me so deeply. Many times, you may not see things as they are; you see things as you are.

Be aware that everything you say and do affects you or those around you either for good or for ill. And sometimes what is meant for ill; can be changed to good.

> *"Everything I do and say with anyone makes a difference."*
> —Gita Bellin

THE SPIDER ATTACK

I am thirteen

I ENTER MY YOUNGER SISTERS' ROOM. As soon as I step in the door, I hear my younger sister Dana screeching. I hurry to where the screams are coming from into her bathroom.

Dana and my other two sisters are scared. They're pointing to a spider. Not just any spider—but the biggest, blackest, hairy, scariest spider that I've ever seen! I get a wad of Kleenex and bend over to squash it. They all shriek. "No! No! It will bite you! It will hurt you. Don't touch it! Please don't touch it!" I jump back. All their screaming has me convinced. The fear is contagious.

They have their little shoes out trying to smash it, but miss target every time. One of them sprays it with hair spray. The spider stops moving for a second but then continues on its journey. More screams and jumping up and down! My youngest sister sprays it with deodorant—it stops for a second and then continues on. Screaming and screeches again! One sister throws a shoe and hits it, crippling a couple of legs, but it keeps moving. She tries again to slap it with her shoe. Yay! Another hit with possible damage to another leg, but the spider continues moving.

We get body cream and squirt the spider. Now, it's covered in white cream so heavy that I think this must be it. It will slow down, so we can kill it. We watch in anticipation waiting to make our next move. Then it starts running fast—faster than before. We jump! We scream! We jump up on the bathroom counters in fear that the wild spider, covered in cream will run onto our feet. It's as if this spider can't be stopped.

Our attack escalates. We are now in war mode against the spider. We throw bath power on it. We coat it down so heavily that the shape of the spider can't be made out. No movement—I think, finally, it's stuck. I start to go over with shoe in hand to smash it. But, No! There it goes! This wild spider completely coated in white is running around the bathroom. We jump and scream!

By now, we're laughing and giggling in hysteria. This is beginning to be fun, besides there are four of us and only one spider. No matter how big and scary this thing is, we begin to feel our power in numbers. The ordeal is scary and fun at the same time.

Then my father's voice, "Girls what in the world is going on in there?" We yell, "Daddy, there's a spider in here and we can't kill it! We're scared because it will not die! No matter, what we do, we can't kill it!"

Daddy walks in, looks at the spider and all of us. He laughs. "What have you all done to this poor old spider?" We tell him of all the torture and warring methods that we've used on this spider along with the fact, that no matter what we do, it keeps on moving. He laughs as he bends over, picks it up, and in one swoop drops it into the toilet and flushes it away.

We all run over to see the spider covered in cream and powder twirl down the toilet. "Let me see! Let me see!" Truth is, we're a little sorry to see it go!

As easy as that! The spider attack is over! Daddy, our hero saves us from the big scary spider.

At times, something might seem scary only because you make it so, when actually it's all in your mind and easy to solve.

MAKING A PATH

I am twelve or thirteen

I LOVE TO LOOK DOWN AT my backyard. It's full of trees and they are beautiful! It's fall and the colors of the leaves are incredible.

I'm standing at the windows and looking out to the back of my backyard. I'm high up and looking down. I notice many large, flat rocks over to the side of the yard where it begins to slope downward. The rocks are scattered throughout the area. Interesting, I never noticed them before.

I run out the front door then around to the side and down then to the back where the rocks are located. These rocks will make a really great path through the trees. It's always been a bit difficult to walk down between the trees. A path of flat rocks will help a lot.

I try to lift one rock and it's very heavy. I hope I'm strong enough to move them. I bet I am. Sure I am strong enough! I move one rock up to where I think the path should begin. I am perspiring. This is hard work but I am determined to do it.

After I line up the flat rocks through the trees, I'll have a path to walk on and it'll be easier to get to the backyard without sliding down. Plus, the path will look pretty meandering through the trees. I'll be able to look out the windows and see my path from above.

I keep working, dragging and pulling the rocks to form the path through the trees. The path takes twists and turns through the trees and down the slope of yard. It's difficult work. The rocks are big and heavy and I am becoming tired. My back is hurting but I keep on working. I am a ballet dancer. I am strong! I'm not going to let these rocks get the best of me. Besides, I have my plan. My plan is to make a path with these big flat rocks through the trees.

I step back and review my work as it progresses and to scope out where it's best to place the next rock. I go back to the beginning of the path and walk it, to test the distance from rock to rock, step to step, to make sure it flows easily. After my testing and evaluations, it not only works but looks great! The path of the rocks going through the trees and down the hill looks like a picture! I like it!

I keep working to complete the path and to use up all the rocks. It takes me the whole afternoon. Finally, it is completed. I am both exhausted and exhilarated at the same time.

I go back to the beginning and walk my completed path. I go from rock to rock. It works perfectly. The rocks are placed just right. I feel good! I am proud of my work! It feels great walking the path that I designed on my own. It was a lot of hard work but it was worth it! I can't wait to show my dad. He will be proud of my path, proud of my idea and all my hard work. I go inside. Daddy is not home. The next week, I have school, ballet classes, homework and friends. I forget to tell my dad about the path, I made in the backyard.

Then one day, I'm standing at the large picture window looking over the backyard to see my dad throwing all the rocks off my path.

He'd begun at the bottom of the path throwing all the rocks to the side. He was at the top now, the beginning and getting ready to throw the last ones off the path. Pretty soon there will be no path at all! I would not even be able to remember where it had started, where it had been or where it finished. I run out the front door and around to where my dad is. But, I'm too late. It's done! The path I worked so hard to create is all scattered.

Before I can open my mouth my dad looks up and gruffly asks, "Do you know who lined these rocks up?" I proudly respond, "I did! I made the path. Didn't you think it was pretty? I wanted to show it to you. I worked really hard to put the rocks in a path through the trees!"

Dad says, "I can see that you worked hard. These rocks are heavy but having them in a path will mess up the drainage. So leave them alone! Leave them like they are."

"Can I make a path somewhere else in the yard?" "No!" He answers, "Leave these rocks alone. Do you understand me?" I reply, "Okay." When he sees the disappointment on my face, he says. "Well maybe, a path can work if it's on the other side of the yard. I'll think about it."

I understood that there was a reason to tear my path and all my hard work apart. I pondered that I might make one on the other side of the yard. But it was too far and too much work to drag those heavy rocks clear to the other side of the yard. I tried one day. I tried to find another place where I could put my path. I tried to find a place where my path could stay put and please my father, but the other side of the yard didn't need a path. It wasn't the same. The other side of the yard didn't slope as much and I wouldn't be able to see the path looking down from the windows above. So there was no reason for it.

I knew where the path in the backyard needed to be because I was the one who played there. It needed to be exactly where I put it. It looked pretty and it worked there. It seemed like the best place to me but not to my father. I wasn't able to find the place for a path that would please both my father and me. I'd stand at the big picture windows overlooking the backyard and see the rocks scattered all over and think. They would look much better if they were arranged on a path.

My father and I saw the backyard from two very different perspectives. My father is an engineer. He was viewing the backyard from the perspective of an engineer which was to make sure that it was laid out to function efficiently.

I was a child with a creative side—an artist. I saw the backyard as a place to play and wanted it designed for comfort to do this. My creative artist side wanted the backyard to look pretty from the windows above.

A path I can create, stay on and please my father may never occur. Sometimes the most difficult thing to do in life is to find your individual path. Actually even when you feel that you aren't on your path, you may still be on it. The looking, creating, tearing it apart, finding a new path then rearranging it again, may very well be the most important part of the path. An important part that once experienced hones and enhances your skills and direction, to further assist you. To that time you know for certain that you have found the right path.

Once you are sure you are on your path, you can find your passion. You become excited and focused. Life has real meaning and you have an understanding of why you are here on earth.

The more centered you are in your being and soul, the easier it is to be connected to your higher self—that guides you about how to locate your true path. Then when your path turns or twists and even takes a totally new direction, you have an inner knowing that you'll eventually arrive at your destination.

"Wisdom comes to those who are calm and tranquil in spirit."

WEARING THE 'RIGHT' SHOES

I am thirteen

THAT GIRL IS SO PRETTY! She has so many friends. She's so popular. I wish I could be like her. I wish that I was her. I don't understand why she's so popular and I'm not? I wear neat clothes and I'm pretty, well, sort of. She's older than me. Maybe next year, I'll know what to say and how to act so that I will be popular, too.

In the school where I moved from, I was popular like this girl, but I don't know anybody in this school. It seems as if everyone already has their friends. It doesn't seem as if anyone wants to get to know me. It feels like there isn't a place for me in this school. Everyone has their group of friends and there's just no room for me. I feel all weird and gawky, as if something must be wrong with me. It certainly was easier when I was in elementary school and popular.

I watch this particular girl and her group of friends. When I pass them in the hallway between classes, I turn and look to see what they're wearing and how they're standing. I even try to overhear what they're talking about. They always seem to be laughing and the cutest older boys hang around them.

I try real hard to look good and be 'cool'. I spend hours blowing my hair dry, so that it will be straight and not frizzy. Unless it rains, I look pretty good. Except my face gets broken out with pimples at times, my skin used to be pretty with no pimples. Now some of the time when I look in the mirror, I don't recognize myself. I just hate myself when this happens. Pimples make me feel like I'm the ugliest girl in the world.

I spend hours reading all the 'teen' magazines. I'm looking for how to act and be a teenager in this world. I think these magazines must have the answers. I hope they do anyway. The girls in the magazines don't have frizzy hair and they don't have pimples.

I read in 'Seventeen' magazine that if you want to have a lot of friends, you need to smile a lot. You need to say 'Hi' to everyone. Perhaps, I will try doing this.

So for the next few days at school, I smile at everyone and say, Hi! It seems to be working kids are saying Hi, back and smiling at me. Plus, with all this smiling, I feel happy inside. Okay, I have found the magic trick, just smile and say Hi! I keep doing this very enthusiastically. It appears to be working. Then a group of guys pass by me and ask, "What are you so happy about all the time? What's your problem? Is your face stuck in a smile?" Then they laugh at me.

I feel devastated. I'm so embarrassed. I wipe the smile off my face and feel too intimidated to say Hi, anymore. This incident crushed my already fragile self-esteem into nothing.

I look around at the kids in this school. Upon further observation and examination, I discover many of the 'popular' kids don't smile much. They look all angry and sullen. So I decide to try on this look and attitude for a while. But trying to look angry and sullen only intensified my unhappiness. Unfortunately this hung on for quite a bit.

One day, I'm in the girl's locker room before my gym class. I'm getting ready to put on the ugliest green gym suit that there could ever be. When I notice that the really pretty, popular girl and her friends are still in the locker room. Their class is before mine and they are still over by the mirrors, doing their hair, talking and laughing. I walk over and stand beside them, look in a mirror and begin combing my hair.

I recall what 'Seventeen' magazine had said about being friendly, to be popular. I think this is my chance. I'm going to give it a try.

Besides, I have on a new, cool outfit and new, really cool shoes—the ones that the neat older kids are wearing.

I'm combing my hair. Then I take a chance and say, "Hi, are you just getting out of class? Don't you think these green gym suits are plain gross?"

The girls look over at me, shocked that I have said anything to them. They look me up and down focusing in on my shoes then ask, "Who are you? What are you? You have cool shoes on, but who are you? Who said that you could wear cool shoes? We don't know you? Who do you think you are? We think you are gross!"

The girl that I thought was the prettiest the one that I admired so much was the cruelest.

I respond, "I'm trying to be friendly with you. Why are you being so cruel?" They reply, "Why would we want to be friendly with you? You're only an eighth grader. Eight graders are dorks!" They begin laughing and continue to laugh, as I turn and walk away.

I walk back between the lockers. I locate my locker and sit on the bench in front on it. I slowly begin to get my gym stuff out of the locker. I'm aching inside. I'm embarrassed and my heart is pounding inside my chest. It feels as if my heart is breaking. I feel so alone. I'm trying so hard to make friends, but I guess I don't know the rules or something. I almost start to cry but luckily, I don't.

I just become more into myself. I feel more and more that something must be wrong with me.

I knew those girls were being rude. I knew that I would be just as old as they are someday, but knowing this, didn't much matter right now.

This incident hurt me deeply inside. I spent days, weeks and months depressed over how much it hurt to reach out then to be harshly rejected, while trying so hard to be accepted and to make friends.

After this experience, when I passed that girl in the hall, she didn't look pretty any longer.

As an adult, it is easy to look back and see the dynamics of this situation. Really, even as a thirteen-year-old, I saw them, but it still hurt intensely. That, particular group of girls were trying so hard to be 'cool' and accepted that they did not have any concern for anyone else. I am sure that I have done the very same thing to someone both with and without any intention.

At the time, I was trying so hard to be accepted that I lost myself. I temporally believed that wearing the 'right' shoes would make someone like me. I wore my insecurity as an invitation to hurt me. I was rejecting myself before anyone could get to know me. I was so needy that the other kids could feel my insecurity. Especially since, they were feeling insecure too. They used this opportunity to relieve themselves of some of their own insecurity by insulting and hurting me. This temporarily made them feel secure, safe and what they thought was 'cool'.

All I needed to do was to 'like' myself.

Children do this to other children and as adults we continue to use this method of trying to make ourselves feel important. We try to take the power away from others and believe that this will make us feel powerful. It won't for long, actually doesn't and never will.

This incident and others similar to it that I have experienced in my life while growing up and just living in this world have made me very aware of other's feelings. Of course, when I feel bad or negative, about myself, I may revert back to this type of behavior. But the more I am aware of it, the less I will have the need to do it. This behavior damages self and others. When I feel good and positive about myself, I am able to be aware of other's feelings and take responsibility for the way I interact with them.

Every interaction we have with other's can either affect them and us—positively or negatively. As we treat others, so we treat ourselves.

Others can reject us only when we reject ourselves.

Become aware of this. Gather your power from your higher self— the God source. There is no limit to the power that comes from the God. Let us all be kind to one another.

SHE SITS ON ME UNTIL I CAN'T BREATHE

I am thirteen

MY YOUNGER SISTER TAMMY IS tall, much bigger than me. She's mean, too! I know, how really cruel she is. She fools a lot of people including our parents because she pretends that she's sweet.

She enjoys starting fights because she knows that she can win because she's bigger than any of us. She says really cruel things to me when no one else is around. She's careful that way, to wait to say ugly things and to behave cruelly only when no one is around. She calls me ugly and if I have a pimple, she laughs and says that my face looks like a bumpy road.

She really hurts my feelings. I don't let her know it because I know that the reason she's cruel is to watch my reaction to the things she says and does.

When she says cruel things, I yell back at her. She chases me. She runs very fast, but I can run faster down the stairs to my room. I close the door and lock it before she can get me. Most of the time, I beat her to the door and this makes her really mad!

When she gets mad, she'll get quiet while she plans her revenge.

If she catches me, she throws me down on the floor and sits on me until I can't breathe. One time, when she was sitting on my chest I really thought I was going to die. I don't think she would have cared. She would have figured out a way to prove to our parents that it was my fault. That's her greatest talent, doing horrible things and getting away with them by passing the guilt onto some unsuspecting person. She does this constantly and seems to always get away with it.

Other kids see what she does and when one of her friends catches on to her plotting, she dumps them and accuses them of doing what she did. It amazes me how she gets away doing this so much of the time.

She has my parents completely fooled. She can cry on cue. When she realizes she may get into trouble, she can really turn on the tears. She manipulates by crying. I've seen her crying her eyes out and then in an instant turn around and smirk with a nasty smile. She scares me! I try to steer clear of her. She's not my friend. She's actually no one's friend. She uses people to manipulate for her gain.

If I try to do something mean in return, it always back-fires on me. She can turn it around so it looks as if I'm to blame, no matter what I do. She's a master at this kind of manipulation.

One day I'm standing on the upper landing of our entry hall watching her. She had just come in from outside and her feet were all muddy. She tracked through my other sisters' room to get to the bathroom and into her room and left muddy foot prints all over their carpet.

Mother walks in and sees the muddy tracks and starts scolding my other sisters. Tammy comes out of her room and tries to look so innocent. She's smirking behind mother's back. Because I am standing up higher, I have a view of it all. She's just standing there and letting our two younger sisters take the blame. Mother is getting very angry at them because she had said for no one to go outside in the wet snow.

Dana is crying and saying that she didn't go outside. Mother is stating, "Well if you didn't go outside then why are there mud prints all over the freshly vacuumed carpet in your room?" Mother is really angry.

As I'm watching this scene from the living room above, it shocks me to realize that Tammy is not only going to let her younger sisters take the blame but she is smirking in pleasure for doing so. It makes me feel sick to my stomach. Finally, after observing for a while and after I realize Tammy isn't going to admit to doing it.

I state, "Mother, Tammy is the one who tracked through the room." Tammy glares at me. She can give the scariest looks like she could kill you.

Mother asks, "What? Why would she go through their room to get to hers?" I respond, "Look at her boots." Mother goes into Tammy's room where she has hidden the boots. Sure enough there they are—the muddy boots.

Tammy is starting her 'crying game'. She's whining to mother, "I didn't mean to do it! I didn't know my shoes were muddy." The little liar, I had watched her look at her feet before she decided to go through their room.

I don't think my mother ever truly can or will comprehend the plotting that Tammy does. She accepts what the little liar says, and then says to all of us. "Do not go outside anymore today, none of you!" Then she made all of us clean up the mess that Tammy made. So that's how she does it, the little monster gets off again.

Tammy knows that I know what she's up to and she doesn't like me for knowing this. I see through her and this makes her angry. She tries to make me look bad in my parents' eyes. So that she'll look better.

I avoid her at all costs. She's not a person to trust. She only cares about herself while she pretends to care about others. She's always buttering-up mother and for some reason mother buys it.

Tammy plays tricks and games with people's lives. She may get away with her tricks and lying on earth. But God sees and knows everything.

When I think back to that day of her tracking in my younger sisters' room and letting them take the blame, I remember the look on Dana's face while being falsely accused. It was pitiful how hurt she appeared. Tammy looked on smirking. It was clear she didn't care and showed no remorse and certainly no empathy—only anger that she had been caught.

Tammy grew tall quickly. I could tell that she felt uncomfortable being tall because she would slump over. I am petite. I believe that caused some of her hate towards me. In my opinion, I believe she adapted this behavior of hers because it makes her feel safe and it is an attempt to get the love and attention that she so badly needs to help her feel okay. In my opinion, she will do whatever she feels that she has to, to get love and attention from our parents.

She grew to become an attractive tall lady. I believe that she is still uncomfortable with her appearance and she still has the same personality trait of trying to make something look one way when it is really another. She can always make sure that she comes out looking good no matter what she has done. She is compelled to be the center of attention.

As an adult I still avoid this sister and always will—she still seems to get away with her hurtful games and manipulation. My awareness is that she must not feel lovable to behave so harmfully to others. She must not love herself or she could not lie and play games with people's lives. She must do these things to get attention, to prove she can get away with doing things and to feel powerful and in control. She hurts others but is really hurting herself much more. I forgive her because I can see and understand her pain, but I will never trust her and will always avoid her. Actually my opinion and perception after observing her for years and being the beneficiary of her harmful actions, she possibly is a covert narcissist and has sociopathic traits.

A covert narcissist is deeply fragile and insecure. They may appear shy but they manipulate others sadistically to cause pain and make themselves feel better by doing so. They are like a shy lion sneaking up on their prey, rather than the lion that roars before attacking. Sociopaths try to figure out others, so as how to manipulate them. Perhaps, their time would be better spent to try and figure out themselves and their distorted perception—that others are to be used for their personal manipulation, gratification and gain.

SOLITAIRE

I am thirteen

I NEED TO TALK TO MY mother. I need to ask her about everything. She must have some answers for me. I'm so confused and weird feeling. I feel alone at school. I don't fit in. Mother must have the answers because she was young and grew up once. She must know secrets that she can share and will help me. I hope that she'll tell me.

My mother hardly ever talks to me except to be angry. "Come to Dinner! Wait until your father gets home, he'll take care of you! Don't eat before dinner or you'll spoil your appetite!" This is the only stuff she ever says.

We moved to a new house and I'm in a new school. I love the house and my new room. But the school is so different. In my old school, I was really popular. In this new school, I don't know anyone and everyone already has friends. Plus I feel real ugly as if something is wrong with me. I want friends but don't know how to make them or maybe no one likes me because I'm weird or something.

The teachers are boring. Nothing is like the other school. I wish I was back there. I'm not going to make it in this new school. So I'm asking my mother, what should I do? She must have some answers.

My mother sits on her bed playing the card game, 'Solitaire', over and over and over and over! I go in and start to sit on the bed. She says, "Careful sitting down because the cards will move."

I'm very careful as I sit on the bed and begin talking to her. She doesn't even look up or answer me. I feel like she wants me to go away, but I'm not going away. I'm going to keep talking to her until I get some answers. Only, she will not talk. She will not give me answers. She just keeps on playing the stupid card game repeatedly.

I want to wipe all those cards away. Maybe she thinks something is weird about me, too. Maybe that's why she won't talk to me. Maybe there is something really, really wrong about me.

MOTHER, TALK TO ME! I shout. HELP ME! She just says, "It will get better at school the longer you are there. Now leave me alone!"

I hate her. I can't stand it anymore! My own mother doesn't like me enough to even talk to me. I go down to my room and decide I'm never going to talk to her again.

Through the years, I always did try to talk with her, share my life and ask for answers. I did all the talking and got few responses. She mostly talked about the weather.

Many years later, I figured it out. My mother does not have my answers. She never did and never will. She feels alone and like she doesn't fit in. That is why she did not answer me. She could not offer any suggestions or ideas. She does not feel like she fits into social groups and friends. She feels the need to escape through her card games.

When I asked her my questions, her silence made me feel that she had some answers. I felt even believed that she was withholding them from me because she did not like me. When the real reason was, she did not have any answers. I thought she did because she was an adult. I still believed at the age of thirteen that adults had all the answers because they were grown-up. I thought mothers had all the answers, but they don't.

My mother tends to be a loner. She appears to be content playing cards once a month with her friends, going to the hairdresser and going out to dinner with my father. This is the extent of her interaction with people. She does not seem to want to be bothered by anyone or anything and that includes me. I don't recall ever seeing my mother mop a floor, clean a bathroom or change the sheets on a bed. All she did was go to the grocery store and cook, and she complained about even doing that. She never talked about when she was a child or stories about her escapades in college. It's as if caring and communication require too much energy for her to expend.

As an adult, I needed to have sudden, minor surgery. The doctor said for me to call my mother and ask her to be with me. I just needed to have someone with me during the procedure and to drive me home. I guess the doctor was used to other women having their mother's with them at these times. It was sudden and short notice. It was an emergency! I called my mother and asked if she would mind going with me to the doctor's office, the next morning because I was going to have a minor surgery and needed her. She said that she was sorry, but she had her hair appointment at that time and could not go with me. Hearing this hurt me very badly, but I never let her know it. Besides I do not believe it would have mattered to her.

People and communication and interaction are too much trouble for her. She does not like to have her routine changed. A change in her plans creates stress and overwhelms her. It was an irritation to her that I even made this request of her. I do not believe nor did I receive any evidence that she ever thought about what I was going through or even thought about me at all. My stress about having surgery didn't seem to enter her mind.

One weekend my father was out of town. When my father is away, my mother will invite one or more of her children to go out to dinner with her. She does this to keep her company and to occupy her time. I had just gone through a divorce. Therefore, I spent most of the weekend with her. It felt good to be with her. I needed to have some attention and nurturing. We went to dinner both Friday and Saturday evenings.

One evening after dinner, we were sitting by the swimming pool talking. As usual, I was doing most of the talking, but what was unusual my mother appeared to really be listening. This gave me much pleasure. I went on and on about the alcoholic marriage that I had just escaped from and my plans for creating the life that I truly desired.

I felt such relief to be with my mother and had the feeling that a true understanding and connection had been felt by both of us on that evening. I needed this release and the comfort of my mother. This was the first time I had ever remembered her being with me in this way.

It was good to have my father gone because he can be so dominating and controlling that he runs everything, and at times does not care about the feelings or desires of anyone else. I can never share my true feelings with him. I am not myself around him. He is critical of me even when I am in pain.

After my father got home the following week, he told me that my mother was very upset by all the 'bullshit' that I had laid on her. He said, "Keep your problems to yourself. We are tired of your problems. We do not have any problems, but you. We do not want to hear about your troubles. Do not upset your mother again!" I stated that I thought she enjoyed being with me. He responded, "She had a horrible weekend. Do not bother your mother with your problems! No one wants to hear them! Do not upset your mother!"

I asked my mother about what my father had said to me. She did not answer me.

My mother shares everything with my father. There can be no 'girl talk' because she will tell him. Then he will 'butt in' and be angry or something. There are no boundaries set in my family.

I was told and experienced repeatedly that my emotions and feelings do not matter. I learned to put everyone else's feelings and emotions before mine. I took in from my parents that I was not as important as they are and I kept repeating this in my relationships in my life.

I brought men into my life that after the 'courtship' was over; put me last just as my parents had done. My feelings and desires did not matter to them. I kept recreating exactly what I did not want in my life and I did not understand why. I pulled unhealthy people to me as if I had radar attracting them, which I understand now that this is accurate. I did have a kind of radar. I allowed them to treat me like a second class citizen because that is what I was used to being treated as. I did whatever I could to please them so they would show me love. I thought that if I could get them to love me then my parents would love me, too.

The men I married were not capable of love, true communication or intimacy. They had so many of their own problems, issues or addictions that there was never time or caring for me, just like my parents, especially my mother. My husband's did not have the time or energy to listen to or help me. It was all about them. They were too busy with their own problems and they accused me of being the problem. I brought to me people who did not know themselves. They were just like my parents are to me. I married my parents repeatedly.

The men I married drank, gambled, and had affairs, lied and more. They did whatever they could to escape and cover up their pain. There was nothing left over for a relationship to communicate, grow, heal and be emotionally healthy. Everything totally revolved around their pain. There was nothing left for me. They were just like my parents. Therefore, I was proving to myself over and over that my parents were correct. I was not lovable and I was not as important as they were. I was the problem, so they never had to look at themselves.

My whole existence was like a big façade—a pretense of a family. I never learned to relate openly and share myself. What I learned was to deny my feelings, emotions and to put others' first.

I have since learned and experienced through friendships and life that there are people with the ability to care. They care about my problems, emotions and feelings and will listen and nurture me. Of course, I respond the same with them because that is what I became really expert at doing.

I learned not to turn to my family to receive what they do not have to give. My parents cannot hear my problems and pain because they cannot honestly look at themselves. They only desire to be around what they call fun, drinking—lots of drinking, eating out, TV and so on. They desire distraction and escape. Any problems of mine are too real.

Of course, having fun is great. But the happiest and most fun you can have is to know who you are and to release negative emotions and feelings that keep you stuck or blocked. Then you will be able to have honest relationships with yourself and others. You will be able to offer sincere caring to others without feeling that it is taking from you.

Then other things you experience in life will genuinely be for the fun and not the escape. Escaping from feelings and emotions only buries them further down. They will resurface by either exploding onto others or imploding into self, causing more damage to body, mind and spirit. Burying feelings creates the need to escape.

Later in life I realized, I am not the loner that I had become by observing my mother's life. Friends and interaction with people are the most rewarding gifts there are on this earth.

Friends and relationships with all people on this earth from the grocery clerk, you see once a week, to your children and lover are all reflections of yourself.

Only in relationship can you know yourself—not in isolation. The movement of behavior in all relationships is a guide to reveal and understand more about self. It is a reflection of both your subconscious and conscious. This refection reveals its content in the emotions and feelings that are shown to you. Poverty lies in running away from relationships. True wealth is having friends and relationships with many. By having many and a variety of friends and relationships, you learn how to genuinely relate on an intimate level with others and most importantly with yourself.

The definition of friend is—a person to whom one is attached by affection. The definition of friendship is—intimacy and mutual attachment. The definition of relationship is—the condition of being related.

You will attract to you the friends and relationships that mirror who you are or who you think that you are. You are able to be friends with others, when you are first your own best friend. When you truly love yourself, you will attract that reflection. I am a whole worthy individual and my feelings and emotions are equal in value to all others. We are all in relationship with one another in some form or another as we live in this world.

My big awareness is that my answers are in me and the most important relationship is the one I have with myself. Interesting that I found the answers in my solitude and I found them mostly on my own. My awareness and understanding are that my mother does not know or have my answers. In my solitude I discovered people, friends and relationships are important to me.

I only need reach out to people in the true essence of who I am and I will have all the friends that I desire. My mother's answers are not my answers. She is so full of issues that she has no time for anyone else. The most important relationship and friendship that an individual has is the one they have with their self. This is the basis for all the other friendships and relationships in their life. All the others are simply mirrors.

In my solitude, I found my answers and I forgave my mother. Forgiving my mother releases me to be free. Forgiving myself allows me to accept my mother for who she is, also for whom she is not and will never be.

I HIT MY MOTHER WITH A COOKING SPATULA

I am thirteen

I'M STANDING IN THE KITCHEN watching my mother make dinner. My mother hates to cook and she states this often. I don't know what my mother does enjoy doing. It seems to me as if she doesn't like to do anything. She always seems to me as if she's in a bad mood. I like to stay away from her and be gone at my friends' houses as much as possible.

I'm talking to her about my day at school. She's just listening. My mother doesn't talk much to me. I think, she thinks that what I do is boring or she must not like me or something. I want her to talk to me, to share herself with me. I want her to be my friend. She usually just talks about the weather or whatever she's making for dinner—how much she hates cooking—or where she and daddy are going out to dinner. That's something she likes to do—she likes to go out to dinner. She also likes to drink and to smoke.

I tell her that smoking is really bad for her. I saw a film at school. It showed lungs in a person after they had been smoking for many years. Their lungs were all black. I tell my mother about this because I don't want her to have black lungs and get sick.

She responds, "I don't care! Smoking is one of the few things I like to do and I am going to continue to do it. So shut up about it!"

She doesn't seem to understand. I ask her not to smoke because I love her and I don't want her to get sick and have black lungs like the person in the film. Besides the smoke stinks and it makes me cough when I breathe it. I hate the smell of cigarettes!

My mother asks my daddy about everything. She will not make a decision on her own. It drives me crazy because I always have to wait until my daddy gets home, before I know if I can do something or not. My daddy works all the time. So sometimes, I have to wait a long time to find out the answers.

I wonder if my father ever gets tired of mother asking him everything all the time. Does he want her to do this or does he want her to make decisions on her own? I did hear him get angry at her and say, "Can't you ever make any decisions on your own?"

Today, I'm asking her if I can spend the night with my friend Linda. As usual, she's says, "Maybe, wait until your father gets home." I respond, "I need to tell her now, because if I can't spend the night then Linda wants to ask someone else to stay with her." Mother says, "Well, I guess she doesn't want you to spend the night very bad, now does she?"

There she goes again trying to make me feel unwelcome. It seems to me that my mother likes to hurt my feelings because she'll say things like this all the time, implying that if Linda really liked me, she would wait for the answer and would not invite anyone else over but me.

Sometimes, I hate my mother!

I ask, "Why don't you ever just say, yes? You always say maybe or no. You never just say yes, you can do something! You always have to ask daddy and then he says, I don't care, what do you think? Then, you say, well it's all right with me if it's all right with you? Then he says, I guess it's all right. Then you say, your father and I think that it's all right. You can do it."

Daddy doesn't care if I spend the night away or not. So why can't you give me an answer? She asks, "How do you know what your father will say." I respond, "Because on Fridays you and he always watch TV. He won't notice if I'm here or not. Please give me an answer. YOU give me answer. I want to spend the night with Linda! Please, say YES! You know daddy will not care. Why do you always put me through this? Can't you ever just say yes, without asking daddy?"

I'm getting more and more upset with her. She does this to me each and every time that I want to do something.

I watch other girls' mothers. They give their daughters' answers without having to ask their fathers all the time. And I tell her this. She says, "I'm not other girls' mother. I'm your mother."

"I wish that you weren't my mother! I wish I had a mother that could answer with the word, yes and who talked to me. You don't care about me. I hate you!"

Then she says, "Okay, the answer is, no!" I ask, "Do you mean that?" She says, "Take this answer or wait until your father gets home!" I get so frustrated with her that I pick up a cooking spatula and hit her on the arm.

It shocks me that I did this. I'm shocked that I hit her and scared of what my father will do when he finds out what I have done. My mother immediately starts crying and yells. "Wait until I tell your father!"

"I didn't hit you hard! I didn't mean to do it!"

I run downstairs to my room in fear and disbelief about what I did and knowing that my father is going to kill me when he gets home.

I call my friend Linda and tell her that I can't spend the night with her. I tell her that my mother will not give me an answer.

My father comes home real late that night—so nothing is said. I don't even see him.

The next day after ballet, my father is there to pick me up instead of my mother. I get into the car and am real quiet.

Daddy starts talking. "Your mother told me about what happened yesterday." I look at him. He doesn't sound or appear angry. He sounds sad and serious. He asks, "How have you been doing?"

"Okay." I respond.

He says, "I'm going to tell you something because I think that now, you're old enough to know."

I'm scared and worried because of the seriousness of his voice and how softly he is speaking.

He continues. "When you were a one-year-old, your mother had a nervous breakdown. She got real sick and we had to take special care of her. So you'll need to be extra nice to her."

"I didn't mean to hit her, daddy. I just got really upset because she doesn't talk to me or make decisions without you and you're never home. You're always working."

He says, "I know. I understand. Will you promise me that you'll be extra nice to your mother and be careful of her?"

"I will. What happened to mother? Why did she get sick?"

He answers that he does not know why or how, just that he came home from work one day and she was sick. "You were only one-year-old and I took you to live with NaNa."

I ask. "How did mother get well or is she still sick?"

Very seriously, he answers, "A doctor cut into her brain, so she would be better, but she gets upset easily. So you need to be careful of her and be good."

My thoughts are racing. 'They cut into her brain?' I don't know what to ask or to say. Hearing this makes me feel really awful that I hit her. I knew that hitting my mother was a horrible thing to do no matter what. Now to find out that she's sick in her brain makes me feel even worse and more guilt ridden. I would never hit her again or anyone else for that matter.

Daddy strongly states, "Make sure you be extra nice to your mother. Try to help her with your younger sisters. Your mother is fragile and gets overwhelmed. You're the oldest. You can be a big help to her."

Nothing more is said.

Therefore for the rest of my life, I denied myself and was denied my own feelings by my father to protect my mother. Instead of having my needs met, I was given responsibility for others' needs, too much for me to handle, too much for any child to understand or to deal with.

I felt guilty for my normal feelings of frustration. I denied my emotions, my needs, my desires, in order to be extra nice to my mother.

My father denied my emotional wellbeing, by asking that I deny my emotions and be more grown-up than I was truly capable of at the age of thirteen. He put the facade of the family before anything else. He put the protection of my mother before anything else. He put the protection of his dream before anyone else—his dream of being a successful man with a perfect wife and family.

The emotional environment that I grew up in was to pretend that things were okay when they were not. I took what my father said one step further. I tried to be a 'mother' to my younger sisters. When I visited at friend's houses, I observed the way their mother's treated them. I could see that my mother did not treat me or my sisters like the mother's I observed.

To help me feel better and to be a good daughter like my father had requested. I tried with all my heart to figure out what to do. I wanted to help myself, my sisters and my father and try to create a family like I saw my friends' had. I tried to figure out what to do to get some love. I wanted to make my mother and father love me more than anything else in the world.

I looked at my younger sisters and decided that I would try to do for them what my mother did not do for me. I took them shopping for clothes, showed them what to do when their period came and many other types of things that I saw my friend's mothers do.

My mother did not seem to care or notice. She wanted to do as little as possible. She gets exhausted just going to the grocery store and picking us up from school.

At sixteen I got a Mustang for Christmas and took over many of the chauffeuring duties. In one aspect, I loved this because I got to drive a car, but I became much too responsible for too many things. I felt guilt. I wanted things to be different. I tried to create in the best way I knew how the kind of environment and family interaction I thought was normal. I did the best that could do as a teenager.

Of course, it was a distortion. Children cannot successfully fulfill the mother role in the family. It created stress in me and denied me what I needed which was to be nurtured myself. It created resentment in my younger sisters, especially the sister directly under me.

One time during some disagreement concerning one of my sisters, I yelled at my father and said that I was tired of being their mother. He yelled back that I must not have done a good job because of the mess this sister was currently involved in. I remember I froze up inside. I was being criticized for doing a job that I was too young to do and should not have been doing in the first place. This awareness made me feel sick into my core. I felt incredible anger and resentment at my mother and father.

I desperately wanted a mother to give me attention, to nurture me, to make me feel loved, worthwhile and to teach me how to be a woman. I observed in my mother everything that I did not want to be.

I did seek and find this attention from a variety of other women in my life. My friend's mothers fulfilled this role, so did my ballet teacher and a few acquaintances of my mother. I role modeled as best I could other women that came into my life. I also read a lot and learned about women through books and magazines.

The more I read, the more I learned and I saw that my mother did not do or say the usual things that most women did. She seemed to have no interests of her own. Nothing excited her. She complained about the simple everyday things in life.

My mother showed no joy in her spirit. Therefore mine was temporarily put to rest, especially when around her. She seemed to be suspicious and envious, if I was happy and full of joy.

My mother said that she wanted me to be happy, but if I was happy she seemed to always say or do something to upset me. I do not think she really liked it when I was happy because she was always so unhappy. I learned to act unhappy around my mother to match her lack of joy in being alive. I thought by doing so, I wouldn't upset her or make her angry at me.

I had the awareness that my mother was envious of my spirit, my joy and my strength. My mother does not, did not like me. She feels little closeness or bond to me.

I do not know what a better choice might have been? I am sure my over responsibility, simultaneously helped in many ways and hurt in others. As the years went by, it alienated me from my sisters and it caused resentment in me towards them. I became tired of worrying about them and sick of having them around. I became sick of the guilt and responsibility laid on me at such a young age. I became tired and disgusted with my mother and her complaining.

I literally did become physically ill much of the time. I felt worn out and overwhelmed by the responsibility I felt for everything and everyone. When I was young, I felt old.

I do understand that my father was handling a difficult situation, the best he knew how given the tools and awareness that he had at the time and based on his own background. We all tried to fit in and to cope the best way we knew to do.

My father's emphasis has always been on making money. I believe he thought that if he made enough money that everything would be alright. Money cannot fix everything. It cannot cure pain in the heart and emotional neglect. Money and material things are great but they cannot fill that gap.

My mother did not and does not communicate with me. I do not feel emotions from her. She feels blank when it comes to me.

My awareness is that since, my mother became ill when I was one and went to live a year with my grandmother, my mother and I did not develop a bonded 'mother and daughter' connection. It was broken by her breakdown and the prefrontal lobotomy that followed. My mother is more connected to my younger sisters, although she does not show much affection to anyone. My sister Tammy manipulated her.

My father was always trying to pretend that the connection was there and that my mother was capable of giving it. She was not. My mother is like a child herself. She is extremely dependent on my father for everything.

I wonder after my father saw how fragile my mother was, why he did not treat his daughters with more care and understanding. I wonder, does he ever realize the harm and damage his yelling and criticism do to a person's self-esteem. There were many times that I thought I would go crazy if I heard him tell me that I was worthless one more time, but then he always did it again. A miracle is I did not go crazy. I did take what he said to heart and did think less of myself. I thought that I was worth little to nothing for part of my life.

I wonder, is that what happened to my mother? She felt like she was not good enough, could not please anyone, so she escaped into her mind. She escaped into a nervous breakdown—into nothingness.

Observing this I vowed never to be like her. I held onto my feelings and emotions with everything I had.

My father was depending on me, consciously and subconsciously, to help in this situation of his. Since I was the eldest, he relied on me. So there was a distorted bond between us. I was like a little adult.

My sister Tammy feeling this must have felt left out. She attached to my mother by being her supporter. It appeared to me that Tammy received the love from my mother that I did not receive. Tammy manipulates in any way possible to be mother's 'good' little girl while she does evil behind everyone's back. I had to be the adult. The rest were children. My two youngest sisters learned to fit in the best way they knew how to do. They were neglected emotionally. Thus, the drama was set to be played and carried out into our adult existence.

The lack of this connection in my childhood has created a need in me, since I did not experience love or a bond from my mother. I took this into myself, to mean that I must not be lovable. That just my being myself does not make me lovable. I flipped into a mode of believing that I must do more, be more, be prettier, cook more, clean more, workout more or do—be whatever more before I would/could be loved. I must be, no needed to be 'perfect' in order to be loved.

Of course this did not work because I did not have love for myself. I could not love myself if my mother did not love me. Therefore, I was not lovable. A deep hunger for love and a connection developed. I have chosen to marry men and have gotten into relationships where the men were emotionally unavailable. They treated me very much like my mother does. Therefore I proved to myself repeatedly that no matter what I do or how 'perfect' I am, I am not lovable. I am not worthy of being loved.

Also even though I vowed not to in marriages, I have taken a more passive role than what is truly me because I observed this behavior and type of interaction between the role models that were in my life. This pattern of interaction was imprinted in my brain. I role modeled what I saw whether I wanted to or not. I did not know of another way to behave. I was on auto-pilot for a good part of my life.

This has brought me much unhappiness because I have been living someone else's truth not my own. For a long time, I did not know who I was or what my true reality was. I tried so hard to please in the best way that I knew how that I lost myself.

I did all the things that my mother did not like to do. I cooked, decorated, loved people and entertaining and having parties.

I joined social groups. I had a career. I didn't have a career. Whatever I did, it did not bring me love. The men in my life did not appreciate me, whatever I was or did because I did not accept and appreciate myself.

I did not see an equal male, female relationship in my parents' marriage. I saw a man and a child, a domineering man and a totally dependent woman. A man, hell bent on working and making a lot of money and a woman, hell bent on avoiding life and living. In my observance of this, I thought I had to be strong all of the time. No matter what, I could not let myself become like my mother. I did not realize that it was okay for me to be fragile and nurtured when I need it.

Men in my life, seeing and feeling this, have taken advantage of me. I have denied myself the experience of having my soft, emotional, needs met by a man. All the men I have brought into my life have been so needy in one way or another with addictions or their own issues that I could have none of my own. There was never time or energy for my needs to be met.

When a parent is consumed by mental and emotional issues, pain or addictions, they are not able to nurture a child. If they are unable to release their own pain and nurture themselves, there is no way they can do this for a child. The child will then carry their parent's pain around inside which distorts and influences their self-concept and esteem. As the child matures into awareness or as they become an adult hopefully, they will be able to look at the pain that they are carrying inside of themselves and give back to the parent that which does not belong to them.

It has taken much awareness on multiple levels to release this pattern from me. By awareness, understanding, acceptance and forgiveness, I've come into love of self and into joy of my circumstance.

I have found myself through this awareness and understanding and I release any resentment that I have towards my mother and father. They were only doing what they knew to do with what they had to rely on.

My mother loves me the only way that she knows how to do. She lives in and from her reality, the experiences she took in and that have created her beliefs about herself and others. She does the best that she can with her imprints and perceptions. She is trying to keep herself safe in her beliefs and her world as she has come to know it.

I am who I am. I learned that I am strong and what others say and do is not about me. It is about them. What others say and do does not have to affect me. I decide my worth, not anyone else.

I am at peace with myself, therefore able to be at peace with others. I accept myself. I love myself and can give love to others and set my boundaries. I am able to receive love from others and know that I am worth it—just because I am me.

I have the ability to experience genuine joy in this life's existence. Now I am older in age but I feel young. I feel like the child, I didn't feel like I could be when I actually was a child.

I can now look at the experiences of what I was handed in my childhood as a gift. I learned a hard way to value my true worth. By others not valuing me, I learned the true value of me. Therefore, I am able to value others. I was given and chose to take the experience of learning to value and love myself.

DADDY TAKES ME TO SCHOOL

I am thirteen and fourteen

I LIKE IT WHEN MY DADDY takes just me to school. He doesn't do it often and when he does, it's special. He talks most of the time about his business. I don't understand much about his business, it's about pipelines, and power plants, etc. but the more I listen, the more I understand. He tells me about what he's trying to accomplish. He shares his concerns about how difficult or how well things are going. He talks to me as if I was his son.

My daddy tends to worry a lot. He thinks and thinks and worries. He talks about all the different possibilities that he thinks may or may not happen. One thing I know for sure, daddy wants to be successful and to make a lot of money.

He tells me that he wishes that I was a boy, so he could teach me about his business and turn it over to me someday. Hearing this makes me sad. I have no interest in my father's business. It's not a type of business that I would have an interest in learning about. It's more about things that guy's like, but I do learn a lot about it from my dad.

I like fashion, art and ballet. My father enjoys these things all except for ballet. My father does enjoy fine décor, art and he wants his girls to dress the best. His business has little interest to me but I like to hear about it because he likes it.

I listen intently as he talks while he drives me to school. I feel uncomfortable at times listening to him but I also like it. I learn from him and I like to learn. I feel uncomfortable because I know he wishes I were a boy.

I tell my dad about the books I'm reading. He likes to read, too. I like to read romantic novels. The author I'm into now is Frank Yerby. He writes novels about the old South that follows families through generations. My dad says that he has read books by this particular author and likes them, too. He comments that in all the books about families through history that it is always the women who ruin the family. He says the women are always the weak ones in the family and they bring the family down by their weakness.

I look over at my daddy and feel sick inside hearing him say this but I agree with him to please him. I want my daddy to like me and not think that I'm like the women that he is speaking about. I want him to know that I am different than those women who bring the families down. So I agree with him. I think that if I agree with him, maybe I'll have a chance my daddy will like me. Why would my daddy say and think like this? He must not like women much.

We continue on our drive to school. Daddy is talking to me about pipes and refineries, BTU's and other engineering things. I ask him questions and, at times I get the feeling that my daddy thinks I'm smart. I try to be smart, to learn and understand what he is telling me.

I learn a lot about engineering and building from my father over the years. I also try to learn to think like a man in some regards, instead of like a woman. I try to act like certain things matter to me that really don't, in order to please him. I sure don't want him to think I'm one of those weak and silly women in the books. I want my daddy to like me so badly, but I am not sure that he does. Nothing I do or say helps, it just seems like he doesn't like me. It's because I'm a girl and there is nothing that I can do about this.

I like all the things that girls like clothes, make-up and boys. I don't like to talk about pipes, refineries, or football all that much. I enjoy being a girl! At times with every word my daddy says to me, I feel not good enough because I'm a girl and that's not good enough for him.

In looking back on these drives to school, I reflect that most times when I was or am around my father I felt inept. I felt as if I do not have a brain in my head. I hide my true feelings, my intelligence and my personality. I am most always in stress around him. I do not believe I have ever been my true and relaxed self around my father. I used to try to be what I thought he could love but now, I have given up. My father will never really see me or know me. He considers me less than him because I am female.

At times, when we are involved in a social event and someone tells him that I am beautiful. He will pass the compliment along to me. He won't tell me directly that I look pretty all that much but he will tell me that someone else saw me and stated that I looked attractive or how smart and friendly I am.

When I was young, my father rarely stated to me that I am intelligent or that he believes in me. I seem to need an endorsement of some kind from others for him to even acknowledge something about me.

I try to pretend in my heart that is the opposite of all this. I try to pretend that my father thinks that I am great. This is the only way I know how to cope and to help myself survive the fact he doesn't like me. This is why it feels doubly awful when I am around him to realize the truth.

As an adult, I can acknowledge that much of the time my father does not like anyone including himself. He criticizes everyone including himself. He does not bother to really get to know me because he knows no one including himself. He treats everyone as he treats himself with little empathy or compassion. He beats everyone up as he beats himself up. He has few close friends and certainly no women friends and this included his four daughters. He thinks we are all useless and has told us all this plenty of times.

I learned to deny my soft femininity around my father. I recreated this interaction with the men in my life. I attracted men who did not value women just as my father does. I would rarely let myself show my soft, vulnerable, dependent, womanly side. I hid it. I tried to be strong while in many instances, I actually was the one holding it all together. I allowed the men to be the 'weaker' sex, if there is a 'weaker' sex? I do not believe there is a weaker sex, just weaker and stronger people. Men and women have different innate strengths respective to their sex. But there can be weak men and strong women—their strengths are just different.

I became the 'man' in many of my relationships. By doing this, I received few of the womanly things that I desired from a man. I became exhausted denying my soft feminine side. The men I attracted had so many issues that there was no time for me or mine. I eventually had to be the strong one and I got so tired of being both the man and the woman. I thought I had to be perfect and that I could have no weaknesses or needs.

I am a very feminine woman and have learned to enjoy these qualities in myself. I enjoy and love being a woman. I have also become aware that men who put down or look down upon women are either fearful of women or fearful of their own feminine nature. Or they had a father or observed other men degrade women and that became what was imprinted in them.

A secure man can appreciate all aspects of the differences in women and men. They are able in their own security to release the need to feel that anyone, women included, are less than.

I understand and forgive my father for his weakness. He cannot see what he is doing because he is blinded by his prejudice against himself and the imprint that was made on him. At times he does not feel equal to, so he has to put everyone else down to feel better than. When an individual feels equal to, there is no need to put others down.

Dad's wife, my mother, was afflicted with mental illness. Therefore, she could not be there for him. To him, she ruined his plans like in the books we were discussing, where the women were weak and the ones who brought down the family.

All this created in me the imprint that I had to be perfect to be loved and not only perfect as a woman but perfect in the knowledge of many things a man would/should know. So I needed to look perfect as a woman but think like a man. I became exhausted trying to be both the perfect woman and the perfect man.

I am aware of the imprint of damage that Dad's criticism has done to me. I own my femininity. A woman can be anything she wants to be in this world and can learn anything she wants to learn. A woman is equal to a man. A man is equal to a woman. Both are equal but they are different.

Then at the same time, I appreciate and am grateful that my dad taught me how to think. I can figure out things that many women have no idea about. I can talk about power plants, etc. But when I used to do so when out with clients with my first husband when he worked for my father's company, it intimidated him. I realized that many men don't like to be around a woman who knows more than they do about certain subjects. Some men are threatened by an intelligent woman who can reason and think. Throughout my life, I have had men become shocked at what I know and how I think. Many have stated, "I can't believe you are so intelligent and look like you do."

My dad taught me common sense and I like to figure out how things work, along with wearing designer clothes. So ultimately, in some regard, it was a win-win, Dad stretched me to heights that I never thought I'd be able to reach or ever be aware of and for that I am grateful.

DARE AT THE FIVE AND DIME

I am thirteen

O N SATURDAYS, MY BEST FRIEND, Renee, and I like going to the shopping center and hanging out. It's the 'in' thing to do. All the really cool kids hang out at the shopping center on Saturday and we want to be cool. Then of course, we like to shop, too. Lots of kids will be walking around talking to each other.

It's great to be out of the house, away from our parents, and on our own for a few hours.

Renee and I take turns spending the night with each other on Friday night. Then one of our parents will take us to the shopping center. This Friday night, I'm staying at Renee's house. So this Saturday, it's Renee's chauffeur, Leonard, who will take us to the shopping center. Renee's mother is away somewhere in mental hospital. I have never met her mother and people talk in hushed tones whenever she is mentioned. So her father hired a nice man to drive Renee around. Leonard is cool. We like him. He doesn't bug us all the time, like parents can do.

Leonard drops us off at noon on the corner by the 'Five and Dime'. He says that he'll be back to pick us up at four o'clock and for us to be at this corner and to be on time.

We have lunch at a department store tea room. We have our usual—tea sandwiches, soup and shakes. Yummy! Then we set out to be hanging out and cool.

We walk to the bowling alley. Lots of the really cool kids are there. We walk around the place and talk to our friends. There are some cute boys from another school. We talk to them. Then we go to purchase some items we want. I get a wallet and Renee gets some shoes. It's fun to shop and get what we want without having parents around.

We head back to the 'Five and Dime'. It's getting close to four o'clock. We want to have time to look at some records before Leonard picks us up. We like the '45's' at the 'Five and Dime'. We begin looking at the records. Bobby Vee and Paul Anka are two of our favorites.

Renee states, "Lots of the really cool kids steal records." I ask, "Who?" She tells me the names of some of the kids that she has heard steal records. I can't believe they would steal because their families have lots of money. Renee states, "It has nothing to do with money. It's just cool to steal records to see if you can get away with it." She says, "I dare you to steal that record!"

I'm nervous. I don't know what to do? I want to take her dare. I want to be cool but I don't want to steal. Stealing is wrong. Renee taunts, "I dare you." I look around. No one is watching. So I slip the record into my sack. Renee walks around to another aisle and puts a record into her sack. We did it!

I'm freaking out scared inside. We walk to the checkout counter because we have some candy we're going to pay for. We're standing in the checkout line and a man comes up to me and asks, "Young lady, what do you have in that sack?"

Oh, no! I'm caught! I'm so scared that I pull out the '45' record and hand it to him. I say, "I did it because of a dare. I'm sorry! I won't do it again!" The man turns to Renee and asks, "Do you have anything?" Renee answers, "No! I wouldn't steal anything." He turns back to me and orders. "Follow me!" I look at Renee. She says, "I've got to go out and meet Leonard. It's four o'clock. Bye, see you later!"

She's just leaving me and this whole thing was her idea. I'm terrified!

I follow the man as I do I turn around and look up to see there's an office that looks down over the whole store. That's how, he saw me put the record into my sack. This man is the manager of the store.

I follow the manager up to his office. Sitting here, I have a view of whole store.

The manager is really mean to me. He takes my purse and goes through it. He says, "What else did you steal? You spoiled, little brat?"

I respond, "I did it on a dare. I'll never do it again!" He goes through my sacks. He comments, "You have money, so why are you stealing? You children are spoiled rotten. There are people that really don't have any money. You steal and you have the money to pay for whatever you want."

He's yelling at me. I'm so scared! I'm thinking—I'm going to kill Renee when I see her again.

He says, "I'm tired of you children coming into my store and stealing. I'm going to call the police!" I ask, "Can I call my parents? Please! I need to have them pick me up. My friend has left me." He says, "Sure she's left you. She doesn't want a thief for a friend!"

I'm trembling. I'm so scared that he'll call the police and I'll be put in jail!

He hands me the phone to call my parents. I call over and over again but there's no answer. They're expecting Leonard to bring me home. I'm afraid that if I don't get my parents on the phone soon. This man will have me taken to jail.

The manager says, "If you'll tell your father about your stealing, I won't call the police. Have your father call me first thing Monday morning. So, I can be sure that you told him. If I don't hear from your father on Monday, I'll call the police. They'll pick you up at your house." I promise him that I'll tell my father.

Finally, my father answers the phone. I say, "I need for you to pick me up."

The store closes and I go outside to wait on the corner for my father to pick me up. I'm all alone and I feel like a criminal.

When I get into the car my father asks, "What happened I thought Leonard was bringing you home?" "Renee had to leave early." I respond. Then I bravely tell him the whole story.

He listens to what I tell him then responds. "There's no reason for you to ever steal." I answer, "I know, daddy. I'll never do it again." Then he says something that I'll never forget. "What will your mother's friends in her Bridge club say if they found out? Your mother will be so embarrassed."

I say, "I promise I'll never do it again. You'll need to call the manager at the 'Five and Dime' and tell him that I told you what happened or he's going to put me in jail." Daddy said that he would call him on Monday morning. He could see how scared I am.

I plead, "Please, don't forget or I'll go jail!"

Daddy says, "They don't put children in jail. I'll call him Monday."

I was so glad to get home and to feel safe.

I called Renee, that little rat! She wanted to hear about everything. She apparently thought that she was super cool because she got away with stealing without being caught. She acted like she thought she was better and smarter than me just because she didn't get caught.

All I know is that I never did steal anything again ever in my whole life. Some of those 'cool' kids did end up in real trouble with the police.

Maybe I was lucky in a way for getting caught.

I sure never trusted my friend, Renee again or anything she said.

The obvious awareness is that it is wrong to steal. Nothing is cool about it. Also, you need to be very careful when you take a dare. An additional awareness is my father along with his concern about my stealing was more concerned with what my mother's friends would think, if they found out that I had got caught stealing.

As I remembered this incident, I thought it so strange that this would even occur to my father. It made me feel uncomfortable that this would even cross his mind. I thought he would be more concerned with me. What I had done, why I had done it and my fear of going to jail. I wondered why he would even care what those ladies think.

Then I remember the reason that I took the dare to steal was to be like the others that I thought were 'cool'. The whole reason I had stolen the record was because of my concern of what others would think of me. I was more concerned with the acceptance of those so-called 'cool kids', than I was concerned with what I knew was 'right and wrong'. I gave up what I knew was the correct way to behave in order to be accepted by others that I felt were doing wrong. Therefore I gave up acceptance of myself to try and be accepted by others.

My awareness is, no one will accept me if I do not accept myself. When I live by my own standards and what I know is right for me is when I will be at peace with myself and able to totally accept myself.

Now I can forgive myself for stealing because I did not understand this yet. I can forgive my friend, Renee because she did not understand this either.

Why do we put so much emphasis on what others' think when what really matters is what we think of ourselves?

Did you see how quickly my friend turned on me when I got caught and how she acted like she was better than me because she did not get caught? She was the one that dared me! What others' think about you can change rapidly. What I think of myself can remain true. I honor my mistakes and learn from them.

My awareness is to accept myself, trust myself and to do only what I know is right for me. I do not listen to others before I listen to what I know is right for me in my heart.

When I accept myself totally, I will care less if at all what others' think. Others will accept me when I accept and honor myself. I will live by my own standards of what I know is right and wrong. No one else influences me nor can decide this for me. I accept myself and know who I am!

PIMPLE ON MY NOSE

I am fifteen

I AM ENJOYING VISITING WITH DAD in the kitchen about everyday things. "Hey Tiger, you look cute today."

Surprised, "I do? Thank you, Daddy!" I was going through the blahs being a teenager and usually felt like I looked icky. So for Dad to tell me that I looked cute made me feel great!

Dad continues, "But you have a pimple on your nose."

Hearing Dad comment about the pimple on my nose devastated me. I had tried hard to cover it up. It was one of those hulking red terrible ones and it had to be on my nose. It was just horrendous, a complete headlight of embarrassment.

Dad continues, "Did you realize that you had a pimple on your nose, and a big one!"

"Yes, Daddy I did." Sarcastically, "Thank you, for reminding me."

"Aren't you going to do something about it?"

"Yes, I am." Then I quickly exit the kitchen to my bathroom to look at and work on the pimple on my nose.

So instead of Dad and I having a nice conversation, he pointed out a flaw in me that not only embarrassed me but shut down our communication. Dad often did that, pointed out a flaw. He would compliment me then take it away in the next breath.

This created in me the feeling that I was never okay and certainly, never close to perfect. And that I must be perfect so that I would not be criticized in some form or another. I became so aware of every little flaw that I didn't need someone to point them out because I did it myself continually in my mind.

Okay, you know those hard pimples that when you poke a hole in them with a pin, sanitized with alcohol of course, then squeeze and clear liquid and blood comes out? Then the next day, they are full of white pus. They are red, painful and awful and you need to work on them a couple of days—layer by layer, squeezing, applying peroxide and alcohol then repeating the process to fully release the yuck inside of them. Well, releasing poisonous imprints, perceptions and belief systems are the same thing and take the same repeated process. Poke it with a pin and it hurts. Squeeze and a bit of relief then repeat again and again until all the nasty poisonous pus is released. Then and only then will the wound created by the pimple heal itself so that the skin is back to normal and is healthy.

Same as with the fractured part of your being that has been imprinted with negative and poisonous imprints. When these imprints are recalled or triggered, it's not until all the pus is out that the wound can close over and fully heal. Otherwise, it's left with poisonous pus to fester and will come back again and again.

It's also interesting that while the pimple is there that it's the only thing I can see when I look into the mirror. It stands out to be seen. First thing in the morning, I look at it to see if it's still there or if it's healing and less noticeable. I do this many times throughout the day and before I go to sleep at night. I think about it often when it's there, then when it heals I completely forget that it had ever been there. That is how we are with most things. When something is irritating us, bothering us, needs our attention, we focus on it as if it runs our life. This is how negative imprints, perceptions and beliefs control us. Until they are seen, understood, accepted and forgiven they control us. Those imprints will continue to bother us until they are recognized because that is their nature and purpose.

My skin is olive and is oily. I suffered and suffer with pimples at times, but the good thing is that oily skin is not prone to dryness and wrinkling like other skin types. So like most everything in life, there is a minus and a plus because we are on the planet of dualities—good and bad—negative and positive. It just depends on where you are at any given time and how you look at it.

As I age, I am happy that I have oily skin. But I still get embarrassed and hate it when I get a pimple and especially on my nose. Because it's like a sign flashing that I am not perfect. Ha! But I have learned to love myself even though I am not perfect. Just as God loves us all and knows that we are not perfect. But in our imperfection, there is perfection.

GOING TO THE COUNTRY CLUB TO SWIM

I am thirteen and fourteen

MY DADDY WANTS ALL OF us to go to the Country Club to swim. He is going to play golf and he's insisting that we all must go with him.

I don't want to go. Sometimes I hate having to hang around my younger sisters. Besides it's hot and sticky outside and I dislike this type of weather. My tummy hurts because I have the cramps and my body feels all swollen and puffy. I just don't feel like going to the club. I don't feel like wearing a bathing suit. I don't feel like sitting outside in the hot and muggy weather.

I run up the stairs from my room and into my parents' bedroom. Dad is relaxing on his bed while waiting for all of us to get ready.

I say, "Daddy, I don't feel like going to the club. My tummy hurts and I don't want to be out in the heat. Please, can't I stay here alone and rest?"

"No, I want all of us to go to the club. We're going to stay out there and after swimming and golf we will eat dinner. We're all going as a family. Now go get ready. Put your swimsuit on!"

"Please, daddy, I don't feel like going!"

"Go and get ready!" he yells.

I run back down the stairs to my bedroom. I feel awful. My cramps are getting worse. I wonder why daddy is so insistent today about us all going to the club together. He has never been like this before. I try on bathing suits. None of them work. I feel fat and awful. Finally, I try on a green one piece then run back up the stairs to show my daddy how swollen my tummy is and how bad I feel from menstrual cramps.

"See daddy, I feel awful and I look so fat. Please, don't make me go to the club and sit out in the heat. It will make me feel worse."

With that, my father grabs my arm so hard that I fall to the ground. He shouts with spit spewing out of his mouth and teeth clenched, "Why aren't you like other children? I'm so sick of you! Who cares if you have the cramps! You're always sick and complaining. I don't care if you're dying you're going to the club! No man will want a girl like you, unless it's for my money!"

I'm in shock and began to cry. "Why are you treating me this way? Why are you saying those things?"

He shouts, "Because I'm sick of you. I'm sick of all you girls! Now, go get ready or I will give you something to cry about! I want you to be like other kids. I'm sick of your problems! It makes me sick just looking at you!"

I feel like I'm going to die inside. My body hurts and now my heart hurts, too. I run out of his room and down to mine. I hate my daddy for saying and doing this to me. I feel humiliated, ashamed and want to die. Why is my father so cruel to me? He must think I'm nothing. Why does he want us to all go the club together? He has never insisted that we do this before.

I shut down my feelings and continue to get ready. I feel shaky inside and on the verge of tears. I hear my father yell. "Get up here, now!"

I go upstairs with my change of clothing and swim things and stand there feeling humiliated by this man who is my father.

I get into the back seat of the car. Everyone piles in and off we go to the country club to swim and have fun!

I sit in the car feeling sad and alone. I feel like no one cares about me.

Arriving at the club, I walk to the pool with my sisters. Hardly anyone is at the pool this day. It's one of those hot, humid days where it's raining off and on. It's not a good day to go to a pool. My younger sisters swim. I find a chair under the cabana and sit in the heat suffering with my menstrual cramps. I feel like I'm going to cry any minute but try to hold my tears in.

One of the cute lifeguards is looking over at me. I feel embarrassed. Why is he looking at me? He probably thinks I'm weird and fat. He probably hates me like my father does.

Then the cute lifeguard comes over to me and asks, "Are you okay? You look so sad. Why is such a pretty girl looking so sad today?"

I'm sure, I blush. He thinks I'm pretty! Oh my gosh!

I respond, "I'm not feeling well today."

He says, "I'm sorry! You look so sad. Come in the pool and play when you feel like it!"

I am so surprised. This cute guy is so nice to me and he's much older, too.

I go into the ladies locker room to find relief from the heat and the blazing sun. It's cool, damp and dark in here. My tummy hurts so badly. I sit down and begin to cry. My heart and my body are in pain. Why did my daddy talk to me so cruelly? What he said hurt me so badly. Is something wrong with me? There must be something wrong with me because both my mother and my father hate me. What is wrong with me and what can I do about it? I wish I could talk to my mother. I wish I had someone to talk to. I feel so alone and I cry.

After sitting outside for what seems like forever, it's time to get dressed then go to the grill and have dinner.

We're all sitting here eating. I don't say anything. I feel dizzy, as if I'm going to faint but I don't say anything because I don't want my father to yell at me again. He's acting like everything is just fine. He's smiling, talking to people and drinking. He's pretending or maybe, he has already forgotten how cruel and hateful he was to me. I have not forgotten. I'm still hurting inside, but no one notices or cares. My mother just sits there laughing her loud, shrill laugh and drinking her liquor. I bet I could die and they would not even notice, unless I messed up their plans.

By the time I arrive home that evening, I'm shivering. I go to my bathroom and throw up. Then I take a hot shower and get into bed. This was a horrible day for me. It was all for my father. So that he could feel like we were a family having fun.

Lying here in my bed, I feel intense dislike of my father and mother. They never see my pain or notice anything about me.

When I look back to this day, I still feel as if it was just yesterday with my father grabbing my arm and saying those cruel things to me. Actually, after that day I never felt the same around or about my father. I shut down more and more and away from him. I couldn't wait until I could be away from him, away from both my parents. I will always remember the hate that I saw in his eyes for me that day. The hate he felt because I did not want to do what he needed and wanted me to do, in order that he felt okay about himself. He was always going for that family image no matter what the cost. The cost was me and my respect for him.

I now understand that he was directing his frustration with himself and my nonresponsive joyless mother at me. Except at the fragile age that I was, I needed my father's understanding and respect of me, in order for me to grow into a woman who would/could respect herself. What I experienced was my father's dislike and disrespect of women.

Only what he was actually showing was his dislike of himself.

I took this in and brought into myself all of his dislike of me and I disliked myself. I beat myself up mentally and repeatedly with his words. My heart cowered and was crushed before him and I lost myself.

My awareness is that my father is so full of his own pain, at times that he has no awareness of another's pain. He works, earns money to make him feel powerful and then he pretends he has a wonderful life. If someone does not go along with his game, he will overpower them or shame and humiliate them until they do.

Many times, I lost myself to please my father. I did not please him or so I thought. He does not see and value me as an individual and he never will. He never will because I am different from him. He wants and needs for me to be the same as him, in order that he feels in control.

I now can understand this and I forgive him. This is all that he knows to do with his experiences and beliefs. He is insecure in his feelings about himself and I took this insecurity into myself.

I release what my father feels about me. It is not me. It is my father. What my father thinks of me is not me—it is him.

You can only do to others what you have done to yourself first.

When you recognize your own uniqueness, you will not need to dominate others, or cringe before them.

By being yourself, you help others be their genuine self.

YOU'RE IN REAL TROUBLE

I am thirteen or fourteen

"WE RECEIVED THIS NOTE FROM your school today and you're in real trouble!" My father sternly states.

I ask, "What is it? What does it say?" My father says, "We'll talk about it after dinner." I protest, "That's not fair. I didn't do anything wrong. I haven't done anything! So tell me now! What does that note says about me?" My father says, according to the note, I did do something and he states again that we'll talk about it after dinner.

I feel so upset and confused. I know that I didn't do anything bad at school that would have gotten me into trouble. What does that note say? Why did the school write a note to my parents and why won't they show it to me right now? What is it and what's going on?

I suffer through dinner with everyone smirking and looking at me. My younger sisters are laughing at me because they know that later after dinner I'll be getting in trouble. And I didn't even know what about.

Then after dinner my father and mother take me into the living room alone. They read the note that came from school. The note is from my gym teacher.

The note reads: 'While coming in from outside, Natalie pulled her gym uniform top down before getting into the girl's locker room. There were boys in the gym at the time and they saw her. We are concerned about her behavior and her showing herself in front of the boys.'

I'm shocked! I never did that! I protest, "That is untrue! I didn't show myself off to some boys. The teacher must have me confused with someone else or she's lying!"

My father says, "Then, why would she write this note and why would the teacher lie?" I state, "I don't know, but it's not true!"

The next day, my father calls the school and the principal asks the teacher about the note. The teacher says that this is a true note and that is what she saw me do.

I'm hurt and embarrassed. Everyone thinks that I take my top off to show boys. It's not true. Everyone believes that teacher instead of me—like because she's a teacher that everything she says is automatically true. Well, it's not true. It feels so awful to be accused of something that you didn't do and to have no one believe you. I wonder why they believe her instead of me. My sisters are looking at me funny and laughing at me. My parents are shaking their heads.

I didn't do it. I didn't take my top off to show any boys! When, we come into the gym, after being outside playing softball. We all rush into the locker room to shower and get onto the next class. We rush in and as soon as we get to the locker room door, we start unbuttoning our gym uniforms. No one sees us and there are never any boys in the girls' gym. I don't know what this teacher is talking about.

I feel torn apart! Why? Why? Is this happening to me? It feels so awful that no one believes me! I'm going to tell the principal. I'm going to his office and I'm telling him the truth.

I go to the principal's office with the teacher. I state to the principal that I didn't do what this teacher says in her note to my parents. I say that I believe she has me confused with someone else. Then, I began to cry, which is unusual for me. It takes a lot to make me cry, but after all the confusion and frustration of the last few days, I'm emotionally exhausted.

The principal is very understanding and says to the gym teacher. "It appears to me that this young lady is telling the truth. Do you think that you might have made a mistake?" The teacher responds, "Well, there were many girls coming in and all at once. I guess that I could have made a mistake. Since, Natalie is crying, "Yes well, I may have made a mistake."

The principal asks me, "Do you feel better now? You're brave to have come to my office to clear this up. Everything's alright now."

"Yes, I do feel better. Thank you, for listening to me and believing me."

Thank God for that wonderful, understanding, insightful principal. He saw that I was telling the truth. The gym teacher was never nice to me after that incident because I had called her out on her error and won. It was all over, just like that! I'd been put through two days of torment by my parents. And all that teacher needed to say was, "Well yes, I might have made a mistake," and it was all over.

After having that experience of being accused of something that I did not do, I have always been careful to look at both sides of an issue. I give someone accused of something every ounce of doubt. This incident showed me how awful and helpless a person feels when they are being accused of something that they didn't do. It is an awful, awful feeling.

Sometimes, I am too trusting and this has worked against me in my life. Other times, my ability to stand back and look at both sides before making a decision on guilt has served others and myself very well. I have always been the type of person to stand up for myself and confront issues straight on.

The fact that my parents were so ready to believe a teacher over me deeply hurt my heart. My father and mother never apologized to me. They just said that they were glad it was all over.

My parents don't seem to see me or listen to me. They seem as if they don't know who I am as a person. If they listened and really saw me, they would have believed me and not the mistaken teacher. I seem to need some sort of endorsement from the outside world before my parents believe me. This hurts and I do not understand why they are this way? This has hurt my self-esteem over the years, until I regained it.

I look back and admire the little girl who went to the principal's office to prove her innocence and accomplished what she set out to do.

I was brave and I stood up for myself. Hooray for me!

The awareness is that persons with authority can be wrong and can hurt and harm others with their mistakes. I know and understand what it feels like to be accused of something that you did not do and how awful it feels!

I FEEL LIKE GIDGET!

I am fourteen

MY FAMILY IS ON VACATION in Miami. The beach is beautiful. The sun is bright and I am so excited!

I'm really looking forward to getting to the beach. I feel like the girl in that teenage movie, 'Gidget' I feel like Gidget!

I work a very long time to get my hair just right. I have a really cute blue bikini to wear with a matching cover-up.

We have a big suite in the hotel. My parents have a bedroom on one side of the large living room. The other bedroom on the opposite side is where my sisters and I will sleep. The hotel is the prettiest on the Miami strip. It's tall and pink.

It's exciting to go down in the elevator myself. The lobby is huge and beautiful. I walk into the gift shop to look around. The lady behind the counter chats with me. She comments, "You know, you remind me of that girl. What's her name? The one in those beach movies, Is it 'Gidget'?"

I am thrilled, so she sees it too. So it must be true! I'm petite like 'Gidget' only I have dark hair. Since I'm on a beach vacation, I worked hard to be like her and it must be working. I feel really teenager-like and cool, but the girl in the movie 'Gidget', she's older than I am.

As I'm walking around the lobby on my own, I feel so grown-up. I am so cool! Dad told me to go to the front desk and get another key then I'll be able to get in and out of the room on my own.

The rest of my family has already gone down to the beach. My sisters are younger and need to stay with my parents. I'm a teenager, so I can be on my own. Besides, I take so long doing my hair and stuff that no one wants to wait for me. So yay! I'm on my own and it feels so cool!

I go into a hotel restaurant and order a hamburger and a coke. It feels so grown up and fun to sit at a table and to eat alone. Through the window that looks over the swimming pool, I can see my sisters swimming and having fun.

After I finish lunch, I walk down to the beach. It's windy, a bit cloudy and the ocean has big waves. My hair is getting wrecked and it looked so perfect. My hair has curl in it and the humid air from the ocean makes it full and frizzy. I feel so sticky.

It's hot and windy. How do those girls in those beach movies stay looking so perfect? I find a reclining chair. The sun is beginning to come out and I want to get a tan. I get tan easily. The sun feels good on my skin.

I'm watching the people on the beach while trying to stay cool, get a tan and look good, but I feel sticky, hot and windblown. Two boys come over. They seem older than me. They ask me where I'm from and would I like something to drink. I answer, "No thank you, I just had a coke."

From behind me I hear my dad's voice. "Hi! What are you kids up to?" The boys answer, "Nothing, sir." Then they rush off. Dad laughs then asks, "Were those guys bothering you?" I respond, "No. They just asked if I would like something to drink. I told them I just had a coke with my lunch, so I wasn't thirsty."

Dad chuckles, "That isn't the kind of drink they meant. You be careful around the guys. You are good looking and look older than your age. So guys will think that you are older and come onto you."

I say, "Okay Dad." My daddy is protecting me and it feels good. It makes me feel safe. Anyway, I don't have time to worry about guys. I'm too busy worrying about my hair and the way I look. I stay on the beach awhile longer then decide to go inside.

The beach isn't as glamorous as I had thought it would be. It didn't seem like in the 'Gidget' movie. It was windy, hot, humid and uncomfortable. How do those movie stars stay looking so calm and cool on a hot, windy beach?

Next time, I'm going to hang out around the pool. The heat exhausted me. Going into the hotel, I feel grimy and dirty. I don't feel like 'Gidget' anymore. I feel like a sweaty little girl.

I go up to the hotel room to freshen up. I shower, do my hair and put on a cool shorts outfit. Now I feel like Gidget again and am ready for more adventure.

My mom and dad are going out tonight. They're going to the club in the lobby of the hotel for some entertainment. There's going to be a piano player in the club and my mother loves to hear a piano.

So how cool and fun! My sisters and I get to hang out in the hotel suite all by ourselves. Dad puts me in charge. He says for us to stay in the hotel suite and to not open the door for anyone but them. He says we can stay up late and watch scary movies on TV. They have their own key, so we should just go on to sleep because they will be out very late and they'll call to check in on us. I say, "We'll be fine. I can take care of everything."

We order dinner from room service. We really like to order dinner from room service and eat in front of the TV. We have stayed like this in a hotel many times before when mom and dad go out and we think it is super fun! We run all around the hotel suite as we play.

There's a piano in the living room and we play it for a while. We do go out of the room and run up and down the hall for a bit. Then we settle in to watch all the scary Saturday night movies on TV. I plan to stay up as late as I'm able, but one by one my little sisters fall asleep. They look so cute sleeping.

I lay in the dark with the air conditioning blowing and the remote control to the TV in my hand watching, 'Dracula'. Boy this is the life! I'm having so much fun. This must be what it's like to be grown-up and it's great!

Then I hear my parents coming in. They have some people with them. I hear many voices and someone is playing the piano. The person plays the piano really well.

Daddy peeks in the room and asks, "Are you still up?" He says, "Finish watching the movie then go to sleep. We've brought the piano player from the club up and another couple in to have drinks. Goodnight, see you in the morning."

After the movie is over, I turn off the TV. I lay there listening to the noises coming from the living room. I get out of bed and very quietly sneak down the hall to see what's going on. I sit on my knees and peek around the corner.

A man is playing the piano and mom, dad and another couple are standing around the piano laughing and singing. Mom is laughing really loud—too loud. She often does this when she's been drinking and even when she hasn't been. She keeps asking the man to play one song over and over again. They're talking, drinking, smoking and sometimes they're dancing.

They're really loud and slurring their words when they talk. I don't like it when my parents drink. My mom and dad are dancing and laughing. Then all of a sudden my dad falls down. He just sits down on the floor and he's laughing. But it's scaring me to see my dad like this. He's not hurt. He's drunk. It makes me sick watching this. I feel afraid and betrayed. My dad looks like a big baby. The daddy that protected me earlier on the beach is now a drunken man sitting on the floor. He couldn't protect anyone now. He can't even stand up.

They're all laughing as they help my dad to his feet. These drunks think everything is funny. I think they're all sickening. I hate them all! I run back down the hall and quickly get into bed. I pull the covers over my head and cuddle up in an effort to feel safe again.

I'll never be like them. They look like fools. My daddy makes me sick and my mother laughs too loud and smokes too much. I hate the way the room smells. They are all gross!

Why do they even drink liquor? It tastes awful! One time after my parent's had a party; I went in and tasted their drinks. It was the worst taste I ever tasted. I'll never drink and fall down.

The feeling I felt seeing my father like that on the floor drunk was one of total disgust. I never looked at him the same way again after seeing him that way. It was awful to feel disgust and embarrassment for a man I loved so much.

My dad was supposed to be strong and protect me. To see him sitting on the floor wearing a business suit, sloppy drunk, looking like a baby, disgusted me straight into the center of my being. I felt the feelings of disgust all through my body. I also felt fear. Fear because my parents weren't perfect. They did crazy awful things some of the time and I didn't like this realization.

I wanted to believe they knew everything and that they were perfect and invincible. I was realizing that I didn't like them all of the time. I was seeing lots of things, that they did and said, weren't what I wanted to be or wanted in my life. It was a scary feeling. It was a harsh reality. It was difficult to accept.

Children are aware of much more than parents think they are. Children see who the parents really are and they will eventually see it all. Many of these observances will make a lasting imprint for good or for ill.

My parents had no intention of letting me see them the way that I saw them that night. They thought I was safely tucked in my bed.

Children see who you are. Who you are is what you are and who that is makes a lasting impression on your children. Children do not see only your 'good' side—or the side that you show to them, or the side you want to pretend that you are. Children see it all and it imprints them for good or for bad.

A BIRTHDAY PARTY

I am two and I am fifteen

I AM WATCHING A HOME MOVIE of a little girl standing in a chair at the head of the table in front of her birthday cake. A doll is the center and the cake forms around her to make her skirt. Her whole dress is made of cake and icing. The icing is fluffy. So the dress looks as if it's really full and lacy with flowers all over it. It's too cool.

The little girl is standing in the birthday chair and is dancing and swaying to the music. Everyone is singing the birthday song to her, "Happy Birthday to Natalie—Happy Birthday to Natalie!" She's wearing a pale yellow dotted Swiss dress with white puffy sleeves. She's very tan—must play out-of-doors a lot. She has dark wavy hair and big brown eyes. She looks so happy! She's the center of everyone's attention.

As I watch, I reflect, 'I wish that I could hold that little girl, kiss, snuggle and play with her. She looks like she's lots of fun. She's so happy and full of joy!'

Many other little children are sitting around the table with their mothers standing behind their chairs. Both sets of grandparents and her aunts are at her party. Everyone has come to celebrate her special day. Her second birthday! There's a 'Happy Birthday' table covering made of paper on the table with napkins, paper plates, cups and party hats with favors. There's a pile of already opened presents.

The candles on the cake are lit and ready for the little girl to blow them out to make her birthday wish. The lights in the room are turned low. There's a lovely glow that shines upon the little girl standing in front of the cake. The light shines on the star of the day. Everyone is trying to get the little girl to blow out her candles. She won't do it. She shakes her head—no!

I am two—I stand in my chair dancing to the birthday song. My cake looks yummy. My mommy is bending over and saying, "Blow!" She's showing me how to blow with her mouth. I giggle and think, 'Mommy you look silly. I know how to blow but I want to dance a little longer. This is fun! I like all the people around me talking to me, giving me presents and showering me with attention. So please, leave me alone and let me enjoy my time. It's my party! I'll blow out the candles when I'm ready!' I stick my fingers into the icing of my doll cake and put them into my mouth. Yummy!

My daddy is taking home movies of everyone at my party but mostly of me. I'm his special little girl! My daddy loves me! My mommy loves me! Everyone loves me!

A breeze rustles through the windows making the curtains fly up. The paper covering on the table blows. Everyone grabs their napkins as my grandmother, NaNa whispers softly in my ear, "Hurry up and blow out your candles before the wind does." I bend over and blow out my candles. Everyone claps. I laugh, so pleased with myself! I'm so full of myself, so content, self-absorbed and confident in my feelings of being loved. In the moment, I'm the center of my world and everybody else's in the room. I'm two-years-old and I love being the center of attention. I have full knowledge that I'm loved and adored. I love myself!

I am fifteen—I watch the film of the little girl's birthday party. Her mother is cutting the cake and passing it out along with ice cream to all the other little children. I think, 'Boy, that cake sure looks good! I wish that I could have a piece. Hey mommy, how about you pass a piece of cake out through the movie screen.'

All the children have their cups of punch, their party hats and favors. It's such a joyous scene with all the little children eating their cake and getting it all over themselves, as the adults try to keep the children clean and well-behaved. At fifteen, viewing this home movie of me at two—it didn't feel as if I was the same person as I am now. I wish I could be that little girl again and feel so loved. I wish I could be that confident, free, happy little girl dancing in the chair—so full of confidence and fun. I wish I could hold her and play with her. She's so cute and full of joy! Where did that little girl go? I want to discover her in me again.

As an adult after my awareness and healing, I am that two- year-old again. I have her spirit shining bright inside of me. She didn't go anywhere. She just got beat up along the way. Her parents would have killed anyone that would have tried to hurt, beat up or harm that little girl in the home movie. So why did they beat her up on the inside with their words and behaviors, perhaps because no one can see on the inside. Or perhaps, they did not know what they were doing and even that they were harming her. Perhaps, they had been beaten up when they were children. So what they did was maybe, all that they knew to do. Every harsh word was like a knife into her heart.

Negative reinforcement beats people down. Positive reinforcement encourages and builds people up. Unfortunately, my parents usually chose to give me negative reinforcement. They told me that I was not good enough. I guess so that I would try harder, do better and achieve more. Any positive reinforcement I received, I hung onto like a life raft. I had a deep need to feel that I was okay, instead of in some way bad, wrong or awful.

For most people, negative reinforcement doesn't work well and then for some it does. They perhaps need a negative challenge in order to self-improve. Negative reinforcement can produce results, but at what cost? It brings stress into the body, mind and spirit. The cost is to the individual's spirit and peace of mind as it stimulates anxiety to spur action and activity. A few people might feel this internally as a challenge to succeed but for me, usually it created self-doubt, insecurity, stress and anxiety that I wasn't good enough and could not succeed.

Negative reinforcement produces fear. It is used for dominance and is about control. It can manifest performance anxiety. Positive reinforcement is about love and produces feelings of happiness, encouragement and possibilities that lead to a joyful spirit. Most everyone is more productive and more creative when they are at peace and in touch with their innate essence. To feel and be challenged is great—feeling negative and less than—not so much. Being in the state of fear damages our bodies and soul. Fear separates us from self, therefore making us easier to control. We are not able to think clearly when we are experiencing fear, anxiety and stress.

The Puritan work ethics and religious dogma that our society has been focused and built upon are based on negative reinforcement. They are based on the concept of instilling fear and control into people. The premise is that we humans need to be punished in order for us to be productive and 'good'. Premise being is that people in general are 'bad'.

My awareness is that we need to feel happy and joyful to learn and to be creative. When we are being creative, we are productive. We then have a better shot at being 'good'. We have been operating under beliefs of the Puritan ethics and religious dogma for a long time. Many results have been negative and produce suffering. People controlling people for benefit and profit—it's time to change. It is going to take happy, peaceful, creative people who are connected to the source of all wisdom—the God source to heal our world.

Those connected elsewhere can try to continue using force, control and negative manipulation as the answer. When negative reinforcement and control are used more than positive, it allows those connected to the negative side to dominate. By making the positive weak by their projection of negativity, they are more able to control and manipulate the positive aspects. Turning people into energy resources for their use and benefit, no matter how negative or self-serving that use or benefit might be.

People who believe that society must be ruled by negative reinforcement are judging people by their own imprinted belief system. They feel negative 'bad' inside. Therefore, they believe others are the same or they want to project their own negativity onto others, in order that they feel better about themselves and in control. Just like a parent who was wild and out of control as a child will be extra punitive to their children. Whether it is needed or not because they remember what can happen and how much trouble they got in to. They may rule with a firm hand fearing what 'might' happen. While the child is more harmed than guided by the parents need to control, which is really the parent's need to control their selves.

God gives us choice along with suggestions about how to live a good and productive life, but we have the choice to live as we will. Satan or evil manipulates us as in what to do. This negative energy wants us under his domination and control. God wants us free and at choice.

It all begins with a changing and flexible belief system with focus based in and placed on the positive. It starts with each one of us, person to person, parent to child into the world and beyond.

My awareness is that our source, our God is a loving, positive, glowing light of all wisdom and love. When connected to this higher source, miracles can happen. Let us step out of the dark, 'the negative' and come into the light, 'the positive', in all that we do on earth.

In my mind's eye, I hold, cuddle and nurture that two-year-old little girl. That precious child full of fun, laughter and joy; I keep, treasure and protect her from harm. I heal her hurts and love her genuinely.

Genuine self-love is not narcissism. Narcissism is without the ability to have empathy for others. Narcissists use people for their own benefit, needs and purposes and do not have genuine relationships. When you don't love and have empathy for self, you have no ability to love and have empathy for others and that is narcissism. There is a healthy narcissism—an adaptive aspect. People with a solid sense of self-esteem are better able to find balance between being overly dependent or overly self-reliant. They can be self-sufficient but also capable of genuine intimacy. They may be better at parenting because they don't have the need to see their children as extensions of self and will give children room to grow on their own terms. Healthy narcissism is keeping healthy and fit, groomed appropriately and striving for self-improvement and success.

Look at self with empathy, understanding and love—heal and nurture self. Then when criticism comes, look inside and evaluate self with understanding. That way you are able to incorporate awareness and change or discard it and hold it outside yourself. There is a time to be self-centered and a time to focus on others. Knowing the difference is to be aware and at balance.

In this awareness, I release all negative limiting beliefs imprinted upon me that changed who I am as an individual. I am in touch with myself in all my dimensions—the child and the adult, my higher self and at one with God. My nature is that of joy! I will stay full of joy with the ability to use all my God given talents in a positive way to heal myself and bring awareness to others. I will keep the joyful, playful two- year-old as a part of me forever. Why can't we be able to keep the spirit of a joyful two-year-old in all of us? I don't see why we can't—do you?

STAYING HOME WITH A COLD

I am fifteen

FEELING ILL MAKES ME AWARE that as humans we are fragile. I might have the flu. My stomach hurts and nose is running. I have a cough and am so tired.

I'm staying home from school to nurture myself. I stay in bed, rest, read, watch TV and eat soup. I comfort and lovingly nurture my human body. I feel vulnerable being in my human body today.

I enjoy watching soap operas, 'Another World', is my favorite. I can watch it all summer long. Then go back to school until Thanksgiving, watch it again and have not missed a thing. But it's still fun to watch soap operas even if they move as slow as molasses. I like to look at what the actresses are wearing and see how they're doing their hair.

It's fun to be home from school even though I do not feel well. I can think, reflect, breathe and ponder all sorts of things about myself and the world. I wonder, does my mind control my body or does my body control my mind? When my body does not feel good, it affects how my mind works. It affects the way I feel and think about everything. Today even if I had a wonderful outfit like the girls on the soap opera and a make-up artist had done my face, I would still feel awful. If I had everything in the world that I wanted right now, I would still feel bad.

I ponder, does my body control me or do I control my body? It sure seems as if today, it's controlling me. This cold, cough and flu will pass. This sick tired feeling will be gone in a few days. I'll be feeling good again soon. I'll be back in school, attending ballet class and seeing my friends. But these days of bed and cuddling are enjoyable. Perhaps, illness is God's way of saying be still, slow down, think and come into self, while contemplating your humanness and the frailty of being human.

I'm getting extra attention from the housekeeper and even my mother and my father. Extra attention feels good.

I look forward to the time when I'll have a house of my own and can stay at home all day doing what I really want to do.

Snuggling down under my covers, pulling the comforter up around my chin, I am me and happily to myself. It feels so good. Even though I'm not at school learning, I am accomplishing lots. Learning and figuring things out about myself and the world. I do lots of thinking when I'm home sick. Time to think on your own is just as important as going to school and learning whatever they're teaching. I like to read books they don't even talk about at school. I like to read books by John Steinbeck. None of my teachers have ever mentioned him and he's one of my favorite authors. School doesn't teach me many things that I want to learn. Perhaps at times, school can be an interruption to education. It feels great to be learning on my own. I love to learn on my own.

As a child I was ill much of the time. From the age of twelve until about the age of fifteen, I had an abundance of colds, respiratory problems and flu symptoms. Perhaps I became ill to avoid going to school. I withdrew to avoid facing more feelings of not being good enough while feeling bored. This may not have been a conscious decision, but it is how it manifested itself in my body.

I stayed home from school lots, so I could be to myself and that time benefited me greatly. I spent much time thinking. I did not feel that I fit into school. I was bored and felt uncomfortable there. My experiences with the school system were, for the majority of the time, negative. I was glad to be out of the school system. I feel that most of my learning, growth and awareness happened separate from what we call our 'educational system'. My true talents and abilities were not discovered, developed or enhanced by this system. Actually, the schools and teachers that I experienced contributed to my insecurity and the feeling that I did not fit into the world. They also made me think learning was drudgery, when on my own I think learning is exciting.

If mother mentioned that her decorator was going to be at our house the next day, the next morning, I woke up with a stomach ache. I loved to follow our interior designer around the house asking her question after question. She was interesting and taught me much. I eventually worked in the interior design field.

My creativity was not developed by the school system. I did not fit in and felt left out. I believe the purpose of education along with teaching the basics of reading, writing and arithmetic is to open up an individual to their unique gifts and talents—to teach them to think, reason and to be inquisitive. I felt stress while in the classrooms by the way the teachers interacted with me. Therefore my body and mind were in 'shut down' mode. I suffered different levels of trauma most every day that I was at school. I was trying to survive, forget trying to enjoy the experience of learning. My brain was operating at half-mast most of the time I was there. When I was in school, I felt like I was in a kind of prison. Life and colors were dimmed. The world appeared gray. I most always hated being there.

When I was away from the school atmosphere and away from my parents, I could learn, think, read and enjoy doing so. When alone, I was out of stress and could explore and stretch my mind. I was able to read, ponder and work on my school projects more effectively. I read constantly. I loved to read and would have book after book beside my bed.

During a prolonged illness, a history teacher gave me homework on chapters with papers to write. I loved working at home. I put so much energy, effort and pleasure into this project. I was sincerely learning the information and excited about what I was learning. Sitting home alone in my room, I worked diligently on this project. Away from the school environment and able to be alone during the day, where it was quiet and peaceful, I could learn quickly and enjoy the process.

After I completed the project, handed it in and the teacher reviewed it, he was very pleased. He told my parents that I had done excellent work and that I was a very intelligent student. Now, if I would only apply myself at school. Therefore, for all my hard work, what I got was in trouble by my parents because I did not apply myself at school. I was blamed for not fitting in.

No one ever looked at themselves or the almighty educational system. It never occurred to anyone that the school was the problem and not me. How did we get so in entrenched in the idea that people needed to fit into some system and then when they don't, it is their fault and not the system created?

A person is more open and receptive when they are relaxed and comfortable in their environment. The educational system might want to focus on this concept. A happy and relaxed student will be open to learning and developing their talents and skills. It might be well advised to incorporate into the school curriculum ways to teach individuals how to relax, to enjoy learning and about real life. Learning is fun and should be experienced as such. Perhaps classes about tools to lead the individual to emotional peace are just as important as anything else they are taught.

Education is not just about making children fit into a 'system' or to obey 'teacher's rules'. It is for the development of the individual as unique. Each one of us has incredible talents and skills just waiting to be unleashed. I understand that learning discipline, arriving on time, and following rules are part of learning.

Freedom equals creativity—control stifles creativity. Much of the time, our most talented pupils have their uniqueness delayed or even thwarted all together by the system that we now have in place.

Many individuals who have created what has given the most to our world did not fit into our school system. Some of our most talented and brilliant—our inventors and artists were labeled 'learning disabled' by the standards of the system we have created. So perhaps, it is time to truly recognize that our systems in the world need to be as ever changing as our own beliefs about ourselves need to be.

Being different is great. Individuality is what it's all about.

Sometimes an illness is far more than just healing the body. It is for healing and freeing the mind to create the time and space to relax, think, change and grow.

The educational system should be a place of honoring the individual for being individual. Individual creativity is what will heal the world.

"Great spirits have always encountered violent opposition from mediocre minds."

—Albert Einstein

PART THREE

CHILD, ADOLESCENCE TO YOUNG ADULT

SIXTEEN TO EARLY TWENTIES—INTO THE PRESENT

GINGER SNAP COOKIES

I am eight, preteen to young adult

SITTING IN THE BREAKFAST ROOM with my Grandfather Mimi is a special treat. He works all the time, so when I visit my grandparents I don't get to see him all that much. Tonight I am sitting with him in the breakfast room while he finishes up his dinner, just me and him. He invited me to stay to visit with him while he eats and I was happy that he did. His doing so, made me feel special. I was his first born grandchild and we have a special bond. I am the only child he ever pulled in a red wagon or really played with much at all—is what my grandmother NaNa told me. We have home movies of him playing with me and in them my grandfather Mimi is laughing and having so much fun. His real name isn't Mimi—it's what I call him.

The breakfast room in my grandfather's house is as big as or even bigger than a regular dining room in most homes. They live in a big beautiful white house with pillars in the front of it. Inside there is a long winding staircase carpeted in dark red that is not only majestic but can even be magical at times.

He is eating dinner tonight after we have already eaten because as usual, he got home late from work. He owns a gas station in the downtown area and a parking lot too. It is so fun to visit his gas station. He has a gum ball machine full of brightly colored gum and he gives me pennies so I can get as many as I want.

After Mimi finishes his dinner, he always has Ginger Snap cookies with his coffee. He called them ZuZus. I don't know why he called them that but since he did that's what I called them too. Mimi and I sat at the big table in the breakfast room eating ZuZus while we talked. I had milk to drink but Mimi let me dip my ZuZus in his coffee just like he did. It's really a delicious combination. I can see why he liked it so much and has it almost every night after dinner.

I feel like the combination of an adult and princess sitting with my Mimi. He talked to me like an adult and treated me like a princess. He usually didn't talk much and was fairly quiet most the time. NaNa talked lots, so I guess he just let her have the floor.

Mimi wore a three piece suit that had a watch fob. When he took the chain attached to the watch out of his pocket to show it to me, I liked it.

After dinner I went upstairs with him to his bedroom. He and NaNa didn't sleep in the same room, but instead had adjoining bedrooms. I sat on his bed while he took off his suit jacket and vest and then put on a sweater vest over his shirt. As he did this, he showed me his many suits and ties. I felt so proud and like I was special for my Mimi to pay me extra attention. He wore really fine clothes and was proud of them. When he was a little boy he told me that sometimes, he didn't have shoes to wear because they were so poor. His feet were even misshapen from wearing shoes that were too small for him.

When he was a young man his father owned an oil company. It was either feast or famine. When he met my grandmother, it must've been 'feast' time because he had a dapper car and would drive all the way from another state to take her out. My grandfather had dark hair, olive skin and brown eyes. His mother had a bit of Cherokee Indian blood, so that might be where he got his complexion and coloring. I have the same coloring and he had pretty sisters with the same. My grandmother was a thin woman with short blond hair and blue eyes. She was a flapper kind of a girl. When she and Mimi met at a party it was love at first sight.

After Mimi had changed into more comfortable clothes, he went through the door to NaNa's adjoining bedroom where there was a sitting area with his chair and a TV. He put the TV on a show that he wanted to watch, sat in his leather chair and lit up his pipe. I sat near him and observed. He was calm, peaceful and nice. Even though I couldn't stand the smell of cigarettes, the smoke from his pipe smelled good. I loved him so much. Just to be near him, I felt safe.

Several years later when I am about thirteen-years -old, I am visiting at NaNa's house. Mimi had surgery and is at home resting. NaNa tells me to be very quiet if I go on the staircase up to the landing or to the second floor. Mimi is sleeping and I should not disturb him. Mimi's bedroom is just to the right of the landing at the top of the stairs. I tell her that I will be very quiet but that I want to play on the stairs. The staircase and landing at my grandmother's are so special and fun to play on. NaNa warns, "Okay, but if you play there, be quiet! Do not disturb Mimi." I promise her that I won't. She further warns for good measure, "Do not wake up Mimi! He needs his rest!" I promised her again that I won't.

I am very quiet as I climb to the top of the stairs then take a couple of steps back down to sit at my favorite place. There I am able to look through the banister, down the staircase to not only see into the foyer but also into the music room and living room. As I pretend in my mind, I am a princess in a castle getting ready to come down the staircase to meet my prince. Then I turn and walk back up very quietly to the top of the stairs and sit down on a step at the base of the landing to look out the big picture window. While sitting there looking out, I hear coming from Mimi's room, "Natalie, is that you?!" I freeze in fear. I woke up Mimi. Oh no! What should I do? I try to be completely still and don't answer. Then I hear again, "Natalie, is that you? Come in and see me?"

"Mimi, I am so sorry if I woke you up. I am playing on the stairs. I tried to be very quiet so that I wouldn't wake or disturb you."

"You didn't wake me. I am just laying here."

I am relieved, "NaNa warned me not to wake you up."

"Don't listen to NaNa. Come in and see me. I would like some company."

"But Mimi, NaNa told me not to wake you up. She will get mad at me."

"I am fine. Please come in and see me Natalie."

"But I don't want NaNa to be mad at me."

I sit on the stairs frozen in contemplation as my mind swirls. I need to obey my grandmother but I want to visit with my grandfather. But Mimi needs his rest and I don't want to disturb him. I want him to be healthy and well.

"Natalie, please come in here. I want some company."

"Mimi, I can't. NaNa told me not to."

My heart and mind were so conflicted. I can feel in my Mimi's heart that he is lonely and wants some company, but I am afraid to disobey my grandmother. NaNa said Mimi must get some rest so he can recover. I was an obedient child. So I walk down the stairs past my grandfather's room as I say, "I love you Mimi! Get well!"

Years later as a freshman in college, I got a phone call from my Mom and Dad telling me that Mimi had died. He hadn't even been sick that I knew of. Hearing this news, I burst into tears and cried and cried. I loved him so much—so much. He was in my heart. I couldn't stop crying and my college roommate became worried. She ordered us a pizza for dinner but I couldn't eat any. Everyone on our dorm floor came into our room because I was crying so hard. They wondered why I was so upset. So, I told them. They hugged and tried to comfort me. I could tell that some didn't understand why I was so heartbroken that my grandfather had died. I just wanted to be alone. So I could cry.

That night I lay in bed with my arms across my chest still crying with tears running down my face when I smelled my Mimi's pipe. I felt his presence and heard his words as if conveyed into my mind, 'Don't be sad my precious little Natalie. I am fine. I love you. Live and be happy. Don't worry about me.' Hearing his words soothed my aching heart. His presence felt so wonderful and comforting that I fell asleep and after that I was sad, but cried no more.

This was the first time, I had felt direct communication from the other side that I was consciously aware of and it was beyond comforting. It was an intense knowing of the divine connection and as real as anything could be. I felt it into the totality of my being.

I was at college and I didn't want to ride with a cousin, who was also there, to my Mimi's funeral. I just wanted to hold him in my heart as I have for my whole life and always will.

My grandmother was on a cruise when my Mimi died. She came home quickly. But one of our family members made the comment that 'Mimi died as he lived—alone'. When I heard this my heart broke in half as I recalled that day when I was playing on the staircase and he called out for me to come visit with him. And I didn't because I was being obedient to my grandmother.

My NaNa and Mimi had been a partying couple when they dated and were first married. My mother was born first. Then thirteen years later, they had a second daughter then a third daughter arrived. When my mother was in college, they had their last daughter. My grandmother told me that Mimi heard how much she screamed while giving birth to the last child. Hearing this made him realize how painful giving birth is and how much it hurt NaNa. After that, they never had sex anymore because he didn't want her to go through pain like that ever again.

Mimi became very religious in his later years and became a Deacon in the church. I don't know all that much about his family other than his father married several times. So he had many brothers and sisters—half and otherwise. Some of the males were in the oil business back in the day and some of his sisters lived interesting lives. One worked for the government in some capacity and died in a foreign country. Another sister was a costume designer in Hollywood.

My grandfather Mimi worked most all the time and provided well for his family. My grandmother had everything a wife could want for, except sex in the later years of their marriage.

I loved my grandfather Mimi very much and often envision him sitting in his chair rocking back and forth as he smokes his pipe.

This imprint of my grandfather brings both comfort and pain along with the awareness that sometimes, it's wise to listen to your heart instead of being obedient. Each time I recall him calling out from his sick bed for me to come into his room to visit him; it breaks my heart and can even bring tears to my eyes to this day. I would give anything if on that day I had gone to sit by his bedside. But I also have an awareness that our connection surpasses anything that occurs on earth and that he knows how much I love him and always will.

LATE NIGHT PHONE CALL

Teenager—Young Adult

IT'S LATE AND I AM in the downstairs playroom that is next to my bedroom watching TV. Everyone else in the house is asleep. It's quiet and I'm having fun being to myself without the nuisance of my younger sisters. Then the phone rings in my bedroom. I run down the hallway to get it as I wonder who would be calling me this late.

We have one of those phone hook ups with two lines that can be switched back and forth from one to another. We children use one line and my parents the other, but we have two different phone numbers. As I pick up the phone, I hear a woman talking, "I love you so much." She saying my dad's name, "I miss you. When are you getting a divorce? When can we be together?" I can hear my dad's deep breathing; he starts to talk then pauses then abruptly and gruffly answers, "I don't know who this is." Then he hangs up the phone.

I am stunned at what I heard this woman say to my father. I know that he heard me pick up the phone because there is a click when doing so.

The next morning at breakfast, I am quiet as I look at him every so often out of the corner of my eye. I know that he knows that I know about the phone call. And I know he knows that I know he is having an affair. He says, "I got the strangest phone call late last night." No one pays much attention. One sister asks, "What kind of phone call?" He replies, "Some woman called telling me that she loves me." He laughs as if how ridiculous, "I have no idea who it was." Dad glances over at me and our eyes meet. I think to myself, 'You are lying and you know who the woman is'. And I knew that my Dad knew that I knew. No one else says anything, not even my mother. We continue eating breakfast. Nothing else about that late night phone call is ever mentioned again.

A year before this, I was at an after party of a Junior Assembly Ball. At the party the older brother of one of my girlfriends was there along with several of his buddies. They had been drinking, crashed the party and were acting like hoodlum big shots. My friend's brother was boasting about just having come from an upscale bar. It was connected to a local restaurant where businessmen were known to meet and to hang out. I knew that my Dad went there sometimes after work. The place was just down the street from his office building.

At this time, I didn't drink at all and my friend's brother was trying to get me to have a drink. I responded, "No thanks, just not into it." It irritated him that I wasn't drinking. He commented, "Do you think you are too good to have a drink and loosen up? You think you are a little princess don't you—with your rich daddy, your Mustang and your big house?" I glared at him, "I just don't like liquor." I knew at times this guy could be a jerk. He behaved that way when I was spending the night with my friend at her house. He would bother us, be sarcastic and taunt us. He ran with a wild group of guys. I walked away from him but he followed and kept talking, "How would you feel to know that your rich Daddy has affairs? He is out in bars with women all the time." I snapped back, "You are lying. He is not! My dad would never do that!"

He laughs, "Oh yes, he would and he does. I see him all the time and I even saw him tonight." I come back with, "That is a lie! You are just jealous and are mean! Leave me alone!" He continues, "Hey little perfect girl, your perfect world isn't so perfect, is it?"

On that night, I became defensive and in denial. My Dad often didn't come home for dinner and was out late at night. Mother would hold dinner for him, but then eventually we would go ahead and eat. She would tell us that he had a business meeting or was working late. I never thought too much about it at the time. I was busy with ballet, school, homework and my friends. Hearing my friend's older brother tell me this was a complete shock and it broke my heart—to have the realization that other people knew this about my dad and my family—even a kid just a few years older than I was. And he was laughing at me and my family. I flipped into defense and denial because it was too horrible to be believed. I put it out of my mind until the night of that phone call. What my friend's older brother had told me was the truth. I was too naïve and in denial to become consciously aware at the time. But unconsciously, I knew. I became consciously aware when it slammed me right in my face by that phone call.

Dad had affairs all the time. He was out late at night much of the time. Yes, he worked hard and sometimes he worked late, but he was also out doing other things, He hated coming home to be with my boring, depressed, complaining, unexciting, not challenging mother. Who could blame him? But I still hated my father for doing this to my mother and to our family. It felt that in his betrayal of my mother that he was betraying our whole family and he was. I tried to deny it. But it was truth.

As I got older I came to understand my father's actions. I don't condone them, but I understand it. He stayed with my mentally ill mother out of duty. He loved her from his memory about how she was when he fell in love with her. And he stayed with her to make a home for his daughters and to have a family. My mother had no ability to satisfy my father in any way. She was like a robotic 'Stepford' wife—cold, automated and dull.

My awareness became clear. I couldn't have had awareness if I stayed in denial. I now understand all sides. I accept what it was and I forgive. Everyone was doing the best that they knew how to do with what they had been given and with their respective imprints and belief systems.

My life was perfect. In what I lived through, experienced and by what was shown to me, I eventually was able to break against, so that I could hold onto the joy in my spirit and come back to it when it was temporarily dimmed.

THEY CALLED ME CINDERELLA

Teenager -Young Adult

I ARRIVE AT THE COUNTRY CLUB early to meet my family for Sunday brunch. I am wearing a perfectly fitted Calvin Klein suit with high heels. As I walk to the entrance of the dining room, our usual family server approaches to greet me and as he does, says under his breath, "Cinderella has arrived." I look at him. "Hi Sam, how are you today?"

"Fine Miss Natalie, and you? You're looking lovely today as usual."

"I'm fine and thank you. Sam, what was that you called me?"

A bit embarrassed, "Cinderella, Miss, is what we all call you."

I laughed, "Really? Why? And who's all?"

He chuckled lovingly, "It's clear as day. Look at you then look at the rest of them and how they treat you. All of us at the Club refer to you as Cinderella. Miss, please follow me."

As we walk to the table, we chat. Sam has assisted my family for years—given toasts at our weddings, served at parties and events at our family home. We loved him. And being around our family so much and often, he saw the inner workings of it as I am sure other servers at the club see through to the dynamics of the families they interact with often.

With surprise I continue, "Okay, so I am referred to as Cinderella by everyone at the club—really?"

"Yes Miss and it's a high compliment to you. You are a beautiful kind young lady and don't you ever forget it. God will have something very good for you in your life someday, just you wait and see."

"Well thank you, Sam. I sure hope so!"

We arrive at my family's table and just as I take a seat, I notice other members of my family arriving. Sam put my napkin across my lap as he winks at me. "Have a nice day, Miss Cinderella." Then off he goes to greet my father and the others.

My awareness is that no matter what you may think or try to hide—no matter the image you try to create—how well you are dressed—how much money you have—some people that you may not realize or even know well—will see through to the truth of a family and its dynamics.

The exchange with Sam on that Sunday at the Country Club helped to heal my heart in the knowing that others saw the dynamics of what I was living in. It both amazed and helped me to feel seen and understood. And it felt good to be acknowledged and understood.

Sam would always give a toast at parties, weddings and events—"May you live forever and may I never die!" Thank you Sam!

LISTENING TO THE RAIN

I Am Twenty

IT'S A PEACEFUL NIGHT. IT'S raining. The sound of the rain beating on the roof is comforting. My sisters are in their rooms playing quietly or asleep. Mom and Dad are out on the town and I am snuggled in my bed watching a movie on television. A perfect night, I am relaxed and peaceful and it feels great.

I hear footsteps in the entry hall along with Dad's bellowing voice and Mother's loud obnoxious drunken laughter. Dad is yelling at Mother. They are arguing. I quickly get out of my warm bed and close the door to my bedroom. My parents' voices get louder as they walk towards their bedroom at the front of the hallway. Dad starts humming some stupid melody as he often does when he has had too much to drink. I pray, 'Please let him pass by my room. Please God! Let him leave me alone.'

I can hear him go past my room heading towards my younger sisters' rooms. He bellows, "What's the light doing on in there? Why aren't you girls in bed? Turn off the lights right now! Go to sleep!"

I hear one sister crying. I hear Dad bellowing at the top of his lungs at Dana. "Turn that light off right now, young lady!" He is slurring his words. I feel sorry for my little sisters. They were in bed and being quiet in their rooms last I checked.

I summoned bravery and stick my head out my door. "Dad, they were in bed. Please stop yelling at them. Someone must have gotten up to go to the bathroom or something."

Dad turned his attack to me. "I told you to get those girls to sleep and yourself as well! I get so sick and tired of dealing with you, kids. Can't you ever do anything right? Can't you do as you are told?"

I respond, "I did as I was told." Dad goes back to screaming at my sisters.

I close my door and open the sliding doors to my outside patio. I can hear the rain louder to help drown out his voice. I sat in a chair near the patio door with my knees bent up to my chest. I rest my head on my knees with my nightgown pulled over my legs down to my feet and quietly prayed, "Please God don't let him yell anymore. Please, I just can't stand to hear his bellowing voice. Please, please, please, I don't want him to yell anymore."

Then my door cracks open. The light from the TV is the only light in the room. Dad can't see that I am sitting in the chair by the sliding doors near my bed. "Natalie! Why's the damned TV on?"

I ponder, 'How could I be asleep with all your yelling?' but respond, "I was just turning it off. Did you have a good time tonight?"

"Yes fine." His mind wondered, "No, your mother is . . ."then he focused again towards the direction of my bed. "I thought I told you to make sure your sisters were in bed? And why is this door closed?"

"Last time I checked they were in bed."

"Can't you do anything that you are told to do? Turn the damned TV off and go to bed right now!"

"Okay Daddy, I will." Thankfully, he closes my door but I can still hear his drunken humming as he heads towards his bedroom. Finally and thankfully, I hear his bedroom door close.

I used the remote to turn the TV to barely audible then stay seated in the chair by the doors listening to the peaceful sound of the rain. I prayed for God to get me out of this family, so I can have a home of my own without any drinking and yelling. I vow to myself to not marry a man who drinks, I hate alcohol and what it does to people. I hate it! Hate it! Hate it!

After one of Dad's drunken tirades, he might or might not apologize the next day and he may even send flowers. I was working part time at a boutique. The next day, Dad sent flowers to me at work. The card read, 'I am sorry for last night. You mother was driving me crazy and I took it out on you. I love you very much, Dad.' The girls at the boutique commented, "You have the neatest Dad in the world. He lets you buy all the clothes you want and sends you flowers. I wish I had a Dad like that! He's like Santa Claus."

On some level, I knew Dad took his frustration with mother out on me. Knowing this, didn't help me deal with it. I was blamed for everything. I became the scapegoat in the family. It hurt my heart and made me feel like I was nothing and that nothing I ever did was good enough. I got tired of being held overly responsible for my sisters. I felt sorry for them but I didn't really like them all that much. I thought them a drag and a burden.

A few years later just out of college, I got married. He was an outgoing, fun, hardworking—'worked to put himself through college—tritely from the wrong side of the tracks'—'Robert Redford' appearing guy and we barely drank if at all in college. When he got out into the business world, he began drinking. When he drank, he got loud and obnoxious like my Dad sometimes did. I would observe him and wonder how I married exactly what I didn't want. I tried to make the marriage work, but not only was he an alcoholic, it turned out he was a womanizer. He gambled and lost most all of our money while he worked for my father's company. He was a complete leech, loser and obnoxious. He lied—lied—lied and denied—denied— denied.

I made certain to not get pregnant because I knew he would make a horrendous father. I spent nine years in marriage Hell. I was overly responsible and tried too hard, while he lived a double life. I gave him the image of respectability, while behind the scenes; he lived the life of an immoral player. He would often sing the song, 'A good-hearted woman in love with a two-timing man.' As clearly he knew, he was actually singing about us.

Unbeknownst to be at the time, he got his secretary pregnant—an overweight nondescript girl. She had his illegitimate child while we were married. He paid her money to try to keep her quiet. But one evening, she called to tell me the whole disgusting story because he had refused to pay her more money. I was shocked beyond belief to have this unfold in my life—one horror after another. While he was doing his dirty deeds, I taught ballet. Did the social and business entertaining duties and maintained the house. He traveled for business, having affairs along the way, charging overly expensive bottles of wine to his expense account all the while being paid a salary by my father's company. I kept the image and home front going while he tore it down behind my back. I tried to save money, while he gambled it away. I did not use the Country Club much, even though it was my membership, not his. He took his friends and family out there and spent wildly. Dad said he was living as if he was his son—the son of a millionaire. I was living like a poor little mouse.

Just days after I kicked him out of the house and he had been crying telling me that I was the only one he loved while begging me not to divorce him. I went to the mailbox to find a card addressed to him. I opened it to find it was from a flight attendant that he had clearly been having an affair with. It read that she loved—missed him—was looking forward to seeing him again soon and thanked him for buying her son athletic shoes for his birthday. He was doing all this with her, while I was living on practically nothing trying to help pay his gambling debts and emotionally trying to endure his legal issues concerning his illegitimate son. He ended up paying the mother of his son off—signing a legal binding agreement that he would never contact the child or the child contact him. There had been a court ordered paternity test that showed this boy definitely was his child even as he kept denying it. He denied his own son. Later in life, I wondered if he ever interacted with his son that he denied. He gave up his son as he tried to stay married to me, while he was having an affair with a flight attendant.

On the night that he got his personal belongings from our house,

I recall him shouting as he stood outside at the end of the walkway, "I always loved you the most!"

Truth is—I actually fell out of love and lost respect for him on our honeymoon. He acted the big shot and showed little caring for me. He drank too much and behaved obnoxiously, while I kept trying like a good little wife. I wanted a good marriage so tried to maintain the image of one. Ha!

I was awarded a divorce from him on the grounds of extreme mentally cruelty in a no-fault divorce state. It set a precedent in the legal system in the state. Even though the greedy bastard pushed the divorce to court, I got everything in the marriage or all that was left, which were mostly indebted assets. During the hearing, the Judge looked over and down from his bench at me, to inquire, "Where in the world did 'you' meet this guy?" I responded, "College."

I had married everything I didn't want, actually even worse than I could have ever imagined. How did I bring this nightmare to me? He wasn't anything like he was when we were dating. During our marriage, I gave him value and support while he gave me nothing and devalued me.

I went to a psychologist to help me to figure it out. I began a deep search to find out why and how I brought exactly what I didn't want and everything I am not into my life. I read psychology and spiritual books. I read the Bible. I went to Al-Anon. The psychologist helped me to understand that what my husband did were his choices and that I could have been the most perfect wife in the world which I actually was and it wouldn't have mattered.

I had been fractured as a child and was overly caring, empathic and responsible. My ex-husband saw all this in me, whether, consciously or unconsciously and it allowed him to do anything he chose to do because he knew that I would cover for him and try to make everything all right. It was in my energy and his energy connected to mine to create the perfect marriage disaster. Our energy vibrations connected to play out this horror.

My father was hurt even devastated that I was in this mess. Also, berated me for being in it, he would yell. "How could you marry such a low life con? Didn't I raise you better than to be in a mess like this?"

When we got engaged Dad told me that he didn't think this man was good enough for me. I didn't listen. I thought I was in love and wanted to get out of my family's house to create a home of my own.

Reality is that I was reared to be in a mess like I found myself in. I had been imprinted. It was in my energy. I had little self-esteem, had a fractured core and wanted to get away from my family of origin. I wanted the love that I didn't receive at home. I tried to be perfect, in order to have it. I was weak, had holes in my energy, was kind, caring, fractured, wanting and needing love.

Dad's dream had been that I marry a great guy, have children and that my husband takes over his company and become the son that he never had. Since I had been born a female that was the best outcome I could offer him that fit into his dream—the perfect legacy for a successful man. Instead, it all fell apart into a mess in front of the whole town.

At other times, Dad would talk to me, comfort me and give me words of advice. He told me not to worry about what other people thought because it didn't matter, to hold my head high and put the whole nightmare behind me. That how I handled this situation, will define me and help me to grow. Dad found out that my husband had always planned to marry a girl from a wealthy family. He had dated a wealthy girl before me and her parents chased him off. He was from the 'wrong side of the tracks' but he seemed an ambitious guy and besides my Dad was from the 'wrong side of the tracks'. So since, I thought that I loved and believed in him, I gave it a shot. What I got was shot in the back.

Being naïve, kind, loving, trusting and open, overly-responsible and fractured, I had no ability to see or to realize the innate duplicity in this con man. Along with the fact, I desperately wanted to be away from my family. I married exactly what I didn't want which landed me back to dealing with the imprints from my family of origin. I had been set up psychologically and imprinted to marry everything that I hated and didn't want.

When that husband was out of my life, I felt enormous relief. I started an art and interior design business. I held my head high and just kept living and trying to understand how I landed in that horror of a marriage. Even though it was scary being on my own, I enjoyed the challenge. I had fun making money, taking care of myself and creating my own life. I felt free.

From what I later heard and from articles in the newspaper, my ex-husband bankrupted several companies and is now in ill-health.

Had I been aware as I have grown to be now, I would have left him after our honeymoon. I stayed too long because I thought it was what a woman should do. It was part of what I had observed in my mother and father's marriage—long suffering loneliness. Along with my naïve, trusting nature and the holes in my energy field that allowed him to con me. My need to get away from my family led me directly into everything I was trying to get away from, only worse.

EVENING PURSE

Early twenties

I WAS GETTING READY FOR A formal evening out—designer dress—the works. While getting out my attire, I realized my satin evening purse had a busted chain, not only that but it was broken in a way that—Oh my gosh! I thought could never be repaired and certainly not in time for my date. It was the only purse I had that would work with my dress. I just had to wear that dress with this particular evening purse!

I had chosen this particular dress just to go with the evening purse. Dad had given the evening purse to me for Christmas which had been his perfectly selected gift wrapping for his generous Christmas check. My Dad had shopped for and selected this elegant designer purse just for me. I liked it but mostly so very much for just that reason.

I rushed into the library where Dad was watching TV and in the brokenhearted frustration drama only a twenty-year-old preparing for a black tie affair with her beau could create—held up the purse that was destined to ruin the whole evening. "Daddy, can you fix it? Please can you?! I got my dress just to go with the purse that you gave me. Please Daddy, I have to take it tonight. I just have to! But I think it's broken for good! Daddy what do you think?"

He turned from the TV with a slightly amused but concerned smile as he took my purse from me, examined it then said, "Go on and get ready. I will see what I can do." Feeling better that my Dad was on the job. I showered then rushed into the kitchen to see Dad at the breakfast counter with his tools out, working on the chain of my purse. There was also a needle and thread involved. I observed Dad's work table as I thought, *'Daddy can sew?'* "Daddy, how's it coming along? Do you think it can it be fixed?" Dad glanced up and said, "Don't you need to be getting ready? Your date will be here soon."

"Okay. Daddy—okay. I am. I will." I rushed back to my dressing area and proceeded to do my hair and makeup. I was nervously frantic. I had no other purse that would work with the dress that I so wanted to wear. I entered my bedroom to get my dress and there on my bed sat my purse. I held it up and couldn't even tell it had been broken. I quickly put on my dress and finished getting ready, putting my lipstick, hairbrush, etc. into my treasured Dad given— Dad repaired purse. Then the doorbell rang. I hurried down the hallway to the entry to find Dad talking with my date. Dad smiled in pride when I entered. His eyes lit up as they most always did when I entered a room. "Dad, you did it, you fixed my purse." I gave my Daddy a big hug. "Thank you Daddy! I love you." Dad replied, "You're welcome honey. You look beautiful. Have a good time."

On the arm of my date, as I stepped out the front door wearing my poofy black satin dress with my treasured 'Dad given—repaired evening purse' over my shoulder, I turned back to smile at Daddy, our eyes met in our special love—my knowing of his pride in me and my respect for and trust in him.

My Dad has been gone for years. Memories often come to me of the various ways in which he treated me that instilled his pride, love and served to create my self-worth as a woman. That imprinted, taught and showed me how I want, need—must be treated by any man and most certainly 'the special man' in my life. Those particular moments of love, respect and pride that my Dad instilled in me created my worth as a woman. My Father, a master engineer who built refineries and nuclear power plants around the world, this former Navy man, pro-baseball player, pilot, yachtsman, golfer, intellectual giant, leader in his industry, accomplished masculine towering man, sat in his kitchen late on a Saturday afternoon foregoing sports on TV with tools, a needle and thread and worked on my purse, until it was fixed perfectly for me, his precious blessed to be his daughter. Because this man of so many worldly accomplishments knew in that moment, his most prized and devout duty was that of being a father—a man that would/could 'fix it' to make everything okay.

On the flip side, Dad wasn't perfect. He also left negative imprints for me to break against, understand and to grow past. Because of his perfectionism and great accomplishments, while feeling loved, I also had the imprint that if I wasn't perfect, I was not worthy of love. Dad was tough on me, held me accountable and would turn cold even harsh and withholding when I displeased him. When those times occurred, I felt rejected, ugly, dumb and unloved. So all my life I have been dealing with these competing imprints. Interesting, huh? As much as my father's imprint on me was that I was protected and loved, there was a conflicting imprint that if I wasn't perfect, I was not worthy of love—part of the duality on this planet and my challenge of growth to recognize and overcome in order to achieve wholeness.

As I have grown into life and full awareness, everything my Dad was as a Father, role model and teacher continues to integrate and incorporate fully in me and my psyche, both the positive and the negative. I am fortunate that the tough way he dealt with me, at times and the way that he held me accountable, created strength in me enough to have the tools to grow past his negative imprints. You recognize the humanity in your parents when you are able to heal your wounds. What a blessed gift.

A dad leaves his mark on the world by the imprint, model and love he gives his children as this gift floods out into the world. A father creates self-worth or not, in his children in everything that he does; by example, by actions, by words and by wordless looks.

My father, for the most part, was the example of a generous provider, a giver and a protector. He was also the example of a cheater, an alcoholic and a man who could spew terrible words of anger and frustration from his mouth. I have awareness, understanding, acceptance and forgiveness . . .

ICED COFFEE

All My Life

MY GRANDMOTHER ON MY MOTHER'S side, I call her NaNa. She didn't want to be referred to in any form of grandmother. She felt that doing so made her sound old to herself which is something she was never ready for. My NaNa wanted to be and to stay young. She actually was young at heart most all of her life, full of energy, young at heart with desires of the flesh, drinking, card games, gambling, much younger men and more.

After my grandfather Mimi died, my NaNa recreated herself from an attractive well-kept society type lady who wore pastel colored shirt dresses and worked in her rose garden to a done-up fashion conscious woman who wore black fishnet stockings, high heels and short dresses. She went on cruises, played in bridge tournaments. Her level was that of master. She dated much younger men. She told me that men her age were way too old for her. She was never the 'traditional grandmother'. She drank Scotch and could drink most people under the table including my dad. She was always ahead of her time and she often confided in me that she would have preferred having a career rather than be a mother or to be married. She told me that she never wanted to have children but did as society dictated to do in that day. She grew up indulged and spoiled by her doting father who owned a bank and a Mercantile store among other businesses in the small Southern town where they lived. Her father taught her to drive at the age of thirteen and bought her a Cadillac as her first car. She graduated from college at the age of sixteen. Her father believed that education was of utmost importance. He made her and her sister go to summer school every year. Her sister, my great aunt Sarah attended Smith College. She was a beautiful, kind-hearted woman and was an artist.

My grandmother was a wild, fun flapper chick. Her dad, my great grandfather was successful and generous to all. I remember him as a man with a warm smile and a twinkle in his eye. He would walk home from his bank and ask people along the way to come home for dinner. He made sure his wife my great grandmother prepared enough food for many. When a young man just getting out of the service, could not come up with the down payment for their first house, he would reach into his pocket to help them with it. My grandmother adored her father and of what I recall of him. I can understand why. I recall him as always being happy actually full of joy and kindness with a smile on his face and a twinkle in his eye.

My grandmother taught me to play cards. I would sit on NaNa's bed playing cards for hours. She was always sipping iced coffee and sometimes, she would give me a sip. She put milk and sugar in it, so it was refreshing and tasty. We played for a penny a point. If I won, she paid me. If she won I would have to help her clean up the kitchen. I didn't mind. I liked to help her. So playing cards with NaNa was a win, win. She kept her bedroom very cold in the hot summer and I loved it. We are the same that way. We liked to be in cold-cold air conditioning.

Even though she was not the mothering type, she gave me a great gift of my childhood. She always made me feel special. By her words, she stated to me every time that I spoke with her that I was special, that she loved me. I was her favorite, how beautiful, smart, talented, wonderful and incredible I am. She thought I looked like Elizabeth Taylor. That is when Elizabeth Taylor was the young actress in the movie, 'National Velvet'. She made me feel great, accepted, cherished, and understood. She did not criticize me. She loved me unconditionally. At the time, the only unconditional love that I had as a child. We talked, laughed and shared while we played cards. She told me about her life growing up, about her boyfriends, lovers, experiences both good and bad. She confided in me. She was wilder than I could ever imagine myself being. She made life exciting.

I could talk to her and tell her about anything and everything and she would listen. She never discouraged me. She accepted me for being myself. She thought I was wonderful and I felt this just being around her. I can hear her words to me and they will be in my heart forever.

When she wasn't travelling, she enjoyed lying in bed in her deep freeze of a bedroom watching TV. I am like her to some extent in that regard.

Once when NaNa was visiting my family, she and I were sitting in the kitchen. I shared with her that I had an abortion and that it haunted me that I did. I had never told anyone in my family or my immediate world that I had done this sin. NaNa shared with me that she also had an abortion before she married my grandfather. That she was dating a guy, got pregnant, didn't want to marry him and for sure did not want the baby. She told me that she never really wanted children ever. Just as she was telling all this, my mother walked into the kitchen.

My mother screeched, "Mother, why do you tell Natalie everything and me nothing?"

NaNa and I just stared at one another. My mother went on ranting and raving which was unusual for her.

NaNa said, "Calm down. I can talk to Natalie because she understands and you don't. What are we having for lunch? Are we going out? I would like to go out."

Mother answers. "No! We are staying here and I am making egg salad sandwiches."

NaNa responds, "I hate egg salad."

My mother states, "Well, too bad because that's what I am making!" She begins the preparation.

I observe. It's clear my mother is jealous of my NaNa and I being so close and I don't care. My mother is cold and angry. I can't talk to her—no one can.

NaNa winks at me as I say, "I am going home, Mom. See you later, NaNa."

NaNa antagonizes, "Don't you want to stay and have egg salad sandwiches with us?"

I am in the utility room, out of view of mother as I playfully grimace at NaNa who is looking directly at me, "No thanks, I need to be on my way!" I was a grown-up with my own house and I couldn't wait to exit my parents'.

My NaNa was fun. My mother was a bore. As I drove away, I pondered, 'NaNa had the guts to have an abortion, way back when it was dangerous and illegal. Whoa! She continually amazes me with her life experiences and stories.'

She confided to me years ago that when she was a young wife that she accidently killed a young child who darted out from between parked cars in front of her car. It was a complete accident and my grandmother said it tormented her for years. She never got over it and probably never will.

She confessed to me on several occasions that she didn't think God loved her and that he was punishing her. She didn't tell me why she thought this way, only that this was how she felt. Sometimes I felt the same way, so I understood her feeling the way that she did. Perhaps, that is why she drank so much Scotch and did escape activities, such as sex, gambling, card games and watching TV. But at the same time, she appeared to be self-aware and honest—at times, brutally honest as I am.

She gave me the gift of unconditional love and acceptance. She was fun to be around, interesting and very intelligent to talk with. I loved her deeply even though she was not the best role model in many regards, but she was so, in many others. She had a vibrant 'live life to the fullest' attitude.

She told me that when she could no longer drive her Cadillac that she felt her life was over. She died at the age of ninety-seven. Her nurse left her room to get her morning coffee and when she returned my NaNa was dead.

I had given NaNa a little cloth angel that she kept by her beside and now I have that angel near my bedside and will as long as I am alive.

I don't know if she felt right with God when she died but I do know God forgave her. My NaNa was alive and lived life to the fullest. She was a complex, interesting, adventurous woman with a good heart. She was honest and self-reflective and when I think of her, my heart fills with love, amusement and enjoyment. She creates a smile in my heart. She was certainly not a perfect wife, mother or grandmother but she was fabulous in her own way—selfish, caring, Scotch drinker, iced coffee drinking, rose tending, always Cadillac driving, bridge player, shrimp eater, travelling, fishnet hose wearing NaNa!

I love to sip iced coffee sitting in bed with the AC freezing cold watching TV, and I often think of NaNa while doing so. Actually, I prefer writing while sipping iced coffee or prefer working out to watching TV.

God loves and forgives, you only need to ask.

WITCH BOOK

Early Twenties

IN MY SECOND YEAR OF college, I came home from the University, where I first attended and was taking classes at a local University and living at my parents' house. They had moved to a new house just a few years earlier. It was a show house in our town. It sat on a hill. It was sprawling and on one floor.

During this time, I read everything about anything I could get my hands on. I was a voracious reader. I ordered books, one after another, and would have a stack of them by my bedside in varying degrees of consumption.

One night while asleep—I think, I was asleep because it was in the middle of the night and I felt as if I was paralyzed when a dark entity appeared. I felt a frightening evil energy and my eyes turned towards the sliding glass doors. The drapes were drawn in my large bedroom and a dark shadow like image was in front of them. I was frozen as if paralyzed and could not move one muscle. I tried to scream but couldn't. I felt intense fear into a depth that I have never felt before or since. As fast as it came, just as quickly it was gone. I have never forgotten that image and I can still feel the fear when I think back to that night. It prompted me to read everything I could about spiritual things, evil things and entities, from evil witches, to curses, terrestrials and everything else.

I ordered one book about 'witches throughout history' and delved into it. There were photos and words in the book about curses, rituals, and evil that made me physically ill to read and to view. It was as if the energy from the book jumped out at me and it made me feel deeply sick into my gut, even what felt like into my soul. I always feel everything in my gut. That is where I process energy.

I recall sleeping extremely late one day after reading that book the night before then walking into my family's kitchen. I felt so nauseated and sick from the words and images in that book that I could barely stand up or eat. It was the strangest kind of feeling. It was as if it had permeated into my very being. I had never felt this level of dread, sickness and ill-will. I was rail thin at that time and needed to eat but I couldn't. The thought of food made me gag. It was like I wanted to throw up but had nothing in my stomach to do so. I knew it was the energy in and from that book that was affecting me in this manner. It had come out of the book and entered me. I felt haunted and depressed on a level I can't even explain. I felt evil intent in and from that book—an energy that enjoyed and thrived on harm and destruction.

I sat in the kitchen sipping water as I pondered why I felt so hideous. I knew that I had to get rid of that book. I quickly got the book and threw it with all my strength into the trash can outside. As I did, I strongly rebuked the energy in the book in the name of God, "Get out of me and my life in the name of God! I am a child of God and in the name of Jesus Christ, you can't have me!" I actually didn't realize at the time, what I was saying. The words I said just came to me. I was determined as I could be, to deny that book, its energy and any power it had over me.

After doing this, I felt immediately better. I showered, ate and felt normal again. This experience was part of my process of learning about energy and how and where it affected me and how it can come from anywhere, an object, person or place.

I never understood what it was that I felt that night in my room. But the house my parents' lived in, while beautiful and elegant made me, whenever I was in it, feel ill most of the time. I never liked being there. I felt like I couldn't fully breathe while being there. The energy in it was heavy and dark. My Dad had sold his company and retired soon after moving there. Mostly what my parents did was drink, go out to dinner and watch TV. My mother smoked and I detest smoking. The smell of it nauseated me. There was no life in that house and when I lived there or went to visit, I never felt comfortable and was always happy to leave.

I only lived in that house a few years before I got married and moved away. I like houses with light colors, bright rooms, mirrors and to feel light and full of life. I spent as little time as possible in that house of my parents'. I was always relieved and happy to walk out the door.

Only one time during a divorce, I stayed a week at my parents' house. I was feeling lost and depressed. I needed to connect with my parents and family. I enjoyed snuggling in my old room and being in that house around my parents, sisters and niece. I let myself relax into it. I didn't want to go back home after my visit was over. I had merged with the heavy energy in that house and with my most always depressed alcoholic parents. It took mustering inner strength to leave after wallowing in that energy. You see, I was depressed at the time, so my energy merged in that time frame with my parents' and that of the house. After I left, I realized how much better I felt to not be there. I realized that when you are depressed, you can be taken over by similar energy and it builds upon itself. This was wise information that I gleaned as I realized how insidious depressive energy can be. It attaches and can suck you right into it. I would have sunken to the lowest of low had I stayed any longer on that visit. I can't live in or be around negative energy.

I am very sensitive to energy. Even to this day, I can see a certain horror movie and the impression of it will enter me momentarily. And I will need to consciously throw that energy away just as I did with that witch book. The older I get, the less I can even stand images like such as that. Although some of it, is a lesson in the display of evil and it's interesting to observe, if one keeps it outside their energy field. Evil is insidious and seductive and it can arrive in what appears an innocent way or even a beautiful, comforting or interesting way. At first, it may appear good as in a beautiful house or engaging person to lure you in.

I have entered places; such as houses, public places, been around people or even entered a room and immediately knew that I did not want to be there because something felt wrong. It felt negative, off and perhaps even evil. Places carry the energy of the people who resided or live there. Places can take on the energy of depression, unhappiness feelings of loss, angst, addictions and evil. It's all about the energy.

Our minds and our energy field can be permeated by words and images that stimulate thoughts either negative or positive and repetition of it can create and change a person's thought processes and even their field of energy. Evil can attach to us, to things in this world and reside in the energy field.

This is why the media and continual advertising are so powerful and can be used so effectively and often—as in politics. Evil knows the human mind can be imprinted upon and so uses this. So that is why it's important to keep positive images, positive thoughts and words as food for your soul. Some people are so impressionable that they can watch a television show and think that it's the way to live. Watch a commercial and have the need to buy whatever it's promoting or selling.

Haven't you ever entered a place and felt comfortable then entered another place and felt instantly uncomfortable? It's energy coming at you either for good or ill.

It's wise to honor your knowing, intuition and feelings and get away from negativity and strive to be with people where the energy is positive.

MOTHER SAID!

Early twenties

ENTERING THE HOUSE JUST BACK from college classes, I turned the corner to go into the hallway leading to my room, only to meet Tammy face to face coming out of my parent's bedroom.

Tammy glared then stated, "While you were gone, we asked mother who she thought was the prettiest. Who has the best and prettiest parts of their body and Mother said that you do on most all of them!"

I continued walking towards my room. Tammy always gave me the creeps. I never liked being around her much less to be alone with her, but she followed me, screaming, "So see, Mother said you have the best body parts. Mother thinks you are the prettiest!"

Entering my room, I turned to Tammy, "Well, that sounds very strange because she never tells me that I'm pretty. I actually thought she thinks I'm ugly."

Tammy glared in her usual smirk of hate expression then said sarcastically, "Well she doesn't. She thinks you have the best back—best eyebrows—best face shape—cutest figure—prettiest hands—best legs—best hair and the best everything! We asked her about each of our body parts and this is what she answered. Your body parts are the ones, she thinks are the best and the prettiest!"

"You're being silly. Now how about getting out of my room and leaving me alone." As I thought to myself, 'Bizarre, why would mother say things like this to my little sisters? At the same time, it made me feel good to hear that she thought me pretty, since I thought Mother thought me ugly. I thought mother hates me and doesn't like anything about me.'

Tammy taunts as she walks out of my room headed to her room. "Mother thinks you are the prettiest! Daddy loves you the most! I hate your guts!"

I thought, 'Good grief!' I shouted, "Mother doesn't think I'm the prettiest. You are crazy! Now leave me alone. I need to study!"

Tammy screamed from her room. "Just ask Dana and Jeannie, we all asked her and this is what she said! Just ask them!"

"Okay, fine! Now, please be quiet!"

I couldn't stand being around Tammy and avoided her as much as possible. She was like some evil witch, from everything I had observed of her growing up. I didn't trust her. She was always lying, crying and manipulating. If she got into trouble, she would blame others, causing more trouble and causing one of us to get into trouble instead of her.

I didn't believe mother said this about me. Later that night, I went into Jeannie's room and asked, "Did you ask mother who had the prettiest body parts?" She nods sadly.

"Why would you do that?"

She shrugs. Jeannie is the youngest is fairly quiet and a bit overweight but she has beautiful long straight brown hair. I have nothing in common with her, always felt sorry for her, tried to be kind to her but she was usually hateful to me. So eventually I steered clear of her. She answers with a blank face, "Tammy started it. We sat on Mom's bed and asked her questions. She said that you have everything the prettiest."

"That is stupid and silly. Mother didn't say that!"

"It's true and it's what Mother said."

"Well, I don't believe it!"

Jeannie is sitting in her bed writing in her diary or some such. I sat down at the foot of her bed. As I watched her, I felt sorry for her. I felt sorry for all of my younger sisters. I loved them, but didn't like them and got really tired of dealing with them. "Jeannie, we all have pretty things about us. Look at your beautiful hair. I wish I had hair like yours. Mine is curly and terrible." Her face brightens momentarily then she shouts. "But it's true. That's what mother said!"

Next I went into mother's room. She's sitting on her bed glued to the TV. "Mother, why did you tell the girls that I have the most pretty body parts?"

Mother looked up from her TV program and stared blankly at

me. "What? I don't know what you are talking about. Well, maybe I did." She shrugs, "I really don't recall. They were asking me all sorts of questions about which one of you is the prettiest, which had the prettiest hair, skin, so on and so forth. Tammy was doing most of the asking."

She was in her usual fog but I persisted, "Why would you tell my little sisters something like that?"

She stares blankly, "Well they asked." She shrugs. Then she goes back to watching her program on TV.

I observed her for a moment as she escaped back into her TV fog. Then I go back to my room.

As I think back, my mother was clueless. My poor sisters, what kind of a mother would ever answer questions such as they were asking? She was probably watching some TV program and barely listening to what they were asking. They were trying to get attention, trying to be noticed to feel cared for and her answers only hurt them. It makes me want to cry. I always felt so sorry for my little sisters. I both loved and hated them. I most always felt they hated me, especially Tammy. I tried to be kind to them, to protect them, to help them and all they ever did was to try to make my life miserable. Now after what mother told them, they will only hate me more.

Looking back at that day, literally makes my stomach hurt. I am in college, dating, happy and trying to live my life. And I continually had to deal with my sisters, along with my mother and my father. I wanted to get away from that house more than anything.

During the time I was looking for a wedding dress, I would bring home veils and dresses from the carriage trade shop where I worked. One day, I showed mother some of the veils, I was considering. I would try one on after another to show her but she would barely take her eyes off the TV to look at me. I came out wearing the one that I liked the most.

In excitement and anticipation, "Okay Mom, do you like this one?" Mother turned from the TV as if I was bothering her and shrugs. "It's okay."

"Mom, I really like this one! Do you think it looks good on me?"

She answers, "It's alright but nothing special."

I persist. "Really, don't you like it on me? The ladies at the shop think this is the one. They love it on me. They think I look beautiful in it."

She turns from the TV to look at me. "I think it looks ugly. You look ugly. You are ugly."

Hearing my mother say these words was like a knife into my heart. I am trying on wedding veils and she tells me that I look ugly even that I am ugly. I instantly exit the library and go into my room. I look at myself in a mirror wearing the veil that I like the most and that the ladies at the shop love on me. I thought I look good in the veil. It suits me. This is the one I will choose.

I wore that veil and loved it. I received many compliments from others but not from my mother. I will never forget what it felt like to hear my own mother say what she did. That I looked ugly in the wedding veil I had selected. I pretty much ignored my mother at my wedding because of her statements. Most mothers enjoy the process of their daughter's selection of wedding dress and veil, but mine could care less. She didn't want to be bothered and thought I was ugly to boot.

As an adult, I am aware and understand that my mother was mentally ill. We had to pretend she was 'okay and normal', but she not was okay and certainly wasn't normal. Something was so off with her that it was off the chart bizarre, but she 'appeared' normal. She was attractive, well-kept and married to a successful man. Therefore she appeared to have it together. Even though I knew better, I expected her to act 'normal' and was for some reason was surprised and hurt when she didn't. My Mother was never okay. She had a prefrontal lobotomy when I was two years old. I felt most all my life that she hated me, except for a very few moments of closeness.

Mother was unstable and deeply insecure. Insecure people rarely give compliments to others because they are too insecure to do so. My mother was a critical person. She criticized everything and complained a lot. She noticed the negative instead of the positive. She was full of negativity and depression. Positive people focus on the positive aspects in others. Negative people focus on the negative.

At first glance by my mother's expression and behavior, one might

think that she was cold, aloof and arrogant. Others thought her kind. I think that is because she has quiet Southern manners. She talked little and rarely if ever argued or voiced a strong opinion. People who weren't around her much thought what a nice pleasant woman. Truth was she wasn't fully in her mind and certainly not her emotions. That day when she told me I was ugly when I showed her my wedding veil, was one of the most emphatic opinions I had ever heard her express. I always suspected but later knew for certain that my mother was jealous of me. She was more against me than for me. She could be very hateful and cruel.

Later in life, I was told by my father and some women that were friends of my parents that my mother didn't want me to get a big head. Apparently when these friends would complement me to mother, she would tell them not to tell me. And she would not pass the kind words onto me. Had I heard more kind words and compliments, it would have helped my self-esteem. It wouldn't have given me a 'big head'.

My mother was a kill joy. Anytime, I was happy or excited, she would kill my joy. There are other people in the world like this who aren't necessarily mentally ill. They are just negative, depressed and unhappy people. They get jealous or envious of others or can't stand it when someone is happy, if someone seems to have more than they do or who is enjoying their life. Therefore they say or do something to kill their joy.

My father provided materialistically everything a woman could ever want or have and my mother was never happy. She never acted excited about anything. When Dad sold his company, he wanted to take a trip to Europe and mother said that she couldn't go because she would miss her hair appointment. Dad was so frustrated that he said, "Hell, bring the hairdresser with us!" And he would have done so, had mother wanted to. Mother really never desired or wanted anything but to drink and watch TV. She didn't even enjoy eating. I never heard her say, 'This tastes great. I love this!' or anything of the kind. She started drinking when we were older. She actually didn't drink much when we were little, except when Dad and she went out. But when we were more grown up and on our own at five o'clock there was a glass of wine in her hand. There she would be sitting in the library drinking and watching TV. Mom and dad did eventually go to Europe and many other places but Dad had to insist and prod her to do so. Most other women would have been ecstatic to be able to do and to have all that my mother did.

One evening as usual, Mom was dressed to go out to dinner. Dad was in the library watching TV. Mom walked into the bar to pour them each a glass of wine. Instead she returned to the library passing it by and as she did telling Dad that she had a headache and needed to lie down. She went into their bedroom. In a bit, Dad went in to check on her. She told him, "I have never felt this bad. My head hurts. My stomach hurts." She pulled the covers up over herself, laid her head on her pillow and never became conscious again. She had a stroke. My Mom died preparing to do her two favorite things—dressed to go out to dinner with my dad and drink wine with him.

I see my Mom in full awareness and that she was not a mentally and emotionally well person. She had been emotionally maimed by doctors. It was not her fault or was it just as it was to be? I don't know and never will, until I am reunited with her in Heaven. On Earth, it was as it was. She was doing the best that she could with what was left of her brain after the lobotomy surgery. And I was doing the best that I could to have her as a mother.

I accept where God placed me on earth and understand that we were all doing the best that we could with what we were given and where we found ourselves. I forgive my mother.

I know that she loved me in the only and best way that she knew with what she had to deal with in her marred mind.

THE GIRL ON THE TRAIN

Before I existed then most of my life

A S A YOUNG MAN, DAD was riding on a train with some of his buddies. He noticed a young, beautiful, vivacious upscale girl with dark hair, olive skin and brown eyes traveling with her mother. He is instantly smitten by this girl and proclaims to his buddies, "That's the girl I am going to marry."

His friends laughed at his proclamation and responded, "No girl like that would pay attention to a guy like you!"

Dad responds, "Just watch me."

Dad pursued my Mom for years. He was from the so-called 'wrong side of the tracks' while my mother lived in a large house in the most upscale area.

Dad went into the Navy and my mother attended Stephens College. Dad asked for Mom's hand in marriage three times and finally the third time, her father granted him his blessing. Dad would tease or was it really teasing or perhaps wishful thinking, "If only, I hadn't asked that third time."

The beautiful girl and the sailor just out of the Navy married in a ceremony in the living room of the bride's parents.

My mother was silly, spoiled, beautiful and joyful. Dad was tall, dark, handsome and full of ambition with an intense appetite for success. He knew the moment that he laid eyes on my mother that she was the girl for him. It was love at first site. Dad usually got what he wanted.

My Dad took home movies of my Mother just after they were married as she was at the helm of a motor boat that he had bought. She was laughing, making faces at my Dad, being silly and having a good time. She appeared a fun person. This was the only glimpse that I had of what my mother was like before she was forever changed.

When my mother was a little girl, she was referred to as the 'Song bird of the South' in the local newspapers. She starred in dance recitals and articles about her were often in the newspapers. She tapped danced on her grandfather's counters in his mercantile store. Her mother treated her like a little doll dressing her up in all sorts of cute little costumes.

I have Mother's dance book filled with pictures and newspaper clippings beginning before she was two-years-old until about thirteen years of age. When she was a toddler, she looked like a gorgeous little butter ball child full of happiness and fun. As she grew, she was still pretty but a lost sad and lonely look appeared in her eyes. There is a photo of my mother about age thirteen where she looks like a lonely little princess wearing a beautiful dress with eyes full of sadness. I used to study these photos to try and see who my mother once was, to try and understand her and to try to figure out what had happened to her.

From what I have been told, her mother played the card game Bridge every day and pretty much ignored my mother, except for when she was showing off her dancing efforts and dressing her up like a doll. Her mother would take her to her Bridge games and have her sit still as long as she was there. When my mother was a little girl, her parents partied a lot. Her father worked lots to make a living and became very successful. Her mother apparently played Bridge daily. My mother was an only child until she was thirteen. Her mother as the story goes didn't really want to have any children but there was no birth control in those days. NaNa was focused more on having fun instead of the emotional and physical needs of a child. My mother finished high school, went off to a girl's college for two years then married my father. I was born three years later. One year after I was born, Mother had a nervous breakdown and was given a prefrontal lobotomy by Dr. Walter Freeman.

Walter Freeman is known as the father of the lobotomy, an infamous procedure that involved hammering an ice pick-like instrument into a patient's brain through their eye socket. The horrifying procedure often left patients in a vegetative state and is responsible for an estimated 490 deaths. I believe he did this procedure on one of the Kennedy children, the actress Frances Farmer and on my mother— among others. My mother is considered to be a success of this barbaric procedure because she went onto have three more children and to be a housewife.

Dr. Freeman came to visit my family when I was in junior high school. He stayed in my room and I slept in the playroom. I stared at this man who cut into my mother's brain and made her something different then she was born to be. He looked through my books in my room - one of which was, 'The Winter of Our Discontent' by Steinbeck. He commented that I must be a very intelligent girl to read a book such as this at my age. He was going around visiting what he considered his lobotomy success cases. He travelled in a beige Winnebago. Soon after that he died.

I recall standing at our dining room window and watching as he drove out of our driveway. He gave me the creeps.

After Mother died, I got the photos and records from George Washington University hospital of my mother before, during and after she was given this procedure. When I saw them, I felt a pain and horror that I cannot fully express. I could barely breathe and I immediately went to seek counsel with a minister whom I talked with at times. I cried uncontrollably. He, of course had no answers. Just that, perhaps had this procedure not been done that she might have been in a mental institution for the rest of her life which was the same answer my Father always gave. Then he said, "Some things that happen on earth, we will not fully understand until we can ask God."

After that procedure as lives go, Mother had a good one. She had three more children, housekeepers, beautiful homes, classy cars— all the clothes, jewelry, trips, out-to-dinners, etc. that anyone could want. But my mother never wanted much of anything, but to drink, smoke, play cards and be left alone. She hated to cook, although she was a good cook.

She did enjoy dancing with my dad and they danced well together. She liked 'Big Band Music'. A joyful memory is when Mom and Dad would play the music they liked and would dance in our living room. All four of us little girls would dance with and around them. Then Dad would take turns dancing with us.

Dad took care of Mother very well for the rest of her life. He did love her and never left her. Many men would have exited that terrible situation as fast as they could, but Dad honored his commitment to her and to their love.

The young man who saw that lovely girl on the train did attain her as his wife and loved her for the rest of her life in sickness, in health and for always.

My awareness is—it was what it was. I had no control over it. I was placed in it to live it out. My understanding is that everyone did the best that they could under the circumstances. I have come to accept this. I forgive all concerned. Everyone thought that they were doing what was right and best at the time.

My mother escaped into mental illness and the fullness of her was taken from me forever. I needed her. I needed a mother.

Was what happened to my Mother, perhaps to show and teach me to never lose my feelings and emotions—to forever hold onto what she lost?

I AM A MURDERER!

In my thirties

WHEN I WAS IN HIGH school, I didn't know what an abortion was. Only the sleaziest of girls went 'all the way'. I didn't know of, or ever even heard of a girl getting pregnant. If one did, it was hidden and taken care of by her family to an outcome that they alone reached and it was done in private.

I didn't have my first 'French Kiss' until the night of my high school prom. The first man that I 'went all the way' with, we were engaged and got married. As an adult, I can look back and know that I missed nothing by not having sex at a young age. In that area, I was able to be a child, instead of pretending or playing at being grown-up.

When I was in college, one of my best girlfriends from high school got pregnant by her longtime boyfriend and I was appalled to hear it. No one that I knew of got pregnant before they got married. This couple quickly married because to have a child out of wedlock just wasn't done. It was shameful to everyone concerned.

I dealt with the issues of sexuality as an adult and even then they were at times very difficult. In my thirties, I got pregnant. The man and I were in love, but I wasn't out of my first marriage even though we had been separated for years. My ex-husband dragged it out and forced it to court. My first marriage had ended in complete embarrassment and scandal and the whole town knew about it. It would have added more shame for my family and me if I was pregnant, not being completely divorced and not married. The man I loved and I, couldn't get married, until three months after my divorce was final and it was not even as of yet final. So for the sake of image, we killed our baby.

The man I was dating told me that he would do whatever I wanted to do in this regard. We were planning on getting married anyway, but after much discussion, we opted for abortion.

It was the most difficult decision that I have ever made in my life. I changed my mind several times before actually having the abortion. Even as I was getting out of the car to enter the medical facility, he and I were still discussing it. One of my thought processes in deciding to have an abortion was that it must be okay because others were doing it. Then there was 'Roe versus Wade', a ruling that deemed it okay to abort a baby. This created distorted thinking in me to think that if the government said it was okay then it must be okay. As if having an abortion and killing a child, had a government stamp of approval. Therefore even though in my heart and soul, I knew it was wrong. I made the difficult and horrendous decision to kill our baby. Even as they were putting me under anesthesia, I was protesting in my heart. The doctor feeling my angst said, "Relax, it will be over soon."

I went to court to testify in my divorce on Monday of that week, which was eventually awarded to me on extreme mental cruelty in a no-fault divorce state. Then on Friday of that same week, I had an abortion.

That doctor performing the abortion was incorrect. It was never over. I suffered emotionally for years because of this decision. The man and I married the following year, but our having made the abortion decision, irreparably harmed our relationship. I couldn't get past it and he wanted to forget it. He did suffer but he didn't want to think, talk about it or to deal with his emotions. I needed to deal with mine. I would have intense crying spells concerning this decision. I felt tormented in my heart. I prayed and asked God repeatedly for forgiveness, until I was finally able to put it into some sort of perspective. But I will never get over it and when I think of it, still to this day, I feel like crying. Abortion is murder. On my death bed, I will still be asking for God's forgiveness for this decision.

Many years later, I told my father about my having an abortion. I am not sure that he believed me or that it really sunk in. He just stared at me and said, "Of all my children, I wanted you to have grandchildren." Hearing him say this, of course made me feel worse than I already did, in some regards, but not in others. In some ways, I was glad that I didn't have children. I had such a horrible childhood in some ways that I didn't want a child to be brought into this world to suffer as I had. I wanted a child to be born into a marriage with a loving couple. I never felt that I had that.

These were my beliefs based on the imprints that I took in from my family of origin.

Children are gifts from God no matter how or where they enter the world. I believe that whatever circumstances a child enters into is theirs to break against, to heal from and is their opportunity to become more of who they are meant to be.

I don't want women that make the decision to have an abortion to have to sneak into some back alley and have it done by some hack or in less than sterile and safe circumstances. But at the same time, if having an abortion carried shame, it might curtail some from getting pregnant in the first place. That there is shame associated with getting pregnant out of wedlock.

Why is abortion a government issue? Shouldn't this most serious decision be made between a woman, her doctor, her family, those in her life who understand her situation and her God?

I believe in a woman's right to choose as there are circumstances in life and that of the unborn where an abortion might be the decision neede be made. I am not stating that abortion is the right thing to do, as this is not my place, nor is it the place of the government. It is deeply personal and a decision of seriousness that matches few others, as is also the decision to bring a child into the world.

There is a right or better way to live, such as a couple of mature age, fall in love, get engaged, marry, buy a house then when they are settled, financially responsible and secure in their relationship, have a child. This is actually the best/better/easier way. Sure there are many other ways, but when you do things 'right'—they have a better chance to turn out positive for all concerned.

When and how did abortions become such an ordinary and easy decision to make? Was it 'Roe versus Wade' that did it? But the woman that forced the decision concerning this ruling being made into law, has since changed her mind.

How did we as a country become so lax and promiscuous? Was it when the government started paying for unwed mothers and their issue? Is this when many decided that having a 'government baby' was the thing to do or even a 'lifestyle choice' that was desirable—that the 'government' be a child's father?

I was in my thirties when I had an abortion and even then I didn't realize how deeply that I would be affected for the rest of my life by this decision. So how in the world can a young person in high school, or even younger understand or have any idea about the importance or how profoundly deep a decision it is to have sex, get pregnant, choose to have an abortion or to bring a life into this world? You need to be able to provide and care for yourself before you bring a life into the world to be under your care and supervision.

Sex creates life. Human life is the most valuable creation there is. Life is the most valuable, important, precious and profound thing on our planet. Abortion is killing a growing human being. Abortion is killing a life.

My awareness is that I made the choices that I did, based on where I was at the time. I made a choice guided by shame and image. I made a decision that instinctively I knew was wrong, but based on the fact that the government deemed it okay. I went with the government's decision to kill an unborn child. Had I not had the government's blessing, I may not have had the abortion.

I understand all sides, mine, the father of the baby's, society and the governments. I accept the choice that I made and have lived with it ever since I made it. I forgive myself and all concerned and I turn it over to God.

THANKSGIVING

Mid-thirties

MY ENTIRE FAMILY IS SEATED around the table in the dining room. The table is filled with turkey and all the trimmings. Dad opened a special bottle of wine. It's a joyful family celebration. Before we begin eating, we go around the table and each one of us states what we are thankful for.

Then we dig into our Thanksgiving feast. One of us girls makes the suggestion that we reveal the worst thing that we did and got away with when we were living at home with our parents. That our parents didn't know about. After all, we were all living in our own homes now, so what could Mom and Dad do—ground us?

I don't recall which one suggested it or who went first or what anyone confessed to, but when it was my turn.

"When I was fifteen and had just gotten my driver's permit, it was a Friday night and Mom and Dad went out for the evening. I had a friend over spending the night and we were babysitting my little sisters. We watched movies popped popcorn then got bored and were looking for some excitement and adventure. It was a cold wintery night and there was a bit of snow and ice on the streets but even so, my friend and I decided that it would be fun to take the car out for a drive."

Mother gasps. "What? I don't believe you would even think to do such a thing!" She glances across the table at my Father.

He says, "Go on finish the story."

I continue. "Well believe it, mother. Because after we had done our usual Friday night fun, we were ready for some real adventure. So we talked about loading all the kids in the back seat of Dad's car then driving around the neighborhood." I glance at Mom and she shakes her head in disbelief.

I continue, "Really Mom!"

She replies. "I don't believe you. You are making this up just to shock us."

I continue, "No, I'm not. We talked about doing it. Changed our minds then we decided to go ahead and do it. The little girls jumped up and down and begged that we do. So we loaded all the kids wearing their pajamas into the backseat of Dad's car. I got behind the wheel. My friend sat shot gun and off we went. We went driving around the hills of our neighborhood in the dark when there was a bit of ice and snow on the streets. We drove around for a while just fine and it was fun. Then, in an instant we hit an ice patch and the car slid a bit off the road. I'm scared but everyone else thought it was fun and were squealing with excitement and laughter. One of the car's tires got stuck in some mud. I gunned the car and it didn't move. I am freaking out inside, but try not to show it. Now everyone else is, too. The little girls are screaming that they want to go home and they are cold. So I gun it again and thankfully, am able pull the car back out onto the street. I drive the car down to the end of the hill, turn around and head back up to our house. I pulled in the driveway and was very careful to park Dad's car in the exact place where it had been. Then we all get out with excitement and full of exhilaration at what we just did and run into the warm house with everyone exclaiming how much fun it was. Everyone promised not to tell you." I look at Mom and Dad. "And I guess no one did." I look into Mom's face, "And you and Dad never knew or suspected that we did that?"

Mother exclaims, "No and I don't believe that you did. You were too mindful and good. You were the most obedient child. You never would have done something like that and I don't believe that you did. You are just making this up to shock us. You were too good and responsible. You never would have done something like that!"

My sisters chime in. "Well, we did it!" It happened!"

Dad says, "Well son of a bitch! No! We sure didn't know!" He laughs, "You little devils! You are all grounded!"

And everyone laughed.

My awareness is that as a child, my mother always told me how bad I am and how I ruined everything. Now, when I confessed to something I did that was dangerous, irresponsible and bad, she didn't believe me. Even said, I was making it up because I was too good and responsible. I was stunned, talk about confusing and conflicting messages.

Then I have awareness and understand how much both my parent's relied on me and had confidence in me. And I fulfilled what they expected of me on most every occasion. Therefore, when I confessed to a time that I didn't do as they expected, Mother didn't believe it.

The truth is that I was most always overly good and responsible. And Mother never told me or thanked me when I was being so. She just expected it of me. Thinking back to this makes me angry until I understand that because of my Mother's issues, I had to be just as I was, responsible and good. I was placed to be so.

But still it felt crazy and confusing and made me feel conflicted inside to hear my mother state that she did not believe it when I was confessing something bad that I did. It also made me realize just as I had thought that I was a kind, caring, good and an overly responsible child. I am proud that I was so, even though it wasn't fair that I carry such burden and responsibility as a child. Only doing so taught me much and prepared me for life.

A BIRTHDAY CELEBRATION

Big 40!

I AM SO EXCITED! IT'S MY birthday, my husband and I along with my family attend a dinner show at a local nightclub. I am tan, feel great, wearing a white skirt, peach silk blouse with strappy snakeskin Calvin Klein shoes. It's a beautiful evening. I feel and look fabulous and it's my big 40!

The entertainment at the nightclub is great. The food is, too. The nightclub is a place we frequent often. We know the owner and they take special care of us. My father spends lots of time and money there and we are a 'prominent' wealthy family in the town. There is a birthday cake with thirty-nine plus one candles and everyone sings Happy Birthday to me. We head back to Mom and Dad's house for the opening of my presents. My parents have, of course been drinking. I even had a glass of wine with my filet.

I sit on the white sofa surrounded by presents. I open them one by one. It's such a happy night. I had asked my Mom and Dad for a check, so I could purchase a fabulous piece of furniture that I so wanted.

I begin to open my presents. Everyone is talking, laughing and drinking. I notice Dad staring at one of my sisters with a serious and angry look on his face. Even as I notice this, I push it out of my mind. I so want to have a happy night and thus far it's going well. I pray to myself, 'Please God, let everything stay fun.' as I continue opening presents, thanking everyone and talking about how much I love everything.

I thank Dana for what she gave me. Immediately after I do, in a drunkenly slurred voice, Dad gruffly states, "Here we have Dana a mentally ill good for nothing. Then we have Tammy divorced from a nut job, left with three kids, then . . ."

I talk louder and so do my sisters, mother laughs to drown him out. We all try to ignore him hoping he will shut up.

"Dad, I am going to open the gift from you and Mom now."

He turns to me. "Okay baby. I hope you like it, but you already know what it is."

I quickly open my birthday card from my parent's and in it is a check to purchase the piece of furniture that I want. Happily I exclaim, "Thank you Mother and Dad! Yay! I'll go to the store tomorrow to get it."

Dad states gruffly, "Okay, you do that." Then he looks at Mother, "And over here, we have the woman who bottle butts around all day doing nothing." Everyone is getting tense. We can feel what is coming. He turns to Jeannie. "And this one is pregnant and her husband is a good for nothing SOB!"

I stand up. "Dad, it's my birthday. Stop saying these things to my sisters and mother. Stop it! You're ruining everything! You are ruining my birthday!"

He shuts up for a minute then turns to me. "I am not the one who ruins things. It's . . . all of them." He looks around the room, "They are losers!" One of my sisters begins to cry. I state, "Don't say another word about anyone, Dad or I'm leaving!"

But Dad continues in his drunken angry mood, tearing everyone down then starts in on me. "You aren't much better!"

With that I yell, "I am leaving!" I stand up as the gift I was opening falls to the floor. I rush to the front door as my husband quickly gathers up my presents.

Dad shouts, "Go on! Leave then!" I sarcastically shout back, "Thank you for a really great birthday! Then I slam the front door hard, go outside, get into our car and cry out in torment, "Why does he do things like this? I hate him! I hate him!"

My husband opens the back door of our Mercedes to put my gifts on the back seat as I state, "I don't even want those. I don't want anything! I hate all of them!"

He gets into the car and hands me the birthday card from my parents with the check in it. "Yes, you do want them and you will want this. Just relax. He will forget what he said tomorrow. You know how he gets."

I state, "I am sick of him and how he gets! Hurry! Let's get out of here!" He turns the car around and drives out the driveway.

I continue, "How can they stay in there and listen to him. Now that I am gone, they will turn on me and talk about me. They are all so messed up! How do they put up with it?"

My husband responds, "They put up with it because they don't know what else to do. They want his approval and his money. That Tammy is the worst. She kisses his butt every chance she can. She needs him to take care of her boys. She uses him like he was her kids' father."

"I see what Tammy does. She makes me sick. They all make me sick! Dad will forget what he said because he's so drunk! But I will never forget! He ruined my birthday and for what? Why did he say all those horrible things to my sisters? And they just take it! I hate him! I hate my whole family!"

This imprint of this night will stay with me for the rest of my life. My Dad ruined my 40th birthday celebration and he never apologized or said a word about it. It was as if he hated us all.

Dad would get very drunk at times and rant like he did that night.

He would attack everyone and usually I would be the one who stood up against the verbal assault in an attempt to protect my sisters or whoever his target was and sometimes it was even his friends. When he would get really drunk, you never knew where it might go or how it would end. On occasion I would be his target but even if I wasn't I was always collateral damage. When I was Dad's target, no one stood up for me or tried to divert it. They enjoyed it when I was yelled at. And my standing up for the others did no good and they did not appreciate it. In fact, it backfired on me. I eventually became the family scapegoat. And they would even become angry at me when I would stand up to Dad in their defense and would then side with him against me when he turned on me as I protected them. They would do anything to stay out of the line of fire except to confront it directly. It was the height of craziness. Even when Dad would lay into Mom, I would defend her but she would never defend me.

I am aware and understand the dynamics. The dynamics were those of classic abuse survival. It was all about their self-protection on some convoluted level. They were too weak to confront it head on, so I became their shield, while at the same time they resented me for doing so and showing my strength. Dad and I could go face to face. I would get right in his face. I would tangle with him and the others would either hide their heads or placate him. I would state truth and confront him about his actions, behaviors and about how they harmed us and the others would placate and dance about the issues or hide in their rooms. I hated them for their weaknesses. And they hated me for my strength.

I know and understand that this is why Dad respected me and not the others. But it took many years before I became completely aware with understanding, acceptance and finally forgiveness. Dad liked to argue, it got his juices flowing. Mother didn't and neither do my sisters. They whine, cry, hide their heads in the sand and just take it. Tammy stands back watches and figures out how to manipulate situations for her benefit. I slam back or confront which got me lots of heat at times, but I couldn't live with myself were I not like I am.

I am the truth teller in the family and for doing so, I became the scapegoat. It hurt me for years enduring this, because it seemed so wrong and unfair. But now, I am proud of myself. Being the way I was/am concerning confronting abuse, it saved my life in more ways than one. I am strong and a fighter.

Also I realize and understand that part of my strength in confronting and standing up to Dad was the knowledge of how much he loved me. My sisters did not have the feeling of strength in Dad's love as I did/do. They were afraid of him and I never was. I could/would be exactly who I am and tell it like it is. Part of it is my nature to do so, but also part of it was the knowledge and the strength of my Dad's love for me. I knew no matter what, he would always love me deeply.

I recall my sister Tammy saying once when she was very drunk, "No matter what I do or accomplish, Dad will always love you the most." And it was/is true.

The next day, I went to the store and purchased the beautiful Burl wood secretary. Even with sadness in my heart, I acted excited in the store that I was able to purchase such a fine piece because it was a birthday gift from my parents. I pretended that I had a fabulous fortieth birthday. I talked about what we did, dinner, the entertainment, but of course, left out the dramatic abusive ending. The abuse and horror of my birthday was secret and unto our family, like all family secrets that eat away destructively at every individual hiding in them.

I still have this piece of furniture. I love it as a gift from my parents, but I also recall that night and what accompanied the birthday money given to me to purchase it. It stands in my house as a bizarre example of love/hate . . .

Now I am full of peace and happy to be away from my sisters and don't desire to interact with, or to see them again. I honor them in their individual struggles, their placement in our family and set them free. I choose to stay away from those who are toxic to my being. Some people are like clouds, when they go away, it's a brighter day.

I feel an incredible burden has been lifted from me. While I miss my Mother a bit and my Dad the most, I have relief that they are not here any longer. I carried so much of their burdens while they were on earth that it weighted me down my spirit and into my soul and now I am free! And truth is, this is what my Dad always wanted for me and that includes my ultimate Father in Heaven!

ANGELS WALK THROUGH ME

Early Forties—Alone In My Pain

WHEN I MET MY SECOND husband whom I loved dearly, he was an executive with an oil company. Oil crashed and he got into real-estate. It was exciting and a challenge dealing with life's changes together, but it was also a rough emotional ride. His partner in the oil business committed suicide. While we were dating, I got pregnant and had an abortion. This decision was the most difficult, worst and wrong of my life.

We sailed at the lake, partied and had a great time while we were dating. After my first marriage to Satan, I was ready and needing to have some fun and to cut loose a bit. I was also building my interior design business. After we married and life became real, his drinking became too much to handle. I sometimes enjoyed wine on the weekends, but not all week long. The party never stopped with him. He also smoked. I found myself married to a man who did things I hated and even was allergic to. Out of concern and respect for me, he did smoke in the garage but the nasty cigarette smoke still infiltrated our house. I had continual illnesses with respiratory issues. Adding to this, it was not unusual for him to lose his car and sleep on the sofa in his office.

One evening when I was helping one of my designers write up an order, while sitting at our dining room table, out of the corner of my eye, I spotted my drunken husband. He was wearing his GQ business suit crawling around the corner to the entry hall towards us with a drunken smirk on his face. I am sure in his drunken state he thought he was being cute or funny. Thankfully, I was the only one that saw this disgusting scene. It was continual drama and chaos because of his drinking. He promised to stop drinking—tried, failed then tried again and failed. Finally, I could not handle it any longer. I had him removed from the house by court order. To do this broke my heart. I divorced him to save myself, but I cried, cried and cried. Think Diane Keaton in 'Something's Gotta Give'—only ten times more. I sat on the floor of his closet with his perfectly lined up suits, just so many inches apart. Mr. GQ was emphatic that they be such and whaled in my suffering. I wrote notes of love and tucked them into the pockets of his suits. Even being in pain and suffering so intensely, I had the awareness that I was fortunate to be able to feel so deeply, to be sober in my spirit and have the ability to love deeply and to feel the loss of it.

I filed for divorce and during this time discovered that I needed emergency surgery to have my left ovary removed. I was frightened into the core of my being and wondered if this was punishment for my having had an abortion. What should have been a relatively uneventful operation turned into an ordeal. While removing the ovary, the physician cut an artery on my left side. I lost a very large amount of blood. He told me later that I had the worst case of endometriosis that he had ever seen and he didn't know how I lived so long with the pain. I had not signed a release to be given blood because it was during the time AIDS was being discovered in the blood reserves. And the doctor told me that I didn't need to ask my family to donate blood because the operation would not call for it. But it did. I lost a large amount of blood.

When I was in recovery, I came out of the anesthesia and in my state of grogginess commented to the nurse sitting beside my bed that I couldn't feel my legs. This prompted her to immediately get the doctor that operated on me who was also a longtime family friend. I looked up to see that my bed was surrounded by doctors. They were looking at my legs and checking my vitals. My doctor told me that my blood pressure was not building like it should be. He was worried that he might not have closed up the artery completely. He wanted to go back in. I asked where on my body he would go back in. He answered where we went in before. I placed my hand on my lower abdomen over the incision and had an intense knowing that if the doctor went back in that I might die. So I stated firmly, "No, I will be okay." My response concerned him greatly. They had one of my sisters and even the man I was divorcing trying to convince me to have another surgery. And my answer was, "No, I will be fine." Dad even inquired if he needed to call in specialists.

They rolled my bed to a quiet place in the recovery area. Even though, I felt a bit unsettled—I felt peaceful. I would go from sleep then wakefulness. A beautiful dark-headed nurse tapped me on the shoulder and said, "You do know that you will be fine, don't you? Just rest, I will take good care of you. My name is Natalie—like yours. I am the head nurse." She placed her face close to mine and I looked into her kind eyes. I felt deeply comforted speaking with her. I fell asleep and when I woke up. My blood pressure was normal. Everything was fine. So they wheeled my bed into my private room.

The next morning, I awakened to see my doctor sitting in the arm chair across from my bed staring at me. "Well, good morning. Dang! You gave us a scare!"

"I'm fine. I knew I would be."

He responds, "How did you know? I was worried. We all were."

"I just knew. And the head nurse Natalie- she really made me feel better. She's beautiful and has the same color hair as mine."

He replies, "Head nurse—named Natalie? I have been at this hospital for thirty some years. There is no head nurse named Natalie. I know everyone here."

I answer, "Really, well she talked to me and comforted me, then I was okay and recovering."

He shook his head as he glanced at me as if I was crazy. "You must have been dreaming." Then he checked me over to come to the conclusion that I was fine.

I knew I had not been dreaming and the beautiful head nurse named Natalie, had been there.

During my recovery at home, I was so weak because of the blood loss that I could barely walk across a room. I was used to being as fit as a fiddle ballet instructor with an excess of energy. Now, if went out for an ice cream cone, it exhausted me. I was weak, going through a divorce and so alone—so alone, so, so, so alone. My family paid me little attention. I think my parents visited me once during this ordeal. My mother complained when she needed to take me to the doctor for a follow-up visit, since I couldn't drive for a week or so. To them, I was even more of a failure—second divorce and now so weak I could barely move. They liked to drink and party, so I was just no fun for them to be around. They didn't like people who are sick.

One night I was lying in bed feeling as down as I had ever felt in my life—lost like never before—like a failure—too tired to work—looking liked death—thin, pale and weak. I felt worse than I looked. I was heartbroken and aching deep into my soul wondering what was to become of me. In my thirties—was I done for? Was my life over?

I don't recall if I was reading the Bible or had it lying on the bed near me. I was reading everything I could about spirituality. Books were stacked on the floor beside my bed and on my nightstand.

Resting back on my pillows, my heart felt as if it were breaking in two. It felt as if I was being deconstructed emotionally and physically—that everything in my life, including my emotions and body were being taken apart. Suddenly I felt a cool breeze enter directly and purposefully into the middle of my chest, near my heart, pass though my body and out my back. It was a strong breeze of intense love that filled me up in such comfort that I can't put it into words. Instantly, I felt renewed. I jumped up and searched to find from where this cool breeze might have come. No windows were open, no air conditioning was on. There was no place in the room from where this breeze could have derived.

I got back into bed feeling a bit perplexed but so much better. I felt relieved, comforted and my energy for life had re-emerged. As I rested back on my pillows, I had the innate knowing that the cool breeze was a message from God—my Angels—guides—something or someone of comfort letting me know that all will be okay. That they are with me and not only care but love me deeply, completely and fully. I rested back on my pillows in peace.

I then picked up my Bible and let it fall open to Psalm 27—'The Lord is my light and my salvation; whom shall I fear?' As I read the entire passage, the knowing of what had just occurred became anchored solidly into me. 'Know that no matter who forsakes you, know I am always with you.' It continued to sustain me through my aloneness and time of healing, even through to this day. I have the imprint of this memory as a comfort and a certain knowing that I am not alone. I turned my life over to God in that timeframe. I asked that he guide me for the rest of my life. I gave my life completely over to him

ITALIAN RESTAURANT

Adult

NEWLY DIVORCED AND STILL NOT completely recovered from surgery, I was feeling so alone and very down. My grandmother NaNa, was visiting my parent's. They were taking her to one of our family's favorite Italian restaurants. I decide to join them hoping for some comfort and nurturing. I so needed to be around my family to feel some sense of connection. It was usually fun when NaNa visited. None of my sisters were going, so I wouldn't have to deal with their noise and issues.

I followed the maître d' and as we approached the table, I could hear Mother's hideous drunken laughter. They were at the table already drinking and by the way they were behaving had been drinking long before they arrived, which filled me with a sense of dread.

Dad said, "Hi Tiger, I saved you the seat next to me. Let me pour you some wine."

"No thank you, iced tea is fine." As I took my seat, I noticed a couple sitting at a table just to my right and they looked over at me and smiled. I smiled in return.

Dad commented. "No wine? You are always such a stick in the mud. A glass of wine would do you some good and help you to relax." After Dad states this, Mother lets out one of her loud hideous drunken bursts of laughter. Dad was sitting at the seat by the wall. NaNa and Mother were across the table sitting beside one another. I am directly across from NaNa, on the inner seat near the other tables in the restaurant. I think to myself as I listen to their drunken bantering. 'Yeah, just get drunk all the time like you, Mother and NaNa—no thanks. I may feel bad but I still want to feel.'

The waiter approached and I ordered iced tea.

Dad asked, "What looks good to you, NaNa?"

She answered, "I don't know. I don't want much, just enough to fill my little spot."

Dad states, "Hell, back at the house, you complained that you were starving. So order something and eat all of it! I'm damned sick of hearing about your little spot."

NaNa always complained about being terribly hungry but after a couple of bites would stop eating. She drank instead. The older she got, the more she drank. Even though, she was a hoot. It made me disgusted to see her drunk.

"Hell, if you order it then eat it!" Then he turns to me and in a kinder voice, "What looks good to you, honey?"

"Spaghetti and meatballs is what I want."

Dad agrees, "That's what I am having too. Sure you don't want some wine?"

"No, thank you." I knew that alcoholics didn't like to be around someone who doesn't drink. They want everyone drinking—drinking and drinking. Along with this, my mother and NaNa smoked. I could smell it on their clothes. This was back when smoking was allowed in restaurants. It was difficult to eat surrounded by the smell of cigarettes.

Dad continues, "I don't see why you won't join us and have some wine."

NaNa chimes in, "Leave her alone, didn't you hear what she said? She said no thank you." Then she smiles at me, "Darlin', you have whatever it is you want to have."

NaNa and Dad begin arguing. Their voices get louder and louder. Mother says little, but every once in a while her hideous drunken laughter assaults my ears and she says, "Oh Momma", to something NaNa says. Along with her sporadic laughter mother would smoke. She would hold the cigarette down by her side after taking a puff because she knew I hated smoking and how it affected me.

Dad orders another bottle of wine while we have our salads. I hated being there with the drinking, smoking, arguing and the hideous inappropriate laughter. I pondered leaving but had already ordered. I didn't want Dad to yell at me. All of it was making me sick to my stomach. I was feeling even worse than I had felt when I first entered, if that was possible. My heart and soul were aching.

The main courses arrive. NaNa picks at her food. Dad notices and starts berating her for ordering something then barely touching it.

I keep eating my spaghetti and meatballs while hoping they finish quickly, so that I can leave. Thank God, I had my own car instead of riding with them like Dad suggested. They are getting drunker and louder. I feel like I could start crying but continue eating my dinner. All of a sudden, I knew I must leave the table or I would scream. So state cheerfully, "Excuse me I am off to the ladies' room. Be back in a minute." I stand then turn to pass the table to my right and behind me. The man at the table says, "Miss" and motions for me to come towards him, which I do. "Yes?"

He asks, "What are you doing having dinner with those people? Do you feel the need to punish yourself or what?" The lady with him smiles in concerned kindness at me. "You are a beautiful, lovely woman. Why are you putting up with them? They are disgusting drunks."

I am stunned to hear his comments and questions, embarrassed that he noticed the horror of my family. Then at the same time, it felt good to realize that someone else sees the horror of them. I respond, "Thank you, I am okay." He shakes his head. As I walk off, he said, "My advice is to get away from them and to stay away."

I stare at my reflection in the mirror of the Ladies' Room and sadly think, 'It is like I am being punished to be around my parents. It's like being in Hell."

When I pass by the couple on the way back to my parent's table they both smile kindly. While I wish that I could join them at their table and finish my dinner there, instead of where I was.

That evening was one of many that turned into a nightmare of drunkenness and arguing that I had to endure while trying, wanting and needing to connect to the people who are my parents. But there can be no real connection with alcoholics. Their connection is with alcohol and escaping their pain and issues. My Dad and NaNa argued lots. NaNa was selfish and could be very irritating, but she could also be kind and carry on interesting and intelligent conversations. My mother could do neither. Dad blamed NaNa for what happened to Mother. Dad blamed others instead of just realizing who mother was and her weaknesses. He had to find someone to blame for his wife being mentally ill.

I had been married to two alcoholics and attended Al-Anon meetings. I well knew that alcoholics didn't like to be around those that don't drink. But I kept going back to the place from where my pain derived to try and get what I would/could never get from them—acceptance and nurturing. They couldn't accept or nurture me because they couldn't accept or nurture themselves. I kept wishing and hoping they would change, but they didn't. They had little to give. They needed to drown their pain in order for them to survive, instead of facing the truth. Truth is my mother was extremely mentally ill. She drank to escape and my Dad drank to escape her. While NaNa could be a hoot; the older she got the more she drank and the fun exited.

I needed to become well-aware of these facts, understand it, accept it and forgive them and to stay away from them. What I wanted and needed, they didn't have to give and never would.

It took me many times before and after this Italian restaurant night to be able to finally keep the pain of whom and what they are outside of me. But, of course when I was going through a rough time, was when it was the most difficult to do. That is when I needed nurturing and would keep trying for it even in the place where none could be found. At times, Dad and NaNa gave me love and attention, but I never knew when it would be pleasant or a revisit to Hell. So for most of my life, I kept hoping for the best and instead mostly got the worst. That little bit of kindness and nurturing that I got on occasion kept me hooked into coming back and trying to get more. Mostly being around them made me feel like something was wrong with me and like that man at the restaurant asked, "Was I punishing myself or what?"

Another time, in a restaurant with my mom and dad, it got so bad that I walked outside to get away and to get some fresh air. Both our waiter and the hostess came out to see if I was okay. I recall the waiter commented, "I don't mean to pry, but I don't know how you stand it—being around those people. I have served them often and they are always like this. Let me know if there is anything I can do to help." I almost started crying while standing outside a restaurant with my drunken parents sitting at a table inside while our waiter tried to comfort me. Those people were my parents but who were they really?

Smoking—my parents both smoked. My dad eventually quit and after doing so, he hated mother's smoking as much as I did. I would beg her to stop and ask her to read about what it did to your body. She came back with, "It's one of the only things I enjoy in life and I am not going to quit! So shut up and stop talking about it."

As my life progressed and I become more aware, I steered clear of situations such as this. I moved out of state and saw my parent's rarely. I could barely stand to be around my mother—the older she got. And after she died, I saw my Dad a couple of times a year and my sisters rarely. As Dad aged, he got mellower and was verbally and emotionally affectionate with me—when it was just him and me alone out to dinner or talking at his house. In his later years, he must've done much self-refection and he stopped drinking almost completely. He had stopped smoking years ago and had tried to get mother to stop but her response was, "It's the only thing I enjoy in life."

For most of my life, I rarely drank after observing members of my family and ex-husbands—liquor pretty much disgusted me. Now I might drink wine with dinner. I enjoy the taste of wine as it accompanies food. It's fun to let go and allow myself to feel tipsy when I am with people I trust. When drinking, I have fun or feel sexy. Drinking wine doesn't make me angry or abusive.

SHOOTING AT LOGS IN A POND

Adult

I AM DIVORCED AND LIVING IN my house alone. I loved being alone in my house. But one night, late at night, while in bed I heard the fence gate at the side of the house squeak open. I jumped up and looked out the side windows of the house. I heard more noises. As I turned on the outside lights to the side of the yard, I dialed 911. I went back into my bedroom, closed the door and kept the 911 operator on the phone until the police arrived.

The police looked all over. No door or window was tampered with but when they came in from the back yard, they told me that the gate to the right of the house was open. There were footsteps on the side yard and in my backyard. They said that when I turned the outside lights on, it must have scared whoever it was away. I was freaked out. So I turned on all the outside lights to flood the yard and kept them on the rest of the night. The policemen inquired if I had a gun for protection. My answer was no. The police patrolled and watched my street and neighborhood for the rest of that night.

The next day, I called Dad to tell him what had occurred.

Dad said, "I'm going to pick you up. We are going to the ranch. You need to learn how to shoot a gun for your protection."

At our ranch, Dad drove the truck far out to a back pond where he showed me how to load and to shoot a gun. I practiced by aiming and shooting at logs in the pond. It was so fun! I found that I was a good shot. Dad was impressed. I loved practicing so much that I wore my dad out. I didn't want to stop. Dad sat in the truck while I stood nearby, shooting at log after log. Dad did place some beer cans on tree stumps for me to also practice on. But my favorite was to shoot the logs in the pond. I was able to hit my mark most every time.

I noticed that Dad looked at me in pride as I was having fun practicing my aim. Dad and I could have such a goodtime, just the two of us. We had much in common. We enjoyed learning, striving to master skills and new adventures. I loved the tomboy side of me and so did Dad.

Driving across our land back to the ranch house, "Well Tiger, from the looks of it, I'd say that you could hit someone dead on if they were coming at you. The best strategy is, if you hear someone in your house—get your gun, cock it, get down behind your bed, face and aim at the bedroom door. If you see someone at your door, shoot them in the legs. Immediately after, shoot them in the torso. Shoot to kill. If they are in your house and in your bedroom, they are there to hurt you, so hurt them first."

"But Dad, I don't know if I could really shoot at someone to hurt them—to kill them?"

"Hell Tiger, are you kidding? If someone is in your house and entering your bedroom, you shoot to kill. Do you hear me? It's either you or them by that point! And of course, call 911! But don't be weak and let someone get too close to you, so they can overpower you. You hear me? Shoot to kill!"

"Yes Dad, I understand."

"Here keep this gun, it's yours. Keep it beside your bed."

I respond, "Okay. Thank you."

Dad continues, "When we get back to the house, I will give you more ammunition for it. Keep it loaded, but with the safety on."

Dad spent time at length teaching and watching me load and unload the gun, taking the safety off and putting it on. I loved learning. Dad had many guns of all types both at our in town residence and at our ranch.

Knowing how and being able to shoot a gun, when and if I ever needed to protect myself gave me a secure feeling.

That is part of what a Dad does, teaches you to protect yourself physically. Thank you Dad!

Emotionally, Dad taught me some about how to protect myself but also left me open to be taken advantage of and to be overpowered. He didn't do this intentionally. He did it unknowingly. His way of relating to me taught me that I was above most others in the world, but not good enough for him which served to confuse and fracture me internally. At times, I felt better than others then my self-esteem would crash and I felt like I was not good enough.

When you don't feel good enough and not equal to others, you can flip from feeling better than others to not feeling good enough. This means you are not in balance and not feeling 'equal to'. It creates up and downs and insecurity at times, then over valuation at others—which is an imbalance in the belief system that leaves a person fractured internally. While they may appear outwardly arrogant at times, they feel weak and insecure at others. This is done to compensate for not feeling equal to others. And this is how my dad related and what he created in me.

Had he been aware, he would have taught me to protect myself emotionally as vigorously as he had taught me to protect myself physically. But did he really and fully know how to do this? He was passing down to me the way that he internally coped and it became imprinted—until I became aware that I am equal to all others, not better than or less than but equal to.

FEELING LEFT OUT WHERE I DIDN'T WANT TO BE

Adult

THE TOWN APPEARED EMPTY WITH very few cars on the streets. It was Christmas and I had nowhere to be. I got tired of being home alone, so I looked up a movie to go see. I felt so very much alone, aching and desolate in my soul and unhappy. I was divorced. All of my family was at my sister Tammy's house. She had not invited me. She never included me in celebrations for her sons, holidays or any events that were held at her house, even though I had allowed her to live with me and my new husband at a time, when she needed a place to be. In the past, I had also cared for and baby sat her sons often and gladly.

My dad would call and say, "Come on over!"

I would respond, "No, I was not invited." It would upset Dad terribly but he allowed Tammy to do this to me—to break up our family. I was not going to go to a house where I was not invited and be around a person who meant nothing but harm to me and had for all of her life.

This year was tough, I had been through a divorce and was recovering from a rough surgery and was still not feeling my physically strong self.

I had spent many holidays alone and not with my family. I wanted to be with them and then at the same time, did not. They drank lots. Mother smoked and laughed way too loud. Several would get drunk. Insults could be hurled. Arguments and snide looks from the arrogant and jealous Tammy—so on and so forth. So while I was lonely and alone, and wished I had a family to be with on Christmas. I didn't. I prayed to God that someday I would.

Sometimes it was better to be alone, lonely and feeling left out from where I didn't want to really be. Even though, my heart ached—terribly.

HOME MOVIES

All my life

WATCHING HOME MOVIES MADE FOR an entertaining family night. It was fun to watch all four of us little girls at varying times of our lives as we played, celebrated Easter wearing our pretty little pastel dresses, white socks with shiny new shoes. At Christmas with a room full of toys from Santa and presents galore that filled up the whole room. There were many happy family movies—birthday parties, riding our bicycles, playing on play equipment in our backyard, not to leave out jumping on our trampoline.

My sisters always got angry while watching the movies because there was more of me than there was of anyone else. I was the first one born and my Dad took movies of me continually. It was like I was their little doll. He even made one reel of a whole day in my life taken from the moment that I woke up until I went to sleep that night.

My sisters would complain, "We are tired of seeing Natalie. When do I come in? When will I be born?" I was the first born and as each child came after me, there were fewer movies. Until the last baby, I think there were just a couple. Dad became very busy building his business and with four children, didn't have as much time to take home movies.

It's also interesting even educational to watch the home movies. As I watched the ones taken when I was first born, the older and more aware I became, I studied the faces and feelings displayed. I became keenly aware of the expressions on Mother's face. I was a premature tiny thing with long skinny arms and legs. There is a home movie showing my Mother nursing me. My Grandmother and Aunts were visiting. As Dad scanned the room with the camera, it showed their faces happy and lit-up. Then he focused on Mom and me—a tiny, skinny baby nursing then he framed in on Mother's face. Mother's face had a faraway look in her eyes—more than just tired after giving birth, but dead, distant and empty as if she were just going through the motions with no real connection to the baby in her arms.

Watching this along with my realizations, made me feel sad along with becoming more aware, I could see no connection between her and me even though I was in her arms nursing. There was no love, happiness, energy or joy in Mother's face. Nope! No joy of becoming a mother could be seen in her. It also appeared to me as if the tiny baby was sucking up her Mother's sadness instead of receiving love and nurturing. This realization broke my heart. There was no life in my mother. My mother doesn't like life and would state this often. Everything about life was too much trouble in her eyes.

At first viewing, home movies can appear like a happy family enjoying their life, but much more can be seen if examined closely with awareness.

The stage is set—a sunny day in the backyard after Easter Sunday church with the director and producer continually heard off camera giving instructions, "Girls, show Daddy your Easter baskets. Tammy smile at Daddy and look in the direction of the camera." But this little actress doesn't take direction well. Tammy sits in a swing with her head down almost touching the ground then just when the cameraman about gives up, she looks up to flash a mischievous grin. Tammy and I swing higher and higher showing off for the camera with our skirts flying up in our faces, intent in our competition. I jump out of the swing and land perfectly on my feet. Tammy is too small to jump. She stares at me in jealousy and anger then she cries.

"Girls go stand by Mommy and smell the roses." The set is encased in a wire fence, first built to keep me from escaping blocks over which of course, didn't work. Now, it's adorned with pink, white and yellow roses that Daddy planted, tended to and of which he is proud. We gather around Mommy who is holding baby Jeannie in her arms. We twirl our skirts for the camera. Mother's a bit upset because the yard behind us has sheets hanging up to dry which detracts a bit from our perfect Easter movie setting. A backyard filled with roses and four little girls dressed in Easter attire holding colorful straw baskets full of bright green grass, pastel eggs and chocolate bunnies.

A bit later, there's a location and costume change. Now the four little actresses are barefoot wearing brightly colored shorts outfits. Three walk beside Mother up the driveway. The Director pans the camera up and down Mother's long tan legs surrounded by the commotion of little girls. I am helping Mother push the stroller that holds Jeannie as I am the only one tall enough to reach the handle. I place my hands next to Mother's. The camera pans down to find sweet little Dana with her thumb in her mouth and Tammy is acting the clown with arms and legs dancing trying to garner more camera attention than everyone else. We wave and smile as Daddy comes in for a close up of each one of our faces. Last scene is Jeannie smiling through drooling; her chubby cheeks framed by dark-straight-hair which prompted Daddy to call her 'his little Eskimo baby'.

What looked like a precious family and it was—oh, how it was, also revealed glimpses, if one was watching closely of the drama and ending that would eventually occur.

Five-year-old me helping Mother, three-year-old Tammy acting the clown to garner as much attention as possible, sweet Dana lost in all the commotion, Jeannie being pushed in a stroller. What a sweet appearing family in these home movies merging the personalities of the little stars.

My mother would eventually say to the little five-year-old girl who helped her push a stroller that Easter Sunday: "If you had never been born our lives would have been better! Just look at what you have done to us! You are harming our family!" I never understood what she meant by any of these statements. They made no sense and only hurt me, until I became an adult and could realize in full awareness why she was projecting her feelings in this way. She was the one who harmed our family when she became mentally ill. She was given a prefrontal lobotomy. That changed everything in our lives and our family forever. I became her scapegoat because I pointed the truth out of which she would never be able to see in awareness. After being hurt, ignored and told I was the reason for everything bad that ever happened. As the years progressed, one day, when I was soon to move out of state, I passed mother's car on a road. I looked over to the lane going in the opposite direction to see a woman with short-reddish-brown hair driving a white Mercedes sports car and thought to myself, 'What an ugly arrogant bitch'. This woman had a look on her face of arrogance and superiority that was beyond the pale. At the same moment, I thought this—I also thought, 'That woman is my Mother'. Driving past, I felt no connection to my Mother. I felt nothing but disgust.

My awareness of this memory is—by that time, I had been so hurt and grown so far past Mother that she appeared a complete stranger. And that was fine. She and I had little in common. I came to earth through her body, but that was about it. While at the same time, I had love and a connection to her that was ingrained into my soul. Only that was the mother/child energy connection and had little to do with her personality.

Throughout my life, I would use mother's friends, wives of my father's friends—business and otherwise and my friends' mothers as role models. I wanted to grow up to be nothing like my mother. So I modeled other women. Some of the women were fine ladies and I

became friends with them. They took me under their wing. I always wondered if they could see or knew how emotionless my mother was and how cold she was to me. A wife of one of Dad's friends said to me one evening when we were dining out. "You are the most beautiful and kind and we can see how the others treat you. I want you to know that I see."

During the time, I was preparing for my first wedding; I was given many wedding showers and parties by these women. One couple, pretty much business but also social friends of my parents took a special liking to me. He was a senior executive in a large company. She was his second wife. Before that had married, she had been a model of some sort in New York City. It was clear living in New York City, they were snobby social climbers. They dropped well-known names all the time. And from what I observed in her behavior, she was after my daddy. She flirted with him much of the time. Daddy owned his own company and had more money than the man to whom she was married. She wore overly large jewelry. I found her interesting, entertaining and crass. She had a stepdaughter with this man and they wanted her and me to be friends. I didn't know the girl but we were about the same age. So I thought, okay I will meet her and see.

They invited me to accompany them and their daughter to travel to New York City in their corporate jet combining a business trip with shopping. We stayed at a penthouse that took up an entire floor in one of New York's finest hotels that overlooked Central Park. It was entertaining and fun. Only the more I was around the daughter, I didn't like her much and the more I was around the man and woman, I didn't like them either. The woman was cruel to her stepdaughter. She criticized everything about her—what she wore, what she purchased and what she said. She even made fun of her behind her back and said things in front of me to her such as; "Why don't you have taste like, Natalie? You need to dress more like her," which made the daughter cry and made me embarrassed.

She was even worse than my mother was, because at least my mother didn't talk much. We shopped Fifth Avenue, dined at Tavern on the Green and 21 Club among others. All entertaining and fun but being in their company was horrible. By the end of the trip, I was so happy to be away from these braggadocios, cruel to their daughter people that when their private jet landed and limo dropped me off at my house, I felt great relief.

This woman offered to give me a shower before my upcoming marriage. I wasn't responsive because I didn't want her to. I had more than enough of these people in New York City. Mother asked me to tell her what I wanted and who I would like to invite, but I didn't do as mother asked which, isn't like me. I was reared to display perfect societal manners. I told mother that I didn't want any more showers that I had enough of them and for her to tell this woman, but I guess mother didn't do as I had asked.

One evening this couple was at my parent's having drinks before they were to go out to dinner. The woman came into my bedroom, sat down on the end of my bed and started talking about the 'Silver Shower' that she was going to host on my behalf in their penthouse. She complained that mother would not help her or give her any input. She said, "You know how your mother is? She doesn't talk. She is no fun. She dresses horribly and shows no excitement about anything. So how about you and I put this party together?" I glared at this woman as she went on. "You do want a 'Silver Shower', don't you? It will be the most elegant one that you have been given. Your mother's other friends don't have my style." In an instant, I responded. "I don't want you to give me a shower, silver or otherwise. But thank you for offering. And don't ever say anything bad about my mother again." She stared at me in disbelief then said in surprise, "You don't want 'me' to give you a sliver bridal shower?" I responded, "No, thank you!" With that she stared at me for a pause then exited my room mumbling something about my being an ungrateful spoiled brat.

The next day, both my parents were furious at me for talking to this woman as I did. I told my Dad what she had said about mother but he didn't believe me. So even when I defended my mother, I still got into trouble and was made the scapegoat.

The awareness's here are so many—my parents' defensiveness and denial. I could/can see how they projected onto me, so they did not have to deal. They just wanted to have their fake friends and to party.

I am/was proud of myself and my ability to see through to the truth of these people. A wedding shower from this woman would have been really more for her than me; to show off her house or whatever it was that she wanted to show off. Or for her to boast and gloat that she was giving a shower for the daughter of my father. So what if I received more gifts and even if they were all silver—to endure these people would not have been worth it.

A few years later, Dad told me I was correct about these people and they broke off their 'friendship' with them.

I WISH YOU HAD NEVER BEEN BORN!

Age One To Mid-life

WHEN I WAS AROUND SIXTEEN, I would try to talk to my mother, but she rarely talked. I needed a mother's input so badly. Mother would play the card game Solitaire repeatedly. I would get so frustrated that I would talk louder to try and get her attention and at times, I even screamed. Nothing worked. When Dad would come home from work, he would tell me to stop bothering my mother. So Mother must have complained to him about my trying to talk to her. My mother was more like a child than an adult.

When I was somewhere in my forties, I was home visiting. Dad and I were alone together in his car. I was going through a divorce and was distraught. I felt as if I could collapse and needed to hear words of comfort, advice, something or anything to try and understand why I was having such a difficult time in life. The man I was married to turned out to be a control freak. He didn't want me to work, to workout, to join community organizations. He didn't want me to do anything and wanted to know my whereabouts at all times. When we dated he was fun, encouraging and happy. We went snow skiing, traveled often and had fun. After he thought he 'had' me, he became an old man and didn't want to do anything. I wanted out of the marriage and away from him so badly that I could scream!

"Hell, how do I know why you are where you are in your life? Your mother and I have nothing to do with the choices you make. You marry losers. Men use you. Marry you for money—my money. You marry jerks! No man wants you unless it's for my money. This is not how it's supposed to be. I wanted you to marry a great guy and have grandkids. Hell, I should just wash my hands of you. Your mother and I are fine. The rest of the family is fine. It's only you with problems."

My Father is saying words like this to me, while I already feel broken hearted and lost. Hearing these words come out of his mouth today makes me feel as if I could die. "Daddy, I try so hard and nothing works out for me. I don't understand why."

"If you don't understand, why would we understand? We have nothing to do with your problems." His voice gets louder, "Hell, I wish you had never been born! If you hadn't been born your mother wouldn't have gotten sick! We don't have problems until you enter the picture."

I stare straight at Dad's face as he stares ahead at the road then something clicks in me. Even as my heart is breaking to hear these words come out of his mouth. I know that he doesn't mean them and that he is a sad, angry and frustrated man. He is projecting his frustration onto me.

He turns and looks at me, as I softly ask. "Daddy, do you mean that?" His eyes tear as he answers. "If you had never been born, your mother would not have had a breakdown. If you had never been born, she would be okay—like she was when we first met. She was more like you are then. She was happy and full of—of life and now . . ."

"You said this is not the way things are supposed to be with me. So you think at the age of one that I caused her to have a breakdown and caused her to have a prefrontal lobotomy? Was I, at the age of one supposed to experience that? Do you ever think about what that did to me as a baby, to have a mother become catatonic then put into a mental institution? Was that supposed to happen? In less than a year,

I lived with my grandmother, mother had a prefrontal lobotomy and when she comes back, she is not the same. She is like a robot. Was that supposed to happen? Was that 'supposed' to happen to me when I was a baby?"

Tears enter my Dad's eyes almost as if he had never thought about the affect all that had on me as a one-year-old.

I continue, "That surgery cut her feelings for me. So I didn't have much of a mother before and I sure didn't have one after. Was that supposed to happen? Are you are blaming me for her weakness and frailty? That is cruel, wrong and insane. Is that what a father is 'supposed' to do to his child?"

Dad's face is frozen as he stares at the road ahead.

I go on, "How did I cause her breakdown? By just being born? Perhaps, it was you that caused it because you wanted a child? It was her hormones or her emotions that caused it. What were you doing at the time? You never tell me how she was behaving before you found her catatonic. It's like you have no memory of it. Did she behave strangely? Did you see it coming? On the day that you found her, what was I doing? I was only one. I was a baby and there alone with her. What must I have felt as a one-year-old when my mother became catatonic?"

Dad doesn't answer. He just stares ahead.

"All my life, I had to endure not having a mother and being blamed for her becoming ill. I was only a year old! Thank God, I lived with my grandmother when I was one to two; at least I got love and attention from her. When Mother came home, she was not the same person and you kept having children one after another trying for a boy. Mother could barely take care of me and you had three more children. That in itself is insane! You and mother created this mess. I was left trying to survive and to get nurturing, guidance and attention from a woman with no ability to give it. You told me at the age of twelve to be good and kind to my mother so as not to upset her. I was not responsible for her at the age of twelve. And I certainly was not responsible for her at the age of one. I had to stop being a child to worry about my mother. Nothing about this is normal. Mother didn't rear me. The maids did. I never really had a Mother! None of us did!"

Gruffly Dads snaps, "Shut up! I don't want to talk about it, any of it!"

We rode in silence back to my parent's house. When I got there, I immediately packed up my things and left to drive back to the state where I lived. On the four hour drive, I cried most of the way, but as I got closer to my home, I felt better and better. I loved living in another state away from my critical, cold and mostly unloving family. The next day, I went to aerobics and worked out hard, perspiration flowing with emotion and energy pulsating throughout my body as I processed my pain. Then after a hot shower—physical and emotional relief!

I was already going through devastation in my life dealing with my emotions during yet another divorce. Now I had more pain heaped upon me by my father. No comfort or understanding could be found when I was in the worst of times. That is how my life usually was with my parents. I was blamed for whatever happened and given little to no comfort. I had to pull myself up on my own. I honestly do not know how I survived it. Except as I was struggling thought it, I would pray and repeatedly turn it over to God. Ask for protection and healing, and cry until I could cry no more. I would work out until exhausted but afterwards, I didn't feel exhausted it energized me giving me the energy to keep on keeping on. Working out was a life saver, keeping me physically fit, but also mentally and emotionally fit. I became stronger and stronger inside but always wondered how much more I could take before I couldn't take anymore.

With each marriage and divorce, I became stronger. When I was fractured, weak and needy, insecure, predator-like men were attracted to my energy of kindness and caretaking nature and my family money. When I became stronger and eventually very strong, weak, insecure men were attracted to my strength. Weak, insecure men eventually become resentful. Either way, it was lose—lose for me because when strong, I attracted weak men. When weak and lacking men were the last thing I wanted or needed in my life, after living in my family of origin that I had survived and escaped from. Either way, I added to their value while they deducted from mine, all the while they sucked off my energy.

Dad eventually called and apologized to me for those words that day in the car. He and I always had a bond that went deep below his frustration of hateful words, I knew in my heart that he didn't really mean what he said, but it still hurt me into the core of my being. His apologetic words were, "Of course, you didn't cause your Mother's breakdown. It had nothing to do with you. You were so cute, so beautiful the most precious child. In the airplane, taking you to your grandmother's, your ears hurt and you cried and cried. I love you so much. You were the cutest little thing that ever lived." Through tears, "I don't understand why you of all people, my most beautiful child with a heart of gold can't find true love. That is what I always wanted for you. Forgive me, Tiger for hurting you."

Of course, I forgave him. I was the truth teller in my family. Therefore I became the scapegoat. I would put it out there and be told repeatedly that I was wrong but then as it eventually turned out I was correct. I knew what I knew to be truth, wasn't afraid to say it and it was as if I had to speak it. It was as if I was compelled to, as if driven by some force and as if it was my duty and place in life to do so. I wondered at times, if part of my father's anger at me was a kind of envy on some level that I got out of bad marriages, instead of staying to live in Hell as he had. It takes a different kind of strength to get out and again another kind to stay.

I moved to a different state because of this marriage and even though the marriage didn't last, I was so glad that I had moved away because I genuinely believe that it saved my life. After the divorce, I stayed where I was. Had I not and gone back home, I know that I could have self-destructed even died.

I could only stand to be around family members for a very short time. They drank too much, many smoked and at times, some of them did drugs. Some were promiscuous. I detested their behaviors. My father had affairs on my mother and some of my sisters lived a similar life-style. They all 'appeared' respectable but it was mostly façade. We had money and lived an enviable life-style. It all looked so pretty and nice on the outside. No one wanted truth and they all hated me for stating it as I saw it.

I didn't want to drink to drown my pain or escape in other ways.

I wanted to feel, to heal and to process through it and to process it out of my life. They laughed at me for not drinking and told me I was a 'square'. It didn't bother me in the least. Instinctively, I must have known even then that to feel pain and be aware of the cause then you are better able to process and release it. Drown it in alcohol, stuff it, try to escape from it or try to cover it up and the pain remains stuck.

After Mother died and Dad's mourning for her diminished, he had one affair after another with gold-diggers—women my age and younger. I told him exactly what those women were and he told me I was wrong as he usually did. That I was full of it! We would email back and forth and he would get so angry with me that he would block me. Then he would unblock me and tell me I was correct.

He called me almost in tears when he found out the truth about one woman, admitting to me that I was correct. He was upset with himself and wondering how he could have been so blinded. I had told him the moment that I met her that she was no good.

While being chided, humiliated, alienated, blocked and laughed at and even worse—I was eventually proven to be correct.

My dad was looking for the love that he never had and never could receive fully from Mother because of her mental condition and sadly I don't think he ever found it.

In the later years of my dad's life, when he was in a wheelchair and had gone through woman after woman, I was visiting him and he looked me straight in the eyes and said, "You always tell me the truth about everything and you are always right. I wish that you had been my only child and that I had left your mother." The first time he told me this I didn't say a word just stared into his face and thought, 'My poor sisters, no wonder they hate me so much. They could feel the energy of Dad's love for me and so could Mother. That is why they tried to alienate me from the family and from my father.'

My dad, his special love and connection for me had inadvertently set me up to be alienated from my sisters. They all resented me as did my mother. It was the underlying factor in my life with my family. Jealousy and envy were continually coming at me from my sisters and my mother from all angles and at every turn.

As I grew up, my father would hold me at a distance when around other members of the family. When it was just the two of us, he would tell me, "You are my first born and my special girl. I love you more than anything in this world. He told me the only woman he thought was beautiful in this world was me." Thank God for those times and those words because they got me through so much else that was so opposite.

During the last years of my father's life, each time that I visited, he would reveal his heart and regrets and tell me things such as this. That he wished he had left mother when she had her breakdown and taken me with him. He never told me any more information about her breakdown other than what he always had—which was that he came home from work and found her in a catatonic state. That he took her to the town where her parents' lived. Mother was put into a mental institution there. I lived with my grandmother and grandfather for that year.

They could not help mother in that particular institution, even after electro-shock treatments. Therefore they sought the best care they thought available at the time and sent her to George Washington University hospital. There she was given a prefrontal lobotomy by Dr. Walter Freeman, which severed the nerves in her frontal lobes which served to release the stress from her emotions but rendered her without emotional affect. She was like a real life 'Stepford wife'. She looked the part, but was not really there. She had no joy, talked little, repeated herself when she did and did errands as if on remote. She could not come up with solutions to the easiest things that I had to help her with and kept to myself. Secrets between her and me, so Dad would not be disappointed in her—as in simple solutions such as adding a can of bouillon soup to make more gravy when cooking a roast. She had few interests but card games. She was usually a good cook but hated to cook. She had housekeepers. Drank too much and laughed way too loud. Most of the time, when I was around her, it freaked me out, especially as I got older because I realized more and more that she was not all there. She was cheap and miserly. She clipped coupons and was always trying to save money. As a teenager and young adult, I would laugh at her for doing, since she wore incredible jewels, drove a Mercedes and lived in a magnificent house and Dad would have given her anything she wanted and he could well afford to. But later in life when I was practically broke, I recalled her money saving ways and incorporated them into my life. So that was a beneficial awareness from her. She kept Dad on the straight and narrow. She nixed many of his schemes, ideas and extravagant spending which many times was good. Her negativity and his love for her served to rein him in, in some regard.

After her death, he spent money like water, took gold-diggers on Yachts to the Mediterranean kind of spending and invested in a bad business venture that lost almost half his money. In trying to make more in his old age and trying to feel vital and still in the business game, he lost plenty. But this was Dad's nature to keep trying, to create, to build, to provide and to care for—in order that he feel important and worthwhile. Everything in his life had turned to gold until his last business venture. In his old age, he got soft, lost his cunning and ability to read business deals. I told him repeatedly that this business venture was not good but he did not listen to me, until it was too late.

Therefore even after Mom's complete breakdown, Dad kept to his goals and plans and kept trying to have his dream, his family and to have a boy. But it was not in God's plan. God had other plans.

In Dad's last years, he realized he could have made different choices. But had he left mother, she could not have functioned in the world. She was like a child. Dad loved my mother and he gave her a good life and treated her like a queen except for the cheating part. And I don't think she was even aware that he cheated on her. He confessed on one of my visits with him that there was one woman he loved that he had an affair with and almost left mother for. He knew mother would not be able to function and by that time they had four children.

He was frustrated with his grandchildren and my younger siblings. He allowed them to manipulate him and in his later years he saw what was going on, didn't like it, but it was too late by then.

I was the child who saw it all from the beginning, lived it then was blamed for it. We all suffered in our individual ways—all three of us and also my sisters.

I was the only child born before mother's breakdown and I have little to no connection to my siblings. I am very different from them. When I am around them, I feel like I felt when I was with mother— dead.

I wonder how different my life would have been had Dad left mother and taken me with him. I will never know. My life was what it was and as God planned it to be.

I used to hate my dad for cheating on my mother. I used to hate Mother for not talking to me and being so passive.

As an adult, I can see and understand the situation from all sides. My mother was mentally ill. My dad didn't receive the love, comfort and stimulation that he so desired from a wife. I didn't really have a Mother and Dad while he loved me deeply was frustrated and took it out on me. I had to be overly responsible and lose some of my childhood to be mother-like to sisters.

I was not responsible for any of it. But I entered this life to experience this mess and to learn to love myself through it all. I learned to see all sides of issues and learned to forgive, therefore releasing the imprints from me and allowing me to heal. I am fortunate in that I have the ability to express my emotions and I do not stifle them. I have known great pain but also have known great joy because I have the ability to feel all my emotions. My mother's ability was taken from her. I think possibly what my mother suffered from was post-partum depression and little was known about this affliction in that time frame. Today, most of the clinical presentations in patients with post-partum mental illness could be relieved by anti-psychotics, mood stabilizers or antidepressants. In addition, intramuscular injection of lorazepam is also effective in patients with catatonic features and post-partum depression or psychosis. In that time frame, my mother was given the cure of the day—a prefrontal lobotomy which forever changed her.

My dad was angry at me because he had in his plans for me that I be happily married with children. That is what I wanted for my life also. He wanted my first husband to be like the son he never had. But I would not bring children into a bad marriage. When I realized, I was married to men with addictions or other fatal flaws, I instinctively knew not to have children with them. I did not live the life my father wanted me to live and it made him angry. I did not stay in marriages when I was unhappy. Not that he wanted me to be unhappy but I rebelled against the norm of Dad's expectations. He even called me his 'little rebel'. I would not live emotionally lobotomized in a bad marriage.

I forgive both my mother and father. I see them as individuals with their imprints and paths to live. We three merged on earth to have these experiences together.

Now that both my parents are dead, I feel free in a way that I never felt when they were alive—like a rebirth on earth. After I mourned their passing, I was able to let them go. I processed both the good and bad imprints. I got angry at them even hated them at times and then I came to forgive them and to love them fully. I hold onto the positive imprints and release the negative—as those are not mine to hold onto. They belong to my parent's.

Dad told me often during the years, "When I die, I want you to celebrate. I want you to live happy! That is my wish for you!"

I feel both parents close to me. I know they both loved/love me dearly and are proud of me.

God is my ultimate Father. He wanted me to be born, to experience all that I did on earth and to grow more aware and past the experiences in the life that I landed in. We come to this planet to expand our soul, to learn to forgive and to love and the pain and tension that we break against—is what allows us to do this.

My Father in Heaven wanted me to become more than what I was when I arrived on earth. I am blessed.

YOU ARE A WHORE!

Adult

"YOU ARE A WHORE! WHY aren't you married? Why didn't you give me grandchildren?"

I stare at my father as he drunkenly shouts at me.

I respond, "Why would you call me a whore? What is wrong with you?"

He slurs his words as he states, "I asked bishop, why my most beautiful worthy daughter wasn't happily married and didn't have children. He said it's because you are a whore. You've been married three times. You date all the time."

I state loudly, "I met that bishop only once. Who is he to say anything about me? I date but that does not mean I have sex with any of them. I am leaving. As usual, you are drunk."

I exit Dad's house slamming the door as I do. I drive to the hotel where I am staying. I am so happy to be out of that house and to not be around that raving drunken man. Later in Dad's life, he had hooked up with this bishop fellow. I met him once and thought him phony. In fact, he gave me the creeps. His appearance is like that of the old evil preacher character in the movie, 'Poltergeist'. Dad, I guess counseled with him and while he did—a good part of the time, he was dating gold digger after gold digger—my age and younger. Dad took this 'bishop' on trips, dinners out and their association in my opinion was always suspect. Now because of what this 'bishop' character stated, this fool of a man—my Dad, is calling me a whore. The insanity of alcohol must be rotting his brain.

Safe in the peace of the hotel room, I feel so much better. I take a hot shower to rinse the evil stench from Dad's house off my body. Dad keeps his house so hot that it must be what Hell feels like then with his drunken bellowing and insults—it is too much to deal with.

The next morning, I have an appointment with the gynecologist that operated on me years ago. When I pull into a parking space just outside the medical building, I am suddenly overwhelmed with what my father shouted at me and all the hurt that I have suffered because of my family. It's a bone chilling winter morning, grey sky and dreary as I sit in the car feeling as desolate as the weather full emotional pain. I cry. Then get a grip, pull myself together and go into the building.

After my examination, I am sitting in the doctor's private office, across the desk from him. He states, "Well, your health is great and you look great. Your moving away was great for you—best thing you could have done. But what's wrong today, you look so sad? Why so sad?"

His asking this—that someone even notices how hurt and sad I am makes me break down in tears. I have known this doctor for years. My mother went to him when she was alive and he knew most of my family. He continues, "Hey, what's wrong?"

"Dad called me a whore last night."

His face reveals shocked surprise, "You are the farthest from a whore there could be. Why would he say something so stupid? Was he drinking?

"Yes, he was drunk."

He knowingly nods, "Perhaps, he's distraught over your mother's death. Natalie, don't let what he says bother you. He's a drunk. Stay away from him as much as possible. I know he's your Dad . . . but . . ."

I continue, "He sits at home, listens to music and drinks. And if he's not doing that, he's dating women my age." I blurt out, "My mother was mentally ill. She was given a prefrontal lobotomy when I was a baby. I am blamed for everything. I am so sick of my family."

Calmly, "Natalie, I knew your mother was mentally ill. She had no emotional affect. You had nothing to do with it. You are emotionally stable and happy—certainly not like your mother or the rest of your family."

Surprised, "You knew mother was not all there?"

"Yes. Of course, I knew. She was my patient for years. I would see your parents at the Country Club. It was clear that she had blunted affect and also that she was an alcoholic."

I breathe a sigh of relief, "His comments are helping me to feel better. It was comforting to realize that others could see the truth of the horror that I lived in.

Later I asked Dad about why he would listen to that bishop and what he said about me. That bishop had no idea about me, who I am or my life. Dad just shrugged. He never mentioned that night again. I felt like the bishop preyed on my dad and they connected in a dance of need of sorts. Higher ups in some churches like to associate with moneyed individuals. Dad needed comfort and when he couldn't find it in alcohol, I guess he used this bishop. When I met this bishop, I got chills of foreboding even seeing his face and feeling his energy. When I shook his hand, everything about him felt off. My instincts, intuition and every bone in my body told me he was phony. I will go even further to say evil hiding behind the mantle of the church. He did nothing to bring my family together or to guide us to healing. I know Dad donated money and bought places for mother and him to reside after death even as we were not a family of the religion that this 'bishop' worked for and represented. It all felt very strange and sordid.

MY FATHER'S CANE

Adult—Present Time

I COULD HAVE IMAGINED THAT ALMOST one year exactly after my father's death, I would be using one of his canes. My dad died in April, the day in that year was Good Friday.

Daddy used canes for years because of an injury when he was in the Navy. A bomb had hit on the submarine he was on. When Dad was running away from the explosion, he turned to look back and was hit in his neck and spine. This created a degenerative spinal disease to develop as his life progressed. He had been an athlete in high school and was recruited to be a pitcher, but he hurt his arm and couldn't pitch any longer. After a few years of college, he went into the Navy where he acquired this injury to his upper vertebra. He was a large, vibrant man and it wasn't until later in his life that he needed to use a cane to steady his walk. He eventually ended up in a wheelchair. One day I asked, "Dad is it horribly difficult being in a wheelchair when you were once so active?" He replied in a gruff tone, "No it's okay. I manage." I rarely saw him frustrated concerning his disability. Although in private, I am sure that he had his moments. Dad rarely if ever let me see him down, depressed or hopeless. I guess that is why he wouldn't tolerate it in me. He wanted me to have a strong core because he knew in life that internal strength is what makes or breaks you.

While in the Navy, Dad flew planes but he was also on a submarine. Going from the different altitudes also wreaked havoc on him. He told me stories about being in the Navy infirmary and how lonely he felt. He said that he had never felt so alone in his life and that it was the worst feeling in the world. Healing can be an alone process . . . When he got out of the Navy, he asked for Mom's hand in marriage repeatedly—on the third attempt, her father said yes.

Through the years, I would buy him antique or usual canes for gifts. He had quite a collection. After he died, I got some of his canes. I placed the black one with the silver handle to lean in a corner of my powder room. There, I could see it easily as I walked through the hallway past the powder room door. It gave me comfort to see it in there. It gave me the feeling that Dad was watching over me.

On April twenty-fifth, one year after Dad died, I had an accident. I slipped and fell on an unmarked wet concrete floor in a local wine bar. I broke my left elbow and sustained three hairline fractures in my tailbone. 'Unmarked, wet floor, wine bar wounded warrior'— not really funny, but . . . ' And no, I was not tipsy. I had one sip of champagne with a friend who I had picked up from the airport and we were celebrating. It was near closing time and the employees in the wine bar had prematurely begun to clean up and mop. Yes. I sued and yes, they settled with me for their negligence.

I was dealing with so much at time. I was still healing from the death of my Dad. My sisters were continually suing me concerning Dad's Will. Then I fell and had another lawsuit to contend with. I still don't know how I dealt with it all. But I knew my Dad was with me. I pulled Dad, Mother and God close to me every night before sleeping and often throughout the day.

During the healing, I was on crutches for a bit. How horrible are those things? I needed to 'baby' my left hip completely for a while and I also had my arm in a sling, I had to use one crutch under my right arm to take pressure off my left side. Using the crutches threw my walking gait off. After starting rehab to strengthen my left leg, I realized I was really having difficulty walking normally. This was frustrating beyond belief. Being a former ballet dancer and used to being fit as a fiddle, I was scared because I seemed to have little control over movement in my left leg to walk naturally.

The first day after I came home from rehab, I 'crutched' by the powder room and noticed Dad's cane. It was as if it was calling to me. I decided in that instant to toss the crutches and to use my Father's cane. Even though he was 6'2" and I am 5'3", the cane worked perfectly for me. I began practicing immediately—by walking up and down the entry hallway using my dad's cane. It was exactly what I needed. It offered support while I strengthen my left leg to regain my natural walking gait. I felt tremendously close to my dad during this time using his cane. Each step I took to regain my natural walk and balance, it was as if Dad was with me. Just like when I was taking my first steps and he encouraged, balanced and guided me. He was with me now. My parents told me that I learned to walk at nine months and after I did - I ran everywhere. Mother could barely keep up with me.

Now I was resting my hand on the same silver handle that my dad used for years. After two days, I was walking more naturally and in a week, I could walk without the cane. I used it a week longer just to feel my daddy close to me for comfort and moral support. Dad used to tell me he loved to watch me walk and to move. I have a fast gait and he told me that he loved the energy of my fast-paced movements.

I was blessed to be born with my Dad's will of iron—to keep on keeping on. By breaking against his internal strength all my life, I triggered my own. It's one of my greatest gifts from him.

Mom used to say, "You and your father are just alike—both have heads as thick as a brick wall, stubborn as can be." When Mom would say this, it was usually when she was irritated at one or the both of us. Dad and I would look at each other shrug and smile. Dad and I are/were a lot alike and our hard heads could butt in real style. But actually that stubborn-will served/serves us well at times.

During this time of recovery, I decided to venture further into town to run an errand. I had spent two weeks almost completely in bed and without driving. Only recently, I started driving myself to rehab and doing errands but only in my area and was now ready to get back into the world. I knew that I needed to push myself so as to not become fearful and isolated. So I forced myself to step further out. With my dad's cane in tow, off I go. As I near my destination, I hear a big pop and the tire light comes on in my car. I slowly enter the parking lot and park in front of where I was heading. Get out and realize that both tires on the driver's side of my car are blown out. The tires were fairly new. Clearly, I must have run over something. Here I am using a cane, it's hot outside and I am a far distance away from my house for the first time in almost a month. I momentarily fill up with fear and stress. Then settle my mind and call a tow truck which arrives in record time after I explain my circumstances. The man driving the tow truck was as kind a man as there could be. Here I am with sling on an arm and using a cane, barely able to lift my left leg climbing into the cab of a tow truck. The man stood behind me guarding me as I did. While we ride to the car dealership with my car in tow, we chat and I share with him my ordeal of the past month. He listens with understanding and says, "Just have trust in God." I replied, "That's what I am doing." Then we both burst out into laughter concerning the ridiculousness of it all. He tells me to keep my smile and to keep laughing.

My new tires were put on and I was home in record time. But why did this happen at just this time, one thing after another putting more stress and challenge on me? Was it to further expand me? All you can do after dealing with the issues at hand—is to trust in a positive outcome, laugh in amusement and let it go. What's that saying? 'If you find yourself walking in Hell just keep on walking'. That is what I did. With each issue I dealt with, God had my back. As fast as it fell apart, it came back together with adventure, magic and more awareness along the way. Kind people were put on my path to assist me—complete strangers with like heart and belief.

As I continued dealing with rehab and this whole ordeal, I could hear Dad's words in my mind's eye as I pushed, faltered, got frustrated, scared then kept on . . . "Keep at it Tiger! You can do it. I am here with you. I am proud of you."

Dad had been a wounded warrior and my accident and what it took to recover gave me a new appreciation for what it is to deal with and recover from physical trauma. Dealing with this just one year after his death, was a lot to process on the physical, emotional and mental levels. But the strength that I had honed from my lessons in life got me through it. In the exact moment, I replaced my crutches with his cane. I promised Dad that with the help of his cane, his eyes watching over me and the energy and grace of God that I would regain the walk that I was born with and he loved to watch. I fully recovered in record time and in my doctor's amazement with no lingering effects from my injuries. None! I am physically fully restored.

To add to this time of trauma—dark night of the soul—testing of my spirit—just six months after I had fully healed from the fall and was beginning to feel relief—I went to my dermatologist for my yearly examination. To discover I had a place on my forehead that was cancerous. This place was above my right eyebrow. My dermatologist sent me to a MOHS surgeon to have it examined. Because of where it was, they scheduled me with a plastic surgeon to close the opening after the surgery. I was in full panic mode before the surgery. I had no idea how deep the cancer was or how intensive the damage would be to my forehead.

In two years, my dad had died, I was still dealing with the emotional effects of this, my sisters were repeatedly suing me, I had fallen, recovered and was in the middle of suing the restaurant where I fell. And now, I was looking at having my forehead possibly disfigured. My father was gone -the only one on earth I had to turn to for strength. My physical abilities had been threatened and I was now facing losing my looks. Talk about overwhelming stress upon stress.

I was wired, anxious and I became depressed. I wondered how much I was going to be put through and if it would ever be over. Would I ever feel like me again? Then who was I, anyway?

I prayed and prayed and finally turned it over to God. At times, this was easier to do than at others.

A friend took me to have the MOHS surgery early on a winter morning. They only needed to go in one and half times, so the cancer had not destroyed much. But I still was left with a large hole in my forehead. That afternoon, I went to the surgery center for a plastic surgeon to close it, to leave the least effect on the appearance of my forehead and face. God lead me to a gifted surgeon.

After the surgery, I felt like I looked like Frankenstein because my forehead was swollen with a red suture line over my right eyebrow. The caring surgeon called me every morning for a week to see how I was doing. He promised that the swelling and the scar line would disappear. I was going to look great again even better. The upside was that the surgery raised my right eyebrow that was lower than the left one and served to tighten my forehead—a light in the darkness.

After a few weeks, it did look much better. In months, it was barely noticeable. Today the scar line is barely, if at all visible. I don't even need to put makeup on it, to cover it up.

Everything I had broken against as a child, young adult and throughout my life had prepared me for this sequence of events of my dark night of the soul without my father here on earth to sustain me. I had almost lost everything several times in my life, but never like this. Nothing had ever felt this alone and low. In this timeframe, I remembered back to when angels had walked though me. I asked and prayed that they please do it again. But they didn't. I heard in my mind's eye, 'You know we are with you and you will be fine'. Therefore, I focused on recalling that feeling of love that had once filled me up in comfort and grace as I pulled God, my mother and my father close to me every night. As I lay alone in my bed, I could smell the fresh fragrance of my mother and heard my father's words, "You can do it, Tiger! I am with you all the way."

Things can appear horrible and like everything including your life is falling apart, right before more awareness is recognized. I learned how strong and resilient I am. I felt, knew and renewed my faith and strength in God. I realized the hate that my sisters have for me, so I cut them completely out of my life which I should have done a long time before. Doing so, has freed my spirit in ways that is incredible. I feel younger now, than I even did when I was a child living in my parent's home with the burdens of my mother, my sisters and my father weighting me down with their imprints. I have awareness, understand, accept and forgive them all. I let them go.

I choose only to keep the love of my mother and dad as comfort to guide me in the rest of my life's journey. Of course, I do have happy family memories that I enjoy at times.

Embrace challenges in life as opportunities for self-reflection and transformation.

"You have power over your mind, not outside events. Realize this and you will find strength."

—Marcus Aurelius

LAST CONVERSATIONS WITH DAD

Adult To Present Time

FULL OF ELEGANT THINGS, THE expansive living room with various seating arrangements of white upholstered furniture atop Oriental rugs—various styles of artwork—rich mahogany accents and a black grand piano positioned by the fireplace is empty, except for my eighty-five-year-old Dad sitting in his wheelchair. He is positioned near a round game table in the corner by the windows overlooking the swimming pool. I sit comfortably in a high-backed club chair across from him. My once tall dark and handsome athletic dad is, now gray-haired, shrunken and frail. He takes a sip of wine then stares with a face full of regret into my eyes, "I should have left your mother after she had her breakdown."

I take a sip from my glass of sparking water then turn away to stare pensively to the left—past the large room out into the long hallway. I take a deep breath and turn back to look at my dad, "Daddy, you've told me this so many times. If you really felt that way, why didn't you leave?"

"If only I had."

"You would have taken me with you, right? Dad, you wouldn't have left me with her?"

Dad smiles warmly with love in his eyes, "Of course, I would have taken you with me. I wish you'd been my only child." His voice trails off, "You're the most like your mother, before . . . before." Then he looks me in the eyes, "You're beautiful. You're my first born—the light of my life."

I reflect, 'I was designated the pretty one but rarely felt that way'. Then I ask, "Really? I didn't realize that you even really thought I was pretty or much anything. You rarely gave me compliments, except in front of people when you were bragging and showing me off. Most of the time, I thought you didn't think much is good about me at all."

He chuckles, "Like you? I adore you. Pretty? You are gorgeous. We argue, but it's because we are so much alike."

I laugh, "Alike in some ways Dad, but also very unalike in others."

Dad replies, "Everything about you is right—inside and out. I think two women in this world are beautiful."

Surprised, "Really who?"

He answers, "You first and maybe Elizabeth Taylor when she was young and on a good day."

I laugh, "Really?"

Dad continues, "I didn't and couldn't compliment you because your mother and the girls are so jealous of you. It's best you stay away from your sisters. I see the cruelty in Tammy. I see how she treats you."

"Dad! Do you realize how it's been for me with a mother who couldn't show me love and sisters who hated me? Why didn't you do anything about this way back when you could?"

Dad's face reveals deep emotional pain that he's having difficulty controlling. "I did the best I knew how to do. I did the best I could to cope with your mother, your sisters and to keep the peace. What should I have done, left and not talked to any of them? Not that I didn't think about it."

I contemplate, 'So instead you drank and had affairs—like doing that didn't harm us,' but I say, "Your affairs—did you love any of those women?"

"Yes, there was one I loved and almost left your mother for." He shakes his head, "I don't want to talk about this any longer."

I reply, "Dad, too often you don't want to talk about it and you brought this up. It's time we talk about it."

He worriedly rubs the side of his face. "Your mother couldn't have survived being on her own, so I stayed. But your mother—your mother . . . she . . ."

"But Dad you had three more children after her breakdown." I observe as Dad sinks back in his wheelchair and takes a sip of wine. "Did mother have post-partum depression? She got ill over a year after I was born, but she had no history of mental illness and they didn't know much about post-partum back then. But Dad, I got mother's records from George Washington Hospital and her diagnosis read schizophrenic catatonic. That is severely mentally ill. Did she behave strangely or unusually before you found her in a catatonic state?"

Dad shrugs sadly, "No. I came home and found her like that—catatonic. She didn't even know who I was."

"But there is no history of mental illness in her family. How could she just become catatonic without any previous symptoms or unusual behaviors? I just don't understand. I always thought it was post-partum depression until I read her records from the hospital. What could have caused her to become like that, Dad?"

"I don't know. No one did. I did the best I could to get her well. If the doctors hadn't done what they did, she might have been in a mental institution for the rest of her life. I took her to a hospital near her parents and you stayed with your grandmother. That doctor is who recommended she be transferred to . . ."

"But Dad, a prefrontal lobotomy—that operation changed her permanently. Today they would use antipsychotics, mood stabilizers or antidepressants."

"I know, honey, but we did the best that we could at that time. What they did cured her or they thought it did."

"But left her like a 'Stepford wife'. And why did you have more children with her in that condition? She was not capable of caring for me—let alone more. Sure she picked us up from school, looked nice and gave the façade of a mother, but she barely interacted on any real level. If you hadn't provided housekeepers, mother couldn't have functioned. She hardly spoke to me. She was like a child herself. I was only one-year-old. Did anyone think about me? My mother was gone!"

Dad's eyes fill with tears, "I am sorry—so sorry. You were so cute, so precious." Dad's voice breaks, "I did what the doctors thought best for your mother. I wanted a family—a son. I had my plans and where I wanted to go in life. Your mother let me down."

"Dad, mother got sick. She didn't let you down. But I understand how you feel because I felt like she let me down, too. Did you think I caused mother's illness by my being born? I always thought you blamed me. You told me if I hadn't been born that she would not have gotten ill."

"No! No, you did nothing. You were the most beautiful precious child there could ever be with your beautiful dark wavy hair and that smile—a real beauty. You were feisty, intelligent and fun . . . more wonderful a child than any parent could ask for."

"But Dad, I've been hurt so much by all this and for all my life."

He looks down then up at me, "I know you have and I am so sorry. I am forever sorry. But your mother and I were in it together so I had to do what I thought best for us all." He motorizes his wheelchair back and forth. "How about pouring me some more wine?" He holds up his glass.

Out of obedience, I take his glass and cross to the bar to pour him more wine. I pour myself more sparkling water.

Dad mumbles, "I wish I'd spent more time with my little girls when they were young.", then loudly states, "If I'd broken up the family, what would that have accomplished but to destroy the family and hurt everyone?"

I state, "I don't know the answers Dad, but I have been hurt all my life by this situation and by my sisters. I was kind to my sisters and all they ever were was cruel to me. I babysat their kids. I took care of them and gave to them. I allowed Tammy to live with me after she got out of college when I was a newlywed. What have they ever done for me, but to hurt me? If I were walking through the desert dying and needed water, if Tammy came by and had some, she wouldn't give me a sip. She would let me die and enjoy watching me do so."

Dad motors his wheelchair back and forth then back to the game table. "I know your sisters have not treated you right. I see it. But you were born out of love and when your mother was herself. You are the best of the both of us . . . the others . . . well. Your mother loved you very much."

I hand Dad his wine and he takes a sip then says, "She just didn't know how to show it. Your beauty, intelligence and strength intimidated her. You are everything she once was, hoped to be and would never be again. Your sisters are jealous of you and so was your mother."

I reflect, 'So Dad saw and knew this all along.' I sit down at the game table and state, "So what you're saying now at this late date is that I have been tormented and punished all my life for being me. Tormented and blamed for being born and you recognized this all the while it was happening?"

Dad's eyes tear up. "I see how much you have been hurt and I'm sorry. I see how Tammy manipulates. I didn't at first, but in recent years I do. She is a cruel, cruel conniving person and it's hard for me to admit this about her—Dana with her drugs and having mental issues. Jeannie's head is somewhere in outer space. I can't relate to any of them."

"Dad, I can't either. This family has been a nightmare for me. Tammy is the ring leader. She manipulates everyone—Mother, Dana, Jeannie and you. I never felt loved by anyone but you." My eyes tears up.

Dad chokes up. It's been a nightmare for me, too. I see what and who Tammy is and what she has done. Your mother was weak—fragile. It was Hell living with her all those years. Yes, I loved her, but . . ." He sighs, "I worked hard and tried to provide a good life for you all."

"And you did in many ways Dad, but . . ."

Dad takes a sip of wine then in a strong voice, "When I die, make sure to go to my safe. I gave you the combination, didn't I?"

"Yes Dad, several times, I have all the codes and combinations— keys to the house and everything." I feel sick inside as I realize, 'Dad is frailer each time that I see him.'

Suddenly, Dad's voice is full of life as if he was in his hay day and his eyes twinkle mischievously. "I have a surprise in the safe for you, so go there first thing. I want all my children to be taken care of. But I want the most for you. Take your inheritance and have fun. Don't mourn me and don't be sad. I want you to smile that beautiful smile and be happeee babeee!"

My heart smiles to hear Dad's vigor back in his voice and to see the light in his eyes. "Dad, ever since you were in your forties, you've been saying, "When I die and we all know that you'll never die.""

Dad chuckles sadly.

I continue, "I'll be grief stricken when you're gone. You're the only one who has ever really loved me."

Dad replies, "Of all my children, I want you to live for me and be happy! Keep your chin up, Tiger. Have a party! I keep cash in the safe and other things, so don't you forget."

I teasingly inquire, "Okay Dad, but how much cash?"

He playfully responds, "Enough for some fun and I want you to have it. It will be in my safe, in an envelope with your name on it and labeled private."

I state, "I recall you showing me your money in the safe all my life, always lots of cash—a hundred thousand or more."

Dad winks playfully at me.

"But Daddy it makes me so sad and even afraid to think that you might not be here someday."

Dad replies, "Baby, it happens to us all. But I'll always be with you, no matter where I am."

"Will you leave me your Angel that's always on your shoulder?"

He laughs through a smile, "Of course, I will."

I respond with heavy heart, "That might help."

Dad's mood changes as he travels back and forth in his wheelchair. His voice tone turns gruff, "Damn, Tammy's sons lost all that money and the little jerks didn't have the guts to tell me. The broker called to inform me the account was empty—one million gone. I made one little brat sell his house and the other his car and give me their commission back. So they did pay back a small part of it. And what they don't pay back, Tammy can pay back out of her share of the Estate."

I grimace, "Those boys are exactly like their father."

Dad finishes off his wine. "They're certainly nothing like my sons would've been. Those kids couldn't even figure out how to put together a model airplane. They don't think. I don't know what's wrong with them."

"But Dad, you pretty much raised Tammy's boys."

He shrugs, "All three are losers and all little shits."

I continue, "What did you expect? Didn't their father do drugs and at one time, wasn't he a male stripper? Then Tammy and her affairs with married men and almost losing her business because of affairs with clients."

Dad gets noticeably upset and his voice gruff, "I get so tired of taking care of people and cleaning up their messes."

Dad drinks his wine then motors his wheelchair back and forth as I think to myself, 'Poor Dad, mother was dead weight for him all her life. She was a burden. Then my sister's sons—the 'sons' Dad had hoped to have all his life turned out to be spoiled rotten brats. In Dad's blindness, he didn't realize that he was part of the reason that they became what they did. Their father dumped them on my sister. I don't think he ever even paid child support. Dad graciously took care of all his grandkids like they were his own children.'

Dad continues, "Lost all that money and didn't have the guts to tell me. Losers, the lot of them!" Dad shakes his head with a face full of disgust. "How could I have been so wrong?" He raises his voice in frustration, "Why didn't you have some children? You're the one I wanted grandchildren from. Why didn't you find a good man and give me some grandkids? You are the perfect woman, kind, beautiful, intelligent, loving, sensitive and joyful. You are quick on the uptake, direct and honest, and then you marry losers. You are the type of woman a man wants. I just don't understand it."

I think to myself, 'Now, you tell me.' But say, "Dad, I always wanted children but after I realized what my husbands were, I made certain that I didn't have children with them."

"Well, you were right about that. Why in Hell couldn't you find a guy that deserved you? Your mother and I talked about this often. You of all women with everything going for you picked damned losers—our most beautiful, intelligent girl and no children."

"Dad I don't know why. All I ever wanted was to be married and to have a family. Dad, I don't think I have ever really felt or been loved."

Dad looks into my eyes as his eyes well-up with tears and as my eyes fill with tears also. Dad takes a deep breath then a sip of his wine.

I continue, "Now I'm glad that I don't have children. Do you think your other daughters married such great picks?"

Dad chuckles sadly, "Worse than yours. That guy Dana married—what do you think about him?"

I answer, "I think he looks like he's been frozen in the hippie generation and can't get out."

Dad chuckles then we laugh together as we share one of our in sync knowing glances, then he concurs, "I think the same way."

"Dad, I have nothing in common with any of them."

"I know. I understand." Dad face saddens, "But I want my family back together. I told Tammy and she promised that she would make it happen."

I reflect to myself, 'Dad, you were the one that allowed it to be torn apart' then say, "Dad, don't be silly. It will never happen, after what she's done. She's the one that did the major damage in tearing our family apart and you allowed her to do it. She would have to admit the truth and she never will. She knows that I know the truth about her. She needs to keep me alienated to keep her what she thinks is safe. She is full of ego and greed. Just make sure to protect me from her because she will do everything she can to hurt me."

Dad's face reveals how weary he is. "My Will is airtight. She can't do anything or take anything from you, but watch them like a hawk. I have been noticing things about my Estate attorney that I am not happy about. He's slow as molasses. I have to keep my boot on his neck for him to get anything done. I want you away from your sisters. They will try to eat you alive. They are jealous women. Stay away, but watch it all carefully. You have the brains to figure it out, if they do something underhanded and wrong."

"I will Dad. I've never met your Estate attorney but when I talked to him on the phone, I didn't care for him. Something is strange about him . . . unprofessional."

Dad says, "The best thing you ever did was to move out of state. You're the one with the brains and beauty. Of all my daughters, you're the one who deserves happiness after all you have been through. I hope you get the golden ring. I am so sorry—so sorry for my mistakes and weakness."

I go to my Dad and hug him tightly. He looks into my face with tears in his eyes. "I wish you had been my only child. I always have. You always tell it straight, the truth and are always right. I wish I had listened to you and not the others. Always know I love you very much. You are my first born—my beautiful . . ." his voice cracks, "And the most special, always were and always will be."

I look into my father's face, "I do, Daddy. I will. I love you, too."

Dad then turns his motorized wheelchair to the left and takes off across the room. Gruffly shouting behind him, "I'm tired. I am going to bed! Will you shut off the lights and put the glasses in the dishwasher before you turn in and do anything else in the kitchen that needs doing? And don't break anything! It's crystal."

"Yes, of course Dad." I watch as his wheelchair becomes distant in the darkness of the hallway and vanishes around the corner. I think to myself, 'Dad you drive me crazy. How long have I been putting crystal in a dishwasher and have I ever broken anything?' Then I recall when I was trying to tell Dad the truth about some gold-digger that he was dating and how he covered his ears and made a face like a little child because he didn't want to hear what I was revealing. And what I was saying all turned out to be the truth. People are so confusing, complex and often in defense and denial, until they can't be or can't endure the pain any longer.

Full of conflicting thoughts, I turn the lights off one by one. I pause to look at photos as I think to myself, 'Every visit lately, Dad tells about his many regrets. He's told me all this many times before. Telling me how much he loves me, mixed in with all the other stuff that hurts me.' I pick up a photo of mother and gently run my finger over it. 'Mother, you always told me that being on earth was like being in Hell. It must have been the Hell that you created in your mind because you had everything that a woman could want on earth. You were true to daddy and he cheated on you, but I don't think you ever even knew he did.' I put down that photo and pick up one of the whole family. 'Dad must've been so lonely married to mother all those years. His affairs were out of his loneliness. His desire for a son overwhelmed him. He used Tammy's sons—his grandsons in that place.' I shake my head as I continue talking to myself. 'Families have so many layers and my family certainly is a multi-layered mess.' I carry the glasses into the kitchen then load the dishwasher. I wipe the counter tops while my mind is in over drive. 'All those gold-diggers, Dad went through after Mom died; my age and younger, disgusting women playing an old man for his money and to make it even more bizarre, one looked a bit like me. The one he bought the hundred-thousand dollar engagement ring for. Only to finally come to the obvious conclusion that she was only after him for money. She was a real witch. I think she was forty-eight. Daddy—Oh Daddy, what were you thinking? Searching for the love you never had and looking in all the wrong places.'

I head through the darkened hallway to the back of the house passing the door of Dad's bedroom. From his bed, Dad shouts, "Goodnight Angel! Don't mess with my thermostat! I'm cold!"

"I won't. Goodnight Daddy. I love you."

"I love you too, Tiger, more than anything."

I am emotionally exhausted as I enter my old room filled with large wooden furniture and windows heavily draped floor to ceiling. I shut the door. It must be eighty degrees in this house. I'm suffocating. I turn on a fan and stand in front of it for a bit then aim it directly towards the bed. I strip off my clothes and put on my nightgown. I go into the bathroom just off the bedroom and wash my face. I brush my teeth as I reflect. 'Dad wasn't happy married to Mom, Who could blame him, but she wasn't happy either—except Mother never seemed happy. When I discovered Dad's cheating when I was in high school, it changed my feelings for the both of them. My respect and trust vanished. My security was forever shaken. I was angry at him for what he was doing. I was angry at her for not being more than she was. Only it wasn't her fault, she had been irreparably damaged by what was done to her by the mental health field. What they did to her was actually done to us all.'

I turn off the light, get into bed and stare at the ceiling. 'Was Dad strong or weak for staying married to Mom? He spent most of his life taking care of his obligations and providing for those he loved. Dad's cheating on mother showed me everything I didn't want in a marriage and it was exactly what I got. I used to love too much. And now, do I even have the will and ability to love and be loved? But even though Daddy was unhappy in his marriage after Mom died, he was lost. Mom was his anchor. His reason for being, she was his someone to look after and to make a life with and for. And as hard as he tried and looked, he never found it again. Interesting, Mom said I looked like Dad and Dad said I look like Mom. I guess I'm a mixture of them both and they saw each other in me.'

I turn onto my side to face the window. The drapes blow out from the wall as the heater comes on. Even though I am suffocating hot, I shiver as a cold chill runs up my spine. 'I am going to melt in here and sleeping in this room gives me the creeps. This house always felt haunted or as if it had a curse on it.' I flip onto my back, 'God, please help me turn off my mind and to fall asleep.' Only I can't sleep, my mind is spinning full of thoughts. 'When fractured and insecure, weak men sensed my need and thought they could control me, while doing as they liked, I provided their stability and image. Then when I became strong, weak and insecure men desired my strength. They thought I would take care of them and give them higher value. Only weak men that desire strength in a woman, also resent that they do. Where are the strong men that will add to my value and accept my strength, while also having the ability to nurture me when I need it—like a real man does for a woman and as a woman does for a man? That is what my dad wanted for me. He, of course had no idea that he and mother and the environment I grew up in had fractured me. This was the very reason and cause that prevented me from drawing to me, what he and I both wanted for myself.'

In the middle of the night as I sleep, I feel a shadow-like image of a woman hovering near the bed looking down. I feel a hand stroking my head as if to comfort. Startled, I sit up and look around as I say, "Mom?" I lie back down as I smell the fresh fragrance of my mother and fall peacefully back to sleep.

1 Corinthians 13:6-7 (KJV)—Love does not delight in evil, but rejoices with the truth. It always trusts, always hopes always perseveres.

NIGHTMARES OF WARNING

Adult

I TOSS AND TURN IN MY sleep in my large iron bed covered in shades of white and full of pillows. It's a bed made for a princess. And this princess is fighting off demons in her sleep. I sit straight up in bed half asleep, "Tammy's going to kill me. She's going to kill me." I am frozen in fear and shiver as I look around the dark room. I awaken a bit and pray, "God please, please protect me. Come close to me and protect me from evil. God, protect me from Tammy." I relax a bit then snuggle back down under the covers.

The next day, the doorbell rings and a vase full of roses are delivered. I open the card and read as my face lights up.

'Always know that you are loved above and beyond all others'.

—Dad

I burst out crying, "Oh Daddy, please don't die. When you're gone, I will have no one on earth who cares about me." I place the roses in the center of the white marble table in my living room then sit on the sofa and cry.

I wipe my eyes then dial the phone, "Dad, I got the roses. Thank you. They are beautiful."

"Always know that I love you deeply and forever. That's important for you to understand and to hold in your heart forever and always."

"I will, Dad. I will. I love you too, very much."

"The will to live, the will to die and the Will one leaves after dying. The end of one life can mean the end or the beginning of another's."

—Ayn Dillard

PART FOUR

THE PROCESS TO RELEASE IMPRINTS, PERCEPTIONS AND LIMITING BELIEFS

THROUGH MY AWARENESS IN RELEASING the imprints, perceptions and limiting beliefs from my past and present, I developed 'a process' which has worked miracles for me. I am not a psychologist or a psychiatrist. I took child and regular psychology classes in college, studied kinesiology, have done tapping, meditation, been in therapy and read extensively to learn for my own benefit. Years ago, working with clients in a stress management practice, I further defined, 'The Process'. I am sharing it as a way to assist in releasing imprints and to heal the limitations that knowingly or unknowingly, you are placing on yourself.

There are many programs that are effective. They work for many and I support them. I have used several modalities including step programs during my journey. 'The Process' is a flow to arrive at joy. It is a mental and emotional process. I found it to be faster and easier for me than others or it can be used in conjunction with other modalities. Different ways to awareness and healing can be effective at varying times and in various and different combinations. No matter what the healing modality, ultimately it's you who does the work or not. It's your choice whether to heal or to stay stuck, blocked and limited.

'The process' is a mental flow to move you forward in your life to self-awareness, to release negativity and stress on whatever issues you become aware of and are causing you discomfort. The key is awareness. Nothing can change without your first becoming aware. Awareness is like a light coming on in your consciousness. In a moment, you get it, see it, work through it and it feels great. Then like a light, it may burn out. Or like a light with a switch, the switch may be turned off then turned back on again. Awareness is a continual process. It will take you deeper and deeper into a brighter light each time the awareness switch is flipped.

When you are feeling mental and emotional pain or discomfort, it's a message. If you want to affect shift and change, you must be willing to endure and become more uncomfortable before you come into awareness and peace. It's a process. You will go from pain to peace as you flow through it. This is what life is about anyway—feeling all your emotions. The sooner you recognize and let go of the hurt—the faster and more often, you will be at peace and joy.

The only way you can affect change in a muscle is by using it. The only way you can affect change in your mental state is by feeling your emotions then processing them both intellectually and emotionally which will flow into the physical. 'The Process' will take you from your emotions into your intellect then back into your emotions allowing you to become able to be in an authentic relationship with yourself—your mind, body and spirit. This will assist you to create more positive and authentic relationships in your life, but most importantly with yourself. The more you are able to think through your heart and think through your emotions, the more at balance and in present time you will be.

It is a movement, a shift in perception. A progressive series of acts of awareness aimed at a conclusion. The conclusion is for understanding, acceptance and forgiveness to release limiting and negative imprints, beliefs and perceptions that create the discomfort in your mind, body and spirit. When you aren't aware of your imprints, you are controlled by them. When you don't process your feelings and emotions, they control you. Releasing negative and limiting imprints will bring you to love of self along with forgiveness and the ability to have love of others which will enable you to be open and clear to experience joy. Joy will expand the more you allow in.

It can take minutes, days or years depending on you and the imprint or belief that you are dealing with at any given time.

Release the weight of negative imprints past and present to be free and in the flow of your true destiny. Change is difficult at first, then it becomes messy and finally—it is glorious!

THE PROCESS is: Awareness—Understanding—Acceptance—Forgiveness—Love of self and others to Peace and Joy!

Dictionary Definitions Of The Words Used In THE PROCESS:

The reason I give the dictionary definitions of the words is to make sure that the meanings are clear. Individuals reading about and using the process will know exactly what the words mean based on the English language.

1. **AWARENESS**—to become informed, to become cognizant. If you aren't aware you can't see or change. If you are in denial or defensive then you will stay unaware in a kind of willful blindness. The opposite of aware is blind, deaf and dumb, clueless, or ignorant included also are the states of being defensive, in denial and deflecting.

2. **UNDERSTANDING**—the knowledge and power to perceive in self and others. The difference between knowledge and understanding is empathy. The ability to see from all sides and points of view. Once there is understanding, there can be reasoning and discernment about feelings, events, circumstances, situations, and people involved. To look at the cause with intelligence, empathy and sympathy. To acknowledge the value and reason of all sides.

3. **ACCEPTANCE**—to acknowledge it is what it is. See it—own it including your responsibility in it. Definition of RESPONSIBLE—duty to deal with something, being

in control, accountable, or to blame, opportunity or the ability to act independently and make decisions without authorization. Opposites of acceptance are projection, rejection and deflection.

4. **FORGIVENESS**—to cease to feel resentment. Release the hope that the past could have been different and accept it for what it was and is. Let go of resentment of self and others. Let go of wishing it were different or that what has occurred can be changed. The past is what it was/is.

5. **LOVE—FOR SELF AND OTHERS**—passionate, ardent— unchanging devotion for and to. To have a feeling of great attraction and affection.

6. **PEACE**—state of tranquility and calm. Freedom from fears and worries. Absence of war, freedom from disorderly disturbances such as anxiety, fear or depression. The same as quiet, freedom from noise or interruption. Calm—the absence of violent motion Tranquility—marks the present moment or situation, a permanent condition. When at peace, you are able and can be in the moment and in enjoyment of present time

7. **JOY**—bliss, the opposite of pain, grief, depression, anxiety, or sorrow. Rejoicing, it is a deep spiritual experience. A complete filling up of bliss. Joy expands the more you let in.

What you are feeling at any given time is up to you, but that's not as simple as it sounds. People make this statement often. Some use it as manipulation to make another feel guilty for feeling what they do.

When clearly they have done something that would, could and did make another feel bad. But the truth is that when you have something that triggers hurt, fear, stress, anxiety, insecurity, etc. it's for the purpose of awareness of why it does. This is where self-reflection enters. Some people are too fearful to look at self in honest reflection, while others enjoy it. I happen to find it fascinating and without it, I couldn't have survived, healed and found purpose in my life. Doing so, has been my life's journey and the only way I was able to travel through this lifetime without collapsing or complete destruction.

When you are genuinely able to self-reflect after that perhaps most of the time, what you are feeling is up to you. But it might take lots of digging into your psyche to understand why something bothers, 'triggers' you or also even as to why something brings you joy.

When your pain becomes overwhelming, when you find you are living in a repetitive kind of Hell and your life is not what or where you want it to be, not what you want to create. When you have the awareness and can accept that you are operating out of imprints, perceptions, a belief system and pattern that is not your own. That you have taken on a way of living and thinking from someone else, experiences or circumstances from your past. You will decide to release the negative imprints and beliefs that are bringing you what you do not want. Un-brainwash yourself, tear apart embedded belief systems, re-evaluate imprints, break against them for understanding. Once torn apart they can be realigned. Then you will be free to create flexible, ever changing beliefs and observations to assist you in moving towards achieving your desires, being at peace and living to your full potential.

Constantly changing, flexible beliefs and observations of self and others leave you open to change with the capability to create a truly fulfilling and peaceful life. What was meant for negative and evil can be turned to positive and good. That may have been the purpose in the first place.

MEMORIES AND IMPRINTS

OUR MIND IS MADE UP of memories. Who we are and what we believe and how we live is comprised of our imprints and memories. Who and what we are is driven by our memories either consciously or unconsciously.

When a memory, or 'imprint' enters your mind, pleasant or not, it's something that your heart, mind and spirit want to revisit. It may be for the pleasure and joy in the remembering. Or if negative in its imprint and intent has surfaced to trigger that which causes you pain, in order that it to be revealed, examined then released. But it's impossible to release that which you are unaware of. Some imprints and memories may keep returning to your mind as if screaming, 'Please get rid of me! See me! Become aware of why you keep remembering me! So you can release me and be free!'

In our lifetimes, we have many experiences and memories. It would be impossible to recall them all. Therefore, why do certain memories stay with us or reenter our minds repeatedly more than others? Have you ever wondered why you have certain memories that stick with you? Why you recall that which you do and the way in which you recall it? It could be that something in present time triggered the memory or it could be that the imprint needs to be revisited, in order that it be seen, acknowledged, understood and released. A strong realization and truth is, what you aren't aware of, you can't change or grow from or actually even have joy in. Therefore, awareness is the key to healing, releasing and also joy. You will block your joy, if you focus repeatedly and continually on the negative.

Some people will block memories, deny imprints and pretend their life, their parents and families are perfect or even ideal. Some will idolize their parents. As they try to keep the negative and unhappiness at bay, so they think. I have never met anyone with a perfect family. But most families are or may be perfect in their imperfection. Most parents are not evil but we are all guided and flawed by imprints that do damage and are carried forward.

Some people stay stuck their whole life living imprinted and being guided by the imprints made on them by others. They think they are this or that because their parents or others of influence told them this and that, and they took it to be truth. They think life must be lived in this way or that way or that something is one way or another and the only reason they think and live in this way is because they have been imprinted.

Children are for the most part formed by the age of seven. We are learning, impressionable and observing continually in those formative years. Imprints made in those tender years are the most covert and deep. Therefore many of the imprints that guide your life, you may not even know or realize that they are doing so, until you become aware.

It may take some kind of trauma, death, divorce, birth of a child, an illness that triggers you to become self-reflective with the desire and need to dig out the negative imprints and to shift your perspective. When the pain or internal conflict becomes unbearable, you will be triggered to find out why and to either let it go or to keep on stuffing it down so that it will/can be repeated.

Some people live in denial, stuffing down imprints, emotions and the feelings attached to them with drugs, drink, food, sex or avoidance, defense and denial, along with other physical and emotional addictions and ways to cover up. They look to escape rather than to deal with their pain, their issues and what they are truly feeling deep inside, no matter how badly they get off the rails or fall off the cliff. They may even feel comfortable in their depression— for example. So they wallow in it. Some may even revert back to infantile reactions and behaviors when wounds are triggered. Or they pull so much into self that they become chronically depressed. Others have extreme anxiety and don't understand why they do. Depression and anxiety oftentimes go hand in hand and often times are caused by suppressed imprints and memories. Some spend a lifetime trying to figure it all out, why they think and behave as they do. It takes looking back in genuine and honest self-reflection to uncover imprints, perceptions of them and beliefs that we no longer want to have directing our thoughts, choices and ultimately our lives. You may temporarily feel more pain by doing this, but then you will have release.

To assist in triggering memories, look at photos, videos, etc. from the past. They will often bring to mind what happened preceding the photo and after—both joyful and negative.

Think back and without filtering, answer these questions:

- When did you feel the most happy or joyful in your life?

- When did you feel the darkest or most down in your life?

- Next:

- What is a happy, pleasant or joyful memory that immediately comes to mind concerning your parents, caregivers or childhood?

- What is a worst, unpleasant or painful memory that comes to mind concerning your parents, caregivers or childhood?

- What is the first statement, phrase, belief or warning that comes to mind that you were told often in your childhood or as a young adult? That you may even hear repeatedly in your mind's eye to this day.

- Who was it that conveyed this message and why do you think that they did?

- Now concerning each of these memories—what is your awareness about them? What is there to understand? What is there to accept? What is there to forgive?

In this process to awareness, you can of course recall and work it out in your mind. But I found that to write it down helped especially in the beginning. Then I can refer back to what I wrote and think even further back and go deeper. The more you become aware, the more it will trigger other memories for further awareness. Also the very act of writing your thoughts connects them to your mind and consciousness in awareness.

As I became more aware and adept at using the process, I now can do it in my mind more quickly. Of course, it depends on the severity of what I am looking at or dealing with in any given time. It's become second nature to me as it clears my emotional system and mind.

It takes bravery and strength to revisit trauma and negative experiences and to relive them. The weak prefer to close their eyes to truth and to stay where they are, no matter how stuck or painful where they are may be. The weak cannot forgive. Forgiveness is an attribute of the strong. The weak need something to hold onto for justification of their unhappiness, anger and lack. The strong want to dig it up, figure it out, and then to let it go. So they can move past it and go forward. The weak don't want to see truth and become aware. They prefer to hide their heads, deny, become defensive or run away. The strong and the brave have a burning desire for truth and to become aware. I think more often than not, most all of us want and prefer to be on the brave and strong side of ourselves.

"An unexamined life is not worth living." attributed to Plato but actually stated by Socrates at his trial. Socrates believed that philosophy - *the love of wisdom* - was the most important pursuit above all else. For some, he exemplifies more than anyone else in history the pursuit of wisdom through questioning and logical argument, by examining and by thinking. His 'examination' of life in this way spilled out into the lives of others, such that they began their own 'examination' of life, but he knew they would all die one day, as saying that a life without philosophy—an 'unexamined' life—was not worth living.

When you are ready to ask, who am I? Why do I think as I do? Behave as I do? Make the choices that I do? What am I comprised of? When you are ready to hear the answers and desire change in your life then you will become brave enough to become the change.

Questions to ask of self to assist in becoming aware:

Why am I in this family?
Why am I in these circumstances?
Why am I in this situation?
Why am I with this person?
Why am I around these people?

What will/does my being in this family—or in these circum-stances—or in this situation—or around these people teach, reveal and help to grow, stretch or to expand me?

There will come a time when you realize that your parents didn't really know everything and were not correct about everything that they did know. In fact, much of what they knew or shared was not only wrong but was not good for you to be around. Your parents may have been wise and correct about some things and dead wrong about others. They may have been kind and sweet in some areas and negative evil-doers in others. They may have lied, cheated, stolen or worse. They may have looked great to the world but been abusive behind closed doors. They may have looked like slobs to the world but been great loving parents. Whomever they were and are, there will come a time, if you are maturing to become wise about self and life that you realize who and what your parents are and this will help you to understand yourself and why you think as you do, behave as you do and perceive the world as you do. When you become an adult, hopefully you will realize your parents are responsible for the imprints that they created in you. They do not have to control your life. Keep the positive ones and break against or let go of the others.

When you examine in self-reflection and awareness then become more aware, you will recognize that where you were placed in life was the perfect place for your self-growth giving you the chance and opportunity to become more than what you were when you arrived on earth.

IDOLIZATION OR VILIFICATION OF PARENTS AND ANCESTORS

WHEN YOU EITHER IDOLIZE OR vilify parents, ancestors or anyone, you can become blinded to all their dimensions, both positive and negative. Every human being on earth is made up of both in varying degrees. We are on the planet of dualities and here to balance the good and evil inside ourselves.

If you cannot see evil or negativity, even deny its existence, are blinded to it, then it can more easily infiltrate and take you and your life over. It can hold you hostage, no matter in whatever insidious place it hides or form that it takes. Isn't that what evil wants you to do, not be able to recognize it? We need to be able to recognize evil in order that we keep ourselves safe, centered and out of its grips. Evil and negativity are things you can break against to reveal and focus on the good and positive in yourself, your life and the world. The dark defines the light.

If you can only recognize and see goodness then you are blinded to the truth and all its dimensions. You blind yourself to the darkness of evil and the havoc it can wreak. If you focus only on the goodness then you can't see the dark. We need to be aware and able to recognize and see both. Be aware; not all people are what they appear. Some pretend to be a walk on the beach, but are actually leading to quicksand.

Conversely, if you only focus on the negativity and evil and can't recognize goodness, then you will be blocked from the positive and joy.

As children, we have a tendency to see our parents as gods and the only authority there is in our lives. Until other adults are introduced into our lives, our parents actually are our only authority, guides and measure of how to exist and to live. Then we have other adults enter our lives; relatives, babysitters, teachers, etc. to observe and learn from as we enter more into the world. But even then, there are some children who may/can see only their parents as their authority and their definition of self. Boundaries are crossed and become blurred. They allow their parents to infiltrate their being and define who they are without the ability to question. And this can be detrimental to the individual's sense of self, self-esteem, self -worth, either by over valuation or under.

Some people may have a need to see and defend parents as being perfect so they themselves have a sense of worth, even perhaps, a grandiose sense of worth instead of developing their own individual identity, separate from parents.

I have found those who claim perfection in their parents and families may be the most damaged, wounded and may be suppressing, hiding or denying the truth of deep seated familial issues. They may be living in internal fear and depression and may flip into anxiety and defense posture rather than recognizing the truth and becoming aware. They block, deny and become defensive claiming perfection and if anyone confronts them. They may even cut them out of their lives. They are afraid to have their vulnerabilities exposed. They have trouble dealing with the vulnerabilities in others, so have issues getting genuinely close to people. People dealing with these issues may stay immature and child-like on some level their whole lives.

There is no weakness in opening yourself up to genuinely feeling your emotions. It's courageous to search and to ask why you have the feelings that you do. Being vulnerable isn't being needy or weak; they are very different. The ability to allow self to be vulnerable is the act of a courageous and genuine person.

Some parents are overbearing and controlling, breaching boundaries, while others demanding in their neediness and some are a mix of all. Therefore an unnatural merging can easily be created in the child. They may become unnaturally emotionally tied to the parent and their parent defines the very essence of who they are or who they think that they are. So they have a strong need to defend the parents as being perfect and to claim that their parents were perfect and loved them flawlessly and completely. Any criticism or pointing out of flaws in family members will be met with denial and a defensive posture because it feels as if it threatens the very core of their being. These are persons oftentimes overly concerned with image. They try to hide behind the façade of what they want it to have been or what they pretend it was or is.

Death and Mourning—Some people have trouble getting past or might never get over the death of their parents. This is usually because they are still trying to get what they never got from their parents when they were children or when their parents were alive. Therefore, they still have a need to seek parental approval in some form or another. To stay hooked into this energy dance can keep a person a perpetual child. Everyone dies, it's a natural passing. After parents die, usually a person comes into full adulthood, if they haven't done so before.

Of course, we miss people after they die. It's human and natural to do so. But to hold onto those who are dead in some sort of idolization and or extreme grief at length, reveals deep- seated issues in the person doing so or within the relationship with the person who has died. After mourning, there usually comes a peace.

I missed my father deeply and at times, of course still do. After his death, I went through grief, anger, pain, hurt, sorrow and a deep ache in my heart. I used 'the process' concerning my memories and imprints of him and by doing so, assisted to relieve the intensity of my pain. I was able to arrive at awareness, understanding, acceptance and forgiveness. Now I most always feel peace and love when I think of him. I also feel his spirit around me often. I let his earth presence go, that I may go forward in what God has for me to do and to experience while I am on earth.

I believe that having faith assists with the acceptance of death. Our earthly body dies, but we have eternal life. To stay in mourning is to stay blocked. It freezes a person in a place of negativity, stagnation and limits, even cuts off the ability for joy in present time.

Some parents, as in any abusive relationship balance, reward with punishment—something good then something bad. This keeps the child hooked and off balance as they hope desperately for the good to return. As they try, deny and endure the abuse or negativity, so that they can eventually have the reward again of; love, acceptance, kindness, or attention. This type of imprint is what leaves people open to getting in and staying in abusive relationships for the rest of their lives on whatever level that they are. It can be repetitive in one's soul to keep the negative energy alive, as in not being able to let go after someone dies, as the one alive still seeks and yearns for a glimpse of love and caring.

After Dad died, a man you can tell after reading my memories that I loved dearly and admired in many ways, I was talking to my ex-husband. The alcoholic whom I divorced and he commented that he was sorry to hear about my Dad's death, but now that the SOB is dead, I can live. I chuckled in understanding of that comment, instead of taking offense or becoming defensive, because my dad could be a real SOB at times, and I well knew it. I had no need to defend Dad or to get angry when someone stated a truth about an aspect of him. My ex-husband knew my dad. He knew all sides of him because he had experienced them.

I can see all sides of my dad. He was a man's man, self-made—successful, had Yachts, ranches, horses, cattle and airplanes. He was kind, generous, fun, adventurous, arrogant, boastful, controlling, intelligent, loving, critical, cruel, insecure, ambitious, athletic, competitive, promiscuous, a womanizer, morally pompous, creative and more. Why would I deny one aspect one him? If I can acknowledge one side, why wouldn't or shouldn't I be able to see and be aware of all of him?

If I were still locked in—blocked in a child-like emotional mindset, I would not be able to recognize all sides of my dad and would not be able to understand, accept and forgive. I would become defensive and in denial because I would have the need to think him perfect—so that I could feed my ego and feel/pretend that I was derived from perfection. Only by so doing, I would be denying the truth and I would stay blocked. My dad was a complex and flawed human being just as we all are and also a talented fabulous human being as most of us are.

An exercise to awareness—Write one sentence or group of words that describe each one of your relatives or persons close to or important to you in your life. Don't filter. Write the first thoughts or words that enter your mind. I will write mine as an example:

Father—Money, power, work, enduring, insecure, arrogant, much of the time cut off or denied emotions, disappointed in mother and in women, controlling, protecting, provider, intelligent, brilliant engineer, pilot, Yachtsman, rancher, dreamer, ambitious, generous, a great giver of gifts, big dreams, bigger than life, talented, intense, worrier, alcoholic, abusive, punitive, achiever, fun, loving, kind, cheater, promiscuous, religious, adventurous, loved life.

Mother—Not there, weak, overwhelmed, alone, selfish, no emotion, no affect, boring, unhappy, depressed, smoked cigarettes, critical, cruel, polite in public, cold, rarely smiled, alcoholic, lifeless, indulged, critical, complainer, cheap, kind, vengeful, vindictive, envious, thought being on earth was hell, escaped into TV and liquor often so she wouldn't have to be present and live, tired, hates to cook, is a good cook, her movements slow, little energy, lazy, dependent, indecisive, did the best that she could in her circumstances—Southern manners or respectability, enjoyed swing dancing with Dad, cigarettes, and Big Band music.

Mother's Mother—loved me, selfish, indulged, looking for fun and attention, loved life, hated life, quick mind and wit, intelligent, liked to party, smoked cigarettes, enjoyed gambling, thought God was punishing her, thought God didn't like her, didn't like people all that much, enjoyed scotch, shrimp, and bridge.

Father's Mother—grace, calm, alone, loving, kind, weak, submissive, close to God, sad, great cook.

Mother's Father—twinkle in his eye, alone, kind, loving, provider, protector, hardworking.

Father's Father—cruel, insecure, and abusive.

These are just some of the traits that I was around and were coming at me daily, especially from my parents. I was imprinted with their traits in one form or another, or I broke against them and tried to be the opposite of what I saw displayed. In regard to my mother, I wanted to be nothing like her. So I overcompensated and became overly responsible, strong and tried to rarely show that I was overwhelmed or lazy. I tried to be what I thought was perfect which was the opposite of what she was in my mind. Trying to be 'perfect' is futile because there is no such thing. I did emulate mother's outward manners which were that of a lady and how to behave in public. This must've imprinted in her in childhood and stayed with her even after what was done to her.

I am a mixture of all the above in varying degrees plus more including my individual traits. 'Nature vs. Nurture' is always at play and in varying degrees. It is impossible to measure in what levels their influence. As you can see by my first written thoughts about my relatives, some had/have a more profound imprint on me than others. Some traits I broke against and others I accepted into myself on various levels.

Now write down yours. Then read with awareness concerning what these examples and perceptions of what you wrote from your memory are saying to you: about how to be—what's acceptable or what's not—how to live, behave and about where you derive your imprints and beliefs about life, self and others. Be aware that you are a mix of them all. Either that you break against what they are, or what you perceive that they are and why. Or you accept them into yourself and behave similarly as you travel through your life and make your choices. It can become your defended way to behave, live and to believe. These are your imprints that create your beliefs about self and life.

Steps to awareness:

1. Write down the ways you think and believe that you are just like or similar to your parents.

2. Write the ways that you think that you are not like them.

3. Write how you once were like them and how you have changed in awareness by; growing up, maturing, living

away from them, observing others and/or just by living your life.

My Example:

As a preteen observing Mother, I thought perhaps, women weren't supposed to be happy or smile much. So I emulated the same. Until I read in magazines and observed other women to realize they smiled, were happy, had interests and enjoyed life.

I was naturally a happy child, but as I grew up, I temporarily took on mother's behaviors as she modeled them to me. While trying to learn to be a woman, I first emulated the one closest to me. The one I saw the most often had the most influence. But Mother's behaviors were not mine. I was trying to be something unnatural to my being and it made me miserable. I am innately happy. I was born that way. I smile lots, move quickly and enjoy moving. That I would rather do many things other than to sit and watch TV, doesn't mean that at times, I don't enjoy lazing around watching nonsense programs and otherwise. But it isn't my life.

Recall at the age of four and five, I climbed a tall fence to get out of my backyard to go exploring. I am full of energy and life. So trying to be like my mother was killing who I am. The less I was around her, the less I emulated her and the less I liked her. And she didn't like me because I was so different from her. We didn't mesh. I didn't understand her and she didn't understand me. Therefore, I irritated her and she frustrated me.

The less I was around either of my parents, the happier and more myself I became. As a child their imprints were happening on an unconscious level to control me as I grew up and away, I consciously begin to break away from their hold.

I recall when I was a young adult in college and lived with my parents. I slept late one weekend morning. I was sitting on the floor in the family room, still in my nightgown, intensely reading the fashion and society section of the newspaper. I looked up to notice Dad observing me with love and amusement in his eyes. I inquired, a bit embarrassed by his staring, "Dad, why are you watching me?" He chuckled then responded, "Because, you look so cute. Why are you so happy?" I thought, 'What a weird question. Why wouldn't or shouldn't I be happy?' I replied, "I don't know? I just am." He smiled then chuckled. "You are so dang cute."

In that moment, Dad took pleasure observing me content and happy. He didn't see that in mother. I am sure that she wore him out with her sadness, negativity and lack of joy. I know that Dad enjoyed and wanted me to be happy. But I came to realize that both my parents and my sisters were envious of my being in internal peace and happiness. Many times, they did everything they could to disrupt it.

My dad thought money and things made a person happy. It was how he was imprinted from his childhood. His parent's weren't happy and they were poor. Therefore, Dad thought if he made lots of money that he, his wife and children would/should be happy. Dad made lots of money and acquired many things but he wasn't all that happy. Money and things are great but they will not make a joyless person happy for long. There are many people with little money who are happy. At times in my life, I have been one of them. As long as I had clean sheets on my bed, worked out and had a hot shower, I was happy. Much happier than living in a large house with everything materialistic, being with a man who is miserable and hell bent on making me as unhappy as he was.

When I became aware and really conscious instead of being led by imprints, the differences in me from my family accelerated. I became even more myself experiencing peace and internal joy most all of the time and on the path to becoming more of whom God intended me to be. I looked to God as my authority and not my parents.

When I moved to another state was when I internally shifted big time. Even though I went through very difficult times, I could still be content in my soul because for the most part I liked me. It was usually when around my parents and family that I didn't like myself. When I was away from my parental and familial influence was when I became just plain happy to be a human being living on earth. Away from my parents, I realized that I deserved to be happy.

I faced my pain and walked through most of my very unpleasant imprints, emotions and beliefs to reach genuine happiness. At those times, when I do fall into pain, depression or sadness, I find the awareness in past memories, imprints or thoughts but current ones also. I go then to understanding, acceptance and forgiveness to bring me back to joy. Sure, I might stew in the pain of the triggered emotions for a while. But knowing how great it feels to be without them, I do what I can to release as quickly as possible. We are continually being imprinted by others. Perhaps not as deeply as when we were children, but people we love have the ability to imprint us. Those with authority over us have the ability to imprint us. Friends have the ability to imprint us. Even the television has the ability to imprint us.

Had I not looked outside my parental models and influences, I might still be trying to emulate their unhappiness and discontent along with not smiling all that much. In order to make my parents feel comfortable around me. I am not like my family members. I am different. I don't mesh with them and they don't mesh with me. I choose to be who I am. They were the rocks I broke against to break me open to my awareness, understanding, acceptance, forgiveness into love and joy.

Also, realize and understand that the harder you try to resist something, the more it can attach, 'resist and it persists', until you step out of denial into full awareness, understanding, acceptance and forgiveness. Then the hurt and pain will drop off and you will become your unique self without the imprints of others guiding you and controlling your life. Negative imprints and memories will either kill you or heal you!

As most of us create a separate identity from parents and family, we become more aware and can see all sides of parents—good, bad, ugly and the in-between. Then we can genuinely accept them for whom and what they are and forgive. Some people can do this naturally as they mature; others need assistance in becoming aware. So they be free and at choice.

Parental love for you and your love for them does not mean that the person or parent is perfect. Each person loves in the way that they were taught to love or how they experienced being loved themselves. The way we love is imprinted, beginning when we are infants, when our parents or caregiver are the only place from which we receive our nurturing and expressions of love. Infant imprints are profound and deep. So if you were abused as an infant, left to be hungry and to cry or if your every need was met before you even whimpered, these imprints will define the way you give and receive love. If your every need was met, before you even had it, you may not learn to self-comfort and calm yourself. If your mother or caregiver was over-attentive, you may have felt suffocated. If you were neglected and left to cry at length, you may have a fear of being abandoned. It's a complex balance between parent and child. And you will not recognize why you love as you do, until you become aware and do.

Children feel the energy from their parents and the issues in the energy both the positive and negative. We learn how to love another from observing how our parents loved or didn't love one another and how they loved or didn't love us. We either break against what was shown and imprinted or we repeat it, for good or for ill. Children learn how to love by observing their parent's interaction in relationship. The bond is clearly between the two adults with the children being just outside that circle to observe. The reflection of the love is then bestowed onto the children. This observance is what makes a child feel loved, secure and with knowledge of how to express love, give love, feel love and live with another. The parental example and modeling imprints a child for their whole life. Until, awareness is triggered.

Therefore you can see why it's imperative that you see your parents in full reality of who and what they are—not how you hope or think they are or how they tell you they are -or even how they tell you who or what you. They are seeing you through their imprints. When you can see yourself without their imprints and beliefs in the way and in full awareness is what and when you are set you free.

Example: Some parents give the image that they are religious, attend church regularly, have you attend church and demand that you do as they say to be 'good'; then do immoral behaviors right before your eyes. Or, you may find out immoral things that they have done and hidden. Finding out discrepancies in a parent such as this can be devastating if you idolize them. Parents are just people doing the best they can with their individual imprints, perceptions and belief systems that hold them in place and guide them.

Another example: 'The Mama's boy'—Either the boy had a mother who 'appeared' perfect or was overbearing or manipulative or so overly needy that she overwhelmed him with her personality. What or whichever it was; boundaries were crossed so that the boy lost himself in his mother. Neediness, no matter what form it comes from, a mother can create a male that can't connect to a woman in a healthy way. Until he deals with the imprints from his mother/ female figure, he is doomed and so are his relationships with women. No woman will measure up or he will consciously or unconsciously hate women. This will act out in his life in various ways. Any woman with normal needs will remind him of the suffocation he felt with his mother and he will not be able to tolerate it. He will pick the woman apart, be emotionally or physically abusive or flee. If he over-idolized his mother, no woman will measure up and this imprint will stay stuck in him. He will not be able to genuinely commit in love to a woman and become vulnerable to love as he was with the first woman in his life, 'his mother', until he has awareness and release. It's not until he becomes self-reflective in awareness, understanding, acceptance and forgiveness that he will have an ability to release these negative, limiting, destructive imprints. Conversely, a male who has/ had a balanced and positive relationship with his mother where she displayed and taught him how to treat women; if she is self-aware, self-reliant, emotionally balanced and allowed the boy to be himself and to separate from her, then he is able to grow into manhood. A mother can be a great example of what a female is to a male. Of course and usually, there is a mix of both imprints, negative and positive and in varying degrees.

Fathers' model to sons how to treat women. A son learns how to regard women or not, by observing how their father treats, honors, loves and respects his wife and their mother. Men teach boys all the time, how to regard women by their example. If a boy sees a man abusing women, he will either be imprinted and do the same or break against it and do the opposite. If he observes his father abusing his mother, the son may try to protect the mother or he may lose respect for his mother for allowing it. If a mother dominates the father, either by her strength or her weakness and the son perceives the father as weak and unmanly, the boy may be repulsed by his father's behavior and vow to never allow a woman to control him. Or, he may be imprinted and become just as weak as his father or when he becomes aware, he may break against that imprint and learn manly traits and how to love and be in a balanced relationship. It's all about the level of awareness and whether the imprint stays or is broken against.

'Daddy's Girl'—Same is true for a female and her father figure. The difference is that usually in the father/daughter connection, unless the father was terribly abusive, the woman does not hate men. As a 'Mama's boy' might hate women, all the while looking to mom as the only real authority in his life. If the father was emotionally or physically abusive, either in her observance of how he treated women or treatment of her, she may grow up to hate men, be fearful of them or manipulative of them, until she has awareness. Being a 'Daddy's girl' is usually not as harmful to future relationships as the harmful connection of boy/mother. A 'Daddy's girl' may have more strength and be able to make her way in the world if her father taught her skills. It may serve to keep the negative men away. Usually, the way a father treats his daughter is the measure of how she will expect or allow other men to treat her in her life. But it may cause her to measure all men against her father and none will measure up which can cause the same outcomes as with a 'Mama's boy'. The difference can also be that women have more of a tendency to self-analyze, reflect and become aware on their own about what drives them, than most men. I was certainly a 'Daddy's girl' and it affected how I looked at men both for good and for ill.

Both a mother's and father's energy is needed as role model that is why it takes a male and female to create life . . .

If you choose to delve deep in connection with another in genuine love, you will be faced with waves of emotions, euphoria as well as fear along with many other emotions with the feelings attached to them and only the emotionally aware, self-reflective and those seeking balance are able to do this. Weak, imbalanced people attach to people superficially, out of need, for exploitation, to attain value, money or something to make them feel better about self. It's the emotionally healthy people who can genuinely love.

Separation from parents—baby to toddler—parents are your world, they create and are your security. Example: Your mother takes you to nursery school or for a play date. As you play with others, you turn back to see if mommy is still there. You may even go over to touch her knee and to say, hi! Then you go back to resume playing with your playmates.

What if when the child needs a momentary connection to mom, an overly needy mom holds onto the child and will not let them resume playing? What if the mother says to the child, 'Don't leave mommy. Mommy needs you and wants to hold you.' And even restrains the child in her lap. The child will either submit and the separation steps will be marred. They may even become enmeshed with their needy mother. Or, they will fight her and pull away to go play, carrying the guilt for doing so or feeling freedom in their inner acknowledgment of their independence.

If the mother doesn't allow separation this will create a feeling of suffocation, dependence or guilt in the child. It's natural to seek independence from parents and to separate. If this is thwarted in some regard, it will lead to issues later in life. As a child learns to separate from parents, they need to check that mommy is there less often. And this is when they become autonomous. If separation doesn't occur, this is what can create, for example: 'The Mama's boy', an avoidant personality disorder, or other disorders and issues in those who can't/won't separate from parents to mature, grow up and create their own life. Emotionally healthy parents will guide their children towards separation; others will lean on children burdening them with their own imprint of need, fear, etc. If a parent will not let a child separate their identity, it can haunt the child for their whole life. They may not be able to connect in a healthy, intimate way in a relationship.

Just as idolizing parents is harmful to self-worth, so is vilifying parents. Perhaps your parents were pure evil and abusive. The reality is they carried this treatment forward from what they were imprinted with as a child or young person. If you vilify them, it makes it difficult to forgive giving them even more power over you and creating continual damage. Once you acknowledge what they are, break against them to heal. Think how sad it would be, being Satan, all that hate and evil inside, never to know love, empathy or peace. Always searching to destroy and to reap destruction onto others to satisfy self needs, would truly be a life of torment and horror.

DELUSIONS AND ILLUSIONS

SEEING IN FULL AWARENESS MAY shatter many, if not all of your illusions and delusions, but it's the only way to healing, release and forgiveness. When you realize that what you thought was your comfort, security and safety and come to find out it was your pain and from where doubt, torment, insecurity and negativity derived—illusions and delusions will fall drop off and you will step into reality, acceptance and understanding of self. It's a great place to be.

Worshiping and covering up the family wounds generation to generation is the complete opposite of healing. If we take our stuff, put it on an altar and worship it and then expect others to do the same, it creates victims out of everyone involved.

Every miracle begins with a problem or challenge. Human beings are complex and as an adult you have the chance, choice and ability to unwind through it all by becoming into awareness, understanding, accepting then into forgiveness to be able to be filled up with peace, love and joy.

INTERNAL MORAL ADJUSTER

NO ONE IS PERFECT. WE all have our flaws and blind sides. We also have an internal moral adjuster which is the center core in each one of us that lets us know when we have done something 'wrong'. It's our conscience. Conscience is a group of laws written on your heart. Mankind has demonstrated that they know God's principles. No matter, if we know the Bible or not, most of us know we should not murder, steal, be jealous, commit adultery and generally not do the things that displease our Creator. But some choose to 'deny' their conscience, in order to gain worldly goods, power over others, or acceptance. Some turn to evil or addictions to suppress their pain of going against their internal moral adjuster. Those hooked on drugs, alcohol, food, sex, the escapists and power hungry are looking for something outside themselves instead of looking inward to whom they really are and to what is written on their hearts. For some, God is not enough and who they are is not enough. Therefore, they must 'feel' in control, in power over others, striving to feel pleasure most of the time or they crave and try to find escape. Some will deny the realization of their conscience in every way possible that they can use or find.

This of course, varies in each person, what is deemed as wrong, immoral or corrupt. Some are able to justify doing just about anything. Their ends justify their means. Some are able to corrupt, lie, con, rape and or kill, etc., while being proud of their ability to do so. And others will utilize persons such as these for their having the ability to do their dirty deeds for them. They are sociopaths/psychopaths set on agenda. They can and will do and use whatever it takes to achieve their self-serving goals. Those with a corrupted moral adjuster will use manipulation, fear, coercion or any and everything that they think they are able to get away with.

Some people have little to no conscience and are so warped with the ability to say and do anything to achieve their goals. They have a total disconnect from their internal moral adjuster. Or perhaps, they were born without a conscience—born of evil. Some people are, you know? They may be able to con and to fool many, but not for long, those who are in tune and in balance with their internal moral adjuster.

Others have a moral adjuster that is clear and precise concerning what is moral—'right from wrong'. What is evil and what is good and if they veer too far from their innate moral adjuster, they feel horrible. It shows in their mannerisms, body language and voice as their energy vibration and the light in their eyes becomes dimmed.

Some as they age and self-reflect realize what they have done 'wrong' and wish to make amends and atonement. As some get closer to death, they may desire atonement because nothing you gain in this world will matter after death. Especially if it was gained by ill-will, lies, con and harm to others. Nothing on earth matters as much as what you carry in your soul—so it's best to guard it. If you have wisdom, you will listen to your God-given internal moral adjuster.

When you are in touch with your internal moral adjuster, you are more able to see another's. Observe not only their words, but their eyes, their voice tone, their mannerisms, along with that 'indefinable' something that reveals their true nature and character. Not what they are 'trying' to be or to 'sell'—not their image, but who they really are. Do they have a light in their spirit? Are they true to their moral adjuster or are they a con unto themselves and therefore a con to all others?

Our internal moral adjuster is created in us by environment and the time we are born, our parents, our teachers, our education, all of our experiences and situations. Ultimately, it's who we are at our deepest core level. Again 'nature vs. nurture' is in play. It's our conscience. It's our soul. It's the spark of the divine in us.

This moral adjuster that guides and forms us throughout life decides who we will become, how we will treat others and how, when and if we will cheat, steal, lie, con and more. In other words, it decides if we will sin and when we do, if we will have a conscience about doing so. Some have moral adjusters that consider it okay to cheat but would not kill. Some would steal, but would not cheat. Others deem it okay to lie under certain circumstances but not others. Some think that if they attend church regularly all is well, even if they bring the person they are cheating with another on, to church with them. Some moral adjusters decide that if no one knows or catches them in their indiscretions then it's okay. If they got away with it then it doesn't count or matter. 'Justification' is a powerful tool of the moral adjuster. I have known some who attend church regularly, but in their personal and business lives commit adultery, lie and cheat, etc., but they seem to think that their 'image' of being a church-goer makes everything acceptable. Their image is all that matters. This is how their individual moral adjuster justifies their behaviors. The moral adjuster is internal but is reflected externally in every action and decision that we make.

Our individual moral adjuster has the ability and can justify all things relative to circumstances and need. That what's right for one can be wrong for another. Some moral adjusters allow for 'live as I tell you to—not as I do'. Some can even make good seem evil and evil be good. It becomes just a matter of degree, need, want, goals, agenda and circumstance—justification.

Those without conscience, with a corrupted moral adjuster or those who don't/won't listen to their moral adjuster or are without a moral compass can be truly monsters of destruction. No moral adjuster is 'perfect', or correct all the time, except of course, Jesus Christ to which some moral adjusters do aspire to be. We were given the guidelines to follow to have a righteous life and to create a 'good' society, The Golden Rule, 'do unto to others as you would have them do unto you' and the Ten Commandments.

Be aware and understand that we all have an internal moral adjuster, you, your siblings, your relatives, your ancestors and everyone in the world. It defines who we are and what we determine to be right or wrong. Conflicts between internal moral adjusters are what create the energy and vibration for either peace or conflict inside us, between individuals and even countries.

RESPONSIBILITY

Definition of **RESPONSIBILITY**—the quality or state of being responsible: such as moral, legal or mental accountability **RELIABILITY, TRUSTWORTHINESS**: something for which one is responsible. To be responsible is to respond, to honor, to be trustworthy—to live to a higher standard.

RESPONSIBILITY IS AN IMPORTANT KEY to living a moral, happy, content and peaceful life—to be responsible makes for a productive and fulfilling life. When there is awareness then it's time for responsibility which includes accountability to understand and to either accept, change or break against. Otherwise, you will be stuck and blocked in blame, denial and defensiveness which lead to more of the same. Everyone has issues and trauma in their lives in some form and to continue to use them as an excuse for lack of responsibility and accountability is immaturity. When you know why you behave in a way or think as you do that creates stress and pain in yourself and others and you don't change it—that is being irresponsible. Those without responsibility to self and to others live a lost life. All of us are accountable and there are consequences in life for lack of responsibility and accountability. If you don't pay your car payment, it will be repossessed. If you don't pay your utility bills, they will be turned off. If a man is not responsible to and for his wife and her to him—best if done in equal parts—the marriage will fail.

I was overly responsible in my marriages and it lead to destruction. When one person shoulders all the responsibility in a partnership or relationship—the burden becomes too much—balance is impaired and weakness seeps in. Sure at times, one may need to shoulder more responsibly because of circumstances. If you aren't responsible to your children, family and live a responsible life—it will all fall apart— they will leave—become unruly with a sense of lack, direction and ultimately failure.

Everything worthwhile and of value in life comes from commitment and responsibility to that commitment. And that includes healing of your emotional self. Fears and limits set by imprints and beliefs are often illusions. It's your responsibility to self to shift in order to live your highest life.

EGO

Definition of **EGO**: a person's sense of self-esteem or self-importance—the part of the mind that mediates between the conscious and the unconscious and is responsible for reality testing and a sense of personal identity.

OUR EGO LEVEL AND VALUATION may change drastically when we are fractured and out of balance. Ego may go from one extreme to the other from feeling down and weak to overly confident triggered by external circumstances or internal self-talk.

There is a syndrome—where you go from feeling less than, to more than, but not equal to. Which is—you feel insecure and less than others—that you are not good enough—you don't matter—everyone is better than you—have more—are more attractive—more intelligent, etc. Then you flip into thinking and feeling that you are better than—smarter than -everyone else is a fool even stupid and you know more, are special and are way above and better than they are. You go from feeling below everyone in the world to higher than everyone in the world. Which means that you don't feel equal to, equal to the challenge, equal to living life in the way you desire, equal to developing your talents and skills, equal to taking care of and grooming your body so that you are the best you can be—equal to being on earth along with everyone else.

When you are feeling less than, you will fall into envy, jealousy, denial and defensiveness. You may criticize and blame others to make self feel better. You beat yourself up with negative self-talk and dark thoughts. You fall into fear of the future. Fear, insecurity and negativity take you over. You fear dealing with tasks and dealing with others. You don't like people and think they don't like you. You are insecure and devalue yourself and everyone else.

When you are feeling more than, you will bloat up with arrogance—will treat others with disrespect, like you are much better than they are—you will boast and brag—you will talk down to people—criticize them to show them that you are better than they are, etc. You over value yourself to the extent that you become unbearable.

Either way, you are not at balance and don't feel equal. You go from feeling like you are nothing to feeling like you are above all others. Continually and repeatedly doing this will wear you out as you beat yourself up in insecurity then bloat yourself up in self-importance. Genuine self-confidence is feeling equal to the challenge. That you self-reflect, learn, evaluate self before pointing the finger outward. Ego and confidence are two different things.

Definition of **CONFIDENCE**—feeling or consciousness of one's ability or reliance of one's circumstances—faith or belief that one will act in a right, proper or effective way—to have confidence is to have trust in self-reliance and ability.

Sure there are days we all feel like a bitch, are grumpy and out of sorts then there are days when we feel on top of the world, can do no wrong and are king of all we survey—simplistically, like the difference between a good hair day and a bad one. When you are at balance, the extremes won't take you down as low as to fall into depression or so high that you become reckless into self-destruction. You will not be blown about by the external winds of change—up so high then down low controlled by every turn and twist. You will remain, more often than not, at confidence and equal to the challenge. Being in internal confidence, you will/can more easily adapt to others and circumstances staying more in balance without the highs and lows. You will be able to focus on issues and solutions, instead of allowing your emotions and the feelings connected to them take you over.

A fractured ego—goes from one extreme to the other, from over valuation of self to devaluation of self. Emotions, feelings and behaviors are unbalanced both internally and externally. When you arrive at balance, ego will remain internally confident more of the time. Confident that you are equal to others, not more than, not less than, but equal to the challenge; when you arrive at this place, there is a big internal sigh of release—like a balloon full of hot air deflating. Because you realize that you are just fine. You are okay, all you need to do is to be yourself, learn about self, develop yourself, accept self, challenge self, be open to learn from others, listen to others, listen to self, respect yourself and respect others. Your competition is first within self then reflected outward. Then you will respect yourself and others. Everyone has their worth, their talents, their value. Everyone is/can be equal to and so can you. Remember, when you are feeling less than or better than, you are not feeling equal to . . .

SELF -DISCIPLINE

RELEASING EMOTIONS AND FEELINGS IS imperative to a have a healthy fully functioning emotional system. Self-discipline is a must to become aware of when and how to display emotions appropriately, and also as to what is appropriate to allow into your emotional system.

Definition of SELF-DISCIPLINE—the power to control one's actions, impulses or emotions—it takes self-discipline, not to yell out when someone makes you angry. The ability to make self do things that must be done.

Same as in food choices, discipline is imperative when deciding how much to put into your body and also what is conducive for a healthy digestive system; the same is true with the emotional system. Once you become aware of triggers, vulnerabilities, wounds and weaknesses, you can be more aware of what to allow in and what to keep out.

When you are healed in an area, watching someone emote or what someone does or says to you, won't affect you as much. You will not be triggered and will be more able to hold the emotional energy outside yourself and to observe with your intellect.

Children, the emotionally weak and the mentally ill aren't able to do this well; they take everything in, allowing it to affect them, even change who they are and how they behave moment to moment or even permanently. Their emotions are in control of them. They are not in control of their emotions or often even their minds. As children mature, many will naturally acquire self-discipline. Those who have been fractured will have a more difficult time with maturation as it relates to self-discipline.

You can still feel empathy for someone or a situation without having it affect you deeply or detrimentally. This was often difficult for me to comprehend and do, when I was unbalanced and fractured. Certain issues with others would devastate me emotionally. At times, I would emote inappropriately and overly so. It's when a person is under stress that you can see what they are comprised of and tell if they can readily process emotions and flip into their thinking mind to find solutions rather than emoting without solution. Although at times, throwing up emotionally is what is needed to release, but done appropriately so. As I healed, I became more able to listen to another's issues, and/or experience something dramatic and traumatic and to hold it outside myself and not become as emotional about it. It didn't tear me apart or flip me into not being unable to think. I was able to process it by using 'the process', in order that I keep myself in my center and in balance. I became able to focus my intellect while directing my emotions to arrive at resolve and to speak forcefully while being in control of my emotions. I can now keep my emotions under my control and filter them through my intellect.

You can't help another when you are just as emotional as they are in a situation. It takes pulling into your logic, your thinking mind to figure out issues and to release emotions. This is mastering true emotional self-discipline. I am not saying to block emotions, deny emotions or to become non-feeling—as this is the opposite of what this book is about. It's imperative that you feel all your emotions in order to process them. I am saying to become disciplined in what you take in and to learn to process feeling and emotions, so that they don't get stuck in your emotional system at length and create havoc in you. Then you will be able to express appropriately and in a timely manner.

At times, you may be overwhelmed with emotion but not be able to express it in the moment, because it may not be appropriate to do so. Therefore, self-discipline is required. You may need to deal with whatever you are dealing with by staying in your logical mind. Then later release the emotion by either working out, screaming in a closed room, taking a long hot bath or shower and going through, 'The process', in your mind, to release it from your emotional system.

Some manage by 'appearing' to deal in the moment, but then turn to addictive behavior afterwards. There is a healthy way to process that leads to integration and release and there is an unhealthy way that blocks and cover ups by using addictions. This is where awareness and self-discipline is required. When you develop and practice self-discipline most anything is possible.

BODY WISDOM

YOUR BODY IS MAINTAINED, REORGANIZED and nourished by what you put into it emotionally, physically and experientially. Your body is a processing organism on every level. If you like, love and appreciate yourself, you will most often fill it with the healthy, positive and good. If you have disdain and hate for self, you will more often fill it with the unhealthy and negative. What you fill yourself with on every level is reflected on every level out into the world as your earthly image.

Processing emotions through our mind and bodies is much like processing the food we eat through our digestive system. If we continually put negativity into our minds, we will become negative, angry, depressed, anxiety ridden, sad or volatile. If we over eat junk food, we will feel ill, have stomach issues, be and feel bloated, fat, and perhaps, burp and have gas. It's an energy release like in the emotional system. If we stuff food into our mouths, too much of it at one time, we will get an upset stomach and may have constipation, 'stuck and blocked' or diarrhea, 'running off'. Just like being stuck in emotions, shutting down becoming depressed or not expressing, or overflowing, crying, angry outbursts and emotional vomiting. Either way or on individual levels, we are out of balance and not digesting or processing well. Unexpressed emotions don't die. They are buried alive and will come out later in uglier ways. Just like waste must be release from your physical body.

Positive thoughts create a healthy mind and emotional body. Nutritious food and in moderate quantities, along with exercise, a person will be more able to have a healthy, fully functioning and robust physicality.

Take care of your body. It is the house where your spirit and soul reside while on earth. It is how you move about and experience on earth. It is the instrument and tool when taken care of properly that processes both emotions and nutrients enabling you to further grow in spirit and to live productively and healthfully in joy. Body, mind and spirit work together in unison for an outcome, and that outcome is you and how you live.

Sure it's fun to overindulge and to do so on occasion is even good for the indulgent side that most all of us have and enjoy at times. Indulging until you gross yourself out is physically fun occasionally and does no harm. I have this thing for chocolate and malted Easter eggs and each year I overindulge and gain about five pounds, then I am over it and the pounds drop off.

It's what you do each day, not occasionally that creates your body. What you put into your mind every day is what creates your thoughts and your emotional being which creates your energy vibration. All of us get angry, feel down or depressed at times. It's imperative that we feel all of our emotions. That is what we are built to do. Emotional and mental health is to process through the emotions and feelings attached to them, to arrive at peace and love with the ability to be open to experiencing joy.

An exercise for body awareness and sexuality—stand naked in a full length mirror and view your body from all sides and angles— back, side and front. Stare into your eyes while viewing your body. Learn to love yourself and see what your body looks like fully undressed. Touch your skin and really feel the touch of you. If you want to make changes as in losing weight or gaining muscle then do so, but first appreciate and love where your body is in the present. Then make the changes as you desire. If you don't like something then change it.

With your significant other/partner—if committed and genuinely in love with one another—both stand naked in front of a full length mirror together. Look at one another in the eyes and all over. Be unashamed—be who you really are—without the clothing that you choose that creates your image to flatter one aspect of your body and hide another. Image creation is fine but when you are in genuine love, it is not about the image. It is about the energy between you and image, clothing, etc. have actually little to do with it, unless it's a superficial union and if so, why are you in it? Touch each other's skin. Be playful like children, caress one another, hug and enjoy the genuine image that is being reflected back at you. Smile at the two of you as reflected in the mirror just as you would were you children. Doing so will serve to make you more comfortable with your sexuality as well as more confident. This is a bonding, healing and nurturing experience with opportunity that can lead to a deepening emotional bond and understanding along with deepening intimacy in emotional and sexual interaction. We all want to be seen, accepted and loved for who we really are, not who we pretend to be or think that we are.

Again your connection is because of your energy, you may think it's her long hair and great body. Sure those aspects attract but the real connection and commitment is in your energy, unless it's superficial and superficial will not endure, unless and until you delve deeper. Photos of one another and together can also be fun and confidence building leading to the making of great memories—only done and shared between you two.

Feeling completely loved is a freeing experience whether it is your loving and acceptance of self or another loving you and you loving them. Becoming sexual with someone without commitment is the game of fools. Sexuality is the physical expression of love and it's just one way that love is expressed.

The fastest way to be free is to feel your feelings. Destiny will lead you to your healing, if you are aware and open to it. When memories come into your mind, look at them, examine them, question why you remembered and thought what you did—the when of it and why of it. Some memories are fleeting and just come and go. Others repeat themselves and appear to awaken you to a higher awareness that will heal your spirit and free your soul. Why do you think in the way that you do? Why do you carry the imprints that you do? Who is really controlling your choices, your life, your health, your happiness?

We make our choices then what we choose makes us.

I wrote the memories that kept entering my mind for me but also for you. My memories will trigger yours. We all have them. They are just different for each of us.

The truth of your childhood is carried in your body.

A healing exercise is to write down your memories as I did mine. When you write, it gives you time to think it through and to process. The very act of writing connects mind to body. Rewrite and reread. Ponder with no judgment, allow yourself to feel what you are feeling. Anger, sadness, happiness, love, joy, hate . . . whatever your emotions are with the feelings attached to them. FEEL them. You cannot release that of which you are unaware and you cannot heal that which you won't allow yourself to feel.

How to further find and define the feelings that will identify the awareness . . . If you are having trouble finding out what you are feeling and why—ask yourself these questions: Am I feeling angry—sad—

happy—fear- hate—guilt—indifference—lonely—anxious—envy—arrogant—insecure—denial -defensive—judged—nervous—tired—frustrated—exhausted—shame—humiliation—creative—love?

Angry—What do I want?

Sad—What have I lost?

Happy—Aware of abundance. Happiness and goodness are linked.

Fear—How, when and to whom did I give my authority and or power to?

Hate—Why can't or don't I love myself?

Guilt—Why am I judging myself or others?

Indifference—What am I afraid of feeling?

Lonely—Why do I believe I am alone?

Anxious—What am I afraid of?

Envy—Why do I put a limit on abundance?

Arrogant—Why don't I feel equal to?

Insecure—Why don't I feel equal to?

Denial—What am I afraid to look at? What am I trying to avoid? The opposite is to be open.

Defensive—Why do I feel that I am not good enough? What am I trying to hide? The opposite is to feel worthy and open.

Judged—What am I afraid of seeing in myself? What don't I want others to see in or about me?

Nervous—What am I afraid of?

Tired—What's draining me?

Frustrated—What is it that I want?

Exhausted—What am I blocking and or avoiding looking at?

Shame—What am I covering up? Why do I feel that I am not good enough?

Humiliation—Why do I feel that I am not good enough? Why am I giving my power away?

Creative—In the flow

Love—Summations of all feelings—Joy!

The above listed are some of the feelings that we all experience day to day and certainly at one time or another. These are obvious questions that you can ask yourself that will help you to identify why you are experiencing a particular feeling.

If after asking yourself these questions, you still cannot identify what you are feeling and why, and are still pointing the finger outside of yourself. Go sit in a room alone and in your mind's eye talk to whomever or whatever you feel the problem is or talk to yourself. I talk to myself in my mind's eye about issues, work it out and view it from all sides. You can also say all your feelings out loud. It might be wise to be in a private place, but get them all out. Shout! Scream! You may want to write your feelings down on a piece of paper. Do whatever works for you. This is for you. There is no right or wrong way to process through your feelings and why you have them, but it is important that you identify them so you can.

"Thinking—the talking of the soul with itself"

—Plato

Review and examine what you have said or written. If you are honest you will discover that many times what you are saying to others is really what you feel about yourself in varying degrees. When you point the finger outward also point the finger towards self and see how it feels to you. Self-reflect to more understand how the person or situation is. Oftentimes, it's a reflection of what you feel or think about yourself. Perhaps, not in exact proportions but none the less it is a kind of reflection. Or, it may be how you once felt, and it is being brought back to you to further release. Or, for you to see how far you have come in awareness and it's time for you to assist others.

We cannot recognize in another that which we are not, or once were in some proportion or capacity.

Own the awareness of the feeling, don't stuff it, deny it or bury it because it will only come back for you to revisit again. It may even haunt you. Whatever you try to deny or hide from will return in either your mind or body. Much illness is created by buried feelings, emotions, and beliefs that cause stress and fear which wreak havoc in your body.

If you are stuck feeling some emotion such as anger, ask yourself:

- What do you gain by staying stuck?
- What serves you to feel the way that you feel?
- What are the benefits of staying in anger?
- Does it make you feel like you are holding something over someone's head?
- Does is make you feel like you have more power if you stay in your anger?
- Do you feel temporarily stronger staying in anger?

I have found that when someone stays stuck in an emotion at length, it's usually because they think that it benefits them in some way. Their thinking this may not be accurate, but it's one way that they find to cope. It can be used an as excuse to not do this and so. If they hold onto their indignant, self-righteous anger then it keeps the person or situation at bay and they don't have to deal with the real issues, such as their part in it, their fear, their loss, or that they become aware by self-refection. Anger can eat a person up inside, if held too long. It can/may help you to feel stronger for a while to get through something in a limited time frame, but if held too long it will block love and joy.

Anger is there to be felt—looked at, used for healing and awareness then let go. And the way to get through anger is to understand, accept and to forgive. This does not mean to forget, but to forgive. You can still remember as in factually but when you forgive, the emotional charge is gone from your energy and out of your body. Why forgive? Because when the charge, the trigger is gone, you are free. The act of forgiveness opens your internal emotional channels for all else to flow and for you to be able to be filled with pleasant emotions. Nothing will block the flow as intensely as holding onto anger.

If you are holding onto a negative emotion, ask yourself why. How do you benefit from holding onto it? And if you let it go, process through it, what would you lose or what would you gain?

All emotions and the feelings connected to them are worthwhile. The difference is that some carry positive energy and others negative. Let the negative flow through you as quickly as possible. When we are clear of the negative, we are open for the positive to fill us up. Would you rather walk around feeling sad and depressed or happy and content?

'I feel ill' or 'I feel sad' take the same charge on our body. They come from the same place, blocked emotions. So it makes sense that our blocked feelings and emotions can make us mentally, emotionally and physically ill. The more our emotions process through us, the more alive we will feel.

The way our emotions flow through us can be compared to our physical digestive process. Example: When we eat food, our body takes it in and separates the nourishing part from the part that is indigestible or waste. Our body then releases the indigestible part through our elimination system. When our elimination process is not working effectively, we feel uncomfortable or may even become ill. Our stomach may hurt; we may have constipation—no release or diarrhea—a running off. We may become bloated and have cramping. Any way you look at it—it is not comfortable to our physical bodies. If this system breaks down, we die. Our bodies must have elimination of waste. Constipation—we explode. Diarrhea—we are drained. Most people don't feel physically good, if they don't eliminate the waste from what they put into their bodies the day before as soon as the very next day. After the waste is eliminated then they feel better and are ready to begin their day. If waste is not eliminated then they may feel bogged down the whole day until it is.

So realize what an emotional body feels like when backed up with negative imprints, feelings, emotions and beliefs bogging it down. The emotional system will eventually sink into depression, freak out in anxiety, anger or fear, or even shut down if the negatives aren't released. If it's full of negativity, there is no place for the positive nurturing imprints, feelings, emotions and beliefs to enter and if they do squeeze in for a second they are immediately overpowered by the negative. Our emotional system needs elimination just as our digestive system does.

Allow yourself to feel hunger. Nothing is harmful or wrong about the feel of a hungry growling stomach. Embrace and enjoy the hunger. Hunger creates in me the feeling of anticipation. Hunger shows that all food has been processed with waste eliminated and the stomach is empty. Actually, the time to eat is only when we feel hunger. If we eat only when we are hungry, the food tastes better and if we allow ourselves be hungry for a while, our stomach shrinks. I prefer to feel hungry rather than to feel overly full. I feel energized when I am hungry. If we keep our stomachs full, we will never get to experience and feel the intense energy of our core hunger. Hunger is a good feeling, I am not saying to starve yourself, but a fast cleanses both your body and your soul. It allows you to be more in touch with your core—your center.

Some people can't tolerate the feeling of being hungry. They feel that they must feed themselves continually. At the first pangs of hunger, they must eat. Many eat when they aren't hungry. They have an intense need to be satiated even stuff themselves to stave off any feelings of hunger. I ask why. Were they overfed as infants? The moment that they cried out in hunger was a breast or a bottle placed into their mouth? Therefore, they have no tolerance for delayed gratification or to feel the inner workings of their body and digestive system. Of course, I am not saying not to feed an infant or child in a timely manner. I am saying that overfed, indulged, stuffing of food with intolerance for hunger pangs can create a self-indulgent, blocked, stuffed up and full to the brim human being. Or perhaps, is it that they were not satisfied as infants in a timely manner, making them eternally and internally hungry and trying to fill up and to nurture self with food?

I have found that if I eat when I am not hungry too often, and or eat until I am overly full too often this is when I begin to gain weight. I feel sluggish, lazy with physical energy lacking because it's focused on digesting the backed up food in my stomach. Same with our emotional digestive system, too much in with no release and you will feel emotionally exhausted, tired, on edge, depressed and unhappy because your mind and emotions are overly focused on digesting what you have put into it.

Our bodies are built to eliminate waste just as our emotional system is created to process and to eliminate emotions. This is why we have the range of all the feelings that we do and why we can express sad, glad, unhappy, grief, joy, devastation, peace, love, cruelty, kindness, etc. We have all these expressions of emotion within us. So which do you choose to be in most of the time? Believe it or not, it is your choice as to how quickly you come back to peace, love and joy. If you want change then become the change.

Just like we are at choice as to what kind of food we put into our body because it matters as to how our bodies will react to what we put into it. If we continually put junk food or food that is spoiled into our bodies, our digestive system will rebel and react negatively. We might even throw up the harmful food. Our bodies will try hard to find some way to release the offending food from our system.

We have the same reaction in our emotional system when it is not working effectively. We may become stuck in our feelings, 'emotional constipation', depression, negativity, or just run off about our feelings to ourselves and others, 'emotional diarrhea'. I think running off may be better because at least there is release rather than staying stuck, but too much running off will drain the person and those around them. Either way, we are not comfortable mentally, emotionally or physically.

If we are continually feeding our emotional system negative input it will react by turning in on us. It's all carried in our gut. We have a gut reaction to food and also to persons, places and things. That is why it is so important to identify why you are feeling what you are, when you are feeling it and to release the negative.

What parents would feed their children food that they knew was spoiled? Only the most demented, sick and evil, but think about how many parents feed their children their negative feelings, emotions and thoughts with little to no awareness of what they are doing. I would say most all of them do this at one time or another. Unless they identify their own imprints with self-reflection and understanding, they will pass them on, both the negative and positive. What is important to realize is that many times the negative makes the deepest imprint with the strongest and longest hold. The only positive in this is that the dark defines the light.

Self-reflection is a key component to a healthy emotional feeling system on every level. Marcus Aurelius wrote, "Nowhere can man find a quieter or more untroubled retreat than in his own soul."

HUSBANDS AND ROMANTIC OTHERS

IMPRINTS AND BELIEFS SYSTEMS PLAY a large and significant influence as to whom we attract romantically, also who are attracted to us and why. A romantic love connection can be for a divine purpose which is the healing of both individuals. Write down concerning your significant romantic relationships what attracted you to them. Why do you think they were attracted to you? Who and what you thought they were and what it turns out that they really were. This is up to you, as to whom and what you consider a love relationship, whether it be husband, boyfriend, etc. It's someone you loved/love and why you loved/love them and why you think that they loved/love you. Okay, so what was the energy of the attraction?

I will use my three marriages and subsequent divorces as example:

First Husband—He sat next to me in a college class and we started talking. He was friendly, outgoing and attractive with a big smile. He invited me to go flying with him. He taught flying to help him pay his way through college. He appeared to be ambitious and hardworking.

His parents lived in a house out in the country with acreage and a pond in the back on the wrong side of the tracks.

My dad didn't like him and told me he was not good enough for me. We continued to date for a two years. He asked me to marry him on Christmas, while we were decorating a tree at his apartment. He was the first man, I had sex with and it was not memorable in the least. We had little sexual chemistry, but I didn't really realize this at the time. Although, I had previously dated men with whom I felt sexual chemistry. I have come to know that the physical connection is part of the glue that holds people together and creates the endurance and deepening of the connection and bond. After he graduated from college and we got engaged, my Dad asked him to work at his company. The truth of it is that Dad tried to like him because I loved him. Also, Dad thought he might become the son that he never had. We married and had a large church wedding and Country Club reception. On the way to our honeymoon destination, I threw up almost the whole time during the flight to Bermuda. A sign, perhaps of what was to come?

On our honeymoon, I realized that I didn't like him much and I may not even love him. He had never been to such a resort, while I learned to ski in the ocean off Puerto Rico as a child and accustomed to being at luxury resorts. I was accustomed to an upscale lifestyle and he wasn't. He behaved entitled, arrogant, drunkenly and obnoxiously. He was too busy acting the 'big shot' to show me much attention or caring. I was embarrassed by him. I had not seen him behave like this before or if I had, I didn't notice it. Perhaps, I ignored or blocked it from entering my awareness, since I was blinded and could not see or discern clearly. On our honeymoon, our innate differences in quality began showing quickly. Not that a person with less, can't marry another with more and it be successful, but in this instance his arrogance, ego, insecurity, ignorance and lack of class revealed themselves immediately. He didn't understand or observe the differences as to how to behave and to relate to others, he was too into himself. I also found that he bored me both sexually and intellectually.

I should have filed for divorce the moment I got home from our honeymoon. The woman I am now would have done just that. But the woman I am now would not have even dated this fake buffoon. Only at the time, I was not fully aware and was determined to have a good marriage and a happy home, no matter what my sacrifice to self. In my blindness, I thought that all I needed to do was to try harder. The longer I was with him, the worse it became. As the years went on, he drank and gambled away our money behind my back, as I was trying to save money. He lied about everything. I created the front for his image, while he lived a double life. He travelled lots in business. I taught ballet, was fit, didn't drink, belonged to arts and charitable organizations and he drank, got fat and hung out in bars. He spent more time with my parents than I did. Drinking, going out to dinner and talking business with my dad and others, and at times my mom accompanied them. One thing mother was always up for is going out to dinner and drinking.

When men paid attention to me, he became very jealous. When we entered a theater one night, as we were being shown to our seats, he noticed people looking at us and commented, "I love to go places with you because all heads turn." Chills went down my spine hearing him say this. He was stating that he liked the attention he got when he was with me. He was not complimenting me. He was all about himself and the attention or whatever else it was that he could suck from me to prop up his insecurity and emotional lack that he hid behind his ego in order that he get value from being with me

In our eighth year of marriage, I discovered he had an affair with his secretary and had a child with her. For about a week, he had me convinced that this woman was lying. That they didn't have an affair, the child was not his and that she was just trying to shake down my family for money. Well, he did have an affair and the child was his. A DNA test proved it. They both worked for my father's company. Therefore, the irony was that my father was subsidizing my husband's immoral behavior. My husband humiliated me and my whole family. He paid this woman off and gave up ever seeing his son to get her out of his life, while professing love for me. I discovered he had affairs even back to when we were engaged. It was a nightmare year. I recall that the month his illegitimate son was born, I got a new Mercedes.

How typical, his guilt must've gotten to him—poor thing. Or was it just for his 'image'. Clearly, it would have been better has I divorced him as soon as we returned from our honeymoon. My first instincts were correct and I ignored them. He, at first appeared a nice, friendly, hardworking ambitious young man, but turned out to be a gold digger, gambler, womanizer, liar and a drunk. Everything I vowed I would never have in my life.

I was in emotional shock and suffered a kind of emotional PTSD. To deal with all this, I entered therapy. He didn't. He didn't think he needed to and stated that everything was just mistakes and he would do better. When actually, he was still too busy cheating, gambling and drinking to have the time for therapy.

One night during the time of his paternity suit, I was crying in the shower. He was in bed in the next room. When I got into bed, his comment was, "How do you think it feels for me to hear 'my wife' crying in the shower?" He had no empathy concerning what I was enduring because of his immoral and destructive behaviors. He was only concerned with himself. My despair and crying over what he had done and his having to hear it, bothered the rotten-soul-less-thing far more than what he had done. He had no empathy for me or anyone. I was supposed to forgive him and have empathy for him but he had none for me. Clearly, he was a narcissist with sociopathic traits.

His parents postured themselves as religious and their practice forbade dancing. They looked down on me for teaching classical ballet, even going so far as to tell me that I was not going to go to Heaven for doing so. While their son cheated, gambled and drank. His mother coddled him. According to her, her son was just a victim of circumstances. I never noticed that he had any real affection for his mother. He only cared about himself and satiating his immediate carnal desires. He was insecure, arrogant, self-serving, ruthless, manipulative, immoral and a con. He was internally empty and nothing could fill him up.

The arrogant greedy entitled fool took me to court in the divorce to try to get what was left financially in our marriage. His mother found the attorney for him to do this. The divorce was awarded to me on extreme mentally cruelty in a no-fault divorce state and I was awarded what was left of the marital assets. I can't think of one redeeming quality in this man or his family. I married everything that I found disgusting. But as a college girl how could I have known what he would turn out to be or could I have known? Did I miss clues because I was fractured with my awareness blinded?

He was looking to marry a wealthy girl and he picked me. He thought once having done so, then he would have it made and could do whatever he wanted. He lived entitled as if he was my parents' child. I stayed in the marriage way too long, because I didn't want to fail. His attraction to me was to a sweet, loving, naïve, trusting woman with a successful father. I don't recall much about his family. Only that his mother talked continually about how much money her employer made and about his upscale lifestyle. And that no matter what my husband did, it was not his fault. He and his family were hypocrites and it sickened and embarrassed me that I married into this.

He had an agenda to take from and to use me. He got jealous when I was shown attention, unless it related to him because he considered me his possession and his source. He spent time with my parents badmouthing me to try and turn them against me and over to his side, no matter what the issue. This whole marriage was an exercise in his tearing me down, while the image of my family and I built him up.

Second Husband—We first connected when I was beginning my interior design business and was separated from my first husband. I called on his office to sell him art. At our first meeting, I thought him interesting, intelligent and nice. He dressed like he stepped out of GQ magazine. Months later we ran into one another in a restaurant then really connected. He remembered me from our meeting in his office, telling me that he was attracted to me that very day, but I was wearing a wedding ring. He told me that he thought to himself, 'The good ones are always married'. He came after me strong. We had an immediate attractions and connection and love developed quickly. We dated while I was trying to get out of my first marriage and working to build my interior design business. We had lots of fun. He sailed in regattas. We went to the lake most every weekend. He got out of the oil business and into real-estate. He was sociable, knew lots of people, ambitious and business oriented. He had a kind and good heart and was romantic. I drank more than I ever had in my life during this time. It was wonderful, finally to be able to relax and to have some fun after being married to the drama, trauma and abuse of my first husband. With my first husband, I had to be on guard and alert, totally ready and conscious to be able to take over the man's role—in order to survive, clean up and get through his messes. Dating this man, I could relax and let him be in control.

I got pregnant before my divorce was final and had an abortion. Deciding to have an abortion was complete trauma. I went to court for a divorce hearing on a Monday and Friday of that same week had an abortion. My second husband and I married a year after my first divorce was final.

After settling into marriage, I realized that he had a terrible drinking problem. I was working in my business and only drank wine with dinner if at all; say on a Saturday night, while he was drinking every night. I went to Al-Anon to help me try to deal with his drinking. He would try to quit then wouldn't, try to quit then didn't. He would make me promises that he would quit then wouldn't. I divorced him because of his drinking, while I still loved him. I got out of the marriage to save myself. We really loved one another, but his addiction destroyed our marriage. He had a choice, our marriage or alcohol and he chose his addiction. You can't have a relationship with a person who is addicted because their relationship is with their addiction. Addictions can overtake a person's soul. After enduring my first marriage, I had no tolerance for addictions. So I knew to just get out and away, if he wasn't going to accept responsibility, become aware, grow and heal himself. There was nothing I could do, it was up to him. I was more than tired and overdone dealing with others throwing up their issues on me. After I kicked him out, he went to AA, got into counseling and sobered up.

His parents were nice people. His dad had been in Patton's regiment and his mother was kind and lovely. He had insecurities concerning measuring up to his dad's expectations—so would often rebel. If he had sobered up while we were married, we might still be married. He eventually sobered up, continued his success in real-estate and we remained friends. Our divorce while hurtful emotionally was easy financially, in that I took nothing from him and he took nothing from me. I just kept the lovely jewelry he had given to me as gifts and which he wanted me to have.

Years later, I was back in my home town visiting and we planned to meet for dinner. I was at the restaurant and he called saying that he would be late because he was in a business meeting. Then he called again and again, each time stating that he would be there in a few. It felt just like it had been when we were married. I ate without him. As I was leaving the restaurant, he called to say that he was so sorry this had happened that the meeting had finally ended and he would love to meet me for a 'drink'. Hearing this, I angrily but also in awareness thought, 'Kowabunga'! Or 'Ain't that a kick in the head!' as my dad would often say. I divorced this man decades ago for his alcoholism, he had sobered up and tonight he was asking me to meet him for a drink! Goes to show perhaps, leopards really don't change their spots. I haven't talked to him since.

At the end of and after this marriage is when I began an even more intense search for healing through reading, etc.

Third Husband—I met him while on a business trip concerning my interior design business. I made sure he didn't drink, do drugs or have addictions. He was divorced with a five-year-old daughter. We could talk all night long about any and everything. He was interesting, romantic and intelligent. He had done many things in his life, was energetic, talented and successful. He sent me flowers every week. We appeared to click.

While dating we had fun—dining out, snow skiing, cooking together, events, riding bicycles, child activities with his daughter, entertaining business types. His daughter and I got along famously. It appeared as if finally, I was going to have happiness, even though I wasn't all that physically attracted to him. I sold my house and moved to the state where he lived. We bought a lovely house and I decorated it. We were married in our house and had a great life for a short while.

As it was beginning to fall apart, my stepdaughter commented, "For a while, Natalie, we had it all."

After we were married, he became very controlling. He didn't want me to work or workout, join organizations or do much of anything. Of course I did what I wanted to, but he would try to sabotage. He had a nasty flash hot temper and at times, an erratic energy that was difficult to be around. He called me often during a day, inquiring as to what I was doing. He was always checking up on me.

I ended up having more of a relationship with his daughter being a stepmom than with him being a wife. I enjoyed being with and doing for her. We had fun. I now had a little girl going through my closet and trying on my shoes and I loved it.

My husband became old and grumpy and was no fun any longer. An example is: The three of us were walking in a Mall headed to go ice skating, I believe. My stepdaughter and I were walking ahead of him. She pointed out a good-looking young man walking past us. She commented, "Natalie, you should date him. He's cute!" So his own daughter didn't see us together and was looking for someone better suited to me. Another example: One Sunday, I was at our pool sunbathing. He was in the family room watching TV as he usually was. When I came in from the pool, I passed by the door and said, "I'm going to aerobics." When I went into my bathroom and was changing clothes, I felt all sexy. So I walked the length of the hallway around the living room and dining room to where he was sitting. I was naked with a glistening tan with my hair down and flowing and when I approached him sitting in his 'lounge chair' he glanced away from the TV and said, "I thought you were going to aerobics." That's how dead he had become in one year. He had become a complete bore. Another aspect in him that I found repulsive was that if I did something he didn't like or approve of, he would try to punish me by not giving me an Easter, birthday gift or some such. He was big on little surprise gifts when we were dating which was fun, but after we married, he would show them to me then withhold them.

Once he thought he had me; he stopped trying, ceased being fun and even became father-like towards me in a punitive way. I had a lovely house, a stepdaughter I adored and was living in a place I loved, but was miserable. It was like being in marriage prison. He told me his first wife had cheated on him and did drugs and he was paranoid that he would lose me. He became critical of me to beat me down. We went to counseling, but he couldn't comprehend what he was doing to destroy us and by that time, I was already done trying.

Out of jealousy, his ex-wife filed a custody suit immediately after we were married and kept us in court most the whole time of our short marriage. I gave up our honeymoon, so that he could more easily handle the legal issues that his ex-wife was creating. He won the custody suit. I was told because of me. The reason he wanted me as his wife was that I created a positive image for him and was a devoted stepmother.

One of the regrets of my life is that while his ex-wife was pounding us with legal situations, I melted down several times and became a screaming banshee. It was probably screaming out in pain fearing for my own eminent emotional death, but I tried not to do this in front of my stepdaughter. I was not always successful because I suspect she overheard arguments between her father and me. I apologize into the depth of my soul, if I harmed her precious heart while venting my frustration.

During this marriage, I became even more aware of how my father interacted with me and how my mother resented it and the harm it did to me. So, I was very aware not to do the same to my stepdaughter. I tried to be very careful not to harm her fragile developing female psyche. But by my being so aware of this aspect in myself, also set me up for being taken advantage of by my ex and my stepdaughter. I put them and their interests before me, at times when I should have put myself first. Therefore, in ways they saw me as a pushover.

My stepdaughter was the light of her father's life, even a bit overly and weirdly so. I was careful not to have resentment of the child. It was not her fault what her parents were or what they were doing, and I was well aware of this because of my past. I was her cheerleader, her friend and tried to give her the best of me for her well-being and, at times it was very difficult for me to do because of her father's and mother's continual war over her. I woke up in the middle of their war and was trying to wave the white flag, but no one surrendered. It was she and I me trying to keep the peace and to have a life.

Therefore even though, this man was packaged differently, he was the same type of man. This man lived in emotional fear, was a complete control freak and would not face or deal with his issues from his first marriage. He was afraid he was going to lose me and what he did was literally push me away. As we fell apart, he focused overly so on his daughter. She became like his 'girlfriend'. My dad astutely commented, "It is much easier to meet the needs of a child than a grown woman. With little girls, you buy them some Barbie dolls and a dollhouse and instantly you become a hero. With a woman, it's much more complex." My third husband couldn't handle complex, but he sure wanted to be a hero. Don't most men? He later lost custody of his daughter in some form and he moved back East.

I was so happy to get out of that marriage. I remained close to my stepdaughter for a few years after the divorce. She even had a birthday pool party at my house with her mother and grandmother hosting along with me. Her father was not invited. Being a stepmother can be a thankless job, no matter how close or compatible you are or how much you give and try. Her mother eventually broke up our connection because of her jealousy. It was something about my stepdaughter's mother thinking that I gave my stepdaughter permission to shave her legs, which I didn't do.

This divorce was intense. He tried to harm and take from me in any way possible. It worked emotionally and some financially, but I felt blessed to have this angry man out of my life. This man was a complete control freak, full of fear. He didn't deal with any of his issues from his first marriage and threw them all onto me. People who have a need to be over-controlling are fearful and anxious. They have a fear of abandonment or being taken advantage of that they can't process. So because of their fear, they try to control everyone and everything. Emotionally damaged and fractured people can easily become emotionally sadistic to others as it helps them relieve their intense pain.

After this ordeal was when I went into deep self-reflection

and more intensive into my search for awareness as to why I kept ending up in the same place. What appeared good always turned to destruction. Soon after this divorce was final was when I began writing this book. So I lived through it all and even lived to write about it.

"What we don't resolve, we often repeat."

—Freud

In the instances of my marriages, the men were not as they first appeared or as I perceived them to be. I was unaware concerning many things about myself. Therefore I brought to me what I needed to look at, in order to become aware and to shift. All the men were insecure; hiding behind arrogance which I mistakenly thought was confidence. Had I stayed in any of the marriages longer than I did, I would have been destroyed and become dead inside.

My first marriage and my last had an agenda and intention to use me. I added value to their image and life while they sucked from me on every level they could find. My second marriage was for love, but he would/could not deal with his addiction and issues. None of the men would look at or deal with their issues. They were too fractured dealing with self to be able to respect and love me. They didn't respect or love themselves. While I tried with everything I had in me to make the marriages work—attended Al-Anon, therapy, read books on healing, they did little to nothing to become aware.

One person can't do the healing for both people in a relationship or marriage. When one begins to come aware and the other doesn't or doesn't even try, then usually it is the end. Both people must work to create the space for awareness and healing. It begins with the strength to look at one's self in genuine reflection. The men I was with did not have that strength. In the weakness of their denial, their choice was addictions, deflecting, blaming, avoidance and continuance of destructive behaviors.

One husband told me that I already had everything so I didn't need anything. Imagine how hearing that crushed me? And their thinking this way, gave them license to do as they wished with no regard to me. When the truth was, I had little to nothing in these marriages—no love, security, respect, caring or fun and certainly no place for me to lean, because they were always leaning on me. They were so wrapped up in their issues. That once they did what they thought they needed to do to 'get' me, they had no awareness or realization that I had needs and desires to be cared for, nurtured, loved and protected. I became the last thing on their minds. Their focus was on self, what they could get from me; their unaddressed issues along with escaping or addictions. Once they 'had' me, they thought they were finished with nothing more to do. They were too eaten up and consumed with self. They didn't love their selves, understand their selves; were too insecure to face their issues and vulnerabilities. So how could they love, understand, become emotionally intimate and come to know or to understand me? They couldn't. What they did was to project all their issues onto me and I took it. Just as I had in my family of origin, until I became aware and stopped it. But until I became aware, I was left on my own. Just as I was in my family of origin to understand their issues, accept them, overcome them, while taking care of me and pretending everything was great. While creating the fake image for their life, my strength had become my weakness, the place for men to suck from, in order that they feel better about self.

Quite a job and I did it well, until I decided enough is enough. I learned that in a love relationship, when you feel like you need to prove your worth in order to be loved, is the time to walk away. I was strength and I had married weakness. Yet, because of my imprints I felt like I was not enough, when it was them who were not enough for me or even worthy of me and my love.

I was better off alone. So I could focus on myself and take care of me. It's much better to be alone than in a destructive relationship. All my husbands were burdens to my life and to me. My role was always that of caretaker, image-maker, pretending everything was great when it wasn't. It was all a cover, doing everything to make them be and feel okay. Thinking if I did this, if I was perfect, and made their life appear perfect everything would be okay and I would be okay. My needs were never met. I had to be the strong one at every turn and it became overwhelming and exhausting. I am a giver, a lover and a caretaker and this is the energy that attracted these men to me.

Romantic relationships are the closest that one comes to the parental relationship and bond. In this union is where negative and limiting imprints and belief systems are revealed. If there is no awareness, they can overtake even destroy the relationship. It's a place, if both are ready, willing, able and aware that great healing can occur with the ability to shift both people into deeper awareness. This allows for healing of both and the creation of a genuine, emotionally aware, healthy and deeply connected bond. It begins with awareness and self-reflection.

Of course there were other men in my life, several long-term relationships, engagements, etc. that did not end in marriage. Many first dates and multiple date adventures along with exciting love connections and affairs that were fulfilling. In some regards, enlightening, full of fun and brought about awareness. A realization is that I loved two men with connections much deeper than my marriages, whom I did not marry, but perhaps all this is fodder for another book.

A soul mate or twin flame connection will not be a walk on the beach, but instead may be the most intensely painful, healing and tumultuous interaction that one will have with the ability to be the most rewarding. It's to trigger your wounds, mirror insecurities and to break you open to further awareness. You have connected for a divine purpose and that purpose is for healing your pain and wounds manifesting into the ability to experience profound and expanding love and joy. It's only in commitment that this fully is able to occur. There will always be conflict in relationship. It's to have trust in the conflict and to work through it. Doing so, you will not only learn about the other person but yourself as well. That is why perhaps; the marriage vows include for better and for worse, etc. and is a union sanctioned under God.

Genuine love is enduring. But having stated this, it does not mean to endure never-ending abuse, disrespect and trauma. You are not to be a punching bag for someone else's issues. If after trying and giving it all that you have to give and it is destruction and doesn't work, it's time to get out, to save self and to heal on your own. Nothing does anyone any good if both go down with a sinking ship. Evil should not be allowed to destroy you. Both partners must be held accountable, be responsible and participate in the healing process. Otherwise, it's like a one-legged horse trying to run a race.

Concerning playboys and men who can't commit; they want all the benefits without accountability or responsibility. Just fun, sex and excitement for these men and when it gets real, they go onto the next shiny thing, always looking for the better deal. Men such as this are afraid of intimacy, to reveal their vulnerabilities, are deeply flawed, fractured or wounded—take your pick. They don't have the emotional stamina or depth to sustain a relationship. They are emotionally shallow, immature and may even be frauds, such as faking their emotions to get what they want. What they want is to seduce, conquer, over-power and to attain. Once they have succeeded, they shut down or leave because they are not capable of going further. They don't want to or aren't capable of looking at self and doing the work that it takes to self-reflect, become aware and to heal. So when this becomes needed in a relationship, and it will in every relationship on earth, they bail. They are not capable of sustaining a relationship. Most remain immature, selfish and childlike for their whole life. They usually won't/don't look at self with much if any awareness. Instead they blame or find fault with the women, when it is they who have the issues. It's as if they are missing the man gene. While they may think that womanizing behavior is manly, even desirable. It isn't. It is childlike. They may do 'manly appearing' activities, such as race cars, surf waves, fly planes, etc., which are escape activities and fun. Doing activities such as these does not make a man—a man. Many will over-indulge themselves in the 'play' arena. They are afraid of growing up and becoming real men. Think the 'Mama's boy'. A mature man will have the desire and need to take care of his love and to become responsible. He will want to commit. It will be his honor to do so. Doing so shifts him into becoming a mature man dealing with responsibility and accountability, instead of 'playing house' like a child.

*"The greatest way to live in honor in this world is to be what
we pretend to be."*

—Socrates

When or if a man with this immature emotional and mental mindset does marry, he marries for benefits that have little to do with love. He will continue on with his womanizing or escape-driven ways, like my first husband did. My first husband never committed to me or our marriage. He was committed to what he could gain by being associated with me. Men who emotionally and physically abuse women are fractured and immature. I suggest cut and run as soon as you become aware. They rarely, if ever change. They are emotionally and psychological unstable. Where they not, they would already be on a path to become aware. They feel unworthy and nothing can fill them up. So they keep searching even when they are with someone. It's about them, not their partner. They never feel satisfied for long. They are trying to feel good about themselves. So, they attract and seduce new people to try and feel worthy—to get a rush. But once they have them, when the need to look at self arises, which is impossible for them to do, they move on. It's a cycle. They need constant approval and always feel empty. This was my first husband. He had little self-confidence and felt no self-worth. He was phony unto himself and therefore a fraud unto all others. A normal man would have been satisfied with having all that he had in life, to honor, respect and care for it, but he felt unworthy so he kept looking for something to fill him up, while tearing down what he had and trying to destroy me along with him. When a person feels empty, they go for cheap, fast and easy thrills and victories.

Of course, there are women that do as such, also. People like this are emotionally sadistic. Trying to have a relationship with a person who can't love is futile. It will not work unless; you enjoy suffering, being used, marginalized and negated—choosing to live in emotional pain.

When you are emotionally intimate, you share your wounds, your pain and your vulnerabilities. If that love is shared with an equal, one who has the ability to truly love, they will protect you in this regard. But an insecure, weak, immature, manipulative predator will use your vulnerability against you to their advantage and gain. This is not love. It is usury and hopefully be seen for what it is and gotten away from as quickly as possible.

This book is about coming into awareness in order that you draw as little pain into/onto yourself as possible. When you do, you are able to recognize it, process through it or break against it into awareness. When you realize that someone is trying to interject or project their pain into/onto you, step aside, pull back or run from it. When you recognize pain in you, run directly into it so that you can have awareness. When you are triggered, look at yourself and use the process as many times as needed to release it. So you will have the ability to experience peace and joy.

Love has nothing to do with what you expect to get only with what you expect to give. "Your task is not to seek love, but to merely to seek and find all the barriers within yourself that you have built against it." Rumi

Looking back now with self-awareness, I can see the dynamics and what the attraction was in each marriage. In my first marriage, meeting in college, I was so unaware that I was blind. It was the energy that I emitted that drew him to me as his place to feed. Also looking back now, in awareness to my three husbands, I realize that I actually only loved my second husband. But at the time, I didn't have that awareness. I entered all marriages with good intention.

After my third divorce is when I entered into the deepest self-reflection of my life with goal and intention to become aware of why my life kept being and ending up exactly as I did not want it to be. I realized it had to be something in or about me. Some say, 'the moment you learn the lesson the test will be over', but sometimes the imprint or belief system is so deep that it takes much self-reflection before it can be seen in entire awareness with the ability for its release.

RESILIENCE

R ESILIENCE CAN EITHER BE POSITIVE or negative depending how and where it's utilized. I had become resilient concerning abuse because of the environment I was reared in. Resilience is positive in that, it helped me to not be destroyed by what I was living in. So I could keep going forward. But I needed to become aware at the first sign of addiction, abusive tendencies or dysfunction when dating or interacting with someone before commitment and or marriage—to address it right then and if they would not look at self then to end it. I had been simmered and steeped in abuse, denial of self, was kind, caring and nurturing and always looked at what I could do to help others. Therefore, I felt comfortable in dysfunction, abuse and around addictions so I adapted. I became resilient to living in it. When it'd have been better had I been intolerant, uncomfortable and knew to get out at the first signs of it. And that is what the men recognized in me. I did get out of my last two marriages as soon as the reality of what I was in hit me and I recognized what it was doing to me but it still took its toll on me.

What if I had realized what these men were made of before I married them and ended it then? What if I had ended my first marriage when I came back from the honeymoon like I wanted to? There would have been much less damage. My life would have taken a different trajectory. Of course, men like I married are adept at creating an environment where women are not able to see clearly— addictions, dysfunction, intention and agenda. Hence, the studying, therapy, healing modalities, research and awareness that has brought about this book. Awareness is the key to knowing self, seeing others for what and who they really are and why the attraction and connection are occurring.

My pain was the breaking open of my shell to awareness, understanding, acceptance and forgiveness.

DESTROY AND DESTRUCTION

WOUNDED, BLOCKED, UNAWARE AND DEFENSIVE, hurting, in denial people are the ones who do the most destruction to others. They have the ability to destroy everyone and anything that they touch because they place no value on human beings, others' feelings, others' resources or belongings. They do not have the ability to feel empathy. It is all about them and their staying 'safe' in their fake image of self. They search to feel a false sense of power hiding behind their ego, insecurity and low-self-esteem. They bleed negativity while they suck everything they can from anyone that crosses their path. They don't like themselves. They don't like people and the extent to which they will harm others is related to their internal moral adjuster.

They are in so much pain, denial or in defense of their issues that they project it out onto others. While they are trying to stay in denial and keep up their false image, they wreak destruction all around them and eventually upon themselves. They can even destroy the purest of genuine love and not even miss a beat because they can't recognize genuine love in the first place.

Nothing is ever their fault. They blame others or it's just their inability to cope, as in they are depressed or whatever their issue or excuse is of the day—it's not their fault. They will not accept and will dodge responsibility and accountability for the pain and destruction they create and cause.

Kill Joys—There are people in the world that purposely kill joy who aren't necessarily mentally ill. They are just negative, depressed and unhappy people. They can't feel or experience joy themselves. So, they get jealous or envious of others and can't stand it when someone is happy or they 'think' have more than they do. They can't stand to see someone enjoying life. So they say or do something to kill their joy. They may even try to take what others have away from them. For example: women who try to break up a happy marriage by flirting, taunting and having affairs with married men. Those who when something happens positive for someone, they belittle it to make themselves feel better. Kill joys are full of envy and jealousy. They either, feel less than or more than, not equal to—so they begrudge others their happiness because they are so unhappy inside. Universal example of a kill joy mentality is Satan's envy of God's power. Satan did all that he could and still does, to thwart and destroy goodness. God threw him out of Heaven to forever walk the earth with purpose of destruction never to know joy.

People such as this are in such pain that they are completely out of touch with their God centered core. They don't feel equal to or they flip into feeling more powerful than with no need for accountability. Therefore, just like Satan couldn't accept God's power over him and wanted to destroy human beings and everything under God's creation. When a person is in intense pain, such as feeling hate or anger, they are separated from self and also from God and not feeling equal. So they destroy themselves, others and everything good in their lives. All because they feel unworthy of love, peace, goodness and joy. When they have the awareness of why they are living in this state of self-destruction. They can understand, accept and forgive which brings them into feeling whole, at one with self and also at one with God.

An example is my second husband—the reason I use my second husband as an example is that we really loved one another. My first husband never loved me and I realized quickly that I didn't love him. Love is the glue that creates the possibility for healing in a relationship. Had my second husband stayed in a program to assist him to stop drinking, we 'might' still be together. We could have worked on our issues and become aware together. His alcoholism, behaviors and self-denial destroyed and negated the possibility for anything positive to occur. When there is an addiction, the relationship is with the addiction not the other person—making healing impossible until the addiction is addressed. He would/could not acknowledge or own up to his actions and behaviors or if he did, he would soon fall back into his escape behaviors. He would not look at himself and his behaviors as the reasons that we could not heal and become whole. To do so would have been too painful and at that time, he was too weak to endure the pain. I attended Al-Anon and tried but I couldn't do it all alone. He kept hiding in the alcohol bottle, doing the same things repeatedly. So I broke against his drinking and got out of it to save myself. It made me stronger and more self-aware by doing so. What's intended for harm can be turned into good.

People often treat others as they treat themselves. As long as we are on planet earth, we will be dealing with dualities—good and evil. It's the tension that keeps this planet rocking and rolling. Recall what was done to Christ.

We all go about our lives in jobs, professions, shopping, dining out, going to fitness facilities, etc.—all the events and acts of living. As we do, we interact with one another—triggering and healing, caring for, disliking, loving, etc. It is what we have come to earth to do. But—"The scars of others should teach us caution." St. Jerome

It's not the circumstances that we find ourselves in, it is how we handle and process them. It's up to us. And I do so understand how difficult this can be at times. Evil thrives on destruction that is its goal and purpose. But God gives us the tools to break against evil by giving us choice as to whether to stay in the destruction or to rise from the ashes. We have the ability to process using all the wonderful emotions available to us. It all begins with self-reflection and awareness . . .

> *"First keep peace with yourself then you can also bring peace to others."*
>
> —German theologian, Thomas Kempis

DEFENSIVE AND DENIAL

EVER NOTICE HOW THE MOST messed up people get self-righteously upset, when you get close to their issues?

Defensive and denial are partners in the deepest blocks towards awareness and healing. Becoming defensive or flipping into denial can be a sign that something, someone or some words have triggered an imprint that you are trying to avoid. Defensive and denial are activated because of fear to feel pain, to feel wrong and to avoid reality and truth. Living in denial is living in a fog.

Some people will do any and everything possible to avoid self-refection. They must believe—'think' that they are 'right' and everyone else is wrong. They feel—'think' that they must do this in order to survive. They feel as if they might be destroyed and even die if they don't. Sometimes, it is necessary to die unto yourself—tear down, break down and take apart something, in order to rebuild it on a stronger and better foundation. But the fear of death of the 'current and in place belief system'—no matter how distorted it might be, can create such fear that defense and denial become life lines. Actually defense and denial are angels of death creating blocks and leading to destruction.

If you flip into denial and become defensive along with being angry about a situation or something said or done, it reveals that you have been deeply triggered. You are trying to make them wrong. So you can feel 'right' and 'safe' in your current beliefs according to your imprints about self, others and your issues. You will do any and everything to avoid admitting the truth about yourself and issues.

Break through the knee-jerk reaction of denial and defense mechanisms to be able to look hard and long as to why you react in this manner. Look at yourself in intense self-reflection instead of trying to point the finger outside self. Pointing the finger outside yourself and at another is deflecting and projecting—a sure sign that your vulnerabilities have been triggered. To look and examine with honesty- coping mechanisms that you use to deflect discomfort is the biggest challenge to awareness and healing. The deepest work is healing our personal wounds—our core wounds. This is where the intensity lies. The only way to clear and release them is to be open to looking at self in honest and deep self-reflection.

Often becoming defensive and in denial is insecurity hiding behind a big ego. It's a kind of self-willed blindness. You wouldn't have been triggered, if it hadn't touched something that you were trying to avoid or hide. Why do you have such fear of being 'judged'?

Defense and denial mechanisms can be difficult to break through, because their whole purpose in being kept alive is to defend imprints and the belief system, in order to stay out of pain and to feel 'safe'— to avoid feeling vulnerable. They come into play to avoid looking at self and to avoid change. Therefore, they will fight hard and long to stay alive. The defended self can be a hard nut to crack. Some people reacting defensively and in denial do so with such intensity that it's as if their very life is being threatened. And to them, it does feel this way. The fear that their defended belief system might not be accurate throws them into a tailspin and the feeling as if they are fighting for their life. Therefore, they will accuse the other side to that which they are guilty. They will project.

PROJECTION—is a theory in psychology in which humans defend themselves against their own unconscious impulses or qualities—both positive and negative—by denying their existence in themselves and attributing them to others.

When a person projects their good traits onto someone, for example: a person with a kind heart may see someone as having the same. When in reality the person on whom they are projecting has a cold manipulative heart with devious motives. Therefore, projecting can be harmful whether it's done with negative or positive attributes.

Projection can be an obvious manipulation tactic and is also used to control, along with shaming and blaming others into shutting up, allowing for continuance to keep doing as they wish. Therefore, the clearer you see yourself in awareness and knowledge in relation to others is the best and safest place you can be in this regard. When you become more self-actualized, you will be more able to see yourself for whom and what is yours and see others for whom and what they are, instead of blurring the boundaries and projecting traits and attributes. With self-awareness and reflection, you will be more able to own what is yours and see what is theirs.

Concerning defensiveness—awareness will need to be done layer by layer. Because feelings of defensiveness can trigger intense denial, anger and the feeling that you want to reject the person, words, experience or situation. You may actually do this by cutting them out of your life. As you point the finger at them away from self either in deflection or projection as you try to shame and blame. They are too close to revealing the truth that will break open or shatter your image of self. That which you believe you must hold onto in order to make you 'feel' and 'appear' what you 'think', is 'safe'. Something is shaking up your status quo and your mechanisms of defense don't like it and will fight like hell to stop being exposed and to not feel the emotional pain. The defended belief system is a major block that keeps truth and subsequently peace, love and joy away.

Example of my Father's denial and defensiveness: All my life I would tell Dad the truth about our family and what I felt and saw, he would sometimes be open, listen and understand. But when it was about really deep things, too close to him, things he didn't want to see concerning our family, he would say it was a lie. That what I was saying wasn't true, and I didn't know what I was talking about. One time I recall I was telling him what I thought about one of the gold diggers he was dating. She was obviously pandering to him and hideous in her blatant use and manipulation of Dad. Yet Dad, couldn't/wouldn't/didn't want to see it. As I was talking to him to try and protect him, he covered his ears with both hands while saying, "LA LA LA". He reverted back to child-like behavior because he was in denial of truth and his immature defenses took over. A grown, intelligent, successful, wise man reverted to this kind of behavior, when his defended beliefs were challenged. A few months later, he called to tell me I was correct. He had found this woman using and abusing his credit cards and lying to him.

The last two years of his life, actually at times before then, he told me that I always told the truth and I am always right. That he wished he had left my mother and I had been his only child. This was very difficult for him to say with his pride and ego. It stunned me the first time that I heard him say this. After sitting back, self-reflecting, and watching our family and how it unfolded, he knew what I had been telling him was truth. He had much regret because he had lived in denial of the reality of the truth and this hurt his whole family and most definitely me.

I do not lie. I am certainly not perfect. But most definitely when I love someone, I don't lie to them. I can't placate those whom I love.

I am a truth teller. I tell the truth of what I see from the purity of my heart. I am very sensitive and empathic. I have to live in the truth of me. It's something placed in me by God. And at times, it's been difficult to live with, in that people often don't want to hear or know the truth. They will turn from it and me. Perhaps at times, I am not good in my delivery of it. I am just doing the best that I can with my abilities on this earth.

Dig really deep to become aware of why you are defensive; look at yourself honestly, don't be afraid to feel the pain. Pain is part of living. If and when you allow yourself to get into the feelings and the imprint that is being triggered, you will be able to more easily see why you become defensive and then release it. Why are you afraid of being judged? Why does it bother you so intensely? It wouldn't bother you if you felt secure in self.

Understand that being defensive is usually because you are not feeling good enough, feeling flawed, unworthy or uncertain and someone has gotten dangerously close to revealing it. So you try to do everything in your power to defend self. But what you are actually doing is defending your right to stay stuck, blocked and cut off from self-growth, truth and ultimately healing and happiness. The longer you stay in denial and defense, the longer you will stay blocked. The quicker you break through denial and defense, the faster you will feel free.

It takes bravery to break through defenses. This is why it's so prevalent in our world today and why so many make statements such as: 'Don't judge me. You have no right to 'judge' me. Who are you to 'judge' me?' Comments such as these are defense mechanisms on over drive and come from persons not integrated and at acceptance of self. People who react in this manner are living in insecurity, intellectual denial and emotional pain. Their defensiveness concerning the fear of being judged by others clearly reveals this. They may as well be screaming, 'I am insecure, am weak, feel unworthy, am really not sure of what I believe or what I am saying or doing. So don't put it in my face because I am too weak and frightened to look at it or myself.' They will then deflect or project trying to point the finger outside of self by shaming and blaming those who have triggered their deep seated issues and insecurity.

Blaming is actually a form of giving your power away. When you blame, it is saying or admitting 'they' have power over you concerning the way you react, feel and behave. Therefore, you are admitting that someone else is so powerful as to control your feelings, mood and even your very being. So how weak does that show you as being?

Some people will even defend the indefensible as in someone may commit an actual crime and their mother may say, "Oh, it was just his circumstances. He hung out with the wrong crowd." Or like my first husband's mother even after he committed adultery, had affairs and an illegitimate child, she blamed circumstances or whatever else and not him. It was not his fault. This kind of blaming with no accountability and responsibility can create human monsters and destroy lives. "Some people will do anything, no matter how absurd, to avoid facing their own souls." Jung

Avoidance is another piece of defense and denial—as in avoiding whatever is brought up avoid the pain. You deny, block, bury, ignore or turn away from all warnings and signals. You avoid doing activities, being around people or expressing yourself because you fear that you will experience pain as recalled from past experiences.

Avoidant personality disorder—Those affected display a pattern of social inhibition, feelings of inadequacy and inferiority, extreme sensitivity to negative evaluation and avoidance of social interaction despite a strong desire to be close to others. Individuals with the disorder tend to describe themselves as uneasy, anxious, lonely, unwanted and isolated from others.

Avoidance coping creates stress and anxiety and ravages self-confidence. It is a major factor that differentiates people who have common psychological problems—depression—anxiety and/or eating disorders vs. those who don't. Simplistic example: You realize that you have gained some weight. Instead of addressing it and looking at your body naked in a full length mirror, you avoid mirrors and wear larger clothing to cover up and continue over-eating. When you realize you have gained even more weight, you become overwhelmed and depressed. You feel like you look bad, whether you actually do or not. It's your perception and you feel hate for yourself—your body—your clothing and that hate of self bleeds out into what you do and onto everyone you come into contact with, in some form or another. You avoid going to the gym until you lose weight because you have a fear of being judged and humiliated. You avoid doing your usual activities and being around your friends. It's about what you fear that leads to what you avoid rather than what is actual. Avoidance coping causes anxiety to snowball because when people use avoidance coping they typically end up experiencing more of the very thing they were trying to escape.

You are overly focused that the outcome of interactions and experiences will be negative. You are self-conscious, have fear of being judged and think everyone is seeing you as badly as you perceive yourself. Most people probably will not notice or care that you gained a few pounds. Most people are more concerned with self and not someone else. This is an obvious example of 'avoidance' on a physical level. Avoidant personalities—blow things up in their minds thinking and worrying that if, in some context and time frame, they had a bad experience that they always will. They idealize relationships then devalue them, avoid making decisions and avoid life's experiences in general.

Reality is that everyone is judging everyone else in each day and every moment. We all make judgments. Judgments from others will not trigger you and you will not become defensive, if you are at awareness, acceptance and understanding of self. It will just cause you to self-reflect and self-reflection is how you grow into awareness. So being triggered can be a positive thing, if looked at and addressed with awareness. What matters is how you look at yourself. It's fine to be different and individual. It's your insecurity about self that triggers defensiveness, denial, vulnerabilities and fear of being judged. Feeling the pain in self-reflection and awareness is the beginning to healing. Feel the pain and release it, so you can feel the joy! Stop watering the weeds in your life and start watering the flowers.

Awareness Of The Positive—Think about and write down the positive aspects that your parents, relatives and others instilled in you that you are grateful to have incorporated and integrated in you.

Using myself as example:

My Dad—taught me to persevere—to overcome—to focus my mind even when I was overwhelmed with fear and negative emotions—to forgive—self-reliance -to work hard for what I want, to take calculated risks—to believe in magic—how to love, protect and care for those whom I love. He taught me the meaning of family and commitment. He taught me to keep my word and to give to others less fortunate, 'Matthew 6'—to continue learning throughout my life. To expect the best, to have the best, to strive for excellence, to be strong, to have a sense of adventure, to care for and appreciate all that I have, gratitude, to be happy, even though he worried a lot, he taught me to look on the bright side, to dress well and to have fine things—to be strong and to rely on myself. Even though my father was tough on me by his being so, it stretched and expanded me to be more than and to endure more than I ever thought that I would be able to. My father had a good, kind heart and I am thankful that I have his heart. Ballet lessons that he provided taught me discipline to move my body and this has benefited me all my life. He made available—classes, trips and adventures. He helped instill in me an excitement about life. That life is one great big adventure—that bad times don't last forever and that good is just around the corner.

My Mother—taught me how to cook from observing her. I love to cook for friends and for those I love. It relaxes me. To keep a clean, orderly, well-decorated home—I very much enjoy decorating a home—to save money whenever I can, to keep myself well-groomed, and to live in joy because watching her have so little; made me know that is not how I want to be and live. She taught me to be a lady and to be well-mannered.

Thank you Mother and Father for your gifts of awareness!

The positive are the aspects to focus on and to be grateful for. As far as the negative aspects, write them down, look at them in awareness, understand them, accept them, forgive them, break against them to change and shift then wad up the paper and throw it out with the rest of the trash. Consider this, what if you never took out the trash in your house and let it build up day after day and year after year. What would you have? Well, the same is true for the negative limiting imprints and beliefs that you carry around. Shining the light of awareness onto darkness shapes you into a better person.

Focus on the positive and when negativity rears its head, see in awareness, break against it, and or put it through the process to release it.

After doing all the above exercises, now look at self in fresh awareness and write down what you think comprises you. What makes you, 'you'? What do you think is positive about you? What do you think is negative about you? Don't filter; just write the first thoughts, activities, likes, dislikes, or words that come to mind. What makes you happy? What makes you feel sad? What do you dislike? What do you like?

Review what you have written. Then you know the drill. What needs releasing, put it through the process as many times as need be.

I do this often and can do it in my head, usually fairly quickly. Sometimes at the end of a day, I use the process on any incident or interaction that bothers/bothered me. I find my feelings and figure out awareness. I understand why or understand all sides whichever applies. I accept and forgive then smile inside and outside because I have learned more about myself.

> *"Since love grows within you, so beauty grows.*
> *For love is the beauty of the soul."*
>
> —Saint Augustine

ENERGY

EVERYTHING ON EARTH IS COMPRISED of energy. Our spirit is energy. The energy of our spirit leaves our body when we die, leaving our flesh and bones behind and lifeless without the ability to animate.

While on earth, we learn to talk and to write in order to

communicate. But our energy is the most profound and powerful way that we communicate with others and others with us. Our energy is and driven and expressed by our feelings, emotions and of course, intellect. Nothing makes you more 'you' than the energy pulsating through your mind and body.

How you feel inside shows on the outside. If you have no self-esteem, it will always show on the outside. You cannot completely hide your state of mind and emotions because they are intimately connected to your physical body. The way you hold your head, your shoulders, and the light in your eyes, your voice, the way you move, even the way you take a step all reflect who you are on a vibration and emotional energetic level. People who value themselves have a sense of energy and pride in the way they move their bodies and maneuver through life. They exist at a higher energy frequency. People with low energy vibration move their bodies as if devoid of energy. Their voices are dead and there is no light in their eyes or spring in their step. It's almost as if they're sucking the energy from the space and everyone around them just to exist. The relationship with yourself sets the tone for every other relationship you have.

We are designed biologically to feel and express emotions regularly, automatically and easily. Emotions are the language of our heart, mind and spirit. They have a physiological and energetic value and reality. They have their own vibration. Our energy is comprised of imprints, emotions, feelings, belief system and memories; all these together create the level of our energy vibration. Our energy vibration can be shifted and changed at any given moment. In fact, each time we shift feelings, emotions and thoughts our energy shifts and changes. We are in control of our energy and when we realize that, it changes our awareness and our life.

Where our mind and emotions are at any given time changes the energy vibration that we emit into the world; therefore, drawing to us that which we will experience. When and as we shift, we also shift others. Our positive energy has the ability to lift others and our negative energy can take others down, unless they are aware enough to break against it or to not allow it into their energy field.

What further makes up the energy of our spirit? Along with

feelings, emotions, imprints and belief system, it's DNA—astrological placement at the time of our birth—personality—circumstances that we are born into and much more. We may have little ability to understand it all, while on the earth plane, including that spark of creation that is our life force from God.

We all carry and emit different energy. There are people who stay overly busy to avoid thinking. They are always doing or worrying about something outside themselves, so they won't have to look at self and to feel. There are people who hardly move. They are tired and lethargic, blocked, weighted down with their imprints, feelings and emotions—holding onto them—thinking about them while mulling them over making them feel exhausted. There are people who balance being busy along with that of quiet time and less movement. They are busy but can stop their minds long enough to feel, reflect, recuperate and recharge. There are people who maintain being extremely busy and active while at the same time have the ability to process their feelings, emotions and imprints as they go along. These people are usually spontaneous in self-reflection with few blocks and therefore, able to process quickly. They are aware, understand and accept at rapid pace, so their energy level is high. They have health in the physical, mental and emotional. Lao Tzu wrote, "Those who flow as life flows know they need no other force."

Transformation involves changing both our thoughts and emotional connections to them that keep us stuck in the past.

Nothing will weigh a person down as much as unprocessed imprints, emotions and the feelings connected to them. People carrying unprocessed imprints will feel exhausted after not doing much at all. They will want to vegetate in front of the TV—fall prey to addictions—over eat—overspend—over-sexualize and may be depressed, anxious, or spew forth negativity and project their anger onto others. They are literally blocked within their emotional system. They are stagnant and most of them will defend their belief system with all the energy that they can muster, which isn't much at times.

Working out intensively in any form will not exhaust a person as much as when they are carrying the weight of unprocessed negative imprints, feelings and emotions. Actually working out physically, will help assist to shift feelings and emotions to temporarily have release and create more energy. But if not addressed head on in awareness, the negative imprints will seep back in, to again to drain the emotional system which is reflected in the body, mind and spirit with lack of life force and energy vibration.

People who are overwhelmed with negative imprints, feelings and emotions are preoccupied in their minds and psyche. They often won't be able to learn well, think well, remember well or take pleasure in present time experiences and activities because their minds are preoccupied with the past.

We all have experienced and know how it feels when we are in stress, feeling down or even depressed and can't think clearly or recall normally. It's as if we are blocked. Stress freezes the mind, body and spirit to be under its control. People who do not process emotions well will feel this way on some level—most all of the time and some for the duration of their life. They may experience little relief except for temporary escape into additive behaviors, substance abuse and other escape activities. They may appear as if their mind is always preoccupied and that they are lost somewhere in their head. They are not hearing, seeing, aware or living fully in present time. Pathology is marked by an inability to change and sustain positive change. Your thoughts and the feelings and emotions that create them are what make you and create your life along with your desire or need. To alleviate stress, depression and anxiety is the ability to choose one thought over another in order to shift the energy. Change your thoughts, you change the energy.

What we are feeling creates the energy we carry and also the energy we emit. This energy is what attracts or repels other people, situations and experiences into or out of our lives. It's our energy vibration. It's the law of attraction and the law of subtraction. Therefore, the clearer our energy field is from negative imprints, perceptions, emotions and feelings, the clearer our choices in life will be. We will then have more energy and time to see, hear, touch, taste, feel, laugh, and love and to experience joy. When we are balanced and not blocked or in fear—what and how we feel is how we know what our intuition is telling us. Move away from the negative energy that holds you from your rightful path to fulfillment and happiness. Our emotions are to serve us and move through us, not control us.

Ecclesiastes 3:1-8 (KJV)—For everything there is a season and a time for every matter under heaven: a time to be born, and a time to die; a time to plant, and a time to pluck up what is planted; a time to kill, and a time to heal; a time to break down and a time to build up; a time to weep, and a time to laugh; a time to mourn, and a time to dance; a time to caste away stones, and a time to gather stones together; a time to embrace, and a time to refrain from embracing; a time to seek, and a time to lose; a time to keep, and a time to cast away; a time to rend, and a time to sew; a time to keep silence, and a time to speak; a time to love, and a time to hate; a time for war, and a time for peace.

Our lives are made up of imprints and memories. Let your life's memories play like a movie in your mind; become aware, review, examine, discard, understand, accept and forgive. You are the final editor of your life's movie. Cut scenes that do harm or let them create tension and break against them to create a more magnificent hero. Change the script lines from negative to positive; speak words that promote healing and positive energy. Ultimately, it's you that is the director, editor and producer. You have the lead role in the movie of your life. You are the star of your life and the purpose of which is to feel all your emotions, so you can flow back to and live in joy.

Let examining your life become a grand adventure. Look at how far you've come and how you've grown. No matter what happened or happens, everything is for a reason. When everything seems unsure, everything is possible. Your power ultimately lies in your ability to discern the truth for yourself instead of being guided by the imprints of others. The eyes from which you see are how you view your world. See the world with new eyes. The ultimate power is to live in the authenticity of self. Whatever your circumstances or wherever you find yourself—it is yours. You are having an earth experience to become awake. Before you awaken, there must be awareness.

Be at freewill. You can choose to live in negativity and fear or choose to live on the positive side and in joy!

Awareness—Understanding—Acceptance—to Peace—Love—Joy!

Plato wrote, "We can easily forgive a child who is afraid of the dark; the real tragedy of life is when men are afraid of the light."

GOD HOLDS MY HAND

In present time

GOD IS ACTUALLY HOLDING MY right hand. I lift up my arm and reach upwards and He takes my hand, when my hand is down by my side God's light shines on my right shoulder.

Me—my hand—God holding my hand, am I worthy of God holding my hand? I have such fear inside me at times. I am scared. Fear—scared—while holding God's hand? I chuckle in uncertainty and awareness, but isn't that the safest place to be—in God's hand? So why fear? Fear—that I am not worthy? Fear of my power? Fear of God's power? But I am part of God's power. God is in me. Therefore, I fear not!

How can I fear that which is created by God? Why do I turn God into fear? God guides my path when I listen and even when I am not listening. I am safe! I am home! I am at oneness with God. I love God. God loves me. There is no fear in love!

I am aware that when I can feel God's hand the most firm and clearest is when I am at peace with myself, my world and at one with the universe, appreciating all humankind.

I am aware and at one with God . . .

THE LITTLE SPIRIT BECOMES AWARE . . .

. . . after all her experiences, hurt, trauma, loss on earth, it was all supposed to occur exactly as it did, for her to become all that she became.

She loved deeply, felt emotions into her core, had pain that she thought was unbearable, losses that she didn't think she could survive, but as it turned out, she did. She learned to self-reflect along with the ability to see all sides and most importantly she learned to forgive herself and others. She became more than she was when she first landed on earth and that was what it was all about in the first place . . .

Daddy threw me in the air. So I learned to fly and my spirit soared!

Books by Ayn

Books may be ordered and Ayn may be contacted for
private consultations and speaking engagements at
www.womenexplode.com

Ayn Dillard—has experienced much, prompting much self-
reflection. She is a self-proclaimed know-it-all and is sharing some
of what she knows with you. She acknowledges that just when you
think you know it all, your inner or outer world shifts. For you to
realize that you don't know much of anything, encouraging you
to dig deeper to discover an even more profound awareness and
wisdom. Understanding this, she shares what she has gleaned from
her experiences and life to assist others to become more aware. She is
a former ballet dancer and former interior designer.